GOING FOR BROKE

John Stone

HENRY REGNERY COMPANY · CHICAGO

Library of Congress Cataloging in Publication Data

Stone, John T.
    Going for broke.

    1. Stone, John T. I. Title.
CT275.S84A33 1976 338'.092'4 [B] 76-7946
ISBN 0-8092-8185-6

Certain names have been changed throughout this book
in order to protect possibly innocent and relatively
unimportant characters.

Published by Henry Regnery Company
180 North Michigan Avenue, Chicago, Illinois 60601
Manufactured in the United States of America
Library of Congress Catalog Card Number: 76-7946
International Standard Book Number: 0-8092-8185-6

Published simultaneously in Canada by
Beaverbooks
953 Dillingham Road
Pickering, Ontario L1W 1Z7
Canada

To John III and George W. B.

Acknowledgments

This book might never have been written without the encouragement, counsel, and assistance of Bill Quarton. My thanks to him and to Ev Harrington, Pete Barnes, John Kasimatis, Bob Konop, and a man with a 'green thumb.'

Contents

Prologue

Dawn was once my favorite hour: Awakening from an easy sleep. Smiling, high on dreams. Ready for a new day. Especially in the Rocky Mountains. Especially at Lone Tree.

Six years ago it was still like that. I remember standing early one morning on a hilltop twenty miles from the nearest paved road in northern Colorado. Below me was Lone Tree Ranch, where, rumor had it, I was conceived, and the sun was making shadows along the west wall of Honeymoon Lodge. Lone Tree was sacred family ground, passed down to me and my brother. Now it was my embryo kingdom in the world of big business. I saw myself then as the crown prince of worldwide recreation—a dream I'd nurtured since my school days in Chicago, at a time when a young and eager Hugh Hefner was leaving *Esquire* magazine to found *Playboy*.

"Some day soon, *your* dream will come true," I promised myself six years ago, reluctantly moving down the hill to the lodge to begin packing, going back to a sedentary, frustrating life in Madison, Wisconsin.

Four months later, faithful to my vision, I started building an empire from scratch. I began as sales manager for an idea. I described my conglomerate to investors as "not just a great business, but a fantastic new way of life." I started with little more than sky, but I figured that with imaginative ability, a facile tongue, and hard work I could build a solid foundation beneath the blue. I became president of an illusion. I double-timed to the top because it was easy to run with enthusiastic partners pacing me. My associates were doctors, ranchers, cabinet ministers, astronauts, politicians, movie stars, sportsmen and bankers. Besides recreation, our businesses included lumber, mail order, trucking, agriculture, manufacturing, retailing, real estate, travel, and banks. Almost everyone I met wanted to participate: some to make their first fortune, some to multiply the millions they already had, others just for the ego trip.

My success was astonishing, even to me. It was unreal. In less than forty months my personal net worth multiplied more than thirteen times to over two million dollars and my companies were valued at twenty million.

Then, suddenly, it all exploded. The intoxicating delusions turned to nightmares. There were moments of real terror as I struggled to unsnarl my tangled lifestyle and deal with the total collapse of a business empire that had spanned the globe from Honduras to Hawaii, Kenya to Holland to Manhattan. Twenty-six banks and a union pension fund were involved, along with some of the larger companies in the world. Most of them, along with my once willing subjects, began howling for my hide.

Today, after running the gamut from middle-class money merchant to millionaire entrepreneur to fugitive pauper, I've returned to my beginning. Once more I'm sitting alone in the lodge at Lone Tree as the sun rises to foreshadow another day. But now I'm only a guest at the ranch; it was deeded to my attorneys to help pay their fees. Lone Tree was the hardest loss of all. My shoulders are braced against the hard oak of my father's chair; my damp palms stain its cold arms. And I'm trembling, as, once again, memories of my financial suicide flash behind my eyes.

I've heard that when you're about to die you see an instant replay of your life. Now I'm beginning to wonder if vision doesn't also improve as you start to live again. When I blink I can see the land lightening outside, and then I notice the handwritten pages of my story resting on the table before me. And, by God, I've stopped shaking and I've even started to smile as I remember how this book began and how it became what it is.

First it was an obituary, written during a private wake for my dead dreams. Later it became an exposé of businesses built of bricks with too little straw, structures reinforced with deceit, progressive betrayal, and the misdirected philosophy that the end justifies the means. Sometimes I felt like saying I was a victim of the times; blame inflation, tight money, and the energy crisis. No way. The real story, I knew, lay elsewhere.

Finally, during my research, I found a Xerox copy of a personal promo I had written three years earlier, when I had intended to make myself so exciting, so intriguing, so marketable that potential partners would gather from near and far to find out what I had to say.

"Stone is a fascinating conglomerate," it began, "hard to find and follow (you only see a blur)—a man of vision who is about to make his company's history the mightiest volume on the shelf of man's recreational accomplishments."

I crumpled that paper into a tight ball and threw it far away. Then I began rewriting the real story of a man who once believed that he could make every dream come true.

1

August 1970

ASSETS—$195,550.00
LIABILITIES—$68,650.00
PERSONAL GUARANTEES—0

It was 10:15, three and a half hours since my groping hand had found the button that silenced the clock-radio alarm. I had overslept, and now it was taking me longer than usual to shave and dress. I washed my face again and again, trying to rinse away the gritty feeling from my eyes. Water finally splashed on to my tie, making spots that slowly expanded instead of drying away. I ripped the tie off and grabbed another from the long rack of color-coordinated silks as I finally began to hurry.

Skipping coffee, which I normally drank while roaming through the house to hug my eight-year-old sons good-bye and tell their mother whether to expect me for dinner, I went straight to my car and backed it out of the garage before the electric overhead door was fully raised. The antenna twanged on the bottom edge. I ran every yellow light on my way to the Janeff Credit head-quarters on the opposite side of town. Not until I pulled quickly into the parking lot and slammed on the brakes did it finally strike me: "What's the Goddamn rush?"

I was not, I realized, anxious to begin another dull day dealing with the money miseries of my small loan customers. For more than a year I'd become increasingly frustrated as operations

1

vice-president of a small, struggling chain of consumer finance offices. True, I was first in line to take complete charge and eventually own the company, but the founder and present owner had given little indication that he was ready to retire; F. F. Sommers was over sixty-five, and getting crankier every day, yet he insisted on being ever-present, making every major decision. Recently the business had begun to show the same signs of financial distress as its borrowers. Janeff Credit had barely made it through the money crunch of '69, and now customer delinquency was snowballing. We had to find new corporate financing, and there wasn't any—no money to expand my innovation, a division selling a full-line insurance package to our customers. No resources to develop loans to small businessmen, who were more willing than ever to pay high rates.

I slammed the car door, clenched my fists, and walked slowly toward the rear entry of the one-story building. I hated the place. In the dark hallway behind my office I hesitated. Inside, I knew, the ashtrays were still full, coffee stains ran along the scattered pile of loan applications, and the one-way glass separating my room from the clerical section was so smoke-stained I couldn't even see what the secretaries were up to.

Since it was Friday, the one day Sommers took off, I wouldn't have to endure his relentless questions about what borrowers weren't paying on time, and why. I could spend the day figuring ways to buy him out, to reverse Janeff's steadily increasing losses, and to build myself an aggressive, innovative business that might provide a good income that was fun to earn.

I had eased into the squeaky chair behind my desk when I realized that all that was impossible. I didn't have enough money to buy Sommers out, much less to refinance the business. That had been made very clear by the banks when I'd offered to co-sign the Janeff lines of credit. They'd accepted my signature but inferred that it meant little more than my expression of good faith, my determination to work long and hard collecting delinquent loans and exercising sound judgment granting new ones. My real intent was to begin buying a bigger share of the credit for keeping the company going, the right to exercise greater personal control over Janeff's future. But my name on the company notes was of little financial value to the banks. My personal net worth didn't impress them. I knew I needed to show many more assets, fast, if I wanted to begin buying the loan company.

"Hell," I yelled at the one-way glass, "who wants to spend the rest of his life as a moneylender anyway?"

The intercom buzzed. I ignored it.

"Get out of here," I told myself. "Go home, take Judy and the kids waterskiing on the lake—do something fun with your neglected family."

I was worried about my family too. Recently, I'd begun holding a prolonged happy hour every evening, sometimes missing dinner entirely, always masking my intoxication with aloofness; too busy pondering business problems to chat with Judy or play with the twins. Both my marriage and my career were stagnating, or worse. It was time to do something about them.

I started to rise, then kicked my briefcase into the corner and hunched over the desk, thinking hard while I chewed the edges of a sun blister that nagged my lower lip.

My secretary came in and studied me quietly for a moment. My face must have told her I wanted to be alone.

"I'll assume you're out for the day," she said finally, backing away while I nodded yes.

I was toying with another idea, the concept of earning a living while pursuing my favorite avocations. From the time I first held a fly rod and was just big enough to get knocked on my ass by the recoil of a Winchester carbine, I had fished, hunted, and explored with my father. In my teens I had roamed to Yucatan and Belize and had climbed most of Colorado's mountains. Before I had graduated from college, outdoor sport had become an incurable habit. Now, at thirty-seven, I was still struggling to satiate my appetite for it.

There had to be many others like me, I decided, thousands of people who worked not just to exist, but to earn something extra— the best of natural surroundings, offbeat adventure, and the thrill of the chase (birds, big game, or the opposite sex). If so, then it stood to reason that I could get rich by making outdoor recreation more accessible to them, not as a guide or a travel agent, but as the leader of a massive movement that would make an all-encompassing sportsman's life available to practically anyone. This could be my way out of Janeff Credit, or the means to find money to buy it, and a new lifestyle might even inject vitality into my marriage.

Although I was aware that I was an impulsive person, I rarely ever tried to curb my enthusiasm for anything I decided to do. Once caught up I usually moved fast. I recalled an article I had read in *Fortune* magazine heralding the seventies as "The Decade of Recreation." I reread the article and made up my mind.

"Do it now!" I said to myself. I dumped the ashtrays and shoveled the paperwork into the drawers of the battleship-gray desk.

"Gotta get a new color," I said softly, as I pulled out a legal pad to begin drafting my Master Plan. My brain was racing. Concepts spilled out so quickly that there was no way I could get everything on paper without forcing mental playbacks. Hours later, exhausted, I stopped writing. I was satisfied that I had outlined a scheme in which my friends and associates could not resist investing their time and money, a concept of recreational endeavors designed to control both buyer and seller. The Master Plan envisioned a holding company and a club—the former to own and operate resort properties, the latter to fill the resorts with its members. It would be a conglomerate patterned after the Playboy empire, but selling outdoor recreation instead of sex.

I knew my plan was neither totally original nor complete. At this stage it wasn't even elaborate, but it seemed to me the perfect solution to my problems. Even Janeff Credit Corporation, with new management under my control, could be used to finance club memberships, land sales, and vacation travel.

Unable to contain my enthusiasm, I telephoned Dr. John Kritchner, an outdoor nut who'd done insurance physicals for Janeff's insurance division when he was a medical resident. Now a practicing plastic surgeon who never let a good thing pass, he would, I was certain, be interested in my scheme.

"Busy with patients now," Kritchner said. "Meet you later for cocktails." His voice was hurried, but his willingness to meet me during the happy hour, which he rarely attended, meant I'd been right. He was very interested indeed.

The clock behind the bar at the Mayflower Lounge, the current "in" spot for wheeling and dealing in Madison, Wisconsin, sat atop an aquarium. The fish were darting from one side to the other, making cloudy swirls along the bottom of the tank. They seemed nearly as anxious as I felt swinging back and forth on my stool, my eyes flicking toward the clock whenever I thought the hands had moved closer to five o'clock. I ordered a second drink, and then, when the barmaid stared raptly toward the entryway, I knew Kritchner had arrived.

I turned to be doubly sure; Kritchner saw the movement and waved as he crossed the room. He was a carbon copy of the dashing young surgeons on television. True, he was losing his hair, but only his wife and a few close friends who'd seen him emerge wet from the shower were aware of his imminent baldness. He was adept at combing the long strands on either side of his forehead into a rakish cover-up.

"Is our trip to Colorado last month really going to pay off?" he said, swinging his leg over the stool beside me.

I smiled and nodded. Kritchner was referring to a fishing trip into the mountains behind Steamboat Springs. The water in the streams had been too low and clear for good fishing, so we'd spent the second half of the week scouting the area for possible investments. At the time I'd thought only about forming a small group to buy a toehold in the Rockies—an excuse to write off future trips as a business expense on our taxes, a little venture to expand very slowly, maybe for my retirement. Now I was thinking bigger, and about today, and I'd added the idea of the club.

"Your idea to get into the resort business sounds great," said Kritchner as we carried our drinks to a table. "And I was impressed with Steamboat. I think it's going to be a new hot spot for skiers."

Kritchner was a ski buff. He smiled, sipping from his full glass before sitting down. Then, as he eased into a chair, his expression changed.

"But why clutter up the plan with this club business?" He frowned.

"Because it generates quick cash."

I explained that I'd gotten the recreation club idea from Dave

Padgett, a Janeff Credit associate, who for fifteen years had successfully run a membership operation involving a food-freezer plan and a furniture discount setup. He charged $520 for a five-year privilege. Most of the members were blue-collar or salaried workers; Padgett called them "Joe Lunch Buckets," and constantly emphasized that they were the largest segment of the population.

"Padgett's enrolled over 30,000 families. Multiply that by 520, John. You get over $15 million."

Kritchner nodded, toying with his empty glass.

"Many members can't pay the full fee in advance, so they're allowed a forty-dollar initiation and the balance is carried on a negotiable installment note. The monthly payments are called dues. The notes are sold to Janeff Credit and other lenders; we take a 20 percent discount and hold another ten in reserve against Padgett's guarantee to buy back any accounts falling three months past due."

"Has Padgett had to repurchase many?"

"No, that's the remarkable thing. Only a few go sour. It's a gravy train. I wish Janeff had enough money to keep buying his paper, or better yet, to buy our own contracts for membership privileges in the recreation club."

Kritchner leaned forward, his expression tense. "Is this all legal?"

"So long as there's no misrepresentation or usury. All we have to do is deliver what we promise."

He nodded.

"And that's easy," I blurted. "The world is full of recreation opportunities, starting in Steamboat Springs. Outdoor recreation offers something really important to almost everybody, the richest to the poorest. If it's handled right we won't even have to sell, just take orders."

Though he wouldn't commit himself, Kritchner finally agreed that we should give the club concept serious further consideration. Sure I had him sold, I knew it was time to listen instead of talk when he returned to the subject of Steamboat Springs and suggested that I call friends in Colorado and begin ferreting out the best properties available.

"There's got to be some good deals in Steamboat," he said. "Lots of people have got to be hurting after last year's tight money." He looked at his watch and stood up, suggesting that we meet again after the weekend.

"Right here, five o'clock Monday?"

"Good." Kritchner turned toward the door, then reversed himself. "I want to bring an old buddy along, Ed Turnbull. I've known him since grammar school and he's the hardest-working bastard you'll ever meet. Ed's dependable, loyal, and sharp."

I nodded—sounded like a valuable man.

Kritchner continued, "He's got just one big goal in life—to move to the mountains. I want him in on this."

"I'm sure we can use him."

Later that night I made the long-distance calls Kritchner had suggested and confirmed our feelings that Steamboat Springs was indeed ripe for resort investment. Rumors were circulating that Ling Temco Vought (the aerospace conglomerate, and primary developer of the area) was planning to spend over $104 million on a resort complex there.

When I heard that, and learned it was not yet common knowledge, I took time out to calm down, smoked a cigarette, and drank two cups of coffee before getting back on the phone. Other friends thought the El Rancho, a well-established restaurant-bar on the main street of town, might be available, and promised to nose around for more prospects.

I spent the next two days polishing my Master Plan, with special emphasis on the club. On paper, it appeared that even with just a fraction of Padgett's membership, there'd be plenty of ready cash to provide not only bountiful membership benefits but other resort acquisitions as well. I figured that by plowing back excess funds into new properties, the club members would always have new facilities at their disposal. Hopefully, this would encourage word-of-mouth sales among members and their friends; how could they help but be enthusiastic about receiving more than they'd expected?

No doubt about it, I told myself, this plan had built-in guarantees: early members would naturally enlist others, whose dues would provide funds for buying ever more properties—which, in turn, would entice additional recruits. It was a controlled monopoly game in which eventual ownership of the board was assured.

By Monday morning I had a final draft to take to the office for typing. I ordered four copies: one for the files, the others to be inserted in plastic binders labeled "Master Plan—Kritchner," "Master Plan—Stone," "Master Plan—Turnbull." Though I wasn't positive Turnbull would attend the next meeting, I wanted to be prepared. If the three of us were to be partners, then let him get a snortful of my style from the start. I examined the finished product, determined to judge it objectively. The Master Plan was damned impressive, I concluded. It contained eleven neatly typed pages of background and operational data, with two-inch margins and six sheets of maps, charts, and titles to give the package heft. I'd also sent my secretary out to buy see-through binders in three different colors to add that irresistible dash of creative excitement. Then I sat back and smiled.

Sommers came into my office and frowned. "What are you working on?"

"A plan to save the company." I carefully laid the folders in my briefcase and closed it. Sommers didn't need to know any more. Later, as I began building equities in my own companies, I'd tell him more, explaining how my successes could only help Janeff. In the meantime, I figured he'd allow me enough spare time to implement my plan—after all, I thought, studying Sommers as he stood restlessly in the doorway, he needs me. Janeff's reputation around the loan industry was too shaky for him to find a decent replacement. And I had guaranteed the company's loans, as well as being the only one with a complete working knowledge of the business. So I also figured that my job was secure, and that if I offered any hint of salvation to the old man I might even exercise some real control.

"Wait until I'm finished developing these." I smiled and patted my briefcase. "Then maybe you'll be able to retire a rich man."

Sommers grunted. "Just be sure you keep us in business." Then he suddenly smiled back at me. "I know you're trying. Keep at it."

"Right." I felt a surge of confidence when I realized I'd elicited encouragement from Sommers without telling him anything. Must be my changing attitude, I thought, hoping that everyone would see I was on to something big.

Kritchner met me at the Mayflower Lounge again, with Turnbull only moments behind. Instantly, even in the dim light, I noticed Turnbull's piercing blue eyes; during the introductions, they never blinked. He was obviously an experienced outdoorsman, loaded with vitality. Sincerity, too: his voice was firm and clear, and his massive, nearly bald head, which seemed to move toward me when he spoke, was set atop 230 pounds of bone and muscle.

Before we ordered drinks I passed out the Master Plans, and when the waitress finally arrived, Kritchner and Turnbull were too deeply immersed to notice her. I watched, fascinated and elated, as their eyes moved slowly back and forth across pages that crinkled with classy newness as they were turned. I waved the waitress ·away.

Turnbull looked up, rubbed his eyes, and said, "Stone, you smoke too much." Then the hint of a smile crossed his face and he thumped his heavy fingers on the folder. "But this plan is absolutely fantastic." With a broad smile, he turned to Kritchner, who, his solemn face barely six inches from the pages, was still reading. "Listen to this," said Turnbull, talking to both of us. "Who wrote this? Is Steamboat Springs, Colorado, really called Ski Town, USA? And is it really becoming the center of North America's newest, finest all-season recreation area?"

"I wrote it and it's true," I told him, grinning.

"Just finished that part," said Kritchner. By now he was grinning too.

I signaled the waitress. At that moment I felt totally content. They were selling each other, and I knew I could afford to sit back, relax, and enjoy a drink. They ordered too, but only Turnbull looked up, to say to Kritchner, "You're right. Steamboat Springs has to be the perfect spot to begin because we can ride the coattails of LTV's new ski facilities, and reap the benefits of their investments and promotion."

Great. Turnbull was paraphrasing my words. But at the same time I began to feel left out. I didn't ski, and the two ski buffs knew it; they were ignoring me. If that's their bag, I thought, let 'em emphasize it, so long as they stay sold. "Steamboat's a twelve-month recreation paradise," I finally said, realizing as the words came out that extra encouragement was unnecessary.

Kritchner frowned; I knew I'd better curb my tendency to over-sell. But Turnbull gave a short nod of approval and turned, still grinning, to swipe at his friend's somber expression. Then they were both smiling at me. I ordered another round. As far as I was concerned, it was time to celebrate.

"Before you guys get loaded," Kritchner said, "how about the properties for sale in Steamboat?" He leafed through the folio to the page mentioning El Rancho. "This all you've found?"

"There'll be more." I figured now was the time to raise the money question. "How much have we got to spend?"

Kritchner reminded me that $20,000 was his limit, adding that he thought that was about tops for the rest of us.

"Right," said Turnbull. "Especially until I dump my businesses here, and the Red Shed?"

"What's the Red Shed?" I hadn't realized he had so many side deals.

"My bar," Turnbull said. "Don't worry, I've already decided to sell out and move to Colorado."

We all began scribbling figures on the blank back pages of the Master Plan and decided, more or less together, that by raising $50,000 to $60,000 cash we could buy a business with a total price of around $150,000.

"That's with a third down. I don't think we need that much," I said. "And anyway we could raise more money if we tried."

No one argued.

"So maybe we can afford to spend a little more, or, if not, at least we'll have operating cash left over." Then I asked if they knew that the installment sales tax laws encourages some pretty good extended payment arrangements. "That's why 29 percent down is the rule of thumb on real estate and business purchase deals. If the seller accepts over 30 percent down payment, he has to pay an immediate capital gains tax on the entire purchase price, and who the hell wants to do that if it can be avoided?"

Both nodded affirmatively.

"Just make sure I have enough operating funds," Turnbull said.

"The club will give us an extra cash flow," I repeated, to be sure they both still bought the whole package.

"Maybe," said Kritchner, shaking his head again. Buying real estate in Steamboat appeared to be a foregone conclusion, but he was clearly still doubtful about the club.

I insisted that we needed both to be successful. "First the bricks and mortar, then the holding company and, Goddamnit, the recreation club." I waved my copy of the Master Plan. "This concept involves tandem endeavors," I began. "One won't work without the other. There seem to be two factions at this table; both of you are interested only in a venture in Colorado, and I'm predicating my decision on the mutual advantages of a resort, or whatever it turns out to be, *and* the membership plan. The tangible, and the intangible, I suppose. Maybe the latter isn't as easy to get excited about, but like I said, it guarantees a cash flow."

"You sure?" After five drinks Turnbull was still totally sober.

"Certainly. It's simple."

"Don't bullshit yourself, Stone." Kritchner shook his head. "Nothing is simple."

It was hard to win with him. Too many words and Kritchner thought he was being sold a bill of goods, too few and his reaction was the same. I tried to hit him in the middle.

"Let me put it another way." They *must* buy the entire plan, I was thinking. I wouldn't settle for less. "We're going to need a lot of cash, more than we have now and probably more than we can count on borrowing. The club will contribute the cash flow from the dues its members pay. And remember, we can form the club with a very small investment. As soon as it's started the club will pay for itself and give us a surplus to develop resort properties."

Turnbull chuckled. "You mean the members pay our way with their dues."

"That's one way of looking at it. It's the best way I know for guys like us to get started."

"And you're planning on running it?" Turnbull chuckled again. "I figured you were looking for a way to get out of the loan business."

"Not entirely. I've got plans for that too." I stopped myself.

"But they come later. Right now, it's outdoor recreation all the way."

Kritchner cocked his head. "How are you going to sell hunting and fishing better than Hugh Hefner sells tits?"

Then he burst into a wide grin, whipped out his checkbook, and suggested that we all write $1,000 checks for an expense kitty. "I'll open an account so we can keep track," he said. "Stone, you and Turnbull better start making plans to head west on a scouting expedition."

"You're the treasurer, doctor." They were now well sold. Hell, we were all sold. We knew we were greedy. We thought we were creative. We were about to make our fortunes in a hand-picked environment. "Snowy slopes, rushing streams, elk herds, clean mountain air. What could be better?" I asked. And then I repeated Turnbull's remark: "The plan's absolutely fantastic."

They nodded, smiling. I had said what I knew they wanted to hear. I grinned back. "I guess we just gave birth to a dream, gentlemen. Time to spank life into it with another drink."

Kritchner snorted and faked a punch at me.

I hurried home to tell Judy—"Everything will change now that I've found the handle to a new life." It was much later than I'd realized and I knew I sounded drunk. "Ok, so I'm high on enthusiasm."

Judy listened from our king-sized bed, where she was propped between pillows, blinking from the bright ceiling lights I'd switched on as I rushed into the room. "Tell me tomorrow," she said, expressionless. Her eyes closed again.

I sat down next to her and tried to work my arms between the pillows to hold her tight and promise that everything I said would soon be true. But she rolled away.

"Please," she said. A toneless command.

I stood up and switched off the lights as I walked toward the glow from my adjoining den.

I poured rum and Coke into a tall glass, stopping two inches from the top to leave room for ice. The bucket was empty, so I went into the kitchen, and then, feeling suddenly light-headed, I poured my drink into the sink and filled the coffeepot instead. As it began to perk I went to look for my Master Plan.

"Can't afford any flaws," I said to myself, intending to review every page in the folio before I went to bed. When the coffee was ready I took a cup into my sons' room, sat in the dark on their toybench, and wished it was morning so I could tell them about the wonderful times we were going to share—all because of the ideas inside the smooth cover of the folio on the bench beside me. I stayed there for a long time. The soft cadence of their breathing was amplified by the darkness, which gradually faded until I could see the outlines of their twin bodies curled in peaceful sleep.

"Fantastic." The word had a different meaning now, and I hoped the intensity of my unaccustomed father feeling would come more often. And that Judy would believe me when I told her about the tingling sensation of knowing I was father to a family, the belonging that made me imagine I could reach out and touch the air around us.

Turnbull and I headed for Colorado the following Monday. Tourist class on United's nonstop Milwaukee-to-Denver flight was only half full. Turnbull took a window seat; I sat on the aisle. While the plane was still at the gate we spread our files between us. On top, the most important item, was an analysis of our cash position. It was all on a single sheet of eight-column accounting paper. Our names were listed separately opposite five headings—we weren't sure of the proper accounting terminology, so we just used whatever words sounded right and impressive. Added together, the columns totalled:

Cash, $4,100;

Pending surplus income (we meant proceeds from the sale of Turnbull's car rental franchise, gas station, and parts distributing business), $15,000;

Approved loans (I'd arranged to borrow part of my share), $10,000;

Disposable assets (this was cash to be raised selling Turnbull's Red Shed and some of my stocks), $25,000;

Net Worth (this was the total of everything the three of us owned, stated at its highest market value, minus debts), $387,000.

I was willing to gamble everything, and figured I could convince the others to do the same.

As Turnbull studied the sheet, he tapped his fingers nervously on the armrest. Finally he said, "Unless someone comes up with additional cash or loans we'll only have $54,100 to work with. What will happen if we find something good that requires more money?"

I'd anticipated his question, and produced another eight-column sheet. This one listed potential investors. "We can almost double it if we want to take in partners. As I said the other night, we can always raise more money."

"Let's keep it a small group if possible," Turnbull said, suggesting that the best approach was to negotiate a lower down payment.

We both wondered if the seller's magic number of 29 percent was really an absolute requirement, and agreed that in many ways it was a buyer's year.

"It's not exactly a bull market, even in real estate," I said.

"I hope the word isn't out too far on LTV's plans for Steamboat," Turnbull agreed anxiously, as he organized his share of the papers. I saw him put a wad of the new partnership checks into his billfold.

"Really classy," I needled, noting that they weren't even imprinted.

"Hell, I'm not even sure the initial deposit has cleared," he joked back. "You've got us an appointment to look at El Rancho?"

"Just the name of the agent." I closed my eyes and pictured the Rockies on the horizon. Steamboat was less than a day away. "When the sun rises tomorrow, Ed, we'll be owning a piece of the mountains."

"Right on," he said. We were beginning to think alike.

We rented a car at Stapleton Field in Denver and drove toward Berthoud Pass on the Rocky Mountain Front Range. As the trees thinned, approaching the summit, I turned to Turnbull. "You still enthusiastic about the whole plan?"

"Damn right," he repeated.

A void opened alongside the car; it was a long way down. Turnbull seemed preoccupied, obviously enjoying the mountain view. "Peace and beauty," he said, not particularly to me.

An hour later we stopped near Winter Park for dinner. He picked a Swiss-chalet-type restaurant, with fireplace logs piled high beneath a sign that advertised fondue. I'd passed it many times: a skiers' hangout—not my style. Now I decided I'd better get used to that; my new partners would never pass it by. We drank beer, and ate, and drank wine.

"Let's see Steamboat with clear eyes and our heads on straight," Turnbull urged. We decided to spend the night.

Next morning we were up early; we skipped breakfast and sped over the last fifty miles. As we passed the entrance to the booming Mount Werner ski area, on the east edge of Steamboat, Turnbull asked me how far El Rancho was.

"Mile and a half."

"Think there's anything available up that way?" He gestured toward the mountain; ski runs made happy creases on its wooded face.

"Doubt it. All high-priced stuff."

You could easily see from one end of the main street of town to the other. For me this was cow country, unchanged in a hundred years except for some asphalt and a few stoplights. I pointed out the real estate office to which my friends had directed us to inquire about El Rancho and other properties. Turnbull looked dubious and said so, probably because it was just an ancient, weatherworn storefront attached to the equally old Pilot House Hotel. To find a parking space I had to swing around the block, bouncing over the pitted gravel road.

As soon as I found a spot, Turnbull jumped from the car and inhaled deeply. "Mountains," he breathed.

He was empty-handed and bareheaded; I carried my new leather briefcase and wore my Stetson. Together we ambled toward the real estate office, looking, I suppose, as if we were about to buy the town. Suddenly Turnbull turned and made for a newly remodeled office complex. He stood with his nose pressed to a window framed in rough-sawn cedar. His hands twitched and I suspected they would have snatched up the freshly painted sign inside if glass hadn't been in the way. I went over to see what he was so excited about. The sign said "For Sale—The Inn at Thunderhead." I looked at the fancy photos attached to it and said, "That's up in the ski area. Wasn't for sale when Kritchner and I were here last month. It's out of our class anyway." I started to walk away.

"How can you be so sure?" Turnbull asked, and strode purposefully into the real estate office.

Twenty minutes later Brian Amsler, the realtor, whose lizardskin cowboy boots and suede-trimmed sport coat didn't fit my general impression of Steamboat at all v·as wheeling his gleaming Toronado toward Mount Werner. He alked constantly, modulating his voice like a professional actoɪ. It was difficult not to be attentive, and he seemed to know it. This guy's a pro, I thought. His pitch was canned, but spun off so smoothly you barely noticed.

"The climate is perfect," he advised. "In winter it provides more ideal skiing conditions than any other area of Colorado. They call the snow 'Champagne Powder,' best on the continent. In summer our country's downright balmy, and the sun and stars are always a little brighter than anywhere else."

I knew there was no use trying to interrupt him until he'd finished the presentation spiel, but he was beginning to sound like a travel poster.

"Present sports facilities will serve nearly 20,000 visitors daily. There are hundreds of miles of trout streams, trails and valleys to explore, mountains filled with wild game, ski lifts to carry over three thousand people an hour up the three peaked mountains and thirty-five miles of runs to come down, the finest hot springs in the west. And all this lying next to the Mount Zirkle Federal Wild Area. Yet there are barely 600 rooms to accommodate the public, standing in line for tables is common at most of our restaurants, and customers crowd three deep at bars. Ling Temco Vought proposes a $100 million, ten-year development plan. And the Inn at Thunderhead is at the hub of everything."

I knew what he meant. It was a helluva property. I remembered last year when my hunting group—we called ourselves the Ridgerunners—my brother George, his favorite drinking buddy, Judy, and I, came down from unwashed weeks in the Mount Zirkle Wild Area to the luxury of the Inn at Thunderhead. We'd stopped first at the old hot springs, rented private baths, and scrubbed ourselves red while scalding water bubbled from the mineral-crusted pipes. Judy and I had made love quietly, standing chest-deep in our private pool, while next door George and his friend laughed and splashed and drank the last of their Chivas Regal. Then we'd changed into clean clothes and headed to the Inn for a celebration. The place had a mystique, maybe because it lay so close beneath the rugged wilderness, or because it appeared to be so vastly superior to anything else in the area.

Now, by God, if I read Turnbull's face right and could believe Amsler's line—and if I believed in myself—it might be ours for the taking. Maybe here was a preordained opportunity. Just maybe, it wasn't out of our class. I was caught up in the silky web of Amsler's words. I had the moxie, the connections. I could get the money, I convinced myself, and as I'd told Turnbull and Kritchner, it was a buyer's market.

The Inn's entrance, bordered by huge torches, had always impressed me. Looking at Turnbull as he pushed himself from the car, I could tell that he was even more excited than when he'd first seen the "For Sale" sign. Here, in itself, is an oasis, I thought as we went inside, a tie with the sophistication of far-off places, yet blending somehow with our vision of its surroundings, the raw woods and gleaming rocks. The Inn was rich and brawny, and even the dirt on its windows couldn't obscure the panorama beyond.

Then, in the lobby, I took a closer look. On the front desk was a hodgepodge of wrinkled papers, dirty menus, numberless keys and unsorted mail. It was a mess.

Amsler saw my frown. "Remember," he said, looking straight into my eyes, "busy means money." When he noticed Turnbull examining the worn carpeting, he remarked smoothly, "The Inn's flooring testifies to many boots." He had an answer for everything.

The manager was out, so Amsler helped the desk clerk find a passkey and led the inspection tour. He showed us the banquet room first. It had a bandstand, a dance floor hidden beneath the carpeting, a separate bar and service area, and an electric dumbwaiter to the kitchens below. Amsler said that it would hold 300 people and immediately began listing the other public areas. There were two bars, two dining rooms, and office suites (for temporary use) that could easily be converted to a third bar, rathskeller, or coffee shop. "All connected to a central service complex that can handle small parties, large groups, conventions, anything you want." I began to wonder if he owned a piece of the action.

Turnbull crossed the lobby to the main lounge. Even though his back was turned, I could tell by the swaying of his head that his eyes were taking everything in. He noted offhandedly that there was lots of wasted space, and while he questioned Amsler about the heating plant, I browsed among the wine racks. Either it was top vintage grape or they got a helluva price. The tags ran eight dollars and up.

"How can twenty-two rooms support a complex like this?" Turnbull was asking.

"*Suites*," Amsler emphasized, and then insisted that we inspect them.

We walked down a terraced hallway easily eight feet wide. All room corridors opened to our left. On the right, out the occasional floor-to-ceiling windows, I saw Thunderhead's backside: rotting and rusting construction materials scattered along the banks of a small stream that looked as if it carried open sewage. Stray dogs wandered among empty food cartons and beer cans.

"A Goddamn pigsty," I said.

Amsler, struggling with a door, didn't reply. The key wouldn't turn. He tried the opposing room: inside was strong warmth from paneled walls, muted appointments, a free-standing fireplace, and logs piled on the sunny balcony.

"Nice."

"You better believe it," Amsler said, winking at us. "Everything but a bidet."

Here was a real estate agent who, besides being a pro, had been around. Dressed like a rich cowboy, maybe—and he did have calloused palms—but there were a lot of city miles on his face.

"Originally from Texas, Mr. Amsler?" I threw the quick question, hoping he'd talk about himself.

"No." He explained he was a native and still a part-time rancher. For a while he'd been the state's public relations man. "You both Wisconsinites?"

"Ed, yes. I was born in Denver. Got a ranch in North Park; it's called Lone Tree." This seemed to impress him. We began swapping brag about our land holdings, both smiling. I think we realized the extent of each others' exaggerations. Turnbull moved back to the hallway, and Amsler broke away to lead us to the office. "The Inn is newly listed," he said. "A fast offer might encourage some special concessions. No price cut. That's set at three quarters of a million dollars, but the terms could be very flexible."

My God. It hit me: $750,000. That was *five times* the amount Turnbull and I were trying to cope with.

"Ed and I would like to talk a little. May we see you in the lounge later?" I asked Amsler, trying to sound relaxed. My palms were sweaty.

Though the main lounge was empty, we chose the most distant corner to settle in. No need for Amsler to know we were thinking about buying the Inn with $50,000.

"That's less than 8 percent down," I told Turnbull.

He collapsed into a chair and rubbed his face.

I knew his common sense was at war with his desire. Broken pretzels crunched under my shoes, and the dozens of cigarette burns in the carpet and the grimy tabletop added to my feeling of despondency.

Turnbull leaned toward me, shoving aside the accumulation of used ashtrays. "This could be a great facility," he snapped at me. "Right now it's obviously all fucked up and the owners are hurting. I think we can steal it."

"Only if we get some pretty wild terms."

By the time Amsler came back, somewhat prematurely, Turnbull and I had decided that we needed more information and more talk.

"Drinks, gentlemen?" Amsler offered, along with a very big smile.

"Cuba Libre."

"Coors."

Amsler went behind the empty bar.

"What about El Rancho?" I whispered. I was uptight.

Turnbull whispered back, "Forget it."

Oh, oh, the snowball's starting to roll downhill, I thought. Then, as Amsler brought the drinks, I told myself quietly, "Yes, forget El Rancho." This was too good an opportunity. If you really want to move ahead fast you have to stick your neck out.

In less than an hour Amsler recounted the history of the Inn: how undercapitalized developers had begun the project in 1968, maybe two years too soon, and how the contractor had been forced to take over to avoid a bath. How in 1969 the Cummins Power Company, buying in for a tax break, had gotten discouraged and sold out earlier this year to Senator Decker, an attorney who was a powerhouse in the state legislature.

"Why does the senator want out so soon?" I was beginning to wonder why there were so many losers.

Amsler explained that the senator had other interests as well as cash needs, and that, of course, his asking price included a profit. He produced a rawhide portfolio. First he explained that the buyer could assume first and second mortgages, as well as a U.S. Government-backed Small Business Investment Corporation loan. The existing financing began with $24,500 owed to Maher-Bonny Construction, followed by mortgages of $85,251 to the Routt County National Bank, $262,024 to the Yampa Valley Development Corporation (the SBIC lender), and an extra $80,000 to the same company. When I asked him about the last debt he said, "It's unsecured and exists only as a book entry to satisfy some technical requirements of the Small Business Administration. Don't worry about it. Actually it's offsetting."

Turnbull shook his head loosely, not trying to hide his confusion. I didn't comprehend it all either, but I knew it wouldn't even be relevant unless we could figure out a way to buy a $750,-000 luxury resort from a bigwig politician with just $50,000 down. I asked Amsler to review the debt structure again. The total was $361,775; that left more than $388,000 to pay the Senator, over half of it up front.

I must have said, "Impossible"—mostly to myself—because Amsler pointed out again that the $80,000 note to Yampa Valley

Development was only a gimmick and would never have to be paid. "So that's an $80,000 plus," he said.

So what? When you're over half a million short, an $80,000 plus means nothing, I told myself. Maybe Amsler saw my discouragement, but he plunged ahead to note the tax loss carryforward we'd be getting. This amounted to over $90,000 and would, he pointed out, "seem to be very attractive, especially to physicians. And wasn't one of your partners an M.D.?"

I decided to try another approach. "Is 29 percent down required?"

Amsler thought we could play with it. "After all," he said, "if this is going to be a quick sale, the senator has to make some concessions. Of course, your personal financial statements will have to be submitted for approval by all the lenders involved."

Turnbull, sensing that things were about to get sticky, asked to see the manager so that we could discuss any existing administrative problems. He also demanded a look at the operating statements of the Inn.

Backing him up, I added, "We're not about to be high-pressured into making sudden moves."

It worked. Amsler backed off, telling us in a docile voice, "There's plenty of time to study details."

"We'll talk things over while you hunt up the manager," I said, feeling sudden relief. We needed time for a long, private discussion—darn right we did—because at that moment I had no idea where the down payment on $750,000 was coming from.

"See you in half an hour, OK?" Amsler's smile was smaller now, but I could tell he still thought we were hot prospects.

Turnbull and I sat staring at each other and, for the first time since I had known him, I saw him blink uncontrollably. He was hyperanxious to own this place, I felt certain, because the Inn had skiing written all over it. I began to wonder about my own motives. This venture was so big it was nearly prohibitive, a helluva challenge. I guess I liked challenges. Lord knows it was time to bite off a fresh chunk of life, so why not? The bigger the better. Sure, why not, wasn't this the stuff dreams were made of? Just as I began to realize I was giving myself a snow job, Turnbull pulled out a clean legal pad and began calculating. I did likewise; it was not the time for musing. What we needed were facts and workable arithmetic.

"No way." Turnbull was straining. "No matter what we put down it's impossible to draw a money tree."

Now I refused to give up. "You've sold me, so hang in there. The Inn is a fantastic find, too good to lose. It seems to me that the four previous owners jumped in too soon, like Amsler said. But with our plans and what we knew about LTV's plans (I fingered my Master Plan folder), *now* looks like the right time. I'll find the money we need." I took a deep breath.

"If we can work a deal," Turnbull said, "it'll fly. You and Kritchner talk to that Doctor Hollis on your list?" He began to sound more positive. "Will Hollis come in with us?"

"If we need him."

"We need him. How much?"

"Twenty thousand. You saw the sheet. Possibly fifty. Maybe more." Hollis was the doctor who'd delivered my twin sons—a trout fisherman, bird hunter, good guy. Twenty years older than the others, but I knew he'd fit.

We went to work with the pencils again.

Then I got the idea. It came hard and fast, a blur. My head pounded, and the more I thought about it the more I was convinced it was the solution. I didn't say anything to Turnbull until I had everything worked out on paper. I had to be sure there were no flaws.

If, as Amsler said, the Inn was appraised for $750,000, and the total debt (including first and second mortgages and the SBIC loan) was $361,775, that left an unencumbered equity of $388,225. In other words, the Inn was mortgaged for only 48 percent of its true value. Mortgage lenders, I knew, advanced as much as 75 percent of legitimate appraisals. And the money market was loosening up. If we could get the senator to carry us with a small down payment for six to nine months, there was no reason we couldn't later refinance the existing mortgages for more money and pay him off.

I explained my idea to Turnbull. "Even if the asking price is solid, no dickering, Amsler did say we could play with the down payment. Now, I think we can psyche the senator into terms on the whole deal if we just demonstrate our ability to pay through refinancing. Let's not hassle him on his price. It's a secure arrangement; the equity is there. We can offer a good interest rate. Hell, it might even be to his advantage taxwise."

Turnbull wiped his face on a sleeve and stood up. He was staring at me, shifting from one foot to the other.

I knew he had questions, but I continued before he could ask them. "Amsler never indicated his principal's initial cash outlay. I bet it was peanuts. If I'm right, the senator won't worry much about carrying paper on this place if he doesn't have any real money left in it to lose."

When I stopped talking, Turnbull stuck out his hand. It felt good when I took it. Eight days ago I hadn't known him, and here he was pumping my arm, smiling praises, and telling me that this was a very important moment to commemorate.

Lunch and the early afternoon were an anticlimax. We talked with the manager, who was somehow related to one of the senator's partners. He answered our questions and gave Turnbull the profit and loss (mostly loss) statements, operating recaps, and advance bookings. He behaved cordially and seemed sincere. He also appeared to believe in the Inn. But when he was certain we were going to make an offer for it, his eyes were downcast—I assumed because he knew Turnbull would be running the Inn without him. He wasn't vital or strong enough, nor could he project the enthusiasm I knew he wanted to feel. He was a nice guy, a helpful guy, but an hour later I couldn't remember his name.

By 3:30 Turnbull and I were ready to make a binding decision. "Are we biting off more than . . ." I started to ask, but stopped immediately lest Turnbull construe my vague doubts as weakness. I was ashamed to be up one moment, down the next. "Hell, no."

"Then call Kritchner." Turnbull bounced on the balls of his feet.

We borrowed the manager's office. Turnbull talked first. His eyes twinkled and seemed many shades brighter than their usual blue. It occurred to me that I had a habit of watching people's eyes for clues to their emotions. It was easy to see that Turnbull's adrenaline was pumping.

"Boy, this is really contagious," I heard him say.

"It's an epidemic!" I shouted, grabbing the phone.

"Buy it," said Kritchner. We glad-mouthed each other until Amsler came in without a knock, smiling too.

I'd always thought offers to purchase were intricate documents, but under Brian Amsler's direction our petition to the seller, Senator Decker, was completed swiftly. There were no guarantees that our suggestion of a mammoth fourth mortgage would be accepted, but the real estate man's manner when Turnbull handed him a $10,000 binder check left little doubt. It would be arranged somehow. My only worry was that we had only seventy-two hours to cover the check.

Early that evening I phoned Judy, wishing I were home. I was suddenly horny. Obviously, big deals were a wild aphrodisiac.

"We bought the Inn at Thunderhead."

"What?"

"We bought Thunderhead." I tried to explain the details but was so elated I couldn't remember them. When she didn't seem excited I rang off. How could she understand? I told myself that there was no way for her to share my euphoria. How could she know that I'd decided at last to force my dreams to come true, by making sure there was no turning back? I knew this was something only a few people ever do, and for a fleeting moment I was scared by the size of it all. Then, reexamining the state of my guts, brains, and stamina, I knew: I could hack it.

2

September 1970

ASSETS—$198,883.33
LIABILITIES—$72,615.00
PERSONAL GUARANTEES—$250,000.00

Our flight back to Wisconsin should have been a journey of triumphant ease, but my head was clouded with doubt and my stomach churned. Once on the ground, we'd have to deposit $10,000 at the bank to cover the down payment check, then hurry to a meeting with Kritchner and Dr. Hollis. Hollis's participation was essential. Without him, and the other investors he might secure for us, the purchase would be impossible.

I looked at Turnbull, wondering how he could sleep. Kritchner was right: He was a cool head. And to pull off the Thunderhead purchase I'd need all the help I could get. My God, what had started as an investment where we'd stretched every asset to justify our low six-figure capital was now a full-blown million-dollar project.

My confidence wavered, even though I knew my heritage destined me to do great things. My father was the Chicago clergyman who sold Cyrus McCormick on the idea of buying half a city block and building a cathedral, across Michigan Avenue from the future site of the John Hancock Building. My mother was the daughter of a Teamster Union founder, a man who refused the presidency of the first major dairy to instead "Go out and help the milk drivers." Today's International Brotherhood of Teamsters was the result.

I stared down at the cipher-covered pad in my lap. The figures translated to read a big fat zero if I couldn't put this deal together. If the senator accepted our offer and we failed to keep our side of the bargain, he'd keep the $10,000 and probably sue for the balance. What if I had to ante up my third of the $750,-000? It would take everything I owned and still leave me over one hundred thousand dollars in the hole.

If Judy discovered the risk I was taking, she'd lose whatever small faith she still had in our marriage. Remarks that "I can't depend on you anymore" and "You've got no interest in your family" would take on finality. The idea of divorce wouldn't be as ridiculous as it had seemed when she'd mentioned it in the past. I needed my family. It was the source of my limitless pride (how many men fathered twins on the first try, when there was no record of such an event in either family's history?) and a comfortable haven from the harsh world of business.

I gave myself a mental kick in the ass. This was no time for depressing thoughts. To maintain the momentum to make the Thunderhead venture go, I had to be an optimist. This I knew. I saw my role as the leader, and the leader must never be a pessimist. After all, it was my Master Plan, and my job to convince people of our ability to make it work. I knew I must sell not only my concepts but my charisma, my ability to promote myself and, thereby, to produce dollars.

I poked Turnbull, woke him, and set about building him up for the task ahead. "You're a key man," I told him. "The managing partner. It's your job to convince the others that from an operating standpoint, the project is feasible. I've got the reputation of a promoter. That could be a disadvantage. You lend credibility, especially now that you're really convinced you can handle Thunderhead."

I watched to be sure he agreed before I continued. Turnbull may not have been completely awake, but it was obvious that he understood; he was smiling.

"The image we project to the senator is the key to obtaining his financing—the second mortgage. I think I can help there." I smiled to show him I was sure.

"You'll smother him in horseshit," Turnbull snorted, beaming his approval.

"We can't afford any leaks about our lack of fiscal strength. Even to Dr. Hollis. Might scare him off too." I kept talking even though Turnbull seemed to be getting bored; he looked out the window, then turned back to pick a book of matches from my shirt pocket, using the folded edge to clean his fingernails.

"This is a helluva deal, Ed." I pitched all the clichés at him: "fame and fortune," "the good life," "the opportunity to build something really big." Though he didn't reply, I could sense that I'd rekindled his excitement.

We sat in silence for a while, savoring the moment, until the nearly narcotic effect of the deal's immensity began to fade. Then, perhaps because we were both aware of our tendency to dwell on fantasy, we simultaneously began talking about practical matters. Turnbull produced a sheaf of papers provided by Amsler and handed half of them to me. The more we studied and discussed the inn's operating statements and pro formas, and LTV's development plans for Steamboat Springs, the more convinced we became that our acquisition was not just an impulsive speculation but a genuinely sound investment. The only problem was finding sufficient immediate cash. But that problem, I hoped, would be solved by my brainstorm of yesterday and the inclusion of Hollis.

Leaving our luggage at the airport to be picked up later, we headed for the hastily scheduled meeting at the doctor's office. It was Madison's largest medical center, and Hollis had been instrumental in its construction.

Obviously we were expected, and I felt like a VIP as a nurse ushered us into the private conference room. As we entered, Hollis and Kritchner were laughing over what I took to be the latest gynecology joke making the rounds of the hospital.

Physically Hollis was medium, in height, weight, and age. He seemed the type who would fit well in any situation, with anybody. He was warm, gentle, and jovial, and he had a special quality that no doubt allowed him to tell dirty jokes in mixed company and talk sex with strangers, yet remain the first choice of many women as a doctor. After pumping my hand and retelling the joke, he said, "There are a few more things I need to know before I sign up."

"Shoot." Confident that Kritchner had already presold Hollis on the venture, I was ready to field any question. I smoothly answered his inquiries about the Inn, attributing its past failures to premature construction, tight money in the late sixties, the natural growing pains of newly promoted resorts, quixotic local influences, and shamefully shoddy management.

Finally Turnbull stepped in front of me and said, "The right time—the right place." He flipped his hands toward the ceiling. "Instant progress."

Kritchner grinned and nodded while Hollis carefully folded the paper on which he'd been taking notes.

"I think I've heard enough," he said, sliding the paper into his desk drawer. "Count me in."

I felt like shouting, clapping my hands, or slapping somebody's back. I kept on talking instead, thinking I shouldn't appear too desperately happy in front of Hollis but, at the same time, certain nothing I said would disturb the happy smile on his face. He seemed too thoroughly convinced the plan was foolproof.

"You were the test case," I told him. "Now I'm sure we can find as many other investors as we need."

"Hold it," Kritchner stepped in front of me. "Who said we needed more investors? Let's not get too many people involved. The company could get out of control."

He looked at Hollis and I noticed he was also at ease, talking freely in front of our newest partner. Hollis was a damn good choice, I thought. He really seems to fit.

Turnbull interrupted. "Look, what difference does it make if we take in a few more good men? We started small and now we have a chance to be big. I can live with owning a little smaller piece of a much larger pie, like they say."

Hollis nodded, still smiling broadly.

"We'll always control the company," I assured them, "as long as we stick together."

The squabbling about stockholders stopped; Kritchner, now

convinced, was the first to suggest new investor prospects. And Hollis (whom we began referring to as "Uncle Willie" after his immediate acceptance of the Master Plan and the Inn) immediately nominated more: his cousin and two of his close friends, all doctors.

"Now we've got more than enough," I said, trying to project a reasonably businesslike image, but inwardly pleased to discover that it was going to be so easy to recruit affluent doctors.

Although we hadn't discussed the merits of a corporation over a partnership, everyone seemed to favor the former. Amsler's written explanation of buying the Inn by acquisition of the owning corporation's total stock impressed the doctors tremendously because it referred to net operating losses and investment credits.

"Sounds like we can earn $146,000 between now and 1976, tax-free," someone observed.

Kritchner volunteered to gather prospective investors at Blackhawk Country Club within the week and to prepare presentation charts. "See that your guys get there on time if they want in," he told Uncle Willie, winking at me.

Everything was shaping up faster than I'd anticipated. I began to ride even higher when, as we left the office, Uncle Willie pulled me aside, requested his own personal copy of the Master Plan, and gave me a playful slap on the butt.

"We're on our way. You guys get the job done, I'll get the money. Now go home and take care of your wife." He said it with the same smile that had accompanied the gynecology joke.

I couldn't wait to tell Judy. This time I'd convince her that we were headed for a new way of life—even her doctor said so. When I got home, I showed her the Master Plan, page by page.

"This proposition is even going to be good for Janeff. Sommers senses that," I insisted. "That's why he's giving me a freer rein. He's betting on me too." Then I explained the Thunderhead purchase.

Judy laid the folder aside and turned toward me. She didn't seem pleased. As she brushed aside a lock of hair, I noticed traces of creases on her forehead.

"Buy Thunderhead?" she said. "How? We don't have the money."

As patiently as I could, I went back over the news about Uncle Willie Hollis and his doctor friends.

Still she wasn't convinced. She shook her head; the strands of hair fell forward again. "How do you *really* know that all these men will give you their money?"

I was ready with my answer. "I bit off a big chunk, honey. Now this is how I'll chew it." I knew that Judy had always been impressed with the way I could convert thoughts to words, and I was determined to make her understand how I felt.

"As I see it, there are several consistent traits in men who achieve greatness. One is best characterized as their inherent, automatic ability to step outside subjective frames of reference and objectively see themselves performing on a stage that encompasses everyone and everything that could in any way interact profitably with them. Using people. I can do this. Simply, I can get outside of my head into what's happening around me and then guide the results. I suppose I've always had the ability, but I haven't always used it. My mother was demanding and insecure. She had to be *used* to be tolerated."

Judy turned away, as she usually did when she thought I was selling her a bill of goods. I continued anyway. "I learned this as a child, and by my teens I was expertly devious enough to always get my own way. Remember our wedding? She opposed it. My mother was a user too, but I outclassed her. Now I'm going to play it smart and reshape our lives." I reached out and pulled her around to face me again.

Judy looked as though she was about to say "Huh?" Apparently I hadn't explained it well enough, so I tried again.

"It's like me sitting in the audience, watching myself act on the stage and fitting my role to a script I know plays best, at that moment, to the people around me. Like being an actor and a spectator at the same time. I create the right illusion by figuring out in advance what others want to see. In the same way, I also adjust the scenario, whenever necessary, to fit the subject's changing mood. Some call it "thinking on your feet." By being a spectator at the same time, I'm able to discover the "hot button" of the audience. And as the actor I'm in a position to push that button and cause the desired reaction. If I'm able to show people what they want to see, in me or my concepts, then I'm able to control them. You call it motivation."

I saw her jaw muscles tighten. "You said it right the first time—*using* people," she said in an unusually loud voice.

I knew I should have kept my mouth shut. "Forget it, Judy. I was just trying to give you an example of the power of positive bullshit," I said. I knew that was the only way to get off the hook: inject a little levity and apply the principles of the stage management I'd just described. "Now let's talk about what to do with the orphan Inn at Thunderhead."

Judy shook her head and began to walk away. "You may believe what you say, John, but I'm still wondering."

I took a deep breath and closed my eyes. Her voice sounded a long way off.

"I'm wondering about a lot of things, and right now I need to be alone."

Her final words were very faint. I opened my eyes. The house was very still, and even with all the lights on the room seemed dim.

During the weeks that followed, talking about Thunderhead was about all I did. The meeting with investor candidates was held as planned. Uncle Willie introduced the first arrival, Dr. Robert Crombie, an obstetrician. Though he looked to be pushing sixty-five, he still served as a volunteer on mercy missions of the good ship *Hope*. Next came Dr. Nicholas Barass, a pediatrician. He was somewhat younger, soft-spoken, and apparently awed by the visual presentation Kritchner was busily arranging. Uncle Willie's cousin, Dr. Rodney Vitner, entered at the last minute, explaining that he'd been held up by an unanticipated call to administer anesthesia. He had also stopped at the bar for a badly needed drink. Vitner was a big man, about my age, with a happy face, an easygoing guy who no doubt would go along with what the rest of the group wanted.

Kritchner opened the meeting with a toned-down version of Amsler's original pitch while I passed out photocopies of the Master Plan, sans the recreation club, which I thought would only clutter up the presentation and confuse the new investors.

Money was priority number one now, and as I'd anticipated, when we explained the corporate structure of the Inn and the attendant tax loss, the good doctors' interest became really intense. It seemed a good time to nail down their investments.

"Someone's liable to usurp our position if we delay closing the deal," I said looking from one to the other.

"If Willie's in, I'm in," Vitner said.

Barass agreed too, and Crombie, after some hesitation, approved, adding hastily, "Only in principle, of course."

Specific talk about money had so far been purposely avoided by Kritchner, who was following a private agenda I'd spent hours working on. It called for the money question to come from one of the new investors, and for me to field it—the relevant item read, "Finance Question, change of pace and face. Stone." Now it happened, right on schedule: Crombie asked for an analysis of the Inn's cash position. I gave the 1970 Thunderhead profit and loss report; reviewed the comparative real estate values, emphasizing long-term growth over immediate income; and closed with the suggestion that a further on-site look would be most useful. Then the clincher: "Why don't we all go to Steamboat?"

Most of the group said they couldn't get away on such short notice, but just as I had hoped, they were completely mollified by the invitation. I'd told Judy I had the ability to anticipate people's thoughts. I'd used that ability now, and it had worked.

We scheduled another meeting two weeks later, at which time everyone was to approve the financial details and sign stock purchase agreements.

The anxious waiting began. There wasn't much anyone could do until we heard from Amsler. Actually, we didn't even have a firm deal unless Senator Decker accepted our offer.

Finally, after three days of lingering agony, Amsler reached me at home. The senator had contacted him to relay a counteroffer. Amsler said it was too good to pass up, but that he couldn't go into details on the phone. We'd be wise, he said, to fly out immediately to put the deal together. Too excited to question him intelligently, I hung up and began dialing my partners.

I left a message at Kritchner's office to phone the minute he got in. I left the same message at Turnbull's auto rental office and the Red Shed: urgent, call immediately. Kritchner should have finished his hospital rounds by now, and Turnbull had to be at one of his businesses. Damn it, why didn't they call? I wanted to pass on the good news and leave for Colorado—today, if possible. We had to move fast.

When he finally called and heard the news, Kritchner was all for haste, too. He assured me he'd have Turnbull and himself ready to go within hours. Now my juices were really flowing. What better way to make a solid impression on Amsler and his client than to have a prestigious plastic surgeon drop everything to be a part of the negotiations? No need for them to know Kritchner had just begun practicing medicine.

I sat down and tried to unscramble my brains, but all I could come up with was the refrain: By God, we're really going to do it! All of a sudden I was actually trying to devise an appropriate name for the three of us. My thoughts flashed from plumed musketeers to Don Quixote's windmills and lances—childish, sure, but a nice break from dollar signs. Then I reined myself in: enough. Locking my mind into neutral, I started packing my bags, feeling foolish when I realized I was humming a tune from *The Wizard of Oz*.

Next morning, as the FASTEN SEATBELTS sign went off, I reviewed our progress. Less than thirty days ago, we'd planned to buy a property with a total price of no more than $150,000 and a down payment limited to $50,000. We had agreed to raise the money among the three of us. Then the Inn at Thunderhead had popped up, and we'd set our sights on a $750,000 acquisition with as much as $350,000 down. To swing it, we knew, it would be essential to corral more investors.

This, in principle, had now been accomplished, and for the time being we'd been satisfied with a smaller piece of the bigger action. But now, as we talked things over and built our confidence, it seemed possible for us to remain the controlling stockholders—and, better yet, without investing our own cash. Hollis had as much as said that he'd take care of the money while we handled promotion and operation.

Kritchner and Turnbull agreed that we three had to be the catalysts in making the venture successful. Therefore, it followed that we were entitled to a larger share of the stock than the others.

Yes, by God, it was happening. I closed my eyes, intending to rest my overheated mind, but instead I began coming up with more titles for our group. Most of them seemed far too outlandish, so I settled for calling us a triumvirate: John T., John E., and Edward J. As I wrote the names on my pad, I noticed that the three Js fitted the logo I'd designed for Janeff Credit years before, a stylized letter J inside a condensed diamond. It had never been officially registered. Now it would be a perfect brand for the triumvirate, which might well assume the trade name Diamond J. Carried away by the thought, I started to fantasize again, seeing the Diamond J logo on everything from business cards to private jets.

Kritchner interrupted loudly. "Ten percent for $25,000 is a fair deal, don't you think?" He looked at me with annoyance. "What are you scribbling?"

"Our symbol of success."

The FASTEN SEATBELTS sign had flashed on, and now the doctor tightened his strap with a sharp tug. "Success is money. And *our* money is dependent on how much of this deal we can hang onto for ourselves. Never mind drawing pictures; look at the arithmetic." He held up an outline so neatly printed that I figured it would throw any pharmacist for a loop. "If Hollis, Vitner, Barass, and Crombie pay $25,000 each, for a total of 40 percent of the stock, we've got most of the down payment covered, with 60 percent ownership left for ourselves. That's *control*—and nearly as big a share as I expected in the first place. And we three should be able to get by with investing less than $10,000 apiece."

"Where does the rest of the fifty grand, plus my operating funds, come from?" asked Turnbull as he rubbed his hairless head with a circular motion.

"I've got that figured," said Kritchner. He paused as the plane touched down and we gathered up our belongings. Maybe because we didn't really believe it, no one brought the matter up again.

We caught a Rocky Mountain Airways commuter flight out of

Stapleton Field in Denver. Though I'd seen the awesome Rocky Mountains from the air many times before, today the view was especially exhilarating; I knew I was about to own a piece of this country.

Amsler met us at the Steamboat Airport. At his office, he asked his secretary to bring coffee, then turned to face us with a smile brighter than the wax on his Toronado. "You're in the right place at the right time," he said, and looked directly at Kritchner. "Ed and John took a long shot on their offer to purchase the Inn. I guess you could say they won."

I wondered irritably when Amsler was going to finish setting the stage and get to the nitty-gritty. He must have noticed my frown, because ever so slowly, he took from his desk a single sheet of paper. Holding it so that we could see the perfectly aligned margins and crisply typed lettering, he began to read. The intensity of his voice rose as he finished the preliminaries and got to the meat of the matter: "The seller shall assign to the purchasers all issued and capital stock of the company. The purchase price of the stock shall be $20 per share, or an aggregate of $300,-000 payable as follows: $202,650 at the time of closing; $62,500 on or before May 1, 1971; $34,850 on or before May 1, 1972. These delayed payments shall be secured by purchasers' joint and several promissory note payable to the order of the seller, bearing interest at the rate of 8 percent per annum and secured by all of the stock as to the payment due May 1, 1971, and secured by a first deed of trust on the real estate described as the Inn at Thunderhead until paid in full."

As Amsler paused, Turnbull and Kritchner both turned to me. I naively blurted out my first question: "He's lowered the price to $300,000?" There was a shrill, incredulous ring to my voice.

Amsler frowned and slowly raised an eyebrow, as if wondering whether I was kidding. Then, with not a trace of a smile, he said flatly, "Certainly not." I heard the others settle back in their chairs. Kritchner took a deep breath.

Amsler, lowering his voice for effect, continued reading: "In addition to his agreement as to sale of stock, seller shall sell and transfer to purchasers the real property described in attendant exhibits, the purchase price shall be $78,225 payable as follows: $19,500 at the time of closing; $31,000 on or before January 15, 1971; $27,725 on or before May 1, 1972."

That was more like it. Even though the price was rising slowly, it was, I figured, only beginning to approach what we'd anticipated. But, shit, the payment schedule was rough. I heard someone fidgeting and wondered who was getting rattled besides me. But I kept my eyes on Amsler.

He looked back without expression, cleared his throat, and went on with the outline of terms. "Purchaser will agree to assume all existing long-term debt of the corporation, including, but not limited to: note in the amount of $85,251 payable to the Routt County National Bank, bearing 8 percent per annum interest and calling for monthly payments of $1213 until January 1, 1978; note in the amount of $24,500 payable to the Bonny Construction Company, bearing 8 percent per annum interest and calling for monthly payments of $250 plus interest until December 1, 1978; note payable to the Yampa Valley Development Company . . ."

I closed my eyes tight to try to clear my head; then I began taking notes. The development company (the SBIC lender) loan balance of $262,024 called for monthly payments in the amount of $1,726. Amsler commented that the interest rate was only 5½ percent and that the maturity was 1994. My God, I thought, twenty-four more years of payments?

Then he listed one last debt: "Note in the amount of $80,000 payable to the Yampa Valley Development Company." He leaned toward us confidentially and added, "As I explained to the others, doctor, this is merely a paper transaction to satisfy the federal requirements of SBIC lending. It never has to be paid."

"What do you mean?" Kritchner sounded suspicious.

"Simply that it will be washed out whenever the SBIC credit is paid in full. The $80,000 debt was incurred to buy stock in the Small Business Investment Corporation. That's mandatory before you can borrow from them. When the loan is paid, the stock may be turned in and the debt cancelled. And no principal reduction is required."

"In the meantime, do we pay interest?" Kritchner probed.

"Six percent."

"They pay a dividend?"

"I don't believe so."

Kritchner grimaced. "Helluva deal."

I was trying to tally up the figures. They seemed to total $830,-000, and I was about to jump on Amsler for trying to screw us. But wait a minute, I cautioned myself, the last $80,000 doesn't count. I guessed the figures added up right. And I remembered Amsler advising us at our first meeting that the asking price was firm; only the terms could be played with. Played with? As presented, they called for monthly payments of $3,189, plus assorted interest for over two decades; $93,500, plus interest due within six months of closing; $62,575, plus interest a year later; and an initial down payment—a grand total of $222,150. At this point, our $10,000 binder was only petty cash, and the anticipated $100,-000 investment by Hollis and his friends was more than a little shy of what we needed. Terms to be played with? Be careful, I told myself, this is no game.

I recalled Kritchner's remark on the airplane, that there was a way to cover the balance of cash needs—too bad he hadn't finished explaining. Lord knows, if he'd made any sense at all, I'd be a lot less anxious now. Since there was no way to get the details from Kritchner in the midst of negotiations with Amsler, I decided instead to work off my frustrations by shooting holes in the senator's counteroffer.

"What do you mean," I demanded, "debt including, but not limited to?" What's your client trying to hide?"

"Absolutely nothing."

"Nothing? Then why the phony $80,000 note?" Kritchner joined in, obviously aware that right now the best defense (and we most certainly were, financially at least, in a defensive position) was a strong offense.

Amsler answered by repeating his explanation that the $80,000 note was merely the usual way of satisfying SBIC rules.

We argued back and forth, the Triumvirate picking nits to throw at Amsler, who expertly batted them aside. An hour later Kritchner stood up and suggested that we quit hassling and have a look at the Inn. "I still haven't seen the place, and you'd better believe I'm not about to buy a pig in a poke, regardless of the terrific terms," he added sarcastically.

Try as I might, I couldn't get Kritchner alone during our abbreviated tour to fill me in on his scheme for raising money. Amsler rushed us from one room to another; his attitude was beginning to worry me. He seemed to be showing Kritchner around only as a matter of courtesy. He'd stopped trying to sell, and he'd almost stopped smiling. Maybe he was beginning to suspect that we couldn't afford the deal and was trying to bow out gracefully. Somehow we had to talk privately, so I suggested that Kritchner might like to see the rest of Steamboat and then relax with a swim and a sauna at the hot springs.

"That will give us a chance to relax our trip-weary bodies and digest the senator's proposal," I said.

Amsler offered to borrow a car for us from the manager. "And we'll meet again in the morning. I reserved rooms for you here," he said, adding that if we didn't want three singles we should advise the desk clerk.

Maybe I was getting paranoid, because I interpreted his remarks as a slur about our travel budget. I wanted to respond, but Amsler had disappeared into the manager's office before I could think of an appropriate retort. When he finally returned it was only to hand me a set of keys.

"It's the blue '64 Ford out front," he said, and with a quick wave he turned and walked away.

"Looks like the brush-off all of a sudden," Turnbull said.

We drove around Steamboat. I wondered if the others felt as low as I did.

Kritchner asked a few questions about the Inn's competition, and then sat quietly, eyes almost closed. It wasn't until we passed the hot springs that he looked up and spoke again. "Hey, the pools look deserted. Let's soak and I'll outline my idea."

Kritchner's plan seemed startling in its simplicity: "We'll sell the rooms at the Inn as condominiums."

We'd never discussed condominiums before. I knew practically nothing about them. Although I wanted desperately to believe his proposal to be the panacea it promised to be, I was confused, and I said so.

"Condominium sales are new to me, too," Kritchner agreed, "but they're a booming business all over the country. Amsler seems like a sharp operator. He, or any good realtor, can handle the details for us. What I'm telling you is a healthy method of raising fast money." He paused and looked at us, apparently detecting some spark of enthusiasm, because his voice sounded more confident when he continued. "The Inn's suites would qualify as condominiums anywhere, and there's an obvious lack of them here. We can't help but sell them."

Turnbull, the veins at his temples pulsing, said, "I know enough skiers in Madison alone to handle all the sales. The idea is great. And it's simple."

I laughed and pointed at Kritchner. "Go ahead, tell him not to say 'simple.'"

He laughed too and shook his head. "No way."

We were all convinced, as we listed the rest of its advantages, that the solution had been found. Condos were a good investment. They paid for themselves. They were a tax depreciation. Plenty of people were hot for them, and why not? Condos surer than hell had more class than hotel rooms. Kritchner and Turnbull blinked sweat from their eyes in the steam from the pool, but their voices were cool as they zeroed in on the financial details.

"Say we sell only five suites at thirty grand each," Turnbull thought aloud. "That's enough to cover the initial payment on the Inn and leaves me almost $28,000 for operating. And we three, whatever Stone wants to call us, won't have to ante up another cent."

"Exactly," said Kritchner. "By the time future payments come due we'll be able to sell more. Maybe we can totally avoid refinancing the place."

My mind was moving fast, sorting questions. I wanted answers, but I was afraid to confuse the issue and lose the momentum Kritchner had generated. I tried to keep it simple, asking only about unit pricing.

"The $30,000 figure is only hypothetical," Kritchner said. "After a cost analysis and local market study, it will probably be higher."

I questioned the legality of representing suites as condominiums. Kritchner said, "Certainly it's legal. It's already being

done. The proper term for such a deal is 'CondoHotel;' it originated in Europe, but now it's everywhere."

When I posed the problem of financing the sales (certainly not
all buyers could pay cash), Kritchner said curtly, "That's no problem. I know a banker, slated to be the next president of Madison's
First National Bank, who'll advise us and certainly grant loans to
any good condo buyers who need a time payment plan."

I was amazed at Kritchner's apparently deep comprehension of
real estate, legal, and banking matters. Then I remembered Turnbull telling me on our last trip that Kritchner liked business almost as much as hunting and fishing, and that he'd never be satisfied just being a doctor. Turnbull had called him a genius and said
he was capable of success in more than one field. I was beginning
to agree, and to feel secure in the knowledge that my partners
were along for more than a free ride.

Turnbull pounded his palm against the pool's surface and
splashed me with water. "Have I got your attention?" he asked
with a grin. "You're supposed to be our idea man, the wheeler-
dealer. Well, listen to this. If we sell all the suites, the total package figures to net us—" here he paused, and then raised his voice
—"$480,000!"

"That ought to take care of the senator," I said. "Now let's dry
off and get Amsler back in line." I jumped out of the pool and
trotted to the locker room without a backward glance. Kritchner's
inventiveness notwithstanding, I was assuming the leadership
role again. That was my job: to keep everyone, including John
Stone, keyed up and moving fast. Actually, I was quite convinced
that Kritchner's brainstorm was the direct result of my influence.

As I drove the Ford back to Amsler's office, Turnbull, sitting
beside me, rubbed his reddened head and quipped, "The hot
springs seem to be a perfect place for our business meetings.
They're supposed to leave mere mortals too limp to do a job, but
with us the effect is just the opposite." He jabbed my ribs so hard
I nearly drove off the road; we all laughed and banged each other
with our elbows. But I got serious as I parked the car, and jumped
out ahead of the others: I wanted the first crack at Amsler. He had
made me feel small, and I didn't like that. He'd brushed us off and
embarrassed my partners, and I didn't like that either. If he

thought he could play psychological sales games with me he'd better learn right now that it wasn't going to work—no fuckin' real estate peddler was going to jack me off! In the few seconds it took me to reach his office, I'd worked up a temper.

Amsler must have sensed my ugly mood. He rushed forward to greet me, nervously working his mouth back and forth in a futile effort to present the waxen grin reserved for cash customers.

"Sit down," I commanded. "Get a pencil ready to take notes. We're ready to wrap up the deal."

Out of the corner of my eye I saw Kritchner and Turnbull appear at my side. They nodded. Amsler started to greet them, but stopped to rummage through his desk drawer for writing materials.

"We're here to finalize our offer on the Inn," I repeated, giving my partners a final opportunity to apply the brakes. But they didn't speak, and I was confident of their complete approval. So was Amsler. He began scratching notes on the back of an unsigned letter.

I listed our demands: the closing date should be the day after Thanksgiving, because we deserved ownership for the full ski season. A complete inventory of liquor, foodstuffs, furniture, and all other fixtures and equipment must be certified prior to the closing. An audited balance sheet, profit and loss statement, and operating statement must be submitted to us by November 1.

"And updated on the closing date," said Kritchner, moving in front of me.

Turnbull stepped up with Kritchner and mentioned the tax certificates, the liquor license, and the employees' files. I hung back, catching my breath, while they both talked faster than Amsler could write. I was astounded by Kritchner's overall grasp of the situation. He really sounded like an exception to the rule that doctors were dumb investors.

I rejoined the lopsided discussion with questions about land boundaries. At this point Amsler seemed to relax a bit. He stopped transcribing, leaned back in his chair, and showed us a smile that, for once, looked genuine.

"I have a surprise for you, gentlemen," he said, and, true to form, paused theatrically before telling us: the purchase of the

Inn included an adjacent piece of land suitable for construction of an entirely new condominium complex.

I was dumbfounded. Turnbull and Kritchner must have been speechless too; the room was very still. Was this guy a mind reader? I was shocked that he should introduce the same critical subject we'd just been discussing in secret.

Amsler broke the silence. "In addition, Senator Decker has decided to throw in the construction plans for a sixty-unit condominium development. They include all the working drawings and are valued at $100,000."

I felt Kritchner's elbow jab my ribs again and turned just in time to see his sly smile broaden into a grin.

"Fantastic." I was too elated to notice who'd said it. Everyone was talking at once.

Amsler came out from behind his desk and joined our group as if there'd never been a tense moment. He pulled charts from a cabinet, spread them across the floor, and squatted down to explain how we could turn a million dollars' extra profit by adding condominiums at Thunderhead.

I forgot to question the repayment terms. Turnbull neglected to argue about interest rates. And even Kritchner failed to explore the suspicious $80,000 SBIC loan, or to demand deletion of the phrase "including, but not limited to" as it was applied to long-term debt.

We went to a bar across the street while a secretary worked overtime to prepare our preliminary contract with Senator Decker. When we returned to sign it, after only two rounds of drinks, we all seemed to be slightly loaded. Big business, high altitude, and alcohol, I had discovered, are a potent mixture.

We read the contract, reread it (primarily to show we were still in full control), signed three copies, shook hands, and adjourned to the bar again.

Amsler proposed the first toast: "To the new owners of the Inn at Thunderhead." He said the words in a loud, resonant voice. They sounded impressive to me—and to the other customers in the bar. People stopped by to introduce themselves, and I noticed the look of envy in many eyes. Now, indeed, I was a leader in the community—and by God, I marveled, it had taken me less than a day.

I was also getting richer. Amsler had said that the condominium plans were worth $100,000, and we were getting them free. One-third of that profit was mine: the Triumvirate owned the Inn.

That night we got very drunk—no telling when the celebration ended. The last thing I remembered was telling a barmaid I'd double her salary by Christmas. Strangely, the next morning, when we caught the early flight to Denver, no one felt the slightest hangover. "Why?" I asked Kritchner. His nonmedical supposition was that men circulating pure adrenaline in their systems were immune to such things.

3

November 1970

ASSETS—$232,166.66
LIABILITIES—$93,210.00
PERSONAL GUARANTEES—$250,000.00

To implement the second phase of my Master Plan, I began scouting Wisconsin properties to help sell the club program. One afternoon, driving to check out a nearby farm Kritchner had been interested in, I suddenly become aware of the sound of fallen leaves crackling beneath my tires. I'd lost track of time: Thunderhead's closing was set for the day after Thanksgiving, and I had fewer than ten working days to finish raising $212,150 and to complete the myriad details involved in the acquisition of any large property.

Turnbull was busy rushing around the country selling his businesses and preparing to take command of the Inn's day-to-day operations. Kritchner, while establishing his new medical practice, had been hard pressed to handle the loan with First National. Hollis and his friends were providing our base capital. I dared not upset their sense of security.

Nailing down the stock subscriptions and CondoHotel sales was my first problem, and I had to do it alone. After that I had to make sure the Triumvirate raised its promised share of the cash.

I upped the asking price for CondoHotel suites to $35,000. That would generate enough revenue to cover immediate cash requirements and the figure still seemed to be in line with competitive offerings. There were sufficient prospects to close five sales immediately if down payments were eliminated, and if the buyers were assured that the Inn's bookings would provide sufficient rental income to make the units pay for themselves. Everyone I pitched agreed that CondoHotels were a super idea, especially with no money down.

I told Kritchner how easy it was "to sell anything to anybody" when payment was deferred indefinitely. "They don't even ask the price."

"The commitment to underwrite the CondoHotel payments could be dangerous," he replied, but then added that the Inn would have plenty of spendable income once we made it a year-round resort. "Most ski lodges," he pointed out, "live on seasonal profits."

"And club members will give the Inn a twelve-month shot in the arm," I said. "I'm ready to organize the club."

Kritchner waved a finger. "Whoa," he said. "First things first." He listed the documents required before the First National Bank would complete our loan.

The stack of legal papers he handed me looked formidable. "This looks like a team effort," I said. "Let's call Ed over. Make it an emergency meeting. The next big investors' gathering is on Monday. I want everything finished so they can write checks."

Turnbull arrived, saying that he thought we needed legal counsel to run interference for our hasty action.

"I know a hungry attorney who has past-due loans with Janeff," I said. "He'll work all weekend."

"Good," Turnbull nodded. Suddenly his eyes widened and his neck arched as if he didn't believe he was asking the question: "Did Amsler call to tell us the senator signed?"

For a moment I was too stunned to reply.

"No."

"Goddamn."

"We don't have a deal yet."

I snatched for the phone.

Amsler answered on the first ring. He began apologizing as soon as he heard my voice. "Should have called you. Decker's signed but there's got to be an alteration of the contract terms."

Turnbull was listening, leaning close to the earpiece. I could feel his tension as he pressed against me. Out of the corner of my eye I saw Kritchner pacing, moving closer every time he crossed the room. Soon he was crowding me too, trying to hear. Amsler said that the closing date had to be postponed. There were minor problems with license transfers and inventory. "December 31 OK?" he asked. "You can mix your business celebration into a New Year's Eve party."

"Certainly," shouted Kritchner, as I cupped my hand over the mouthpiece.

Motioning for silence, I told Amsler that my Diamond J associates must meet to approve the change. "I'll get back to you." I hung up quickly, afraid that he'd detect the joy in my voice. Then, spontaneously, I reached for Kritchner's outstretched hands and squeezed them hard.

"The senator's having trouble breaking his contract with his partner's son-in-law, the kid managing the Inn. That's probably the real reason. Amsler is a bullshitter," he said.

"Who cares? Now we've got time."

"We'll lose a month's prime-season business," Turnbull complained.

"And save a month's interest," I countered happily. "The pressure's off." I felt an urge to pitch the recreation club again, but knew it was the wrong time. Their attention was focused totally on the Inn, and it might be quite a while before they'd listen to anything else.

We sold five CondoHotel units to excited friends that weekend. They signed contracts promising to pay $35,000 each. The contracts served an important purpose. They became liquid assets, almost the same as cash, on our corporate financial statements.

"Because they're the legal tender with which the CondoHotel purchasers are paying for their units," I explained to Hollis and Vitner.

Vitner raised an eyebrow.

"The bankers are accepting them as such. They're lending us

the balance due on the notes that are part of the contracts." I insisted.

The eyebrow stayed up. Vitner knew that we were allowing the stated $10,000 down payment to be paid "whenever convenient in years to come," and that the $25,000 balance was carried on an installment note "which will be paid out of rental profits, as earned, over the next five years."

"That's the key to your sales pitch, the only reason you can sell the CondoHotels," he said, starting to frown.

I ignored him and wondered later, when the frown turned to a broad grin, if he'd been only teasing me.

Three young doctors, buying units at Kritchner's suggestion, said they'd pay the front money now if we needed it, and it felt good to know we had a reserve. Diamond J Associates went halves with two other prospects who insisted on inside partners.

On Monday morning we turned in the stack of documents to the bank and picked up another set of forms to be completed by the stockholders. That afternoon, before the investors' meeting, we passed out loan applications and notes to Hollis, Vitner, and Barass. Everyone was present except Crombie, who'd begged off because his financial advisor couldn't come along. I sensed it was time to find a substitute for his money.

Barass did some fast figuring and asked, "How much is your Triumvirate"—he waved his hands—"Diamond J, whatever you call it, contributing?"

"Ten thousand apiece, plus time and effort." I answered quickly. Then, realizing Barass would allow no intrinsic value for time, I added, "Also, we're paying all expenses until the deal is closed."

"Good," said Hollis. Then he observed, with a grin, "the three young tycoons will be the only ones to lose if the venture flops."

Kritchner grimaced when I slipped in a line about the investors being guaranteed a healthy baby or no charge for the delivery. Barass, his face blank, kept figuring. If he had any sense of humor at all, it was well hidden at our meetings. "I'd like to review the stockholder list," he said.

"Here it comes," I thought, as I had known it would have to.

Until now no one had questioned the equity of the stock distribution. The prospect of someone complaining because the Triumvirate had allocated the shares without consulting all the investors had finally surfaced. I reacted as planned: again, the best defense was a strong offense.

"It's all right here, Dr. Barass," I said, tapping a copy of the predetermined stockholder list as I passed it to him. Reading from the top, the classifications showed that the four doctors were to buy 1,500 shares each, for which they would pay $25,000 cash per man. This represented an individual ownership of 10 percent of the company's common stock. The rest of us, the Triumvirate, got 3,000 shares each, 20 percent, for $10,000 cash and $40,000 worth of work and finders' fee credits.

"But the method illustrated isn't fair, doctor." I pointed to the papers in Barass's hand. Figuring he'd be the nitpicker, I made him the target of my preplanned attack. "The way it's set up, as you can see," and here I hesitated, giving him time to study the figures, "Ed, John, and I stand to take a helluva beating. Do you realize the tremendous tax bite the IRS will demand if they consider our $40,000 credits to be ordinary income? We can't get involved if it's going to cost us $20,000 in extra taxes on money we haven't actually received."

My reference to taxes elicited the immediate sympathy of the other doctors.

"How can we change that?" said Vitner.

"What about you fellas paying less per share?" Hollis asked. "Let's see, we're paying . . ." He stopped to work the figures on his pad. "We're paying $16.67 per share. If you were charged $4.44 per share you wouldn't have a tax problem."

I didn't give Barass an opportunity to challenge the five-to-one price differential. "Good idea, if the accountants will accept it. And before anyone complains that we're not paying enough, let me remind you that we've already earned the company $100,000. I'm talking about the condominium blueprints."

At this point it was easy to see from his expression that Barass was back in line.

"Now we need to propose a slate of corporate officers and directors," I continued; I passed out another prearranged list, this one encased in vinyl binders. It was becoming a regular formula for success: anticipate what would occur, establish the preferred results, and prepare in advance a properly packaged visual representation of the predetermined outcome.

Kritchner, "representing the medical profession," was elected president. I was vice-president. Turnbull became secretary-treasurer. And all present were chosen as directors.

"The next order of business is a payment date for stock subscriptions. How about today." I didn't ask; I told. The iron was hot.

There were no objections.

"And finally, because I'm getting thirsty (the rest had ordered drinks already), I'll turn the meeting over to John Kritchner, who'll explain the CondoHotel loan and collect your signed guarantees." I left the room. From the bar I could hear distant bits of their excited conversation: "Great progress to date," "Fantastic Plan," "Thunderhead," "Fantastic."

I ordered another drink and wondered how much the Inn was affecting my total Master Plan. The first phase—property acquisition—was certainly proceeding better than anticipated. But Phase Two, the Recreation Club, was still on the shelf. As far as I was concerned, the Club had to be the most important element.

Had I lost control when our original venture, a low-budget restaurant-bar investment, had snowballed into the purchase of the Inn? Phase One was more than my partners could swallow now. It's like eating an elephant, I thought; it can be done, but only one bite at a time.

After the Inn was officially launched, and after I'd thoroughly researched and polished my outline for the Club and found new properties to buy, it would be easy to interest the others. I reminded myself to be patient (not one of my virtues). Yes, the Master Plan was sound. My best course for the moment was to direct all my energies toward the project in the spotlight and be sure my partners saw me in positive action. I returned to the meeting room with a fresh drink, convinced that today everything was in its place.

The next day Crombie, as I had suspected, reneged; his accountants were suspicious of my hastily prepared financial projections, and Crombie, because, as he told Hollis, he had a hunch that I was fooling everybody—even myself.

The day after that, riding with Turnbull to another emergency meeting with Kritchner, I began to wonder if I'd inadvertently become involved in tackling an endless series of frustrating obstacles. Goddamnit, don't panic, I said to myself; you've got to keep projecting the image of an assured believer. "We've got nearly a month left," I told Turnbull.

"It's got to fly." He was begging the question.

I figured he was as worried as I was, besides being emotionally worn down by the steady setbacks. Yet he surprised me with a broad smile, and said, "My house and businesses are about to be sold. If Thunderhead doesn't fly I'm out of work and sleeping in the street." When he laughed I had a good gut feeling that our lot was about to improve.

Less than an hour later my premonition was confirmed when Hollis burst into Kritchner's office, interrupting our frantic discussion, and announced, "I'll personally replace Crombie's investment. If Vitner and Barass want to go thirds, dandy, but, if need be, I'll put up another $25,000 alone."

Before I could react, Hollis added that he'd already discussed another problem—obtaining wives' signatures on all the notes. He looked at Kritchner. "Doctor John's wife is balking, afraid she'll jeopardize her inheritance, but she'll sign. I've got a way with women." He grinned.

Turnbull exhaled a deep breath. I shared his relief. Obviously I'd convinced them to let it all hang out at the Inn. Hollis and Kritchner, in fact, were already booking friends into Thunderhead.

The crisis was nearly over, and it was a propitious time to tie up all loose ends. "Why has the CondoHotel loan been delayed?" I asked Kritchner.

"The documentation's incomplete," he replied, opening his briefcase to give me another set of forms.

"Look, John, you known damn well all this paperwork is just window dressing. First National's making the loan on the strength of Hollis because he's a well-heeled physician, and of you because they like to service your wife's trust fund. So why can't they close the loan with what we've presented?"

Kritchner cocked his head and stared at the far wall. "I'll expedite the loan," he said.

The word "expedite" stuck in my mind. I liked it.

Hollis said, "We've got to have faith in the venture." "Faith" was another good word.

On a sunny afternoon, it was impossible to enter the darkened Simon House Bar, another hangout of the local elite, and instantly recognize people.

"John Stone, real estate czar." The drink-laden voice I recognized belonged to Bob Rauterberg.

Rauterberg was a hustler. His eyes always twinkled in his bronze face. His hair was streaked, perhaps graying, probably sun-bleached. He looked athletic, but his round face and his physique were not angular. Women said he was cherubic. I figured he was superintelligent, a good schemer, because I knew that he'd moved up steadily, working for twenty years in the tough world of banking and lobbying, and was comfortable within the staid framework of an organization in which divorce was unspoken grounds for dismissal. Right now, the most important thing about Bob Rauterberg was his title, vice-president of the correspondent banking division of the Marine National Exchange Bank of Milwaukee. I was really up, convinced that my success was about to crest. It was a perfect moment to corral Rauterberg: he was the obvious, if fateful, choice to guide me through the maze of high finance.

"What's the land baron up to now?" The word was out. I smiled, trying to look mysterious.

It took three Cuba Libres and twenty minutes to get Rauterberg aside without tipping my hand to half of Madison's junior jet set, another twenty to settle him down. Finally, when it was time for Rauterberg to be serious—if he was ever to be—he was.

I told him my entire story: real estate conglomerate, club, loan company.

"Great, but . . ." He pursed his lips, nodded his head slowly, ran a finger round the top of his glass. "It involves a lot of money. Things are tight. This morning's Federal Reserve report indicates that rates on government notes may go up. I think we're in for another squeeze." He asked about Thunderhead's financing package, closing his eyes as I answered. "That's a tough nut to crack," he said, raising his lids.

Annoyed, I said, "It's handled for now." I hoped the sharpness of my remark made it sound final.

"Sure, but the senator who's taking a second mortgage, I'll bet he's a barracuda. You gotta have staying power."

Rauterberg had a point, so let him help. I looked him straight in the eye and asked, "Can you set something up in case we need it?"

"Not at my bank. Too risky." Rauterberg explained that he had to keep his nose clean until he'd completed the twenty-year minimum requirement for a pension. He had five years to go.

I understood his apprehension. The Marine Corporation was a banking powerhouse. If Rauterberg screwed up with them, he was through in banking.

"But your deal sounds interesting. I'd like to help, and"—he waved a loaded friend away and went on softly, "I'd like to get in on it." He leaned forward, studying me, his eyes moving over the room before he continued. "I particularly like the idea of including Janeff, especially if it assists the club. That could be just the beginning. Later we can use it for financing condo down payments, land sales—"

"Vacation trips, insurance, sports vehicles." I improvised, picking up the tempo. I was really excited. Here was a banker sharing my ideas, wanting a piece of my action. If handled properly, Rauterberg could open bank doors for me all over the state. My mind began to wander, my dreams to expand. His voice jolted me back to reality.

"John, you can't borrow on ideas alone. Not now." He rubbed his cheeks slowly, pensively. "Get it all down on paper. You're good at that. Show how the clearinghouse for consumer paper (Janeff) ties in with the Sports Club (find a name for it), and the whole thing feeds the resort (Thunderhead)."

"Gotcha," I said, thinking that Rauterberg would be a fantastic ally.

"But be careful," he continued. "I like it, but I think you're a guy trying to make lotsa things happen all at once—maybe too many. How are you managing to keep your job at Janeff while you spend so much time promoting resorts and recreation?"

"We just talked about how the loan business ties in with everything else. A great fit. I've explained that to Sommers and I think he's counting on me to make everything work." I leaned toward him and lowered my voice. "As long as Sommers is in that frame of mind I can keep my job. Later, I'll take control of the company."

"Can you?" Rauterberg rubbed his chin.

"Damn right."

He leaned back in the booth and gazed at the ceiling. I could tell he was trying to make a decision. Then he said, "There may be problems, but I want part of the action anyway." I knew he meant it, so long as it was a transaction that no one could trace. No one comprehended the role of Rauterberg the banker. Before we could say more, he was swept up by a throng of revelers. From the doorway, he shouted to me, "Let's get moving tomorrow."

I took a long swallow of rum and Coke, wondering how Rauterberg could warn me against moving too fast in one breath and then urge haste in the next. I decided that the quality of my ideas eclipsed the risks involved. Risks could be tolerated. It was something like walking uphill on ice—no way you can go quickly without falling on your ass. But if you were careful, deliberate, and prepared for the inevitable backsliding, and if you had guts and a tough butt, you'd make it—maybe even flatten out the ice. I laughed aloud. The cocktail waitress came over; I paid my tab and told her, "It's a better metaphor than the one about eating elephants."

She offered me a half-smile, a look I knew was reserved for drunks. The bar seemed noisier than ever as I left. I imagined Kritchner and Hollis talking again, saying they had "faith" and were willing to "expedite." They were sold.

"Of course." The Master Plan was selling itself. Soon it would become a working model.

The Inn at Thunderhead dominated my Christmas at home, in spite of my resolve to attend more closely to family matters. I found that I had little interest in celebrating anything but the closing. That became a certainty when First National granted us a temporary $102,000 unsecured loan and Turnbull moved to Steamboat Springs with enough money to cover our commitments. Even in the midst of the season's first blizzard, everything was coming up green. The bank promised an additional $5,000 when we had completed the CondoHotel details, and Bob Rauterberg, who'd begun visiting me daily, said he could quietly arrange a $20,000 loan at any time. That provided enough funding to meet our first contractual payment to the senator on January 15 and left Turnbull plenty for operating expenses.

After months on a treadmill of apprehension, the first segment of Phase One of my Master Plan was a reality. I should have attended the closing, simply to savor my success, but I didn't. Instead, while Turnbull (using documents executed in advance) took possession of the Inn, I compulsively began to polish my Master Plan. I was wound up. It was mid-afternoon before I realized it was New Year's Eve.

A hot shower didn't relax me. My stomach was still tight with tension, and my shoulders ached from bending over the Plan. As I toweled dry I could see five colorful plastic-bound folders lying on the bed. Except for title pages, they were mostly still empty. I sat naked beside them and spread them out, certain that when all the pages were in place the parts would fall together.

Folder Number One was a recapitulation of my dream, starting in Steamboat Springs and growing into what I liked to think of as a four-faceted jewel of accomplishment—an "Empire of Fun" where power, wealth, and prestige were foregone conclusions and a healthy hunk of outdoor pleasure was guaranteed. What a sales pitch! Plus a speech composed for the Colorado business community: "We'll start with $250,000 and create billions," it ended. I swung around, sorry there was no one to test it on.

Folder Number Two began to list my business maneuvers. I ticked them off—neatly packaged plans, numbered sales points to make the buyers believe first, pay later. Somewhere in here was a foolproof money machine.

Number Three contained current data on the pregnant holding company and its embryo component.

Folders Four and Five would cover plans for the Club (originally Phase Two of my Plan) and the loan company.

I began pacing around the bed, aware that my Master Plan lacked income projections, alternative financing proposals, and up-to-date appraisals. Pretty words and exciting ideas wouldn't be enough to sell sophisticated investors—or bankers.

My mind was accelerating. If it weren't New Year's Eve, and if I didn't love my wife and weren't just a little afraid to lose her because I was becoming (in her words) "a driven man," I'd have returned to the office and worked all night.

I looked at the gray suit I'd laid out next to the folders on the bed—too conservative, too dull to drape John Stone. I picked another: colorful, but not flashy, deep blue-green to match the turquoise bolo tie I wanted to wear. It made me feel like partying.

No sense getting dressed now; Judy was still at the beauty shop. I snugged the towel around my waist and went to the bar to fix a rum and Coke. I telephoned the Inn; Turnbull said that the closing had gone smoothly. I was making money.

"Damn right." I owed myself a celebration. But first I wanted to enter my new net worth in the Master Plan. When I'd finished making changes—always increases—I lay back on the bed, stretched, and took a deep, satisfied breath. I was worth over a quarter of a million dollars.

I was still fondling the sheet of figures when the front door clicked open. "Judy?" I shouted. "Get dressed and let's go. It's going to be a helluva party."

Judy preceded me into the Elks Club. She wore a long, side-slit, flowered dress, almost Oriental in its simplicity. I'd forgotten what a graceful stride she had. Her legs were perfectly tapered to where the dress tightened across firm hips, then tucked to her tiny waist. She glanced back at me with a casual but very sensual smile, her red hair shimmering in the light as the door opened for her. "Some woman." I had told myself that many times, always—until recently—sure she'd never leave me. I needed her—because she was a showpiece and because she was my pilot, my companion, and the only woman with a fitted place in my dreams.

The bar was packed. It was too early for dinner or dancing. I saw Joe Butters standing close by, a long time neighbor. Though barely forty and officially called T. Joseph Butters, he'd surely and simply been "Good Old Joe" since graduating from law school. He smoked a pipe, moved slowly, and was mellow; his prematurely wrinkled face was always in repose. His legal clients were primarily up-swinging businessmen, but everyone knew he never let their problems faze him. His children were friends of my sons, his wife a pal of Judy's.

We rarely met socially as couples. When we did, it was usually in the company of booze, and only after half a dozen drinks did an interesting conversation ever develop. Butters was "still waters." He had run for political office once; he came from a prominent family and had been married, not happily, for fourteen or fifteen years. And, for certain, he had a mistress. No one could remember him ever being without one.

He was a member of a mysterious club. I never discovered what the club did, except that it met on Thursday nights. That was boys' night out. You didn't take your wife to the current in spots on Thursday night; you just didn't, or you'd hear about it from other members. I had never joined, never even been asked. I was known as "the badass" who picked Thursday night to go pub-crawling with my legal mate.

Joe Butters had to be a good choice for my attorney. I thought about it as I wove my way through the crowd. I needed him now —a second-rater, like the guy who'd worked on the CondoHotel papers, would never do. Butters was shrewd; Butters could keep his mouth shut. He was prominent in the Elks Club and he had many affluent friends. I decided he'd never become an investor; when it came to writing checks, he thought his time was worth more than his money and gave you that instead. But he would add an aura of stability to my operations.

A fresh round of drinks appeared as I reached Butters's side. With a friendly, but uncommon, punch on the arm, he said we'd have to toast my success. He kept shuttling friends over to hear about my accomplishments—I had center stage, and I loved it.

Moreover, I was acting the lead role, as planned. The drinks I consumed kept me glib-tongued but so far steady. I repeated my story of how the Triumvirate, now usually called Diamond J, had performed the impossible.

A few more people and drinks, and I began to sail out of the spotlight. I shouted, bragging and proud, that my Plans included more than the Inn. I was going to own all that was left to buy around Steamboat and then apply my genius to found the Playboy Club of Western Recreation. I knew I was drunk; I knew I was making my wife cringe. I cared, but I was out of control. There was no stopping me.

Most people moved on to dinner, Butters included. Judy had disappeared. I stayed behind, suddenly emotionally drained. The letdown left me weak and depressed, as quiet now as the party was boisterous. Soon everyone was as loud as I had been. It was midnight; I couldn't find Judy.

The next morning I woke before dawn. I lay fully clothed on my side of the king-sized bed. Judy was sleeping on the other side—as far away as she could get. I didn't remember coming home. Strange, I thought, that after so little sleep and so much alcohol I felt so refreshed—no hangover at all.

I fixed coffee and carried a steaming cup into the living room, to the chair beside the telephone. Impulsively I dialed Dave Padgett's home number; he was the man who had first tipped me on the Recreation Club idea. His phone was ringing before I realized that it wasn't 8:00 A.M. yet, and a holiday.

Padgett answered quickly, but his voice was abnormally slow. He talked more softly than I'd ever heard him. Apparently he didn't recognize my voice until I'd almost finished apologizing.

"Don't worry about it," he said, suddenly coming to life. "I've been trying to reach you for a week."

"I've been busy, and partying, and commemorating." I used that line as a tantalizer before beginning another repetition of the story. Out of the corner of my eye I saw Judy come into the room. She watched me with sleep-shrouded eyes, took a deep breath that sounded full of disgust, then turned away without speaking. For a moment I forgot what I'd been telling Padgett.

In a booming voice, he urged me to meet him tomorrow. I

shrugged and felt the corners of my mouth turn up; right now he was more important than anyone else. I needed him for the Club, and he sounded like he needed me. He did; he offered me a job. I was certain that the offer had nothing to do with the Janeff money problem, which he knew about, but then again, maybe he wanted control of the loan company.

"What do you have in mind?" I asked. I was just curious; I certainly wasn't prepared for his response.

"Help me set up Lake, Sport, and Travel Club."

"What?"

"My outdoor recreation club," Padgett said.

Maybe my hearing was bad; either he had my phone tapped or he could read my mind. Then I realized that the idea had originally been his.

I left the house very early the next morning. I hadn't spoken with Judy all New Year's Day, and wanted to spare myself any confrontation before meeting Padgett. Also, I knew he liked to conjure up schemes before sunrise. I drove across town to the converted factory building he owned.

The only evidence of occupancy was a walkway clear of snow, shrouded by a faded and windworn canopy. A sign on the front door read U.S. BUYER'S CLUB. Beyond it, in the reception area, another sign warned: MEMBERS ONLY. I shuddered and stopped to fix a relaxed expression on my face. God knew Padgett's offices wouldn't put me at ease, they were a maze of mismatched paneling.

His secretary answered two phones—one black, the other beige—while sitting on a green chair at a battleship-gray desk and pounding a blue typewriter. I picked my way through a conference room cluttered with stacks of printed forms and promotional brochures. An old paper cutter lay rusting in the center of the long table.

Padgett's private office, where he rose to greet me from behind an expansive imitation walnut desk, had thick red and black shag carpeting. The pecan-finished walls were hung with velvet paintings, primarily chartreuse. The lighting was indirect, and even for this early hour, dim. But Padgett seemed very much at home.

I studied his face. He had to be pushing fifty, and if it wasn't his age, something else was worrying him. His every expression, from his squint to his half-formed smile, was a nervous one, and his voice was too loud for the poorly lit room. He reminded me of a worn-down tour director finishing another hectic day on a cruise ship, about to turn in for the night, knowing that seven hours later he'd be back at the mercy of his charges and that the only way out was overboard.

"John, I hope you'll come to work with me," he said.

"Why?"

"You're aggressive. You've got brains even better than mine. And you're the greatest salesman I've ever met. We're an irresistible combination." He paused waiting for agreement.

I made him wait. I was thinking: He also wants me because I have entrée to money—Rauterberg, the banks, and Janeff, when I put it back together . . . and the stockholders, and my doctors— and because I have Thunderhead.

Padgett began talking again; it didn't take much to wind him up. He waved a sheaf of documents. Before I could examine them he repeated his premise that the techniques used to establish his buyer's club were equally appropriate for an outdoor recreation club. He called it "Lake, Sport, and Travel," as if the name were a foregone conclusion. I could see why when I examined the papers in my hand; they had "Lake, Sport, and Travel Club" embossed everywhere. Padgett, observing my astonishment, said flatly that he intended to promote the club regardless of my participation; he was ready to start today. He already owned land— and the Lake, Sport, and Travel Lodge on Lake Couderay in the north woods. He had a line on other Wisconsin properties, too.

"That's all it takes," he said—his major target markets were Milwaukee, Rockford, and the greater Chicago area. "I'm after the campers." He asked me to consider how many millions were invested every year by tens of thousands of sportsmen, just to purchase camping vehicles. "All these 'Joe Lunch Buckets' with their expensive toys are running out of places to go."

He paused, then added, "Private facilities with a selected clientele." He cocked his head and used a one-eyed nod to indicate that he meant to exclude minorities. His inference was not in character; I'd always figured he'd sell anything to anyone. Then, before I could ask, he explained that certain groups, always chronic complainers, were at the heart of the burgeoning consumer movement. "We can't afford bitchers and gripers," he said. "They're the first to run to the authorities. Every black sonofabitch thinks the world owes him a membership."

I directed his attention back to the documents. "Are these the keys to success in promoting a club?" I asked.

"They'll work for any kind of membership," he boasted. "Took me ten years to develop and made me money for twenty. Now pay attention." Coming around the desk, he spread the forms out in front of me, pointing to them with both hands. "These papers allow me to motivate joiners. They're directed to the four psychological catalysts present in all prospects: greed, sex, ego, and envy." Padgett moved around me and repeated the words into my other ear. His breath smelled like worn-out mouthwash. I leaned away, and nodded.

"There are six forms," he continued, his voice quieter. "First is the official nomination certificate." He tapped a four-page booklet printed in black and gold on parchment-textured paper. The certificate was numbered. "In honor of the _____ family," it began, "the _____ family's name has been submitted for possible membership by an existing club member in good standing."

A resumé of club benefits followed. The club was organized for the benefit of families who wanted the use of private lands and facilities to enjoy hunting, fishing, camping, and snowmobiling. A map showing locations was printed on the second page. Across from it was the club creed, which ended, ". . . add happiness and friendship to our lives." The rest of the page explained that since the club was "Exclusive" and "Limited," character references were required. The final page emphasized the importance of the nomination, a *one-time opportunity*. Once declined, it could *never be offered to the same person again.*

Padgett said that the nomination certificate was designed to stimulate ego and envy—"to make the prospect feel important and to show how he can enjoy the same benefits as his presently more fortunate peers."

I asked him who did the nominating.

Laughing, he replied, as to an applicant, "Impossible to tell.

Our club is so popular, the list's so long, we could never keep track." I figured that sales leads would be secured from commercial lists or paid referrals, but Padgett said conspiratorially that once founded, the club would obtain most of its leads from new members. He showed me a member referral form that stated, "There are limited facilities available, and because of this the Club has chosen to avoid advertising for members. We have elected a method of growth using the same system employed by several other clubs, such as the Elks, Masons, and Moose. To avoid undesirable characters, we ask that Club Members recommend interested friends of good moral character."

Adding that this also appealed to ego and envy, he told me to read the next paragraph. "Any new applicant who elects to make an application and will list five names of friends or neighbors below may submit an initiation check in the amount of $30 instead of the regular $40 as required on the 'Agreement.' "

"Greed!" Padgett bellowed. "They save ten bucks. Those words jab their greedy instincts."

"What about sex?"

"I put people together; the rest takes care of itself. *Playboy* sells it. We give it for free." The club had no salesmen, he said, sitting down; only members, referred to as "membership directors," who contacted sponsored applicants. "Sales and salesmen are forbidden words around here," he said, waving a finger.

I wanted to warn Padgett not to talk down to me, but I figured I'd better keep still until I had learned everything I'd come for. He was already talking about another form, the membership application.

"This is only used after the nomination sheet is complete," he said. "Notice how it requires the applicant to attest and certify that he has 'not been induced to make application for membership by promises of any form of compensation, or consideration for the subsequent enrollment of any parties that he has nominated for membership. Got to have that to satisfy the Goddamn law."

There was a lot of fine print; the only large letters said "Five-Year Membership Privileges." I couldn't find a statement of total cost anywhere on the front of the paper, and when I turned it over, I noticed that most of the previously stated conditions were repeated in the form of a well-disguised installment note.

I was familiar with the note: Padgett had sold Janeff many identical instruments through his Buyer's Club. It was legally enforceable; I'd learned that during battles with his disgruntled members in Small Claims Court.

I also saw that he was using the same cost figures as in the Buyer's Club, a grand total of $520. If the applicant wished to pay cash within ten days, he'd receive a special charter membership for $500. No discount was offered for prepayment of the interest-free contract, which included the statement that "a member's cost for dues amounts to only sixty-seven cents a day for two years."

"That buys a five-year membership," Padgett said as I read the line. Then he held up a fistful of varicolored forms. "Look here: one with general information—appeals to greed, ego, and envy. Another explaining the social advantages—appeals to ego and envy. This, listing discount privileges—greed. And committee outlines—we let the members do their own work arranging picnics, parties, and dances. And hunting and fishing trips. Makes them feel useful, important, and saves money—ego and greed."

Quite a scheme, I thought, finding it hard to believe that Padgett could actually influence members to provide most of the services their dues were supposed to buy. All he gave them was a place, an outline, and lots of encouragement. It was too slick, too pat. Even if it worked, it was a lie. But some of his ideas were stimulating. So when he went into his private bathroom, I slipped the duplicate set of forms into my briefcase.

Padgett began talking from the bathroom about his favorite subject, negative selling. "Make every prospective member realize how difficult it is to join Lake, Sport, and Travel Club," he said as he came back into the office. "Never let him think he'll be automatically accepted. Keep him guessing. Keep him doubting. Make him worry. Look. . . ." He circled a segment of the membership application, and gave it to me. "Read it aloud," he demanded.

"If the family feels they cannot make a decision or cannot see the value of membership, the club member conducting the interview is *required to reject the nomination.* It is important to understand that an applicant for membership is not a member of the Club until he is approved by the membership committee. The applicant may not use the Club facilities and benefits until such time as he is approved and accepted."

I told him I understood. I did. I thought it was great.

The final subject was a financial analysis of the membership concept. Padgett had copied arithmetic used by the Buyer's Club. The bottom line, $135 per enrollment, could be used at the club owners' discretion for expansion, investment in new facilities, or personal business expenses. "Anything except executive bonuses or dividends. They're taxable," he said.

His reference to taxes triggered another explosion about bureaucrats and minorities who, in an effort to stamp out free enterprise, had allied themselves with the consumer protection movement—and, according to Padgett, were trying to immobilize his Buyer's Club business. He raved on about how once before the same forces had moved against his food-freezer sales organization, forcing him to convert to furniture discounting. "Now they're after me again. So I've set up something new: Lake, Sport, and Travel."

We worked through the day without lunch—even without my ever-present coffee, which I claimed aided concentration. When I finally looked at my watch it was after five o'clock. There was no way to judge time in the windowless confines of Padgett's office, and I'd had enough. As I'd expected, he knew a way to sell memberships, and I had no doubt that his methods would prove effective in promoting the "Joe Lunch Bucket" camper club he proposed. But I wasn't sure that there was any way I could espouse his selling philosophy, or that his club was anything like the organization I contemplated. When I stood up to leave, Padgett stared at me. He was looking for an answer.

"I'll think about it," I said—nothing more.

I wanted Padgett to be available, a last resort in case my Thunderhead stockholders refused to support the recreation club phase of the Diamond J concept. Turnbull, Kritchner, and the other doctors were still resting with the satisfaction of owning the Inn, and had balked recently whenever I pushed them toward action on the club.

Kritchner had said, "There's no hurry. A good idea is always a good idea and a bad one isn't worth wasting time on. And I haven't decided which category the club is in."

No good, I thought, the club is too important. It can generate the cash flow we need to keep everyone happy. Otherwise the Thunderhead stockholders might have to empty their own pockets again to pay the bills that were beginning to accumulate, even as our first full ski season got underway.

"And the club will help fill our vacant rooms," I'd told every stockholder at our last meeting.

But still they were not enthusiastic, and now Sommers was beginning to have doubts.

"When am I going to see some results from this Master Plan to salvage Janeff?" he'd asked the same day when I'd called in for my messages. "I thought you were going to produce a lot of profitable membership contracts."

"Be patient, please," I'd asked, noticing how raspy his voice had become.

"Either get it done or give it up and get back to work for me." That had been an order.

So there wasn't much time left, and unless I could convince the Diamond J group to underwrite my club soon, I'd be foolish to refuse a coalition with Padgett. Rauterberg's banking assistance would make my plans viable under any circumstances, and once operative, the club wouldn't need promoting. Just fifty local members would be sufficient proof of the idea's soundness; then all the Thunderhead stockholders would scramble for their fair share. Later I could easily sell part of my interest, recouping any personal investment and realizing a substantial capital gain.

I returned to the Janeff office and worked late, catching up on my work collecting neglected delinquencies. After midnight, driving home, I realized how uptight I was. Earlier I'd pictured myself as a new star in the bright business sky. "Or just a damn comet," as Crombie had put it when he implied that I might be undependable.

"Comet, no way," I shouted into the approaching headlights. I hated nicknames in any form unless they came from my own metaphorical allusions. All my life, on and off, I'd been teased for being a P.K., a Preacher's Kid. The connotation, of course, was that all clergymen's children were wild and bad—drank too much, screwed around, and probably made a career out of violating the Ten Commandments.

Judy and I had talked about this—I wasn't hung up on many of the Commandments. I did a lot of coveting, believed adultery had its place, and figured I could kill under the right circumstances. She could forgive me so far, she'd said, but she seemed to dwell on the fifth commandment. It was important to me too; I would not steal, I insisted. Fast deals, yes, but I wanted to be trusted. More than anything I needed Judy's trust and faith, and I was willing to pay for them by returning the favor.

I wanted to talk, but Judy was already asleep when I went to bed and I couldn't wake her. She only groaned and rolled away when I squeezed her shoulder and kissed her neck. I shivered, suddenly cold when I realized she was unable or unwilling to share my ideas.

It wasn't easy to relax. Memories of my life with Judy crowded my consciousness. She had the smoothest skin I'd ever touched, and yet, though I'd tried many times, I had never been able to find precisely the right words to tell her so.

Now her naked body was very still, her breathing almost inaudible. When I reached out to take her hand I wondered if she would sense the warmth I was trying to find for us. It's funny, I reflected, beginning to be drowsy, how I've always called her hands little. They were actually only slightly smaller than mine. Certainly they weren't the hands of a child. Judy was my woman. I wanted to think through the problems we had, but my mind was running down; I just didn't have the energy. Maybe I was reacting to the splendid trauma of Thunderhead, Janeff, and Lake, Sport, and Travel, I thought as I rolled over to press close against her.

And then I shuddered when I remembered I'd begun to think that she "was" my woman; my mind was using the past tense. That was my last, disturbing thought.

4

January 1971

ASSETS—$326,350.00
LIABILITIES—$97,150.00
PERSONAL GUARANTEES—$320,000.00

Sixteen inches of snow fell on Madison, covering the debris of New Year's Eve, and stopping business dead. The flakes were heavy and formless, wet enough to soak the nap of my cashmere topcoat. The phone was ringing as I arrived at my office, well before the morning rush hour, and I answered it in the dark, wondering who could be calling so early.

"Figured to catch you ahead of the crowds," said Turnbull. "You awake?"

"Smartass."

He started explaining his plans to build additions to the Inn, and I switched on the office lights so I could take notes. I was breathless.

"Ed, you've got balls. Diamond J's getting bigger and better faster than I hoped."

Turnbull intended to double the size of Thunderhead. "Sixteen rooms can be added along the wasted west side of the main corridor," he said. "Amsler will help with preliminary plans and cost estimates. He's branched into the construction business."

"Probably on our commission money," I chuckled. I said I'd talk with the stockholders. "They'll approve."

"What'll we use for money?" Turnbull asked. "Why not re-finance the Inn as originally planned?"

I studied the stockholders' personal financial statements. Their combined net worth was over $2 million, and clearly a third was liquid. So far we hadn't overextended ourselves. "Go ahead," I told him.

Meanwhile, the city was paralyzed by the blizzard. I couldn't reach the doctors, Rauterberg, or even Padgett. I looked out at the deepening snow. Then it struck me: this was just the thing to put peoples' minds on snowmobile racing. I'd almost forgotten my races! I rushed from one file cabinet to another until I found the race plans.

The International Pro/Am Snowmobile Championships might seem like intellectual pablum next to my other business ventures, but one day soon they would be the Indianapolis 500 of snow-mobiling. The public relations possibilities were limitless. I'd come up with the scheme in 1969 when, with Kritchner, I had formed a hobby company to promote speed sports. The first annual races had lost money, sure, but still, the United States Snowmobile Association had called them "the smoothest events on the safest track sanctioned; a real winner."

This season's competition was set for February 11 and 12. Time was running out on me again, but I knew that I could still pull it off—cram six months' work into three weeks by enlisting, even shanghaiing, the services of every friend, partner, and employee. So while the snow kept falling I organized the race, this time thankful that the elements buffered me from all other business involvements.

On the day of the race the crowds were bigger and the entries, when we counted them, more than double the year before. It didn't help much; the race lost money again. I consoled myself, and Kritchner and the other stockholders of "Dash," with the observation that our race was now established. The name and publicity alone were valuable; next year it would explode with profits.

Maybe, I thought, we should move the International Pro/Am Championships to a large metropolitan track like Soldier Field in Chicago. I stood in the middle of the racetrack and thought how much my lifestyle was changing. Literally and figuratively I was in an expansive mood; I was ready to try anything. I collared Kritchner and reminded him of the land option he had purchased from a nearly bankrupt Janeff customer.

"The farm?" he said, screwing up his face. "That was over a year ago. What the hell do we need with eighty acres of cropland? Haven't you got enough to handle? Besides, I'm broke—at least I will be when we finish paying for this loser." He pointed to the grandstands.

"There's no risk involved with the farm," I explained. "The club needs it, and once the property is affiliated with the club you'll recoup your investment from the members' dues and use fees."

Kritchner frowned.

I raised my gloved palm toward his face. "Don't say anything till I finish. Don't you see? You buy the property, the club uses it and pays for it . . . and everybody's happy."

Kritchner's face began to relax.

"And while we're converting it into an adult playground, you can be a gentleman farmer. Maybe even put some land in the soil bank and earn a dividend from the government," I said.

Now that Kritchner was nodding, I began to smile. Then he stopped and stared at me.

"But Stone, you don't even have a club, just an idea."

"I'm ready to begin the club today. All I need is investors and a local facility."

He shook his head. "Never give up, do you? What's the price of the farm? I've forgotten."

When I told him $3,000 an acre, Kritchner stepped back and started to turn away.

"Are you kidding? A quarter-million!" He talked over his shoulder. "Get the club started first and show me what it can do with somebody else's money; then I'll think about sticking my own neck out." Kritchner walked away.

That didn't shake me. I knew he'd buy the farm someday soon. I was beginning to believe I could make every deal in the world.

As he did every March, Feldher Sommers, founder and president of Janeff, began a six-week Mexican vacation. It was a holiday for me too. Lately Sommers had been a real bear, always angry and hypercritical, complaining that I was "all talk" and unfairly blaming me for Janeff's credit problems and its shaky relationships with banks. He had left orders to "forget my pipe dreams and clean up the delinquency that makes the company look bad to the bankers."

Shit. Delinquency wasn't the real problem. The past-due lists weren't much longer than normal. If the banks were skeptical of Janeff, it was because Sommers projected such a bleak future. He was a rotten public relations man, set in his ways and incapable of romancing the money men. I was frustrated with Sommers around, and sometimes I couldn't concentrate. The time was right for him to retire: I couldn't afford the hassle of waiting, and yet I still didn't have enough money to buy him out.

But I thought I could get the money through Lake, Sport, and Travel Club. Founding the club was the solution to many problems, but now, since my Diamond J associates were still dragging their feet, each assuming Kritchner's "show me" attitude, I'd have to proceed without them. So when Padgett invited me on a flying tour of his branches I agreed to go.

Judy and Padgett were both pilots. They shared the use of an airplane, a single-engine Navion that resembled a World War II dive bomber. I had flown a lot with Judy, but never before with Padgett. When we were airborne he seemed to be paying more attention to my pending participation in the club than to flying the plane.

"I need you with me to make it go," he said.

I withheld my allegiance. Up there in the clouds, I was again hopeful I'd find a way to build my dream without him.

By the time we began the final leg of the trip Padgett was living on coffee and No-Doz. At every office he'd discovered serious financial problems; the banks were cutting him off. His quick, darting adjustments of the plane's instruments were making me increasingly nervous. After that I swore to myself never to leave the ground with Padgett again; I decided it was safer to put the club concept back on the shelf.

The Thunderhead stockholders, apparently content, met only

once during that six weeks, when Turnbull flew in to discuss final plans for the addition. Sommers returned with a deep tan and a remarkably improved disposition. He announced that he could "handle the banks." I tried to spend more time at home with Judy and the kids. I should have been content, but I couldn't help wondering if the Master Plan was in a slump.

It took money to make things happen, and even though we didn't need it today, we sure as hell would tomorrow. I tried to reach Rauterberg but discovered he was at a week-long meeting in Chicago.

I made a reservation on the morning flight to Denver. It was easy to rationalize the value of my trip; there was no formal stockholder supervision of the Inn. Turnbull, as resident manager, notified me or Kritchner whenever there was a problem, but most of the time he was alone. "He needs support," I told myself.

Snow was still on the ground when I arrived in the mountains. The Inn was filled with late-season skiers stumbling over construction supplies for our new addition, which was already under way. I studied the latest plans and their cost breakdown and decided I'd have to take Turnbull's word, based on consultations with Amsler, that they were in order.

"I know from nothing about the building trades," I told him. As soon as I made the remark I was sorry: I was the boss, and bosses don't plead ignorance.

And something new was in the wind. Several times during my stay I observed Turnbull in hushed conversation with Amsler and a stranger. Early on the last morning, when I came into the lounge looking for coffee, they were huddled over maps spread across two corner tables. When they saw me they rolled up the maps and started bullshitting about a new crop of single girls that had checked in the night before.

Now I was really suspicious, ready to rush across the room and interrogate them. Turnbull must have sensed my intentions, because he waved hello, and with his back quickly turned to the others, winked very slowly and nodded: our signal that there was no problem. I didn't trust Amsler, but Turnbull did, and I trusted Turnbull, so I poured myself coffee and carried it to the opposite side of the room.

They must be working on a deal with principals who demanded absolute secrecy, I thought. Today that wasn't uncommon in Steamboat Springs, where fortunes were being made overnight. When the time was right Turnbull would tell me about it.

There wasn't much for a nonskier to do at the Inn; I was restless and lonesome. So I called Judy.

"Where are you?" she asked in a monotone.

I told her I realized that I'd forgotten to say good-bye or even give her my destination. I apologized.

"I'm tired of hearing you say you're sorry," she said in the same even voice.

I wanted to yell, "Fuck you!" But I knew that would destroy any chance I had to crack the cocoon she was weaving from the tangled web of my efforts.

I dialed Rauterberg next. His secretary said he was still away, now visiting correspondent banks.

Back home, I paced the Janeff office. Sommers came in the front door; a fast look at his face showed that his suntan and his good humor had both faded. I went out the back door to my car.

Conducting big business without a respectable separate office of my own was ridiculous. A loan company gave the wrong impression, and for now, at least, meant living with Sommers. The atmosphere wasn't right. It kept me uptight.

As I was opening the car door I made my decision. I turned and retraced my steps to the office.

"Let's work a deal," I told Sommers. He was prowling around my office, studying the stacks of loan ledgers.

He nodded. "I think it's time to redefine your responsibilities."

We agreed that I would take a cut in pay and work part-time for Janeff. As long as I kept the collection calls current, I would have the freedom to come and go as I pleased.

"That way, maybe you can make some progress with your big plans." He smiled. "I hope so, because we can all use the profits you've been talking about."

I quickly found a vacant mini-suite to rent in a newly remodeled office building. The sudden move was a happy excuse for a change of pace. I spent the next three days decorating, matching colors carefully and deciding which mounted animal heads and fishing trophies I should hang. I bought a deep-brown walnut desk and several leather-covered chairs.

The first call on my new speaker phone came from Turnbull. "How you doing?" he said in an unusually soft voice.

"Hang on," I said, "while I find my cigarettes."

Turnbull dropped the facade and shouted, "How'd you like to make $300,000 this week?" Then he told me about his secret meetings, which had resulted in a sales commitment to buy Walton Creek Park at half its market value.

Tucking the phone against my shoulder, I quickly spread out my map of Steamboat Springs. Walton Creek Park was a forty-acre tract lying between the new Holiday Inn site and the ski slopes. I remembered driving past the north boundary when I'd taken a short cut from LTV's new gondola lift to the highway. There was only one structure on the property: a unique, mushroom-shaped house with its octagonal living quarters perched atop a central pedestal.

"I can buy the whole shebang tomorrow for half a million," Turnbull announced.

"That's $12,500 per acre!" I yelled back. Steamboat's sky-rocketing land values still awed me.

"And I can resell it for over $20,000 an acre any time," he said.

"What's the angle?"

Turnbull said that the owner was a regular customer at Thunderhead's bar and a casual friend. "He bought Walton Creek Park before the land boom; he's satisfied with doubling his money if the property sells for cash, or on a short-term contract to responsible parties."

"And who's more responsible than the owners of the biggest resort out there?" I laughed.

"We need a $50,000 down payment, but I can bind the deal temporarily with $10,000. Okay to use Thunderhead's funds?" It was an assertion more than a question.

"Just don't let Walton Creek Park slip through your fingers," I warned. "All our present partners will want a piece too. We'll use the same percentages as the Thunderhead corporation."

We didn't discuss money again; we both assumed that I'd take the responsibility of raising the down payment. I began calling the Thunderhead stockholders—after a cursory explanation, they all endorsed the acquisition. I wasn't surprised. They're all overwhelmed by the mystique of Steamboat, I thought—and they believe in me.

But someday I knew I'd need more money than they could provide; even now I was short on funding Walton Creek Park. As long as it was my Master Plan, the task of finding money would always be mine. And my experience was limited. Sure, I'd guaranteed some of the Janeff Credit lines. They ran six figures, but Sommers had arranged and administered them. Thunderhead's past financing was merely the assumption of existing debt, supplemented by the installment sales contract with Senator Decker, that Amsler had arranged. And the loan at the First National Bank had been set up by Kritchner. When it came to handling large-scale money accommodations, I was a virgin.

I called Rauterberg and told him I needed money first, then guidance. He rejected the former. "I can't lend money to individuals or companies I'm in business with," he said matter-of-factly.

"You're not a stockholder."

"But you promised me a share of Thunderhead and Janeff," he said.

"Yes, but this will be a new corporation," I told him, realizing I hadn't explained the structure of the holding company.

"What's the difference? You know they'll all work together. The officers, directors and stockholders overlap."

"Yes."

"Well then, my bank can't make any more loans to you," Rauterberg said. His tone was final. "But I'll start hunting another source. In the meantime, look around yourself. I can't be your only banker friend."

Rauterberg was right. I'd partied with him for years before we'd finally talked about money; I'd been ignoring an important resource.

I began my list of bankers with Bill Lindsey, vice-president of the Mount Horeb State Bank in Mount Horeb, near Madison, and actually a much closer friend than Rauterberg. We hunted together, and Lindsey had been my informal partner in a small scheme to buy cheap land in good Colorado elk country. He was a good bet to help, but he needed a thorough briefing: so far I'd done nothing more than brag about Thunderhead and the snowmobile race and reassure him that Janeff was not broke when he'd heard rumors to the contrary.

I kept writing down names. Finally, aware that I was straining to make a long list, I stopped with eleven.

That evening I drove twenty miles to see Lindsey at his home. He was my age but looked younger. His face was smooth, marked only by fading freckles across his nose.

Lindsey smiled indulgently and asked, "So what do you need tonight?"

The hasty, unannounced visit had given me away. "Money," I said, and then explained the Walton Creek Park project.

Like Rauterberg, Lindsey shied from arranging a loan at his bank. "But one of the bank's directors may be able to help you privately," he said. "Just don't argue with him about the terms."

He was right: one of the bank's directors could help. The man's money was very expensive, and available for only ninety days, but the pressure was on, hard. My stomach muscles tensed when I realized that this was my only chance to acquire Walton Creek Park and earn my share of the $300,000 profit Turnbull promised the deal would earn. The seller was suddenly demanding our full down payment immediately, and every other banker on my list required time-consuming loan documentation and credit investigations. Certainly, I felt, my partners would rather guarantee a high interest rate loan than dig deeper into their own nearly empty pockets, or lose the deal.

"Damn right," said Vitner when I explained the proposition at a special board meeting the following day. "Walton Creek Park's too good to lose just because we're low on cash. Pay the loan shark whatever we have to."

The rest shrugged, then nodded tentatively, and the discussion turned to which corporate structure should take title to the property.

"Not Thunderhead," I said. "There's no advantage in using the Inn corporation to buy Walton Creek Park."

"Right," said Hollis. "Better keep the businesses separate, so that if one gets into trouble it won't affect the others. Walton Creek Park is raw land. It's a risk situation. We'll need huge sums of money to develop it."

I had just started to ask where Hollis had gotten the idea that we'd be the developers when the phone rang.

"Did you get the money?" Turnbull said, shouting this time because we had a poor connection.

"Call me back on a good line," I told him. I wanted to put the call on my speaker phone.

When the phone rang again, everybody could hear his urgent request for money.

"Tomorrow," I said.

"Great. Then I'll get started on our holding company to buy, sell, and develop land and resorts." Turnbull said.

"Just like your plan says," Hollis added.

The others nodded.

"Goddamn. You've done your homework," I said, remembering my earlier doubts that they understood the Master Plan.

Turnbull had more than studied my ideas. He had selected a name: "Steamboat Holding and Development Company," he said through the speaker.

It sounded perfect; even Barass agreed. I visualized the letter-head—I had always been impressed by abbreviated cable designations. "Shadco," I shouted, and everyone smiled.

We discussed the advisability of a limited partnership instead of a corporation: a partnership would allow us all to share the tax advantages of depreciation and development expense.

"Partnerships involve personal liability, don't they?" Barass stared at the speaker phone as if he expected the answer to come from Turnbull. "Better check it out with our accountants and attorneys."

"Why?" I demanded. "The choice is obvious. The profits of a corporation can be plowed back as investment credits. We can grow fast, tax-free. Let's make it a corporation and not stick our necks out." I spoke in a loud voice, not for Turnbull's benefit, but because I wanted to end the discussion before someone came up with another reason to delay our progress.

Two days later I flew to Steamboat. Turnbull and I hired a

local attorney to form the company, and I told him to register the trade name "Shadco."

I took my first good look at Walton Creek Park from the wraparound porch of the mushroom house. Our property was a barren scar in the center of frantic construction; I could see new buildings at all points of the compass. "Perfectly situated to build apartments and duplexes," I told Turnbull. "Steamboat needs rental units. Ask your employees. They're shacked up three to a bed."

"Already have. You're stealing my idea." He grinned.

On our way to the Inn we passed another undeveloped parcel. It was bounded on one side by the highway, on another by the ski area access road, and on the third by the secondary access road.

"Who owns that triangle?"

"Retired army colonel who got rich on California real estate and is getting richer here. He bought up half the good land along Route 40 many years ago. Now he's unloading a little at a time," said Turnbull.

"Check it out," I directed, then added, "Why just one, when we can buy a dozen?"

I was in no hurry to return to Wisconsin. Judy wanted to talk about our floundering marriage again and Janeff's banks were making angry noises. I stayed an extra two days. I decided it was time to build a swimming pool and sauna at the Inn, and Turnbull showed me plans to convert the downstairs dining room into a rathskeller opening onto a gigantic sun deck with an open fireplace.

"Build 'em," I said.

The morning I left, Turnbull told me, "It's a good thing you're on your way. Otherwise we'd be paying for new projects the rest of our lives." He pounded my back as I walked toward the plane.

"Three letters awaited me at the Janeff office; an identical set was stacked on Sommer's desk. I could tell before opening mine that they were all from banks, and the contents of all three were similar: "You are a guarantor of all indebtedness, obligations, and liabilities due or owing from or by Janeff Credit Corporation. The bank hereby demands payment forthwith."

Sommers had not "handled the banks." I was surprised to find myself thinking, "*I* can handle it."

Sommers and I held salvage meetings with the banks. One agreed to assume full responsibility for the collection of Janeff's consumer notes pledged as collateral; the others demanded that Janeff do the work but remit all moneys collected directly to them. We couldn't even keep earned interest, and there'd be no more cash advances—our lines of credit were frozen. This meant that Janeff would have to exist on the cash flow from accounts owned outright, and most of these accounts were delinquent loans previously repurchased from the banks because of irregular payments.

We were being asked to liquidate Janeff. When I explained the situation to Rauterberg he told me to hold on, cut expenses, and work longer hours—without pay, if necessary. He was sure the disgruntled banks could eventually be replaced with more liberal lenders. "And in the meantime," he pointed out, "the pressure will be on Sommers. Now's the time to buy him out."

I made an offer, consisting of an option and, if exercised, provisions to pay Sommers in the future. He accepted. As I signed the agreement I felt his eyes burning into my back. The sensation was somehow gratifying. He hated me, I knew. "So who gives a damn?" I said aloud. As I moved faster and faster, I thought, I talked to myself more and more. "Because it's hard to carry on a conversation when nobody can keep pace with me."

That night as I came out of the shower Judy said, "I don't want to be married anymore." She averted her eyes as she turned out the lamp on her side of the bed.

My body, tingling from the hot water, jerked as if I'd suddenly been deluged with ice cold. "That's it? You just don't want to be married? Ridiculous!" I flipped the switch to the brighter ceiling light.

Judy sat up on the edge of the bed and spoke over her shoulder. "I just can't cope any more. You're under too much pressure, and when you're home it wears off on me." She stood up and pushed past me into the bathroom. The door closed slowly before I could respond, and the lock clicked.

Shivering, I rubbed myself with the towel until I was warm again, and then shouted through the door, "It won't be long now and I'll have what I want. Diamond J will be more than most big men achieve in a lifetime. Then we can both rest." I waited for an answer.

Nothing.

I argued, used every selling phrase that had worked so well in business. I had to talk her out of it—I needed Judy and the twins; there really wasn't anyone else. I seldom saw my brother now that his scientific paths led far away from my flamboyant financial artistry. My mother was close by, but I really didn't like her; she was too totally devoted to herself and to my father, alive or dead. Strange, I thought, that he never spent much time selling me the religion he sold so well to others.

"We've shared too much," I told Judy behind the door. "Remember learning to race snowmobiles together, and laughing when we tried to screw in a single sleeping bag?"

She was, in many ways, more important than any of my businesses. And now she couldn't cope? Well, I'd make her cope—build a dream so big and beautiful she'd never give up her part of it. Reason enough to drive myself harder, because soon my lifestyle would be so fantastic she'd be overwhelmed. Once Judy saw what she was really losing she'd never let go, and I'd have the best of business and love too. "You'll see," I told her as she opened the door.

I finally wore her down to agree to a pseudo-separation. "Both of us here—same house, same bed—but no interaction, no pressure. I'll stay silent and sober and serene."

"I hope so," said Judy, looking very tired and not very convinced.

My problems, it seemed, were snowballing, but I knew that everything depended on my ability to live comfortably, yet secretly, with the pressure that threatened my marriage. "You *can* cope," I told myself.

Efforts to refinance Thunderhead got bogged down; supplications to Colorado banks fell on deaf ears. The resulting cash

crunch required another emergency meeting with the stockholders, and this time they were reluctant to increase their investments.

Barass felt that the economic results of the first ski season
were inconclusive. He questioned our judgment in allocating
income. "Perhaps too much was spent on unnecessary remodeling
and frivolous additions," he said. "In my opinion, the shortage
results from imprudent spending."

Turnbull, who had made a special trip to attend this meeting,
interpreted this remark as a slur on his management. He made
an uncommonly harsh reply. "You want me out?"

"Don't misunderstand," Barass said quickly. "It's only that I
think you're overworked." He knew that Turnbull had plugged
every gap in the understaffed operation with his own efforts,
and that it would be impossible to replace him. "All I meant is
that we should have better communication; then we won't have
so many unexpected financial crises. Maybe we should have regular monthly meetings." He looked at me.

I knew Barass was right, but his steady complaining was beginning to nettle me.

I set about building up the stockholders' confidence. First I
distributed LTV's new four-color master plan maps; next I
showed them a rough draft of Thunderhead's year-end financial
statement. "Better than it looks," I said. "Though it shows a net
loss of $2.02 per common share, there was also a $63,131 decrease
in the working capital deficiency. And, more important, by changing from the declining balance to the straight-line method of depreciation we've been able to cut the stated net loss by approxi-
mately $17,000. That looks better to our creditors."

"We've managed to make all of our payments so far," Turnbull
told them. "All it takes now is one last contribution to make the
senator's past-due payment. Then the road's clear for me to go to
Denver or Chicago, refinance the Inn, and pay ourselves back."

Hollis locked his fingers and stretched his arms. He gave a
contented grunt. "Sounds good to me."

The others agreed. Several checked their watches and seemed
to be ready to adjourn the meeting on a progressive note.

But I wasn't finished with them; I'd saved my best work for

last. I began reading my promotional piece: "Discover Steamboat with Shadco."

"STEAMBOAT—the brightest flower of the rugged Rockies—suddenly blossoming as the finest year-round recreation area in the nation."

And three more pages of my best words about Steamboat's climate, facilities, growth:

"All of it rested in the shadow of the mountain called the Sleeping Giant. Now, as the giant awakes, he sees the place where thousands come to enjoy the mating of nature's bounty with man's creative hand, and we are part of it. Thunderhead, Shadco—the Diamond J Companies—with men of drive, vision, and love of nature, will help make the Steamboat story a mighty volume on the shelf of man's recreational accomplishments."

"That's good," said Hollis. "You reading or talking?"

"Either way, he's a helluva bullshitter," someone else said.

5

July 1971

ASSETS—$480,710.00
LIABILITIES—$105,000.00
PERSONAL GUARANTEES—$790,000.00

The airline personnel had begun to call me John; they knew me not just as a man who commuted between Wisconsin and Colorado, but, as one stewardess not too quietly told another, as "a dynamo who's got to have the most exciting life around—wish I could share it." She leaned over to squeeze my arm, and then watched me over her shoulder as she moved down the aisle. I turned her on, I thought, lighting my cigarette with a one-handed flip of the match. And that was just another indication of the powerful charisma of my mushrooming Diamond J Empire. "And Diamond J is John Stone," I told myself.

So it surprised me as well as shocked me that Judy, as soon as I walked into the house, told me she was getting a divorce.

"This sham separation won't work," she said, settling onto the sofa without taking her eyes off mine. "I want out."

I dropped my briefcase onto the closest chair and sat down beside her. "Why? I can't figure it out." I loosened my tie and said, almost talking to myself, "There's no other guy, I take it. Our marriage has got to be better than most. You're turning down my success without a reason?"

She kept staring at me.

"Why? What grounds do you have?"

Judy's face was expressionless. Her refusal to respond made me ache. I couldn't reach her; nothing. I tried to think about not thinking about the hurt, and finally the concentration on escape was sufficient to nearly numb me. I lit a cigarette and wondered if that's what Judy had meant when she'd said "I can't feel anything" the last time we'd made love. The pain started again.

Suddenly she stood up and walked to the window, where her fingers ran up and down the creases in the drapes.

I tried again. "Why?"

She started bunching the creases into a thick linen sandwich. Then she turned toward the bookshelf and reached for a photo album. "We'll have to divide our pictures."

I ran over and grabbed the album. "Goddamnit, why?"

She stepped backward until her calves caught on the front edge of an easy chair. Her eyes darted from side to side. The voice that spoke was strange, high and hoarse. "Because I'm afraid of you."

The words paralyzed me. Judy and I stood inches apart; I tried to ask her why again.

She slipped to one side, and I could see her confidence growing as she moved into the center of the room. "I don't want to hurt you," she said, then laughed slowly and looked into my eyes. "That's silly. I'll hurt you as much as it takes to get free. So *please* make it easy on all of us."

The muscles in my jaw began to ache as I struggled not to scream profanities. Then, realizing how much I still loved her, realizing that I'd lost her, Goddamnit, lost her, I turned away and walked slowly out of the room.

I started lifting weights and bought a new summer wardrobe. If I was getting tossed back into the marketplace, I figured, I'd better look my best.

I stopped travelling by myself; first Butters and then Rauterberg accompanied me. I had a serious and long overdue talk with Rauterberg. I told him about Turnbull's success in securing an "in and out" line of credit at the Routt County National Bank, and pointedly noted his continuing failure to raise money for me. "You've got to understand, once and for all," I told him. "You asked to come in with me. I expected you to arrange loans in return for the equities I promised and the free rides you take."

He said money was tight, but he added, when he saw my frown, that "things are about to loosen up."

"Certainly hope so," I said, beginning to recount the difficulties we were encountering with the Thunderhead refinancing. "When Turnbull presented the new corporate financial statements and the resumés of the stockholders to Columbia Savings and Loan in Denver, the S and L people were enthusiastic. They even offered to consider financing future improvements and condominiums. But first they want a current appraisal, which we won't have for two months. Meanwhile the suppliers and contractors aren't getting paid. Their bills total more than $95,000, and the work is a month behind schedule."

Rauterberg said he had two "wild" bankers in mind. "They'll help."

"When?"

"Soon as we get home. You can count on it." He waved to the stewardess and ordered a double drink.

Since our trip was made on a weekend, Rauterberg had no opportunity to visit the local bank and do a PR job for us.

"All he does is wander around town," Turnbull complained. "Is there any good reason to pay for his vacations?"

He got his answer at a money meeting. Rauterberg emphasized that our present method of borrowing "short-term" was a very dangerous procedure unless we had inside help. The Banking Commission and the Federal Deposit Insurance Corporation, he explained, disapproved of unsecured loans that went unpaid over a year. They wrote bad reports when these loans were discovered. This meant loans had to be "moved" for one month in every twelve if the borrower didn't have the ability to pay off in cash.

That's where the insider was needed. "As a correspondent banker, I'm often called on to assist participating banks in this accommodation of preferred customers," Rauterberg said. "Remember, you can borrow, pay off, borrow, pay off simply by moving the loan. Reborrow indefinitely."

"Sounds like robbing Peter to pay Paul," Turnbull observed.

"Or loan kiting," I added.

"Whatever you like. Just don't ever cause a bank to be written up. That's what they're all afraid of," said Rauterberg.

I'd learned another valuable lesson.

Rauterberg said we could do it once we were established.

"When's that?" Turnbull asked, knotting his eyebrows skeptically.

"Soon. What do you think I was doing today? Walking around, asking questions. Getting to know Steamboat and what it thinks of you. Checking your operation," said Rauterberg. I could tell by his natural smile that he endorsed our endeavors.

Turnbull must have changed his mind about Rauterberg. "I think I'll have a drink."

But after our return to Wisconsin, Rauterberg told me that both his "wild" bankers were out of the state until late August. It was a big disappointment; worse than that, it created another crisis. Counting on Rauterberg, I had taken it upon myself to promise Thunderhead's creditors that they'd be paid within two weeks.

Now I was in trouble. I saw no chance for an immediate solution, and spent a long and frustrating day telephoning bankers. They were all interested at first, but they must have sensed my urgency, because they sounded more and more reluctant as we talked. I made a mental note—never push, never appear anxious or hurried when applying for loans.

As it grew dark outside, my little office seemed to grow smaller. I left the building and went to Janeff, where I came across a familiar name in the delinquency file: Sid Henry, a professional mortgage broker and an unlicensed attorney. When I'd first lent him money, I'd thought he'd be the best risk in our portfolio; he drove an expensive new car and wore hand-tailored clothes. A year ago I had believed his story about needing the temporary services of a loan company because his regular bankers were away at a convention, and when a file check of the credit bureau had showed nothing adverse, I'd given him $5,000 unsecured.

Henry didn't keep his promise to pay off in thirty days, and it was almost three months before he bothered to answer my dunning telephone calls. He didn't make any excuses—he said he needed another $5,000. He offered collateral, and he told me not to worry about "throwing good money after bad."

Now, nine months later, Henry was still past due on his $10,000 loan. I knew he had successfully raised a lot of money to fund real estate projects in which he had an interest, so I called him at home and offered a deal. If Henry arranged the refinancing of Thunderhead I'd allow his loan to ride without payments until he was able to retire it with commissions earned helping me. And, when successful, I'd give him a piece of my action.

I saw this as killing three birds with one stone—and laughed at my unintended pun. I'd bail out Thunderhead, recover a doubtful loan for Janeff, and get a free education in mortgage brokering from a real sharpie.

Each day ended much more quickly than the one before. That's what pressure does, I thought. It accelerates time.

Turnbull and I kept in constant telephone contact. We shared new ideas, tested schemes, encouraged each other to "keep after the bankers."

Finally our efforts began to pay off: the Security State Bank and the Westgate Bank approved personal loans for me. I already had enough for token payments to keep the builders happy when Turnbull called and said, "I scored with a Chicago banker I've been courting while he vacationed at the Inn. We've got preliminary approval of another $150,000 loan."

I met Turnbull in Chicago the next day. We were forty minutes late to meet the bank president because I'd neglected to ask the location of the Lawndale Trust and Savings Bank beforehand, and I expected it to be downtown, not on the South Side, a hard hour's drive from the airport. I was nervous about the time, and my first glimpse of the bank accentuated the feeling.

The old granite building looked stodgy and ultraconservative. The receptionist was undoubtedly a virgin spinster. It was a hot summer day and she was wearing a high-necked, long-sleeved dress. Barely moving her thin lips, she sent us to the second floor. At the top of the stairs, Turnbull nudged me. I guessed he had heard me sigh when I noticed how much the atmosphere had improved just one flight up. A young brunette who looked more like a model than a secretary escorted us to the president, Urban

Myers. His richly paneled offices, most obviously intended to show quiet good taste, also contained enough sport and travel mementos to make them exciting.

Myers didn't look like a banker; only his tie was conservative. His red hair was stylishly ruffled. His welcome was enthusiastic. I expected him to clap me on the back—he slapped Turnbull's shoulder instead, and told me, "I liked Ed the minute I met him. Pegged him as a fast mover slated to do great things in Steamboat."

Turnbull started to grin, then turned to open his briefcase. "They're really just good ideas today, but here's some of the projects we're starting." He handed Myers a packet of pro formas.

After flipping the pages and stopping just a second to study the index, Myers told us, "If you need more money for other Steamboat ventures I'll probably be able to lend another $100,000 unsecured." He hesitated, looking through the papers again. "All you have to do is pass muster with the executive committee."

Here comes the hooker, I thought.

"No problem," said Myers, seemingly reading my mind. "We're meeting in an hour. Afterward let's go down to my yacht and work out the details."

When I drove Turnbull to the airport that evening he was already talking about finding new acquisitions in Steamboat.

"Looks like the sky's the limit," he said.

I used part of the Chicago loan proceeds to pay off the bank director in Mount Horeb. "Keep him happy," I told Kritchner. "Reserve a place to move loans without the help of an insider."

Two weeks later we bought the Cave Inn, a sprawling corrugated-steel building on two acres of leased land at the entrance to the Mount Werner Ski Area, just across the access road from the Triangle. The Cave Inn, a bar alternately promoted during the summer of 1971 as the hottest flesh market in the valley and a quiet haven for cowboys and construction crews, had been a financial flop.

I had stopped here for a beer one afternoon, thinking as I parked my Jeep in the dusty lot that the place was an eyesore, not at all in keeping with the otherwise aesthetically pleasing new construction in the area, which blended native wood and stone into the high-country surroundings. The exterior was painted a garish yellow, and though some effort had been made to face the front with natural pine planking, Cave Inn still looked like a misplaced warehouse.

Inside, after my eyes had adjusted to the vast dimness, it had still looked like a warehouse. The front section, with several levels, contained a bar, a small dining area, and a kitchen; beyond, there were two lounges with free-standing fireplaces. One was filled with giant pillows. I smiled as I recalled spending an evening there trying to snatch a date from the milling mass of young swingers. Pot smoke had impregnated the pillows like heavy perfume and hung foglike around the fireplace. I hadn't bridged the generation gap, but I had had a helluva time watching the new people in action—profitless action. They'd brought their own invisible high with them, barely spending more than fifty cents on a tap beer as the price of admission. But they had let it all hang out, almost as if they'd been obsessed with proving they had no hang-ups.

This afternoon the Cave Inn was empty except for the bartender and, surprisingly, Ed Turnbull.

"Lucky you came in." Turnbull waved me over. "This is important."

"Coors or Cuba?" the bartender asked as I sat down.

I picked Coors; I had a feeling that it wasn't the time for hard stuff. I'd learned to sense Turnbull's moods, and right now every muscle in his face was knotted. His head was several aggressive inches forward of its normal position, and his stance left no doubt that something very exciting had happened.

Something had: the Cave Inn was going up for sale. So far no one but its managers and the three of us knew. The owner, a local playboy who dressed like a cowboy but travelled in an orange Porsche, was tired of his investment.

"Let's grab it," I said.

"Right on."

We already had two bars at Thunderhead and were planning

another. Yet by my principle of controlling the movement of guests and club members, there was a strong case for adding another.

"Vacationers like to barhop," I said. "Now, when they stray from Thunderhead, we'll direct them down the road to the Cave Inn, which, under our guidance, will soon be the biggest and best bar—no, discotheque—in Steamboat Springs—hell, in the entire state!"

Turnbull grinned.

"We need this place," I told him. "Not only will it make money, but it gives us partial control of the highway entrance to LVT's Recreation Development. Goddamn, Ed. Aren't you surprised LTV hasn't snapped it up? They must realize the location is strategic."

Turnbull screwed his face into a gigantic wink. "They don't know it's for sale."

I turned to the bartender. "I want to meet with your boss today," I shouted. "We'll take care of you." I rubbed my thumb against my forefingers and held them up for him to see.

"Not necessary," said Turnbull. "He's going to be our manager."

I flew back to Madison confidently carrying a contract to purchase the Cave Inn. The owner had already signed. It would be easy to secure signatures from the Thunderhead investment group: they were almost as hungry as I was, already talking about building condominiums and bragging that next winter we'd show a helluva profit.

Everything went as I'd predicted. I made a quick turnaround and was back in Steamboat Springs within seventy-two hours, with checks in my pocket and promises that the remainder was "in the mail." While driving in from the airport, I noticed that Turnbull wasn't wasting any time either; workmen were on the roof of the Cave Inn erecting a new sign. The front door was wide open and I went into the bar. It felt good to grab a cold bottle of my own beer.

I heard Turnbull's voice calling; he'd seen my jeep. He came in carrying my briefcase, smiling tentatively.

"They're all there," I said proudly.

His smile widened. I handed him a beer. As we stood silently, I thought how wonderful it felt to be an empire builder, how easy it was. So I asked, trying to make my voice sound sly, "Find any more good deals while I was gone?"

"As a matter of fact, yes." Turnbull looped his leg over a bar stool, passed a hand across his head as if he had hair, settled his other leg on the bar's rail, and began describing Lake Steamboat.

The telephone rang before he'd finished the story; there was a problem at Thunderhead. He rushed away, and I stayed to finish my drink—then another and another. A year ago, I'd said, "My avocation will be my vocation." Bullshit. My vocation was romancing banks and moneymen, hassling competitors, psyching stockholders. The bigger my recreation empire had become, the further I'd drifted from the pleasure it had promised.

Lone Tree, the family ranch and my special resting place, was just the other side of the mountain, seventy-eight miles away. I could be there in two hours.

I pushed my Jeep along at top speed, seeing my face, in the bouncing mirror, relaxing and losing its nervous pallor. The sun had set. The main street of Walden, the county seat, was nearly deserted. Eleven miles farther on I pulled up at the Cowdrey store; it was closed. I honked the horn, and Paxton, the owner, walked slowly over to me from his home across the highway. I knew he'd open the store for me, but I wished he'd hurry. I wanted to drive the last twenty-one miles into the hills before it was completely dark. I wanted to see all of Lone Tree.

My carton of groceries was airborne some of the way, and my fishing tackle was scattered under the seats. I kept hoping the water in Big Creek was high enough for good fishing. I switched on the headlights and slowed down as I approached Big Creek Outpost, where the road into Lone Tree began. The gate was open but I stopped anyway to call out my name to the caretakers —they wouldn't hesitate to use a couple of rounds of bird shot if they thought I was a trespasser. The Outpost was originally built by an undercapitalized rodeo cowboy with grandiose ideas. After he went broke, the present, more qualified, family took over. They ran a small, rustic, low-overhead resort appealing to outdoorsmen. My brother, and most of the other old-timers with private summer retreats in the valley, hated the Outpost's intrusion. I approved of it: the Outpost operator babysat Lone Tree when I was away.

I came to the rickety log bridge over the stream; as usual, I ignored it and headed for the ford. I downshifted quickly just before impact with the current and the icy explosion of water preceding my joyful whoop and holler. I shut off the engine as the Jeep rolled to a stop in front of Honeymoon Lodge.

"John Stone's finally home."

The coffee was coming to a boil on the wood-burning stove as I came in from my morning wash-up at the creek. God, how I'd slept. The ten hours last night had to be the best and the most I'd had in months. I took a cup of coffee outside and strung my fly rod while it cooled.

Later, I put a dozen brook trout in the spring house, opened a Coors, and stood contemplating my private kingdom.

"A fine day."

I was always happiest at Lone Tree. The area was going to prosper now—the Cowdrey store would be a gold mine when the new highway came through from Steamboat. "If I owned the store, and Paxton's house, and the lot across the road, I'd control the intersection," I mused. It was a perfect location for a motel, service station, restaurant, liquor store. . . . "God damn," I said, "off on another buying spree." The spell was broken. I packed and started for Steamboat, and when I arrived there was a message to meet Turnbull in Madison. The appraisal of Thunderhead had been completed a month early, and Columbia Savings and Loan liked it—our mortgage loan was approved.

Turnbull waved the letter of commitment at the hastily convened stockholders' meeting. "Nothing to do except adjust our insurance, order a new title policy, sign the papers—and we've got $650,000," he shouted. "It's that simple."

He seemed more excited than the rest. I looked around the room. Hollis was leaning back in his chair barely smiling. Kritchner, who was on call, was fiddling with his "Page Boy" transmitter. Vitner's eyes were closed. They all accepted the news as if there'd never been a doubt of it happening.

A surge of pride straightened my spine. I'd conditioned them well: they expected success. They believed in me, just as they believed in our projects. They had faith. Goddamn right.

It took ten days to attend to all the details. Finally, in lieu of everyone attending a Denver closing, Lindsey flew West alone; Columbia insisted that a banker personally deliver the executed notes and mortgages. The stockholders and their wives had guaranteed them without question. Even Judy had signed, saying she'd be the last person to hurt me or my business now. All she wanted was "freedom."

"You've got it."

We paid off the contractors, the suppliers, and Senator Decker, made a deposit with the architect hired to update the condominium working drawings, and told Turnbull to hurry up with his Walton Creek Park development scheme.

Everyone was happy except Sid Henry, the money broker I'd culled from the Janeff customers. He started bitching about his rights to a finder's fee on any and all Thunderhead loans. I calmed him down, promising he could begin looking for a way to finance the condominium and the Shadco projects, and reminding him that his debt to Janeff was still unpaid.

Kritchner came to my office unexpectedly one afternoon. "Brief me on your last trip to Steamboat," he said, but he seemed preoccupied. I wondered if he was going to complain about signing too many notes, or going to criticize Turnbull because the latest Thunderhead addition wasn't finished yet.

"What's your bitch?" I asked.

"None." He still looked very thoughtful. "Do I still have an option on the farm?"

"No. But you didn't waste your money. It's still for sale privately. No commissions. You can buy it."

"Then let's go."

"For the club?" I couldn't understand his sudden interest.

"No, for a mobile home park." He turned and walked out of the office. In a minute he was back, carrying a stack of brochures.

"Look here, if we can rezone that land and build trailer sites we can triple its value. Can you handle it?"

I didn't know a damn thing about mobile home parks. But construction couldn't begin until spring. I'd have time to learn. The club would be operating by then, and would also need the land. I tapped on a map while I thought: either way, trailers or members, Kritchner would make money. "Yes," I replied.

"Good." He started to grin. He was hooked.

A mobile home park wasn't in my Master Plan, but it could be. It was important to encourage my partners' creativity. When they began believing that they could add their own dreams to my big dream, they were partners for life.

Judy reluctantly agreed to bring the kids along on my next trip West. She suspected that it was a ploy to reconcile before we filed for our divorce, and I guess it was. But strangely, when we arrived at Thunderhead, I didn't know how to approach her; I felt immobilized. So I did nothing.

A painful day passed. Whenever I thought about touching Judy's skin again my fingers stung like when I was holding a too-hot mug of buttered rum. It occurred to me that I might be afraid to make a move; she seemed comfortable enough as we rode horseback with the children. But her eyes darted frantically to doorways whenever I suggested we should have time to ourselves at the Inn. The frustration of being so close to Judy, yet still irreconcilably separated, was finally too tormenting, and I began to look for a way to escape.

Padgett was scheduled to arrive three days later; I decided to leave Steamboat now and intercept him in Denver. While waiting I'd have time to investigate the Cave Inn's Colorado competition.

"If the Cave Inn is going to be the biggest bar in the Rockies, I'd better see what the other successful night spots are doing right," I told Judy. "My plan is to search out and duplicate the best qualities of each."

When she smiled, I guessed it was with relief.

"The twins and I will have plenty to keep us busy—hiking,fishing and more horseback riding." Judy patted my shoulder. "I wish you could relax with us, but I know you have your work."

My work began at a nightclub that resembled the Cave Inn from the outside, but most definitely not from the inside. As I was getting ready to leave, the manager, who'd seen me nosing around, introduced himself and asked what I needed. I explained my mission.

"Doubt you want to copy this place," he said, "but my bosses may have something else to offer."

I didn't trust him. He seemed too cordial.

"I want you to meet them," he said. It was all so vague and mysterious that I began to wonder if he worked for the Syndicate. Maybe the Mafia was looking for an entrée to Steamboat Springs.

The people I met at noon two days later were not what I expected. The bar manager introduced his boss, the president of the holding company, an aging gentleman with perfectly combed slate-gray hair, wearing a summer-weight gray flannel suit. After a gentle handshake he turned to present the chairman of the board, who'd been standing out of sight behind him.

"Mr. John Stone, Mr. Raymond Claire." He spoke the second name softly as if I were expected to recognize it under any circumstances. The chairman was wearing off-white boots, slacks, and a turtleneck under a form-fitting green jacket. He dressed and looked like a public figure—probably an actor—but I couldn't place him. He stuck out his hand, palm up for a soul shake.

"Call me Super Nigger," he said.

"Trying to shock me?" I answered, and he did—not with his words, but by the pitch of his voice. It was extremely high and odd. It was the first time I'd ever heard a high-pitched voice sound totally masculine.

"My man says you're into Steamboat heavy. I've been watching Steamboat. I like the style. I need an associate."

"I don't know anything about you," I said, watching for his reaction. There was none.

"Mr. Claire," said the older man, moving toward me, "is the outstanding black entrepreneur of the decade. Haven't you read about him?" He began listing Claire's holdings. "Nightclubs, land development, construction, entertainment. Mr. Claire, if he does nothing else, will help book outstanding musical groups into your Cave Inn."

Claire closed one eye, pursed his lips, and nodded slowly. "I want you to see my operation. Today."

Maybe I didn't want him for a partner, but I damn sure was curious. "May I bring a friend?" I asked, remembering that Padgett was flying in at two o'clock.

"Anyone. We're open to the public. I'll send my car," said Claire.

I used the chauffeur-driven stretched Continental to pick up Padgett at the airport. I'd planned to impress him anyway. He'd been pestering me for weeks about visiting Colorado, and since there was no good reason to refuse, I figured I'd lay it on thick with my projects and progress. That way, if it turned out to be absolutely necessary to collaborate with him in Lake, Sport, and Travel, he'd be ready for a subordinate role.

Padgett brought his wife. I hadn't expected that, but maybe I should have guessed that she'd come along to chaperone him. I knew he'd told her wild tales about the swingers in Steamboat. While she sat wide-eyed on a fur sofa in Claire's "ultramodern total Western reception room" (as Claire described it), Padgett and I were given a tour of his offices. One room after another was filled with people talking on phones in soundproofed cubicles.

"What are they selling?" I asked.

"Real estate. Lots, ranchettes, acreage at my Mountain Development." Claire pointed to a map covering one entire wall.

Padgett's eyes were popping. I could hear him breathing faster and faster. "My kind of deal," he must have been thinking, and I knew he wasn't worried about legalities.

As we left, Claire mentioned casually that he was also in the money brokering business. "I'll be up to see you soon," he said. "Let me know then if you need any assistance with financing."

I let him see a very small smile, while inside I burst into mental laughter remembering that six months ago I'd have dragged him to Steamboat the same day.

As I flew back to Madison with Judy and our sons, she leaned toward me. I noticed that she was reading along with me while I studied my notes from yesterday's meeting with Turnbull.

"Interested in what we're doing?" I hoped she was finally giving me a chance to show her how everything was changing for the better.

"Not really," she said, centering herself in the other seat. "I was only curious as to why you've crossed Dave Padgett off your lists."

"He doesn't fit," I said abruptly. I put the papers back into my briefcase and moved across the aisle to play tic-tac-toe with my sons.

Now that we owned three of the best properties in Steamboat, were investigating more, and had eliminated current financial problems, the time seemed right to begin prospecting for new investors. I organized an inspection and familiarization trip. At the last minute I invited Hollis, Vitner, and Barass, who, I suddenly realized, had never seen my progress firsthand.

The Steamboat Stage Coach Line's Mercedes bus deposited me and my entourage at the entrance of the Inn, and I began the task of getting everyone checked in so that I'd have some time to myself. I needed it. The ride in from the airport had been bumpy and dusty, and my companions, attorney Butters and banker Rauterberg, with six prominent Wisconsin businessmen escorting their wives or girlfriends, were loud and uninhibited, probably from a combination of altitude, too many get-acquainted drinks and the beginning of a three-day free holiday. Only Hollis and Barass were restrained; the rest were certainly not the same people I'd herded onto the plane in Madison.

This was supposed to be serious business. They'd been included because they'd showed interest in our Western operation and they had capital to invest. Or, if nothing else, because they'd be good "carriers of the word." Simple psychology—show them a good time at no charge, and once back in Wisconsin they'd tell everyone about their great adventure.

Getting my flock settled took far too long, considering that their rooms had been reserved and preassigned. Part of the problem was a new clerk behind the desk, but most of the melee was caused by my milling "turkeys." The locals, especially the young people—the hired hands one finds in every ski complex in the country—referred to all tourists as turkeys. By God, now I could see why. As I headed for my suite I laughed loudly: the Inn was "Stone's Turkey Farm." I laughed even harder after I'd sent an echoing "gobble-gobble" down the corridor on my way to a nap.

My rooms turned chilly after the sun set, and I decided to stoke up the fireplace instead of upping the thermostat. When I awoke the fire was out. I glanced at my watch: two hours had, to my horror, slipped by.

The cocktail lounge was jammed. Dressed in Levis and faded shirt, I passed within three feet of my flock, seated around center tables. No one seemed to notice me in my unaccustomed apparel. I observed Vitner ogling one of the waitresses. With his Charlie Brown round head but a happy face, he had a helluva capacity for drink, but once past a certain point he changed from a shy, gentle giant to a bizarre, quixotic pixie. The man I had slated to be sales manager of the recreation club sat next to Vitner. I tried to detect what his glazed eyes were looking at, but saw only the darkness outside the floor-to-ceiling windows facing the mountains.

I sipped my first drink too fast; it felt uncomfortably warm in the pit of my stomach. Even with a full bar the bartender was right there, smiling, to dispense my refill. I assumed he knew I was one of the owners. When I asked him to "half shot me and go heavy on the Coke," his smile remained, but his shrug told me he had only tried to please.

Turning back to watch my tables of turkeys, I brushed against the cocktail waitress working next to me. I moved my stool to give her room. She smiled a quick thank-you. She was busy with a drink order, so I didn't respond.

Hollis and Barass were on their feet, backs toward me and heads bobbing. They were off to dinner. Hollis was a good guy who enjoyed people. Barass, on the other hand, obviously disliked loud, drunken chatter and the kind of men who would bring their mistresses on a business trip. It was all outside his staid lifestyle, and I had the feeling that he would bail out of his investment at an expedient moment in the weeks to come. To do so now would, for him, be in poor taste.

With the two doctors gone, I had a clear view of the others. One executive, seated close to his regular lady friend, had reached his horny stage, as he usually did at some point during drinking sprees. Maybe he used sex as a means to sober up. As long as I'd known him, he would invariably proceed to get loaded, disappear with a woman, and return about an hour later the picture of total sobriety. I'd have to see if it worked for me. Is that what they meant by a "good fuckin' drunk"? I laughed aloud

The cocktail waitress who had smiled at me now gave me a quizzical look, squinting her eyes and tilting her head. I'd seen her before. Of course. She was the bar girl who had tried to take my drink away three weeks before, when I'd been brooding over the divorce after the two o'clock mandatory closing hour. I had refused to leave the bar. She hadn't argued with me but had gone to the bartender instead. I had heard him say, "He owns the place. If he wants to lose his license . . ."

I remember walking out feeling about two inches tall. Later, I'd seen her in the lobby counting tips. "Don't let the stockholders give you any shit," I'd said, trying to make amends for my use and abuse of power. She looked good—small and gentle, with untouched coziness. Her name was Shari.

Now I wanted her. I didn't push. I knew that age, experience, and my reputation as an entrepreneur, coupled with patience, guaranteed my success.

The chill morning air drifted in through the open sliding glass door that led to the deck of my suite. I stepped outside, and standing next to a stack of firewood, let the briskness knock the last traces of sleep out of my mind. The sun hadn't topped the eastern peaks, but the sky was already deep blue; it promised to be a good fall day. A double knock on my door meant that a waitress had left 6:30 A.M. coffee in the hallway per my standing instructions.

I heard tub water running. Shari was stretched out soaking. She told me it was the luxury she missed most, because her place had showers only. I brought in the coffeepot, and had nearly finished it before it occurred to me that she might like some. I shrugged. Hell, I didn't even know if she drank the stuff. Through the bathroom door, I told her I'd see her later, and left. Why disturb a luxury?

No one showed up for the morning excursion to our properties. Turnbull was pissed; his temples throbbed noticeably. I was disappointed, but more concerned about his temper. It didn't happen often, but when Turnbull really blew he disappeared on a three-day sulking drunk.

By noon I was boiling too. Most of the turkeys were back in the lounge, well on their way into party day two. I stormed out of the Inn looking for a way to cool off, and bumped into Colonel Donald Livingston.

I recognized him from a snapshot included in the research material on the "Golden Triangle," my descriptive title for the twenty-acre parcel across the access road from the Cave Inn. The "old man" of Steamboat's nouveaux riches was straight-backed and stocky, with none of the belly you'd expect on a retired sixty-year-old. His hair was cut very short. He looked like a colonel—Marine Corps.

When Livingston heard my name he struck a Western pose, hooked his thumbs on either side of a huge silver buckle, and nodded approvingly. "I've heard about you, Stone. Been looking forward to a meeting."

Livingston and I hit it off, perhaps only because he had something to sell that I'd already decided to buy.

"The Golden Triangle," he said, deliberately using my expression as we drank coffee in the otherwise empty dining room, "is the best piece of land in the county. The Hilton people want to put a hotel on it."

I knew that. I didn't tell him that I already had a "best use" proposal in my locked briefcase.

"They want it bad," he continued. "Eric Hilton himself made an on-site inspection. Very impressed." Livingston stretched out the word "impressed" and moved his lips into a conspiratorial grin.

"Quit selling, Colonel," I said. "All we have to do is settle on mutually agreeable terms."

He was asking a million dollars. The price didn't scare me; Steamboat's land boom was just beginning. The only problem was arranging to close the deal with practically nothing down. I hoped I could talk Livingston into letting me pay for the thing out of profits, but he balked. I offered a lease, with option to buy, as the alternative.

"I'll think about it," he said.

I knew better than to push, so I changed the subject to trout fishing.

"There's nothing I'd rather do," Livingston beamed.

So I invited him to Lone Tree.

I sent my "Turkeys" home alone. Livingston brought along his son; we spent two days at Lone Tree, casting dry flies (the only proper way to fish, Livingston opined) into Big Creek. We'd caught more than a hundred trout before I decided it was time to close the Triangle transaction.

I told Livingston that Shadco and all of its stockholders would guarantee performance. I enumerated the tax advantages of a long-term payment schedule, especially for a man who was already in a high bracket. And I promised him lifetime guest privileges at Lone Tree. Livingston seemed close to saying yes, but I could tell by his long pause and his sudden reversion to a military manner that he still meant to proceed cautiously. Finally he settled for a ninety-day option.

When we returned to Thunderhead, I was surprised to see Butters still there.

"Taking a little vacation," he said.

"Now you'll earn it," I said, directing him to my suite and telling him not to come out until he'd drafted an air-tight option agreement.

Much later, after Livingston signed, I took Shari to dinner. She began telling me about her ex-husband.

"He was gentle," she explained, "but so huge he hurt me."

"What does it feel like to get laid by John Stone?"

"Good."

I laughed. "That's a compliment?"

Shari's head kept bobbing, and I figured she was about to say something to build up my ego.

"Never mind," I said. "Can you type?"

"Yes." She stared at me.

"Good. You're coming to Wisconsin." Then, remembering that the waiter had said they were out of her favorite entrée, I made another prediction: "Someday soon I'll buy you a lobster."

6

September 1971

ASSETS—$582,490.00
LIABILITIES—$121,361,361.00
PERSONAL GUARANTEES—$1,870,000.00

Rauterberg's "wild bankers" might as well have been fantasies. He talked about them whenever I desperately demanded a progress report, but he never specifically identified their banks.

"They've been away most of the summer," he said, using rich men's right to leisure as an excuse.

"Nobody takes a three-month vacation." My voice exploded with frustration. "Don't ying-yang me. I need help *now*, money yesterday."

He shook his head and closed his eyes before he told me, "No way. I can't find loans until you show me a positive cash flow. You're lucky my banker buddies are out of the state. By the time they get back, any day now, you'd better be able to prove how you can repay the money you're asking for. Otherwise, it's like soliciting contributions."

Rauterberg had just shot down my wishful premise that short-term financing could serve in place of equity capital.

He was right. I'd parlayed Thunderhead into properties worth four million, and now controlled the access to Ling Temco Vought's hundred-million-dollar recreation development. But the

Golden Triangle and Walton Creek Park were raw land. The Inn and the Cave were costing more to expand than they earned. My plans for Lone Tree and the farm weren't even on paper.

"Good growth investments, just no dividends today. Why not sell stock?" Rauterberg suggested.

"Tried to," I said, exhaling sharply as I remembered the pointless three-day turkey tour. "They signed tabs instead of checks."

"What about the recreation club? It's good for instant profit," he said, nodding vigorously to show he believed that was his best suggestion.

I agreed. I tucked the telephone receiver under my chin and began dialing with one hand while the other reached for Master Plans.

"I'll canvass the doctors," I said. "Maybe it's time they helped me start the club. You're right. It is a money machine." Enthusiasm fortified the tone of my voice.

Kritchner was not excited. "We've got enough going," he said firmly, and then asked if I'd made any progress buying the farm. Kritchner liked property better than people; the same was probably true of Vitner and Turnbull. Barass was running scared— and Hollis, who'd agree to anything, was useless as an organizer.

My hand shook as I dialed Padgett. I knew it was going to be a shotgun marriage. "Time to move on Lake, Sport, and . . ."

"I already have." Padgett cut me off in a cold voice.

Rauterberg, seeing my face tense, leaned across the desk and whispered, "Tell him I can arrange to discount the membership notes."

"I've got money." I knew that Padgett would never refuse a dowry.

"Let's incorporate today. I've been running the club through my other company." Padgett's words ran into each other, stumbling after the dollars I promised.

Butters was in Steamboat working on the Golden Triangle, so I used another attorney, Tom Kanakis, an old friend who, like Kritchner, disapproved of Padgett.

"He's slippery," Kanakis warned.

"I can handle him," I said. I had no choice.

When I called him back to set a meeting time, Padgett demanded a majority of the voting stock.

"Why not? You've got it. Fifty-one percent of the stock." I cupped my hand over the phone and told Rauterberg, "I don't need stock control to keep him in line."

"I hope you know what you're doing. This can be a gold mine," said Rauterberg.

I cut Bill Lindsey in for 5 percent as a reward for finding loans and running documents, but Rauterberg would have to wait until he produced his evasive associates.

Bill Smithers, the man I'd slated as the club's sales manager, went to work with the sales force I'd recruited: four unemployed Janeff customers. Their initial quota was fifty memberships a month.

"$78,000 by year end," I told my Thunderhead partners, urging them to scout prospects.

Rauterberg finally introduced me to my first "wild" man, Walter F. O'Connor, president of the Algoma Bank in Algoma, Wisconsin. He reminded me of my turkeys on tour. His hair was so blond it looked white atop a baby face.

"And a Sunday afternoon cocktail party is a ridiculous environment for a money meeting," I told Rauterberg, who was having too much fun to notice my anger.

"We'll get together again sometime," was all he said before turning away to refill his glass.

The second banker, James Rosenheimer, came to my office a week later. He surveyed the room before he spoke, head turning slowly as his big jowls slid over his collar. Then, feet still planted, he swivelled his entire body to the precarious point where I held my breath, fearful that even a touch would send him crashing into the carefully decorated walls.

Rosenheimer wore obesity like a badge. "A happy body, a happy banker," he said. But even though he ended every sentence with a chuckle, something told me he was a troubled man.

Rauterberg said that Rosenheimer was president of two suburban Milwaukee banks, inherited when his father died in 1970. "And now he's expanding. Jim needs deposits and good loans."

Rosenheimer chuckled.

"He's also a sportsman. A champion sailor."

"In a helluva big boat," I wanted to add as Rauterberg continued the rehearsed biography. Rosenheimer was actively promoting CUSSA, Central United States Ski Association. His attentive glance told me that a free trip to Steamboat was expected as soon as the hill opened.

"Impressive." Rosenheimer pointed to the framed pictures of John Stone hunting, fishing, and playing in the snow. "How much do you need?"

"What?" I watched Rosenheimer tug to loosen his tie.

"Money. How much? That's what I'm here for, isn't it?" It sounded as if Rauterberg had done a good job briefing him on me too.

"Twenty-five thousand now. Seventy-five thousand by Thanksgiving, when the ski season begins," I said.

"He means financing for Steamboat. And also new lines for Janeff so the club contracts can be discounted," said Rauterberg.

The other banker nodded. "Good move. I just returned from an inspection trip of condos in Hawaii. May be some action there too."

"Tell him more about Lake, Sport, and Travel Club," Rauterberg suggested.

I emphasized the generation of quick profits and, later, the massive capital gains that would result from the tandem efforts of the club and the holding companies.

"What's my percentage?" Rosenheimer asked. "Remember, I can throw some great side deals into the pot."

"You can't expect bankers to help you get rich on their money unless you share," Rauterberg reminded me.

Shari, who was turning out to be more efficient than I had hoped, had been eavesdropping. She stopped them on the way out. "Are you mailing the loan papers to Mr. Stone?" She handed Rosenheimer the address. After they left she lifted my arm over her shoulder and pressed against me. "I'm bored." She looked up and licked her lower lip.

"Don't get horny now," I laughed. "We've got condos to build, land to plat, a nightclub to open, and trips to Santa Barbara and Houston." I stopped to wonder if there was more. Damn right. I winked at her. "Take my car today and find us an apartment."

Butters returned from Steamboat with a lease purchase draft approved by Livingston's Denver lawyers. There was another epidemic of enthusiasm when I unveiled renderings of my plan for the Golden Triangle: giant four-color illustrations created by a draftsman-artist working privately for me. They showed the complete development—a shopping center, a medical center, a bank, and a twin-towered hotel with a Playboy club atop one tower, and Lake, Sport, and Travel on the other.

Rauterberg and Lindsey went wild. "Exactly what we needed," they said. "Our own bank, on the scene."

Vitner made plans to apply for a license to practice medicine in Colorado, and the others began suggesting new investors who "should not pass up this fantastic opportunity."

Rauterberg arranged a second meeting with O'Connor, this time at a barbecue before cocktail hour. O'Connor still looked sloppy, but when he spoke those cold and carefully calculated words, he made sense.

"I earn my money betting on sure things. That's the way Bobby describes you. Package your deals and send them to me. If he's half right"—and he poked two fingers into Rauterberg's chest—"you'll have more money than you can use. Just don't ever try to fuck me." He was smiling, but deep within his eyes I saw something that made me shudder at the prospect of ever having to oppose him.

I summoned the Inn's shareholders to discuss and approve construction of the most modern condominiums in the Rockies. The cost estimate was over two million dollars.

"It'll go higher if we wait," I said.

"So who's waiting?" someone replied.

Completion was scheduled for late summer, 1972. Most of the units would be sold by then, "because there's no competition."

Every head in the room nodded.

"The problem is managing the Inn and the condos at the same time," said Turnbull, moving from a corner chair to perch on the edge of my desk. "Shadco should form a management company to oversee everything."

"Good idea." Hollis looked right and left to see whether everyone agreed.

"And, while we're at it, why not a construction company?" I said. "Then we can skim the profits off the condominiums and Walton Creek Park while we're building."

The heads kept nodding.

Turnbull stayed in Madison until, between the two of us, we had convinced the investors that we should add twenty-four more guest rooms to the Inn, pave the parking lots, and erect billboards on Highway 40.

Barass, who was still worried about money, was the only dissenter. "I can't believe our bankers will always come through," he argued. "It's not normal banking practice to lend more money every month to the same promoters."

When the others ignored him, I knew his time with us was getting very short, so I asked for their agreement to sell new shares to Lindsey, Butters, and Henry.

"They're begging to buy in."

"Why Henry?" Kritchner thought he was a mooch.

"Because he's a money raiser. And, as you know, we're going to need stacks of it. Henry's a backup to the banks," I said.

After the meeting I revised the Master Plan. "Lake, Sport, and Travel is moving. Steamboat's projects are ready to roll," I told Shari. "I've reassigned top priority to the Golden Triangle so that whenever the Shadco conglomerate needs extra cash I can sell segments of the triangle development at huge profits, while keeping the key situations—hotel, medical center, and bank—for myself. Naturally, Shadco will retain first rights to all construction jobs."

"What about the Houston trip?"

"Contact Eric Hilton," I told her. "Set up the meeting. Tell him I'm bringing my staff and ask where's the most convenient airport to land a Lear."

"We don't have a jet." She both said and asked it, wide-eyed, not quite sure I hadn't sneaked out to buy one.

"He doesn't know that. And I didn't say we had a Lear, just

asked where it should land. Remind me to continue your education in positive bullshitting," I said, laughing and swatting her backside.

Eric Hilton, conservatively dressed, rushed toward Butters as we deplaned in Houston. "Didn't expect you to be so young," he apologized when I untangled our identities.

"Problems like the Lear's mechanical failures are helping me age," I tossed in.

He hadn't anticipated my entourage either. Rauterberg, Butters, and I rode to the hotel with him, while Shari, Dave Brunke, who'd left Janeff to work full-time for Shadco, and the luggage followed in a cab.

At the Shamrock Hilton a manager, bypassing registration procedures, escorted us to our suites. My staff left the elevator on Four; I went to the top. The mammoth penthouse the manager led me to held a grand piano, three TVs, a bar, a butler's pantry, and two king-size beds.

"Neat!" squealed Shari when she appeared later with her overnight bag. She bounced from one bed to the other and turned on all the TVs.

"Make sure you stop in your room tomorrow and rumple the bed," I told her. "Hilton may get reports from the maids."

"You thing he's that straight?"

"I'm not taking any chances."

We met the next morning at the district office of Hilton Inns. I was surprised that the hotel chain was a separate entity. "Barron runs that," Eric explained. "We franchise plush motels."

Hilton Inns did not buy land, did not participate financially. They offered their name, their management, and their purchasing expertise, and, I soon discovered, they employed the same negative sales technique that Padgett and I did.

"You'll have to qualify," said Eric. That meant approved plans, earnest money, and an acceptable credit standing.

"Won't be necessary," I said, showing him the renderings for the Golden Triangle and reminding him that he'd already inspected the property. "And I have my lead banker along."

Rauterberg, right on cue, explained Shadco's structure and listed its assets. He pointed to the Playboy symbol and the Lake,

Sport, and Travel logo imposed on the picture of the twin towers —"The first Hilton in the mountains."

Eric Hilton suggested another meeting, scheduled for his visit to Chicago in October. "That will give us time to digest your rather startling ideas." He invited us to any early dinner before plane time. "No business. Just relax."

I didn't like dinner parties, so it was my habit to disappear after the cocktail hour. That way, while others played with fancy food and wasted time with table talk, I could escape to organize my thoughts, and then return during dessert. No one ever questioned my absence. But this time, as I made my way back to the private dining room, I saw Brunke waiting nervously at the checkout desk. He looked pale. As I started toward him, Shari took my arm and whispered that Eric was asking for me.

I seated myself where I could watch for Brunke's reappearance; if there was a money problem, I wanted to catch him alone, before the others were alarmed.

It seemed as if Eric had read my mind. "Your accommodations are, of course, on Hilton Inns. Whenever we're doing business, make sure you stay at a Hilton," he winked.

Brunke, who'd approached from my blind side, whispered in my ear. "That's one $2,000 bill I don't have to worry about American Express approving."

I finished a half-dozen brandies with my coffee and slept happily in Shari's arms all the way back to Wisconsin.

We were ready to apply for a bank charter in Steamboat Springs. Rauterberg and Lindsey had researched Colorado laws and competition; both reached the same conclusions: the convenience and advantage of a second bank must be demonstrated to the Banking Commission. And the board of directors should include prominent local investors.

"Bank charters are political plums," Rauterberg said. "The president of the Routt County Bank has clout in Denver. Building our own power base is the first important step."

"Wasn't Amsler state director of public relations?" Turnbull's question led to a quick meeting with Amsler, who was already involved in most of our other ventures.

According to Amsler, the Routt County Bank president was on most of Steamboat's shit lists because he commanded a lending monopoly, and indeed had heavy Denver connections ready to give rivals a hard hassle. "Up to now they've erased competition before applications could be filed," Amsler said, "but I think the time is right. LTV will probably back us."

I looked toward Rauterberg, who was plucking at his lower lip. "Didn't you brag about the banking commissioner being an old friend?" I said.

"Yup." When he smiled, I knew Rauterberg was pondering the tremendous leverage the bank would allow us. "Wisconsin has been a hard place to borrow money that everyone knows will be spent a thousand miles away. If we own a local bank we'll have it made."

"Damn right."

And I'd be an insider, with carte blanche to the inner sanctum of the moneymen. The benefits would be endless—opportunities to borrow new money from colleagues in the state where my biggest businesses operated, reducing the risk of criticism by state and federal examiners who probably didn't exchange much information between Colorado and Wisconsin, and sharing the profits from the large-scale loan and deposit swapping that helped all banks and bankers' businesses grow. I'd even have a chance to employ the full talents of the swinging bankers among us, whose only restraints at present were working for someone else (Rauterberg and Lindsey) and operating in the wrong state (Rosenheimer and O'Connor). Best of all, Rauterberg bragged, he was expert at arranging to buy or start banks with no money down.

"I'll be the spearhead," he said as he drove Shari and me to the airport. "You nail Livingston. By the time you're back, Amsler will buy us a big board of directors, and the Golden Triangle will have its first construction contract, my bank building."

"Any reason we can't build a Savings and Loan next door?" I asked, and we all laughed.

Shari and I had time for a Beverly Hills shopping spree before catching the commuter flight to Santa Barbara.

"This is my first trip to California," I confessed.

"I don't believe it," she said. "You've been everywhere."

"Not yet."

The customized Continental Livingston drove had an "expressly manufactured for" sign on the dash. He wove an intricate pattern through Santa Barbara on the way to the shoreside motel, "where I always put up guests." He passed and described his numerous possessions: a circular high-rise parking ramp holding "half again more autos than a square one," vacant lots with natural foliage landscaped into "great sites for tall buildings when this village decides to grow into a city," and finally Casa Livingston, "our temporary home," where ancient decay, the blight of the nouveaux riches, was still discernible behind fresh coats of bright paint.

At first glance Mrs. Livingston seemed older and frailer than her husband, until she interrupted the colonel's polite prattle to recite a snappy list of "business matters needing attention." She's the thrust behind the Livingston success, I thought.

"We met and married while both of us were on active duty," she explained later as her husband fixed drinks.

I described my visit to Houston, and the plans to build a Hilton at the "Showplace of Steamboat."

Mrs. Livingston took notes. I took one sip from my Cuba Libre, set it on a monogrammed sterling coaster, and placed my clincher before her on the teak table.

"Now I'll show you how to avoid taxes on the Triangle sale, and possess a reinforced guarantee of million-dollar performance." I opened the embossed folder to reveal the outline of a $1 million insurance policy on Livingston's life. "We'll pay the premiums; you name the beneficiary. You're the owner. Live or die, success or failure, the Donald Livingston estate is worth another million."

The colonel blinked. Mrs. Livingston stopped writing and looked up with the trace of a smile freezing one corner of her mouth.

"And you can borrow the cash value, created by the $100,000 premiums we'll pay annually, tax-free." I let my voice land hard on the last words.

Mrs. Livingston wrote furiously, the pen hectic in her hand.

"Stone, my boy, you're a genius," said her husband.

That night he took us to "the best seafood restaurant on the West Coast"—and Shari got her lobster.

On the flight back to Denver I explained to Shari that I was the insurance agent for the Livingston policy, and therefore would recoup over 90 percent of the premium cost. I had a special commission deal with our office landlord, Danner, who was the general agent for the insurance company underwriting the million-dollar policy. "Less than $10,000 is buying me $1 million worth of power," I told her.

She never criticized me again for "wandering down the hall to waste time with Danner."

None of my associates met the plane in Steamboat. They were all in Denver "at important meetings," read my "Personal and Confidential" message.

As we headed back to the airport, I noticed horses grazing on the Golden Triangle, "the world's most valuable pasture," and wondered if Rauterberg would have balls enough to erect a "Site of New Bank" sign when he returned.

I successfully turned the tables on Eric Hilton when I answered his letter of inquiry about the meeting in Chicago. "Shadco expects more than a unilateral franchise," I wrote. "Under the circumstances I am naturally investigating similar, perhaps more intriguing, opportunities." Eric telephoned almost daily until I set a date "just to talk."

My regular staff, plus Turnbull and an architect, boarded a private turboprop, donated by the president of a large construction company bidding for our business. Rauterberg brought Rosenheimer along when he discovered that one seat was vacant. "It's smart to let Hilton see two bankers," he said.

Eric and his regional vice-president waited in rooms too small for my expanded entourage; they looked embarrassed. I knew I had the upper hand, and held my advantage tenaciously. Numerous franchise requirements were waived while Hilton sent his vice-president scurrying after extra chairs.

"But don't ask me to break precedent on the earnest money," he said finally, smiling. He allowed as how $10,000 was petty cash anyway.

Rosenheimer chuckled, and when he was sure Eric was watching, gave me an exaggerated wink.

Hilton got the message. He nodded to the bankers and didn't say another word about money—no personal financial statements, no credit investigations, nothing. In principle, we had a deal. I proposed that we meet again in Madison, mentioning offhandedly that I'd spotted a prime location, near the capital, for another Hilton.

The construction man's eyes widened. He began to drool. "Or was it sweat in that crowded, overheated room?" I kidded him on the way out.

Rauterberg and Rosenheimer stayed in Chicago for "other business." Turnbull sat next to me on the flight back to Madison. I was a fantastic promoter, he told me, but "we've got to pay out another $300,000 within the month. Henry is fucking up, and your banker buddies are dragging their feet on loans. All Rauterberg will talk about is the new bank, and so far the only thing he's accomplished in Denver is hosting cocktail parties for political mooches." He guessed it might be years, if ever, before we opened our own bank's doors.

I asked about the $100,000 extra loan promised by Myers.

"I've already tapped Lawndale," said Turnbull. "It's up to you now."

O'Conner was buying club membership contracts through Janeff, but said that loans involving the Western ventures needed further study. When I put heat on Rauterberg, he told me that the real reason O'Conner had reneged was an inclination to sell his bank. "He's moving slowly because a low loan-to-deposit ratio is an important incentive to buyers in today's tight money market. There are lots of other people looking to feed their financial faces, same reasons we're pushing the bank in Steamboat. Hope we can do it next year." His last sentence wasn't positive enough to suit me.

Rosenheimer also pulled in his horns. He claimed that the authorities were subjecting him to unfair scrutiny because "someone's out to get me." But he didn't explain who or why.

I wondered whether Rosenheimer's paranoia was justified. Rauterberg shrugged when I questioned him. He looked at Turnbull, who was still hanging around Madison, and asked what Henry was doing.

Turnbull's face reddened. "Nothing, Goddamnit. How many times do I have to explain that Henry only screams about fees and expenses, claims he's working to set up financing for condo buyers and handling details on the construction loan? But he's not producing money, just talk. There's too much talk." He frowned in my direction.

Rosenheimer, saying, "I'm trying to make a constructive move," introduced me to Bill Topp, "a man with tons of money. He's a mortgage 'banker,' not a 'broker' like Henry."

As Topp explained his function, "mortgage brokers" hunted for money; "mortgage bankers" had it available. "The Auer Mortgage Banking Company can help you. But we get paid more—and in advance."

Turnbull and I executed a contract and filed applications on behalf of Shadco, The Cave Inn, and Thunderhead. Topp said he'd call back in ten days to advise "how much, how long, and how much for the Auer Mortgage Banking Company. And how much for me, in advance."

Turnbull flew back to Steamboat "to give the Cave a kick," and I summoned Padgett and my sales manager, Smithers, to a critique of Lake, Sport, and Travel.

"The club salesmen are not filling their quotas. Why?"

Padgett said Smithers was a "bust out," incapable of motivating. Smithers claimed the sales material was "garbage." "Then," I said, "I'll direct the club, recruit and train salesmen, put new tools in their hands, and send them out every morning with faith. They'll succeed."

I demoted the sales manager to "just another troop." He bit his lip and nodded slowly. Then I told Padgett to go back to his buyers' club.

"Leave Lake, Sport, and Travel to me."

Padgett's hands twitched and I wondered if he was going to take a swing at me, scream, or pull rank as the majority stockholder. I stood up and walked toward his chair. He did own 51 percent, but he needed my drive, my investors, and my bankers to raise the money to make everything go. And I was bigger than he was, in every way.

"Look," I said, "right now you need me, and so we're going to do things my way. Besides, I'm tougher than you are."

"Okay, try it. You got a plan?" Padgett was afraid of me, as I'd guessed.

"Money's the carrot in front of the donkey," I said. "Goddamnit, if I have to spend my time running Lake, Sport, and Travel, the asses are going to move—fast."

I inserted a blind ad in Madison's newspapers. It offered low-cost elk hunts, using Lone Tree's cabins and the Big Creek Outpost's guides. Twelve hunters, a full booking, signed up, paid deposits, and joined the club. The membership drive was back on schedule. I gave a party for the new hunters before they left for Colorado.

"Nothing's guaranteed," I told them, waving a drink in one hand, my big-game hunting guide's license in the other. "But I'm going along to make sure everybody has a ball."

My schedule intensified, and I felt the need for an air arm, so I renewed an old friendship with the owner of a flying service on the outskirts of Madison. Dan Bindl had taught me and Judy to fly. His wife, recently killed in a crash, had been Judy's best friend, and would have been my first choice for a lover.

"We've got a lot in common, Dan," I said.

"You're right. And now I need a change of pace." Bindl became my personal pilot.

Shari arranged landing and ramp privileges with United Airlines, and whenever we flew Bindl's red-and-white Bonanza to Milwaukee, Denver, or Chicago we taxied to their gates. And I deplaned just like the passengers on 707's. During these arrivals I always looked forward to waving at the noses pushed against the windows in the commercial jets.

"I can read the looks behind the noses," I told Bindl. "They're trying to recall where they saw me before."

"Obviously you're too important to forget," he said as I hopped to the runway and handed my luggage to the United man waiting to guide me aboard the bigger plane.

The next hundred-odd steps to my seat were the most fun of all. I could feel the planeload of eyes taking a closer look, and hear the excited whispers: "Who *is* he?"

Two or three drinks and about an hour later, I usually told them.

Shari and I made many of the trips together. Mostly we worked on the ever-expanding pile of paperwork that filled both our brief-cases, but sometimes she insisted that we talk about ourselves.

"You bought Judy a ring in Beverly Hills," Shari said one night as the plane cruised smoothly, somewhere over Iowa. She sounded very peaceful—no anger, no jealousy.

But I protested. "I'm not giving it to her."

"John." Her voice was sorry for me. "Don't kid yourself. You still love Judy. I can see that every time you're daydreaming. You've tucked your emotions away, like the ring, waiting until it's safe to wear them again."

I shook my head, but I didn't respond. Maybe Shari was right. I did fantasize about the day Diamond J would be completed and Judy would beg to rejoin me. I worried about Shari, too. I needed her in some way almost every minute, and she was always willing to do any job. But, damnit, she was too beautiful a person to be used.

I felt my lips turn inward—my sad expression.

"Have you two tried counseling?" Shari asked.

"Judy suggested it once. A crock of shit. Anyway, why should I try to resurrect the Judy thing?"

"Because you've got to get your head on straight. And you can't do it alone. And because I love you and want you to stop hurting." Shari meant what she said. Judy reluctantly agreed to seek professional help, and Shari took a vacation.

I went to the first session knowing "nobody's going to pick John Stone's brain." The hour ended with a premonition of disaster.

Later that night I went to tell Judy that she was finally and completely free. A strange car was parked near the driveway of my former home. I let myself in with the key Judy had never asked for and stood in the blazing foyer lights. I could see my bar open, the bedroom door closed. The sounds conjured up a nightmare—a wave breaking onto me, blinding me, tossing me beyond the shores of sanity.

The next morning's newspaper reported that John Stone, waving his deputy sheriff's badge, had been arrested for disturbing the peace. The incident was used to cast serious doubt on the propriety of politically appointed deputies. The sheriff lost the next election, and I filed for my final divorce papers.

"It's done," I told Shari long-distance. "Come back. I need you bad."

As soon as she was back in the office, Shari said I needed more help than she could give. "You can't run Diamond J with just your lover and a misfit." She motioned her head toward Smithers, who was reading a magazine in the reception room. "It takes more than money to build an empire."

So I hired an executive assistant: Darrell Norton, an ex-cop and agent for the Wisconsin Justice Department who'd once scaled the granite walls of a midtown hotel to bust a pimp on the fifth floor. He was separated from his wife. Shari moved him into our spare room, guessing, I'm sure, that his job description included twenty-four-hour duty.

Norton was indeed a help, so I went looking for a second man to run Dash, my snowmobile racing enterprise. I found him cooking in a supper club. Jim Higbie was narrow-shouldered, thin-limbed, and myopic; he had a receding chin. He was lonely and felt insecure with women; his laugh always sounded forced. But I could also see that Jim Higbie was a quick learner, imitative as a parrot. I figured he'd prove much deeper and smarter than he looked the night I hired him.

Higbie believed in me. He had instant faith.

At about the same time, Barass stopped believing. He said my businesses worried him: we owed too much; the $80,000 sham note to the SBIC was still unexplained. "You're too fast for me."

"Buy the fucker out," I told my partners.

Barass demanded three times his original investment. We settled for double, to be paid on the installment plan.

"Greedy sonofabitch." Yet I realized at the same time that Barass wanted no more than I'd been publicly proclaiming the stock was worth.

Rosenheimer said it was time to determine "the real value of Thunderhead." He took Topp to Steamboat on an appraisal trip. Topp looked at the long lift lines and crowded ski slopes and said, "I'm impressed." Then he and Rosenheimer disappeared.

My intelligence network, set up to look and listen for new developments, reported that they had held secret meetings with LTV's hierarchy. Brunke was deliberately dating an LTV secretary. She told us that the "money boys" were trying to buy land: the Glover 40, contiguous to Walton Creek Park, and North Meadows, a condominium site near the Golden Triangle.

"So what?" I shrugged at Brunke. "We can only benefit from their purchase. If they succeed with their development it will enhance the value of our properties. If they fail we can buy them out at fire sale prices."

Brunke winked. "You're right."

I winked back. "Just keep track of them. Be sure they don't turn the tables and make a deal to spy on us for LTV."

Rosenheimer must have guessed I was suspicious, because he lent me more money and promised to introduce me to a millionaire investor prospect. "Now smile," he said.

I realized that the only way to do business with "Fat Boy" was to play games. "He's probably addicted to Monopoly," I told Turnbull.

Word of my successes spread quickly. No one mentioned risks; failure was a dirty word.

"You really are a money machine," said Higbie, smiling proudly.

Ingels came to see me—Elliot Ingels, Madison's playboy tycoon. No one except me guessed that he needed money. Ingels said he was after the development rights to the Golden Triangle, but I knew his real reason was to gain access to my bankers. Nonetheless, I was happy to see him. He was big—big-bodied, big-hearted, big spender. He like big parties, big boats, big deals. He owned a shopping center, apartment complexes, and the plans for a horse racing track on the Illinois-Wisconsin border. His grandfather founded a large bank, since sold, and built some of the biggest buildings in the downtown shopping area. Ingels had a classy pedigree and was wealthy on paper, but I knew he was spread too thin. He was always hurting for money.

I took a closer look at Elliot Ingels. Everyone liked him, but I doubted that he had one real friend. He was a cream puff, and there was a big difference between liking and loving his kind.

In less than a week we'd agreed to be part-time partners. Ingels, because he lacked ready cash, was the junior. But he started to earn his way to equality on our first trip to Santa Barbara; he established immediate rapport with the Livingstons. The colonel approved of "men of quality." Ingels extended the terms of Shadco's contract to buy the Golden Triangle, and Livingston promised to take physical exams for his million-dollar life insurance policy.

Christmas was a lonely and painful interruption in our progress. Shari visited her family in Colorado. Padgett sent a present: Chivas Regal, my brother's brand. Everyone knew I hated Scotch. I gave him a silver fountain pen, "to write membership applications."

I spent Christmas Day in Madison with my sons. Santa bought them a promised ski trip to Steamboat, complete with an Olympic slalom racer as a full-time instructress. Judy stayed in the background, watching me with frightened eyes. I'd put the house up for sale, and now it was nearly bare, my maintenance men had removed most of the furnishings that I'd demanded in the divorce settlement. I wondered if she thought I was trying to take the children too. The idea hurt both of us, and for a moment I wanted to hold her hand and reassure her, but I did nothing.

The house was depressing, and I excused myself early. That night I dropped the Master Plans into my briefcase, and Bindl and I took off to catch the last United flight to Denver.

Our airplane cabin was dark. I switched on the overhead reading light and spread colored folders on the vacant seat beside me. It was like the first buying trip. That was the problem—the folders were still almost empty. My desk drawers were stuffed with ragged sketches, swirling with ideas, but there was no recorded design for the practical evolution of my dream.

I trusted intuition, heeded premonitions, more than I relied on rationale. My emotions supported my goals. The Diamond J empire was inexplicably, but somehow inevitably, expanding; I was worth more than half a million dollars; my original Master Plan was sound. But I'd used a bad metaphor. "Kaleidoscope" was wrong—fragments of colored glass jiggled on prisms never made the same pattern twice. It was time to stop rattling around.

"I need *people*," I shouted. The passenger across the aisle snorted and came awake. I slid into a more relaxed position and thought about the legal sheet in my top desk drawer. It was titled "The Brain Trust Concept"—the foundation for Diamond J.

We touched down at Steamboat; I was off again.

Skiers swarmed through the Inn. They seemed to forget Christmas, celebrating snow instead, always returning like lemmings to the lifts.

Super Nigger's packed limousine pulled up behind me and followed me to the entrance; even the jump seats were filled. Raymond Claire, wearing a white fur car coat, rushed into the lobby after me.

"I need six rooms," he shrilled.

The desk clerk overheard and shouted above the milling crowd, "Whose reservations?"

"None." Claire smiled at me. "John's boys will take care of it."

Turnbull, sweating from tension, swore he'd never juggle rooms again during a holiday: "Not for anyone—my mother, your mistress, or the president of the Bank of America." He was mad at me.

But it was hard to be angry when Claire, in sparkling style, introduced his entourage: a celebrity booking agent (Turnbull recognized him), a team of nightclub troubleshooters recently returned from an assignment in Las Vegas, and a stunning girl with silky hair who was obviously not attached to anyone in the group. She made a beeline for Brunke.

"Doesn't look like *you* need any money," Claire giggled, shifting his eyes to the overstuffed cocktail lounge entrance.

"Might use help at The Cave," Turnbull grunted. "I just canned the manager."

"Say that again," I whispered, not knowing we had a problem.

"The mother got drunk and rode a snowmobile onto the dance floor. Then I discovered he was only pouring ten drinks per bottle." Turnbull's words were clipped, indicating that he could handle the situation without my assistance.

I enjoyed Claire, but I didn't trust him. Still, Super Nigger's company was something special. Vitality gushed from every pore, making his skin glow like fired charcoal. He took himself seriously but laughed in the mirror often enough to let me know we could be equals. He was a gutsy man on the make. We had that much in common. I had stopped calling him Super Nigger—"That's for the troops, Ray."

"OK, Stone; no one else is permitted to use my first name. I'm Mister or Super Nigger." He winked and held his glass aside to be filled. Then he waved the hovering waitress away, leaned toward me and said, "Sell me The Cave Inn."

"No way." Was he kidding? Sell part of the dream? The sonofabitch was watching for a wedge. Spying. He had known about the Cave's management screw-ups before I had, and he had charged into Steamboat with an assault force bent on snatching my property. Not this year. "Sell? Nobody gives away pieces of a healthy empire."

Claire saw my temper flare and changed the subject. "I heard from your man Padgett. He wants to learn to sell land."

"Not his job," I said slowly. I realized that I should have expected Padgett to crawl into Super Nigger's bed even if he didn't like the company.

I went back to my suite. Looking out the glass door, I saw the mountains and one wing of the Inn covered with new snow. I leaned against the fireplace, lit a cigarette, and watched more flakes falling. The continuous pattern began to hypnotize me. I stared through and beyond the white haze.

A year ago I had started New Year's Eve with Judy, and I still couldn't remember how it had ended. Tonight was going to be the real party. In twelve months I had accomplished more than anyone, even I, had dreamed possible. Now I had something to hang a celebration on: Shadco; Lake, Sport; Janeff . . .

The bathroom door opened, and Shari stood there wrapped in a towel with the Diamond J monogram. Her long, dark hair fell damp and smooth behind her straight, lightly tanned shoulders. She looked warm and moist and her big, glistening eyes told me that an hour and a half before party time would be better than a later booze-clouded struggle to satisfy ourselves.

Getting out of the icy Jeep and through the snow to The Cave Inn was easy; moving inside was nearly impossible. Our table was the best—and why not? I owned the place. To reach it I had to shove past most of the bodies in Steamboat. I felt a lot of eyes on me. Turnbull, in quick succession, looked me up and down, gaped, smiled, and announced, "Christ, Stone, that's probably the first tuxedo ever in The Cave Inn."

I grinned. "It's time the place got some class."

The table was a buffet of everyone's favorite booze and mix. The dance floor was filled.

"A tribal ritual." I pointed to the hundreds of dancers pulsating like one gigantic organism.

I kissed Shari at midnight. Then I kissed every woman in sight. Lights blinked from all directions. I locked eyes with Turnbull; then I turned completely around to face him again. "That was the year of acquisitions," I shouted at him, and pointed to a drunken dancer dressed like Father Time. I spread my arms, my hands suddenly huge. "This is the year of people."

7
January 1972

ASSETS—$714,916.00
LIABILITIES—$128,300.00
PERSONAL GUARANTEES—$2,100,000.00

Dash, Inc., began to take up much of my time; I announced, "This year the International Pro/Am Snowmobile Championships will be spectacular." The superlatives began when a Milwaukee public relations counselor introduced me to a prominent manufacturer who said he was determined to make my races "the greatest winter sports event in the world." Appearances scheduled by the governor, by Miss Wisconsin, and by four pro football stars from the Green Bay Packers assured statewide stature; my suggestion that Steve McQueen might turn his racing talents toward our snow added national glamour; and confirmation that a television crew was flying from Japan to film the event for a showing during the Winter Olympics in Sapporo gave us international prestige.

"Snowmobile racing should be an Olympic event," I told the shareholders and staff. Rumors that Steamboat Springs could be the site of the 1976 Winter Olympics reinforced my aspiration to hold a sister race at the Outdoor Sports Arena depicted on LTV's Master Plans. "In four years snowmobiling will be an accredited international competition because of the men from Dash," I pro-

claimed. Euphoria permeated the meeting. "This is the first concrete manifestation of the truth of our dream."

I drove my yellow Olds Luxury sedan, leased by my companies,
to my apartment—with swimming pool, tennis courts, and golf
course out back—also leased by my companies.

Shari met me at the door. I held our kiss longer than usual,
thinking how fantastic the fringe benefits of an entrepreneur
were; then I looked down into her opening eyes and finished the
thought aloud. "We've got it made, because I've discovered how
easy it is to alter my environment."

"I love you," Shari whispered.

When she said it I wasn't sure if her emotion was spontaneous
or maybe just the easiest way to table a subject she didn't fully
understand. Then her hands moved under my jacket and her
fingers played the piano rhythm of "Rocky Mountain High" along
my spine.

"You do dig, don't you?" I said, hugging her. The phone started
to ring.

It was Judy, wanting me to stop by for a disciplinary session
with the twins; they were misbehaving in school.

"I've got a busy week. It will have to be tonight, honey," I said.
I was embarrassed when I hung up—I knew the endearment was
more than a habitual reflex. And I was angry, too. A very special
moment had been destroyed.

The races ran better than anyone, even I, had expected. But
after the accounting was completed the bottom line was still red.

"Who cares?" said Higbie. "Now that we're internationally
prominent, we can move to a bigger track. Next year there'll be
plenty of profit."

Everybody, including Kritchner, agreed, and we began to promote the Pro/Ams a year in advance.

My companies needed more space. Half the Lake, Sport salesmen had to stand during pep meetings, some so close that my
spit sprayed their faces at the peak of my harangues. I discovered
that Padgett was renting secret space for satellite sales groups,
peddling memberships in his Buyer's Club, in Lake, Sport, and

Travel, and in U.S. Home and Sport Club (his private combination of the first two), and also peddling land in the north woods, "just like the Nigger does in Colorado."

"Horseshit. That's not in the Plan," I said as I took possession of the offices. The complex had private rooms for Norton and myself, "the Bull Pen" for Higbie and the salesmen, and a clerical section partitioned off by glass reaching three-quarters of the way down from the ceiling (Shari called it her fishbowl). I sat beside her and studied my staff, whose faults were suddenly magnified by the unaccustomed spaciousness of their surroundings.

I could see now that my affinity for stray dogs, misfits, and orphans contradicted my image. It was time to weed out the losers. I made my way into the Bull Pen, using shock tactics instead of tact. "If this is the kind of work you do best," I shouted, striding among the men who'd worked twelve hours straight moving in, "look for another job."

I passed into my office and, for theatrical effect, slammed the door to rattle the huge framed renderings of Master Plans. My ice bucket was empty, so I fixed a warm Cuba Libre and sipped it as I spread out paper strategies until stacks of yellow legal sheets covered my desk top.

The desk was still cluttered when O'Connor arrived in the morning and stood quietly in front of me. I knew why he was silent. O'Connor had the amazing ability to read upside down. Before he stated the purpose of his visit he knew all my current business.

"Good thing you cleaned house out here," he finally said. "Eight original Lake, Sport members' contracts are three months delinquent. I told Sommers weeks ago, but he said the salesmen weren't servicing their accounts and never sent a repurchase check." O'Connor's eyes narrowed.

"I'll see that it's done today," I said, turning to file key documents in the safe. Goddamn Sommers. He had insisted on bossing Janeff part-time until I had finished paying him off. He hoarded every penny and was too ornery to solve simple, obvious bank problems before they became an irksome issue.

"Padgett wants to discount Buyer's Club contracts," O'Connor said, easing into a chair. "Will you guarantee them?"

"Hell, no."

"Then you won't get your share." O'Connor smiled. "Why not run 'em through Janeff as usual? You can use the income, clean up Janeff's debts, get ready for something big." He tilted his head back and watched me.

"Something big?"

O'Connor's head snapped forward. "A leasing company. How'd you like to start with a million-dollar line of credit?"

He had to be kidding. Rauterberg had said that O'Connor was selling his bank.

"Not yet," smiled O'Connor. He explained that that was only a ruse to test the loyalty and sales acumen of Rauterberg's correspondent banking division. "Actually I'm in the market for more banks. That's the reason for my trips to Florida. I'm raising capital."

"Who from?"

"Important people," was the limit of his mysterious answer. "Just keep your house clean." Turning toward the Bull Pen, he explained with a frown that I'd have access to millions as long as I didn't "fuck up" his record. "I never have delinquent accounts when the FDIC and the Banking Commission examine my bank. That way my loans, no matter what they are, cannot be criticized." He told me to take care of Walter and Walter would always look after Johnny. Then he hitched up his pants and sauntered out.

"Get Padgett in here," I yelled to Higbie.

Padgett, already flushed from rushing across town, turned a furious red when he heard why I'd summoned him. "The salesmen quit?"

"They were deadwood. We're going to change the club's image," I said softly, hoping my steady glare would convey the message that there was no demurring.

"You misused them," Padgett screamed. "Calling membership directors salesmen, throwing wild punches at your damned affluent market, demoralizing the solicitors with your jet-set attitude."

He slowed down to remind me that Lake, Sport, and Travel Club was intended to offer private opportunities for "Joe Lunch Bucket" to go camping. Not high-flying ski resorts, not Hilton hotels, and not in the company of doctors, lawyers, and college professors." Padgett begged me to do it his way. "Use my mind twisters—greed, sex, ego, and envy. Then anyone can recruit members."

The better I understood Padgett the less I trusted him. He was horribly insecure, always fretful that his limited education and hitch in the Merchant Marine were inadequate credentials outside his devious land of "Joe Lunch Bucket." I knew he was already luring Norton into his camp and slipping Buyer's Club side deals to O'Connor. The Steamboat projects needed my attention, but Padgett was dangerous to leave alone.

After he left, still sputtering, I told Higbie and Shari, "The Brain Trust will soon replace him as my source of sales tactics." Then Padgett's only value would be his ownership of the lodge and campgrounds. "And those can easily be replaced by Kritchner's farm and a secret project I'm working on with Thunderhead's newest stockholder." We all smiled.

"The sooner you engineer Padgett's exodus the better," said Higbie, observing that his philosophies would never work for an "all-encompassing club."

I felt like hugging him. Higbie's progress was amazing, especially the way he was learning to put words together. While he kept Padgett under surveillance, Bindl and I flew to Bessemer, Michigan, to inspect my secret project: a ski lodge open year-round, serving Big Powderhorn and Indianhead.

"The area's just what we need to attract members. It's really popular with Illinois and Wisconsin sportsmen," I said to Bindl.

"And close enough for me to expand my charter business," he smiled.

On the return trip we touched down at the Chanticleer Inn.

"Equally renowned as a fishing, boating, and snowmobiling center," I noted. "And another good air route." The idea of flying members intrigued me.

The Chanticleer's owner was a stockholder in Dash, recruited the year before because many considered him the father of snowmobile racing in northern Wisconsin. He was the originator of the world championship of Eagle River. Now I was going to make him president of Dash and use his reputation to enhance the image of the International Pro/Ams.

"And while I'm at it," I told Bindl, "I might as well sign up his resort." When we took off to fly home my briefcase was filled with promotional material about two new club affiliates.

The third was easy. Kritchner's farm deal was set to close without having been rezoned for a mobile home park. He didn't seem to mind that I'd ignored his plans for the land's use. His eyes twinkled after he studied my renderings of "The Adult Playground."

"This is great." He slapped my back.

The next day, when I reminded him that "everyone in Diamond J should share in everything," Kritchner gave me a 15 percent interest in the project.

My final divorce hearing hit the newspapers again and I began worrying about the twins, John, blond, and George, dark. If the names were reversed they'd be miniatures of me and my brother George. For nine, they were mature. They'd been exposed to life, but I knew that their original anger over the divorce had been gradually replaced by bewilderment and an "I don't give a damn" attitude manifested in their raucous behavior at school. I was neglecting them.

Shari agreed.

So did Judy when we talked outside the courtroom.

I had paid a great deal of attention to my sons when they were first born, but I had soon created a convenient sociological metaphor to avoid having to meet their constant, squalling demands on my time. Like Renaissance princes, and like their father before them, I felt John and George should be reared by their mother until old enough to move easily among men. "That's what babies need," I told Judy. "Constant cuddling maternalism, something they can understand, not the frightening energy of my male drive." Later there was going to be plenty of time for camaraderie with Dad. Hadn't my father handled children that way?

And, as my mother said proudly, I "didn't turn out so bad."

I pushed my argument but I knew it was wrong even as I did my damnedest to sound right.

"They need me."

Judy nodded.

I dropped everything and set up a special tour to Disneyland. I asked Judy to come along. "Why not?" She chuckled. "What a way to begin life as a divorcée!"

"The world isn't the way books tell you it is," I told my sons on our flight to California. "Mom and I will never really be apart." I tried to explain my latest concept, "pair bonding," in which certain rarefied couples transcended the obviously unavoidable problems of life and shared a unique togetherness even when violently and legally parted.

Judy shook her head slowly. She learned toward me and whispered sadly, "Your word magic is still too complex for communication with children."

My sons perked up when I announced that after this trip it wouldn't be long before they left to spend the summer at Lone Tree, "to see why Daddy's working so hard." Judy blinked, probably wondering what place I'd found for them in my empire.

Turnbull paged me off the plane when our return flight made a stop in Denver. As we drove the icy roads toward Steamboat, he told me that our competitive activities had already alienated the Routt County Bank president, who was, at the time, the only temporary loan source in town. We were cut off; the situation was desperate. The Inn expansion job would be shut down unless the contractors got paid, *now.*

Henry, waiting at the Inn, said, "It's impossible to arrange another mortgage advance on the Inn until the work is completed."

"What do you mean, another? You haven't gotten the first one yet," I hissed, thinking it was time to share Turnbull's opinion that Henry was an obnoxious bag of wind. So I wasn't prepared for his blanching face as Henry stormed out of the room.

"What in hell's the matter with you?" Turnbull's voice squeaked with surprise. "Better follow and cool him down. Didn't you know he's finally producing? He was instrumental in securing the condominium financing, and we'll have to go through him for a quick loan." He gave me a hard shove.

"No problem."

Henry began smiling the moment I explained, purposefully, that frustration had triggered my outburst. "For weeks I've been wrestling with the question—should the Inn, Shadco, and the other Diamond J businesses continue to operate independently, or should they be under a single corporate umbrella?" The latter, even if loosely formed, was my inclination. "Either way we need an administrative force, an executive committee, if you like, to oversee the empire and to be damn sure we aren't overwhelmed by fantasy. My business is selling dreams. I need your help to give them substance," I told Henry. I could see his answer before he spoke.

"You got it."

Henry went to the bank while Turnbull and I called Butters for advice on dealing with Amsler. My first reaction was to "lock his ass up," but when Turnbull told us he had offered platted building lots in his Steamboat II subdivision as restitution I couldn't resist this new opportunity to expand.

"Henry has connections with prefab home constructors," I said. "Remember what I told you about the need for low-cost housing?"

Butters agreed. "There's slim chance to collect from a man in jail."

I left the Inn on a scouting expedition while Butters told Turnbull how to tie legal knots around Amsler and Steamboat II. LTV confirmed the fact that Steamboat was the site for the next Winter Olympics. They were accelerating maturation of their plans for a high-rise hotel and mall.

"Steamboat's showing the potential for moving beyond mountains," I told Brunke as we drove out to the Inn together.

"But LTV's rushing past us," he said. He pointed out a new condo project. "Our best defense is to lock up the bar leases in the nearly completed mall."

That sounded good, especially since I was carrying a proposition to install automatic liquor-dispensing equipment at The Cave and the Inn. "Might be wise to spread it across town. I've been watching the Buttonbush and the Cameo." These were struggling bars, buckling from our competition, and any day now we'd be able to buy them right.

We stopped at The Cave, intercepting Brunke's secretary friend. "Rosenheimer's back with another man who looks like a professional footballer," she told us. "They visited my boss this morning and requested that maps be sent, somewhere in Milwaukee."

Rosenheimer checked into the Inn alone the same night and set up an immediate meeting with Turnbull and myself. But he didn't say much except, "The wealthy investor man I've been romancing is about ready to buy a piece of your action. You gotta come back to Wisconsin to make him a presentation." Then he sneaked away before I could question him about his side deals. He left me a note the next morning telling me the time and place of the Wisconsin meeting.

While I was gone, Shari heard rumors, spoken very softly, that I was going bankrupt. When I returned, Rauterberg and O'Connor came to question me. They were nervous. Rauterberg refused to sit and O'Connor kept tapping my desk.

"Sommers is behind it," O'Connor said, jumping from his chair. "Get him paid off and out."

"How? I'm not bankrupt, but I'm damn short of cash."

"Rosenheimer'll lend what you need. Talk to him after the Steamboat investor presentation next week." Rauterberg's words were persuasive, but his tone was tentative, and I wondered how he knew about the meeting.

Rosenheimer, Rauterberg, and Topp, his huge, athletic frame towering over us all, joined Turnbull and myself for the introduction to the millionaire, Walter Koziel.

Looks were deceiving. I would have sized the man up as a truck driver, but on our way to the back room of a Milwaukee supper club, Rosenheimer whispered, "Koziel made his fortune inventing Charmglo, charcoal broilers using natural gas, he doubled it selling out to Beatrice Foods, and is now worth over four million dollars—mostly liquid."

The results of that meeting were not good. "Koziel bought

property in Steamboat Springs," I told my stockholders later. "But, Goddamnit, not ours."

"We got fucked," Turnbull said with unabashed bitterness. "He bought Rosenheimer's options on the Glover 40 and North Meadows instead."

"Can we sue him?" said Hollis.

"Sue our banker? You gotta be kidding." Vitner's eyes twinkled. "Take it easy. Now he owes us one."

The next day I called Rauterberg into my office. I tapped my cigarette into the ashtray until the butt had crumbled and the tobacco scattered out onto the desk. Rauterberg got my message.

"I know what happened, but you better cool it. Jim has important connections, and anyway, he's going to lend more money to you and Kritchner."

"Why Kritchner?"

"He's a doctor. We've had problems with state examiners, but they never question doctors."

Rosenheimer delivered plenty of money, but I was disturbed by my feeling that he was a coincidental conspirator in too many shady deals. If there was a message so far in the events of 1972, it was, "Hereafter the sharpies better watch out." By my own admission the Padgett game, and now the Rosenheimer-Topp double-dealing, had resulted from John Stone's naivete and inattention. "But I learn fast," I told Shari. She was watching me, worried.

My primary weakness was in accounting, and now I needed to know where every dollar was working, every minute. I returned to my primary source of available talent, the Janeff Credit loan files, and dug out Courtney Toussaint's file. He had a long record —it looked as if money managed *him*. I remembered that he was tall and nervously thin, always ready with an excuse for borrowing, but also genuinely respectful of the hand that fed him. He'd do.

It appeared that Lindsey had had doubts from the beginning about our Steamboat Bank charter when he called to tell me that after six months' effort he'd arranged to buy a bank in Wisconsin. Rauterberg was handling the financing, no money down, so long as Lindsey had cosigners and was willing to spread the stock around. The bank director from Mount Horeb signed up, and I agreed to do the same with one-third of my stock, privately assigned to Rauterberg.

Within a month the Banking Commissioner was raising hell; he'd seen my name listed as a stockholder and director. He told Lindsey that a promoter-borrower like John Stone should not be in control of a bank. So I bowed out quietly, still agreeing to cosign the note, since Lindsey and I were already partners in the Western ventures. "It's not worth the hassle," I said. "But I wonder how the Banking Commissioner got wind of me. Check it out."

A new trend, recruiting close friends and relatives, tipped me off to the changing characteristics of the club's membership directors. They continued to equate merit with money, but now they were beginning to show pride of participation. They all wanted to be a permanent part of Diamond J. They were gaining faith.

I began building my Brain Trust with an insurance counselor-securities representative. The man was a living digest of pension plans, profit sharing, and tax-exempt investments. He was an ultraconservative with a deadpan face; he replied to questions in a deliberately slow monotone, and he was even slower to make decisions. That was unimportant. *I* made the resolutions.

"Your job," I told him, "is to keep the corporate records up-to-date. We hold a lot of meetings, but no one's been paying any attention to the minutes. We're also beginning to sell a load of stock, but it's not getting transferred on time. Then there's the state reports . . ."

He nodded. "Securities are my business."

"Good. You understand *this* is a training program for the important office of corporate secretary in all Diamond J Ventures."

He kept right on nodding.

Lake, Sport, and Travel needed a full-time president, so I hired another man, the perfect Hollywood image of a Nazi *Oberleutnant*. He was tall and blond with a stubborn, belligerent look even when he was happy. Incongruously, he was a liberal whose constantly moving, red-rimmed eyes were the only clue to his awe of my luxurious playthings. I called him my Storm Trooper and assigned him my dirty work. "Your first task is to scare Padgett out of the office."

As spring started everyone began sprouting new enthusiasm. Butters, who was usually close-mouthed, couldn't resist bragging to Elliot Ingels about Diamond J. Ingels, the picture of nonchalance, strolled into my office an hour later and invited me out for a drink. I suggested the Mayflower Lounge.

He came right to the point. He wanted to be more than my partner. His heart was set on total control of the Golden Triangle.

"No problem," I said. "Shadco can use the money. We'll accommodate you as long as you allow us to retain construction contract rights and a minority interest."

Control was first transferred to a partnership headed by Lindsey and myself, so we could handle the interim financing with prearranged loans from Lindsey's associates. Shortly thereafter Ingels bought the options from us with funds generated by outside investors in Bright Star, a new Diamond J entity which I established to convey ownership through a land-holding limited partnership and a corporation to assume all development liabilities.

Livingston endorsed the restructuring and passed the word to Hilton, who resumed his campaign to franchise a mountain resort inn. Mrs. Livingston was the only problem: she was concerned that the million-dollar insurance policy was being paid for with Mafia money.

I tried to hypnotize her via long-distance and finally said, "Don't be silly."

Then, just to be sure, Ingels and I flew to Denver to nail down the transfer of Livingston's contracts. We stayed at the Radisson Hotel, where Playboy ran a club on the top floor. The managers of both businesses recognized me. The Playboy manager wanted a tip on my proposed club in Steamboat, and the Radisson executive pitched his hotel chain as being better than Hilton's.

"Curt Carlson owns it, along with Gold Bond Stamps," the Radisson manager boasted.

I didn't recognize the man or the companies so I called Brunke and Higbie and ordered immediate research. While Livingston's attorneys drafted new documents, Ingels followed me to a strategy meeting in Steamboat. He listened, goggle-eyed, to the scheming.

"The Thunderhead condominium management subsidiary will service other competitive units, and Shadco will probably enter the auto rental business," Turnbull said, then swung around to face Ingels. "Your Triangle needs a movie theatre and an ice-skating rink." He winked. "Plans are ready for those too."

The headquarters was in Minneapolis–St. Paul, where a second local Radisson Hotel and convention center had been nearly completed, at the airport. The report said that Carlson was one of the wealthiest men in Minnesota, and, by reputation, another man on the make. I decided to visit him on the way back to Wisconsin.

In between I stopped in Denver and rented the nine-room penthouse below the Playboy Club for a year. Kritchner was incredulous when I showed him photographs.

"A better layout than the penthouse I had at Hilton's hotel in Houston," I said. "It's got a white-sand-floored balcony—the highest beach in Denver—and the master bedroom has an eight-foot-wide red-velvet-canopied bed. There's twenty-four-hour maid, room, and valet service, a barber shop down the hall, and a private stairway to the rooftop pool." I was breathless as he started to ask what we were going to do with a penthouse. "I got it cheap. Thousand a month—almost a gift from Carlson, I guess because he wants to move into Steamboat."

"Fantastic," Kritchner finally said. He mentioned numerous friends who'd rent it for fifty dollars a night.

"When and if they're stockholders," I advised with a wide smile. We left the office for a private drink and a leisurely exploration of the full potential of Diamond J. Midway through the conversation, I checked my enthusiasm; Kritchner's constantly changing expression made it clear that he was uneasy. At first I attributed his anxiety to my earlier statement that we might have to use his wife's inheritance to guarantee the latest Thunderhead loan. Kritchner knew I was using him, but he was also cognizant of the free ride my maneuvers afforded him. So up to now he'd said nothing.

"Are you losing your self-discipline in the fantasies of the moment?" He made the delayed protest in a tone that, I imagined, he reserved for seriously ill patients.

The question rattled me. Had I missed an important danger signal?

"Say that again." I wanted to be sure I understood his mood.

"Look, John, Diamond J is no longer a game where 70 percent of the investors don't really care if they make a profit. Today, with millions at stake, mostly guaranteed by the stockholders, it's a matter of life or death." And the doctors were running out of money, Kritchner implied.

In that case, our only reserve was the questionable good will of the bankers.

"Your Master Plan"—Kritchner hesitated. "Your Master Plan, damnit, is riddled with contradictions."

I agreed that there was still no appreciable cash flow, and that, although we lived on easily borrowed money, the interest was fast catching up to next year's profit projections. We were buying our way with constant expansion, devoid of monetary planning.

"So where is the point of no return? When we pass it, failure means living death." Kritchner's apprehension was reflected in the hollow terror of his eyes.

I saw then that I'd created the ultimate personal pressure— talking and acting as if the fantasies most important to my life-style were fact, reality. Then, with personal and financial lives depending on me, I had to make them come true. Or, to put it another way, I was either living in a dream or telling a mammoth lie, and, realizing this, spending enormous energy to make it come true before I was caught.

"We're consolidating our positions," I told Kritchner, "and adding a productive staff." I explained my New Year's resolution —the Brain Trust. "This is the year of people." As his eyes brightened, I explained the most important point. "The bankers helped me devise an easy method to eliminate the need for ready cash from investors. Stockholders can sign corporate notes to expand old companies and form new ones. Our own CPA, Toussaint, confirms that this will add paper value—higher equity figures on financial statements—while giving the established stockholders something for nothing. As Vitner and Hollis already said, it's hard to think of a note in our safe as a binding obligation."

"What are you going to do with the notes?" Kritchner asked.

"Sit on them until they hatch money," I laughed, and when his lips turned upward too, I knew the crisis had passed. But I would not forget the heavy premise of that night. If I weren't careful, my acquisition of properties, companies, and people could become a calamity, an odyssey out of control.

Maybe Kritchner had begun to believe that the result was inevitable, but before it was too late, I had diverted his thoughts.

I slept less than two hours that night, but I was hyperalert with rekindled bravado the next day when Bill Quarton applied for a job. Brunke had sent him. Quarton was a disgruntled urban executive searching for employment with recreational real estate in the Rockies. Brunke had told him that the only chance to earn his way West was to join John Stone: "He's always expanding."

Quarton wore western clothes and boots—not exactly the right attire for an executive job interview. And he showed that he knew it when he stared incredulously at my frontier pants and the red silk bandanna round my neck.

I put him at ease. "What did you expect from a country boy who owns half of Colorado? Yellow peg pants and suede shoes?"

We had a long personal discussion. Quarton was seven years older than I. His recently grown collar-top auburn hair and his tanned face, with pressure wrinkles surrounding mellow eyes, told me that he'd worn gray flannel suits in ivory towers for a long time. His conversation let me know that he wouldn't do it again.

Then, with no hesitation, Quarton told me about myself: "One-fourth Billy the Kid, with a stinging whip and a kiss. One-fourth each Wizard of Oz, King Arthur, and Quiz Kid of the forties. A Renaissance man . . ."

Quarton was a pro; he'd done his homework. I copied down the words to use later as the basis for my personal promo piece, "Something about John Stone." He wanted a job that led West, so I made up a title—Vice-President, Creative Marketing—and gave it to him.

My trips to Minnesota jelled a deal with Radisson. Curt Carlson took his private Gold Bond Stamp Airliner out West, loaded with the entire Radisson executive staff. After a day at the Inn and one look at the Golden Triangle, he suggested that the Radisson chain could run Thunderhead while another hotel was constructed to handle the overflow. Ingels beamed when I asked him to stand between Carlson and me as we announced our partnership.

Livingston was also pleased, so much so that he admitted to a long but useless association with Eric Hilton, trying to suck in wealthy developers. "One hotel chain leads to another," he chuckled, eyeing my renderings. "See you still got the Bunny in her place. Anything new?"

Ingels and I rocked with wild laughter as the combined staffs of Radisson and Diamond J crowded around us. We took turns showing artists' drawings of our Alpine Village, including a Savings and Loan, a bank (Routt County First National might move), an auto service center, a shopping and entertainment mall, a motel, the CondoHotel and a high-rise hotel, and a major medical center, to be designed by the architect of the Common Market Convention Center at Yarmouth, England, and administered by Shari's father.

Later, during dinner, Turnbull found me in the office and gave me some private good news. "Columbia Federal Savings and Loan has approved a $1,900,000 mortgage on our condominiums."

As soon as the snowdrifts melted off the roads, I headed for Lone Tree to sketch plans for a new Diamond J compound.

Ray Claire was waiting when I got back to the Inn, accompanied only by his regular assistant. Over dinner he told me that it was time to say good-bye, that there wasn't anything more he could do to help me now that Radisson was moving in.

"I've got problems of my own now," he said. "Sure would be nice if you opened that bank." He exhaled a long stream of smoke through his nostrils, and I got the impression that he wanted to ask me for help. Instead he warned me to watch The Cave Inn. "You're getting screwed, John," Ray Claire said. He paid the tab and motioned to his assistant to bring the limousine.

I never saw him again, although I knew Padgett kept in touch while looking for assistance for his land sale schemes. He accused me of dumping Super Nigger. "But you'll never get *me* out," he shouted.

Higbie and my Storm Trooper smiled. They knew Padgett was planning a campground in the Wisconsin Dells, and would need money to pay for it. In the meantime every move, every side deal with O'Connor was reported to me.

My biggest problem now was Shari. I could tell she was unhappy with the hours we kept. While I worked late, she went home early, to lie trancelike, watching television. On several occasions I found her staring at the snowy screen long after the midnight sign-off. Her moods worried me. I knew I'd used her, and she was too good to be used.

Once, when I asked what was wrong, she said she wanted to get pregnant. "Not married, just have your baby."

She winced when I laughed and told her, "There isn't even time for John and George."

I loved Shari, but she was unhappy. I sent her away, to live in the penthouse and be my eyes and ears in Denver. "You're the only one I can trust," I told her at the airport. I tried not to cry as I walked away.

Moving ahead enthusiastically was a habit, but I was unaccustomed to loneliness. I began prowling the pick-up bars with Quarton. Women turned, and others stared from the booths when we walked in. We were older than the regular crew, better dressed. And we were unique: we never looked back.

Quarton told me about himself. Sober, I was his boss; drunk, I dropped my guard. He was proud of his animal instincts and his native intelligence, which he said was more important than the college education he'd wasted his time on. He'd rebelled against the classic upbringing of an ambassador's son, yet he was well-spoken and his manners were perfect, even when he was drunk.

We bragged unashamedly—"the last of the American aristocracy."

Sometimes, stubborn beyond belief, Quarton refused to leave the office and the new club brochures he was creating. One night

I went alone to the Loft, the entertainment center of my apartment complex. I was already high on home-poured Cuba Libres.

I blinked in the dim light. "I'll be damned." It was like looking into a smoky mirror, but I thought I saw my female counterpart sitting at the bar, straining to take on the world.

"Beautiful." I moved closer and saw that she was the kind of woman who needed no pedestal. Every sun-bleached, naturally deep-blond hair was in place, falling just below her shoulders—a perfect frame for her radiant face. She seemed completely relaxed, yet her sleek body, swaying slowly to the rhythm of the music, soon gave the conflicting impression that it throbbed with barely controlled energy. As I sat down beside her I noticed that her eyes were light blue, flecked with brown.

Much later, without looking at her, I said, "I'm Steamboat."

She laughed. "That's an idiotic first move."

We talked. Soon I knew that she could easily cope with my lifestyle, even before she said, "If you want to get drunk, let's do it privately."

I discovered that she lived right down the hall from me, had ever since I moved in. In my kitchen, we talked until dawn. I don't remember what we said, but somewhere among the liquor-laden vibes I got a sobering premonition that here was my new mate. Her name was Sue, and I scribbled those three letters on my scratch pads over and over for many days until there was time to take her on a real date.

"How about a trip to my ranch in the mountains?"

Sue's face wrinkled into a silent laugh. "Be patient, John."

At first it was hard to believe my reaction. Nobody could tell John Stone to be patient. But suddenly it was easy for me to say softly, "No problem."

When the Lake, Sport, and Travel membership drive began to lag again, I hired an expert, William McCaskill, whose book *How to Get Through to People in Selling* taught "the secrets of eyeball-to-eyeball success—the power-packed techniques that smash through obstacles and objections."

McCaskill got a full-time contract from me; as he said, "My

track record is impressive." Numerous large companies had asked him back a second and even a third time, and an Illinois banker told me that he was "sound as a dollar." So sound, in fact, that he'd lent him large sums to expand his sales consulting business.

But I was disappointed from the moment McCaskill moved in. "If Padgett sees himself as the Masters and Johnson of sales, Mc-Caskill has to believe he's the Freud, Kinsey, and Reuben of sales management," I told Sue. We were at dinner, after I'd spent ten frustrated hours watching the Brain Trust concept collapse. "He's the most disjointed egomaniac I've ever seen in action."

The next morning McCaskill began interviewing the executive staff.

"I'm going to eliminate your hang-ups, bust the barriers to success," he told us.

When my turn came, I was amazed that most of the Brain Trusters hadn't walked out already. McCaskill fancied himself an emotional detective, finding clues everywhere, even in my flatulation patterns.

"I fart more than I jack off," I answered facetiously, knowing the interview was a ploy to discover the personal secrets of John Stone. McCaskill had the darting eyes of a gossip.

Somehow, probably because we were learning to laugh with him, McCaskill seemed to earn his way during the following weeks. The membership directors confessed and studied in the A.M. and closed sales in the P.M.—regularly. While they hustled, McCaskill gave our promotional material his beauty treatment. Kritchner's farm became the "Family Man's Country Club" in specially drawn cartoons that portrayed it as a place where Junior carries firewood, daughter trots water pails, and Mom photographs squirrels while Dad saddles the horses.

Kritchner said he'd be God damned.

Another brochure told "How to enjoy middle life freedom." The cover showed an overweight couple trying to frug, but inside was the real story of playing after forty without looking foolish. "Lake, Sport, and Travel Club has special places for timid members to practice skiing, tennis, and golf. Rookies will find themselves in good company," it read. The final form stressed that Lake, Sport's members were "the right kind of people—lusty, full-bodied men and women, the unfrightened ones, who get an extra delight out of fine people and thrilling events."

And we had a new creed: we were "an assemblage of strong-minded persons who believe in taking care of themselves."

"Maybe the doctors will like it," quipped Quarton, his mischievous eyes twinkling.

My Storm Trooper said, "I'm not sure I want to be president of a sanitarium."

Nonetheless sales continued to increase and I found myself facing an enigma: McCaskill had many ideas that were great because they worked, but he was also antagonizing the hierarchy of my Brain Trust with his repetitious psychological prattle. I finally decided that since he was basically full of shit and his best suggestions were already integrated with my system, McCaskill must go. The problem then was how to remove him, since his contract ran for a year.

Only after I threatened to apply McCaskill's wages toward delinquent payments on his Janeff loan did the master salesman agree to work part-time, drafting sales brochures at home. Before he left he looked me up in his book of capsule analyses and said I was a "maverick."

Rauterberg said, "McCaskill's got you pegged right," when I explained my decision to ban professional sales motivators from Diamond J. "And I'm not a cornucopia," he complained, when I told him we needed letters of credit to backstop mushrooming construction costs in Steamboat.

"We need them now, or the work will fall behind again." I pointed to a new rendering of the Thunderhead condominiums on the wall behind my desk.

"It's crooked—the picture, I mean." Rauterberg brushed past me to straighten it. "Look, John, your greed for acquisition, of people and property, is dangerously ahead of cash flow again."

I stood up and trapped him in the corner behind my desk. "The hell it is." I showed him the latest membership sales report.

"The club isn't carrying you yet." Rauterberg thumbed the pages.

"I know that, but we haven't reached the point of no return, and I won't reverse myself without a reason. Here's something else." I pulled another report from the file, a new scheme pirated from Padgett's discourses with Ray Claire. "If Diamond J options 10,000 acres of land with a title release clause of $200 per acre, we'll have a $2 million gross to play with after selling the land for $400 an acre."

When I turned to find the schematic diagrams, Rauterberg escaped to the center of the room.

"Well, what do you think?" I shouted.

Rauterberg agreed that anyone would buy mountain property at that price.

"And Janeff will handle the paper."

"Where's the land?"

"I'll find it, faster than you gave birth to our bank," I sneered playfully. I knew that subject still embarrassed Rauterberg. "Now get Rosenheimer in here."

Rosenheimer showed up the next day with the letters of credit, which I hand-carried West.

Shari met me at the airport. "Just in time," she said, warning me that there was another fire to extinguish. "Steamboat's lost the Olympics, and Elliot Ingels is afraid land values will plummet."

"Scared shitless, I'll bet. Sometimes I wonder if Ingels is big enough to run with the big boys." I looked toward the snow-capped front range and thought back to when I was a kid, playing King of the Mountain.

"The world is full of mountains," I told Shari as we drove downtown, "but there's room on top for very few people. Everyone else has to stay in the valleys."

She cocked her head. "And you think you have a divine right to the top?"

"No. But I'm strong enough to climb the sides and toss off the incumbents."

We smiled at each other. Shari understood. It was a good metaphor, but I realized that the life of an entrepreneur was more complicated than a kid's game. And I could feel the steering wheel slippery with sweat.

Fortunately, Ingels and his associates, waiting in the pent-house, were desperate for a sense of accomplishment. So they accepted my premise that the Olympics represented only one-third of Steamboat's publicity power.

"1976 is also the Colorado Centennial, and, of course, the U.S. Bicentennial. That's the year everybody will travel, regardless. And besides, the Olympics aren't really out until the formal referendum in November." I invited them to move on to the Inn.

Ingels's enthusiasm bounded back as he said, "That's where the action is. And we can all see firsthand that everything's . . ." He hesitated, looking around to be sure there were no dissenters. I finished the sentence for him:

". . . still on the rise."

8

July 1972

ASSETS—$891,316.00
LIABILITIES—$139,400.00
PERSONAL GUARANTEES—$3,250,000.00

Bindl's Bonanza touched down on the mountain airstrip with only the faintest feeling of contact with the earth.

"Just like everything else," I told Sue. She agreed that our lives had become unaccountably easy as the summer began. I reached back to squeeze her knee and thought how well she suited me. "Let's sneak off to the high country as soon as we check in at Lone Tree." I turned to see her smiling back at me while she unhitched the seat belt and packed construction drawings into her oversized purse.

"Love you." She made the words with her freshly moistened lips moving wide and slow in mute exaggeration.

I tightened my hold on her knee and silently imitated the phrase as our eyes met. This was the way to live.

My first impression of Sue had been my most perfect premonition ever. She was a tough lady in both literary senses. I nodded to myself, picturing the sensually magnificent authority she had showed as she commanded the restoration of Lone Tree astride the snowflake Appaloosa mare I'd given her as an engagement present. She was subtly ageless. When we traveled with the twins, she was often mistaken for their mother, or sometimes—undoubtedly because their bone structure, coloring, and blond hair were so similar—as little John's big sister. Occasionally strangers guessed that she was my younger sister.

"Any way, you're fantastic," I told her, glancing at the marquise diamond I'd bought her. My entire body was warm, satisfied that she was really mine. "Always. Everywhere."

Sue's ability to blend in astounded me. In the same day, I'd seen her mix beer parties exploding with acid rock with champagne formality on Ingels's houseboat yacht, and then fly all night to Colorado, where she slipped into leather ranch pants and stalked the trout streams at Lone Tree.

While I crisscrossed the country, Sue had finished rebuilding Lone Tree. The contruction crew, sons and brothers of stockholders and my staff, felled my trees and scrubbed my logs until they glistened—and hated Sue. She pushed them, hard, until even Higbie and Quarton seemed ready to rebel sometimes.

The new lodge and the outbuildings were the products of imagination, aided only by the freehand sketches in Sue's purse. And yet I knew they'd be more beautiful than the Inn or the Towers at the Golden Triangle.

Our station wagon headed into the mountains. I felt Sue's body tighten against me as she shouted to the driver. "How you coming with the new construction?" Her eyes widened; they showed unbending simplicity of purpose—to please me. But there were also new worry lines at the corners.

Sue shouted to the driver again. "I asked how the work was going." Her voice was higher, and sounded strained. I was concerned that she might be trying too hard, trampling the workers' enthusiasm.

And then the boy said with a wide grin, "We're done."

Sue hugged him. "Great."

I sighed loud enough for them to look my way. For sure, these were my halcyon days.

Riding into the mountains toward Lone Tree, I began a songfest. Nobody knew the complete words to "Rocky Mountain High," so we settled for a medley of old-fashioned cowboy ballads, some of which I had to sing alone.

"The old man of the mountains," the driver called me. He winked at Sue, suddenly his buddy.

"Without a worry in the world," I said, thinking that even the financial pressures were under control. The bankers had seen to that. I had even forgotten the investigations of O'Connor's mysterious Florida connections, and Rosenheimer's sly trips to the East Coast.

"Beautiful," I said. I suppose the others thought I meant the mountains, but it was much more than the countryside that turned me on, made me feel like soaring above the valley we crossed. Nothing was impossible now; every part of my life was a piece of that beautiful big picture. Even my destructive former marriage and the wars with my other women had been settled, smoothly veiled in a new philosophy that some good always comes from bad times, *if you know how to manipulate them.* Judy and I were divorced, but we were friends now, I convinced myself, "pair bonded." Shari seemed content to manage my affairs in Denver. And Sue exuded more confidence every day that she was indeed "my mate."

There was no reason, I decided, to hide the past. I wanted Shari and Judy to see the new growth of Lone Tree; they were still a part of it. I knew that I could call my three women together, honestly, without hassles.

Quarton, when I told him my plan, said I was out of my mind.

"It's part of me to do the unexpected," I told him. "The impossible."

Judy and Shari didn't think my invitation was so strange.

"Why not? We're all adults," said Judy. "And after all, Lone Tree's been part of my life, too. One day it will belong to our sons, I hope."

"It'll be fun," Shari laughed. "We all have something in common, you know." I had expected that response from her. As far as she was concerned, life was a lark.

Sue frowned when I first told her, but then cocked her head and smiled. "OK with me. You're mine now; that's what counts."

I nodded and reached to pull her toward me.

She tugged my earlobe. "Just don't ever forget. You are mine."

And I knew she would bend her beliefs to keep me.

Three days later, after a hectic effort to finish the last-minute details of the new lodge, Higbie delivered my ex-wife and ex-mistress to the compound. His expression changed quickly as the Jeep bounced over construction debris scattered on the driveway. First amusement, then apprehension, as he saw Sue standing beside me.

Sue initiated the greetings and quickly settled Judy and Shari into the same cabin.

"Unbelievable." Higbie shook his head as he unloaded the luggage and followed the three women.

I pulled on my waders, grabbed a fly rod from the rack, and went off for some fishing, calling over my shoulder, "To get away." I laughed and thought, not because I'm afraid of a scene, but to give everybody a chance to get acquainted with their new roles.

Later, when I clumped back into camp waving a long string of trout, it seemed perfectly natural that the three women were animatedly talking, all smiles, around the picnic table. I felt like hugging them all and telling each one how important she was to John Stone and Diamond J.

But there were moments during the next three days when I began to think Quarton had been right—I was crazy. Shari insisted we talk business.

"This is my only chance to tell you about what I've been doing for the company in Denver," said said, pulling me out of the kitchen where I'd been helping Sue and Judy with the breakfast dishes. "And since there's no phones to interrupt us, maybe, just maybe, you'll pay attention."

Sue stared and Judy shook her head when I tried to be funny. "Don't talk like a wife."

An hour later, while the other two were horseback riding, Sue exploded.

"You're acting like an ass."

I asked her why.

"Because none of us likes to be reminded of what used to be or might have been."

The next day Shari told me I was too aloof. "Who do you think you're kidding? I think you still love Judy and, at the same time, you'd like to have your moments to sneak off with me, and having us here together is unfair to Sue."

Then Judy said, less than an hour later, "You haven't changed a bit. You still think you can manipulate people."

And Sue insisted it was not appropriate to make love with the other women sleeping next door.

"What the hell does that mean?"

"It means I'm turned off, John."

I breathed a deep sigh of relief when Higbie drove Judy and Shari back to Denver.

Morning and night I could see heavy cumulus clouds on the horizon, but it never rained, and even the mountain breezes were soft.

"It's too damn peaceful," I told Sue one evening as we watched fresh flames climbing the pile of logs in our new fireplace.

She smiled, knowing from my mischievous expression that I was going to say something exciting or funny next.

"Maybe you should have started a brawl with Judy and Shari before they left." I grinned and winked and then, seeing Sue's eyes pinched and hurting from a little too much of the past, squatted at her feet and told her, "Sorry, hon, I get stupid when I live the lazy life. I've got to get back into action."

So I eased back onto the roller coaster and, thankfully, the jerks into the high points weren't so gut-wrenching anymore. "Either my hide's getting tougher or I'm building an immunity to trouble," I told Higbie and Quarton when they suggested I was beginning to take too many chances. When Rosenheimer got caught charging five-figure personal expenses on his bank's credit card and stood to lose control of his banks, I promised him the future presidency of Janeff Credit. "When it's mutually convenient."

"A smart move," counseled his friend Rauterberg during one of our frequent telephone talks. "Jim's contacts are valuable, and damnit, even if he runs into trouble now and then, he's a shrewd operator."

The next day Rauterberg called again. "See me smiling?"

I could hear that he was about to laugh.

"John, you can stop worrying about Walt O'Connor. He just called me from Florida, and said he'd be back soon . . . to take care of you."

O'Connor had the habit of disappearing to Florida, and it was reassuring to know that he was returning to grant my loan requests. I'd had doubts; Rauterberg had warned me previously that the bank examiners advised caution—"John Stone's borrowing habits are suspicious."

Rauterberg chuckled. "You can relax. Now let's have a party."

"Right!"

But, "just in case," I decided to bring my own "golden goose" into the picture. Jack O. W. Rash had been my father's physician.

"He's a hard man to describe," I told Turnbull, whose job it was to play host to the doctor while he spent his vacation at the Inn. "Rash is a rich conservative; when he helped his friend Goldwater run for president, he spared no expense."

"Then he's not a tightwad."

I cleared my throat. "Hard to say. Rash's tremendous liquidity is due to investments in Treasury Bills and Federal Land Bonds. But he's certainly no swinger."

"Then why the enthusiasm about his visit to Thunderhead?"

I wondered. Rash had been my best friend for two decades. He was eighteen years my senior, but there was no age barrier. Very simply, I got along better with Rash than with any other man. One of the reasons was our mutual reluctance to demand large favors from each other. That's why I'd never asked him to join Diamond J. Certainly I'd kept him advised of my progress, mostly by telephone. But when I visited him at his winter retreat near Palm Beach or at the home farm in Kentucky, we stuck to more relaxed subjects: fishing, jazz, politics, or Irish setters.

"Jack is old-school South." That was the best handle.

"Sounds like an idiotic idea for another freebie," he grumbled, but he started to laugh as soon as I explained that Rash intended to pay for everything—"even the dog damage."

"What?"

"He always takes his five Irish setters along."

"I'll be Goddamned. First your harem, now a covey of bird dogs."

Turnbull got serious again when I warned him that there should be no sales pitches, no tricky maneuvers.

"If Rash volunteers to join the Diamond J investors, that's something else," I said, smiling.

Turnbull kept me regularly informed, usually calling late at night after Rash had retired. He liked Rash, so it was easy to show him a good time. "Even the dogs are having fun," he told me. "And I'm not soliciting him." Then there was an early-morning call. Turnbull's voice was steady, but there were frantic undertones.

"I hope the doctor's interested in the Inn by now," he said, "because we're going to need lots of extra money soon. The condos are going to be finished a year late."

"When did you find that out, for Christ's sake?" I couldn't believe it.

"Late last night. There's a problem getting structural steel. I tried to call."

I'd been on a celebration drunk with Ingels, Quarton, and Butters to commemorate the latest Bright Star development contract. My mind was still too fuzzy to discuss the details of the problem. "Find out why, *exactly*." I was sobering up fast. "And make damn sure Rash stays happy. *Impress* him. I may have to fly out now and ask him to buy into the project."

Because, damnit, maybe there'd be no choice. I'd have to butcher my golden goose. A year's delay would cost us nearly thirty, no, forty thousand a month—we'd moved so fast we hadn't realized that Amsler had neglected to insert a penalty clause in the construction contracts, and now there was no way to recover losses due to the delayed completion date.

Turnbull got back to me two days later. This time he was obviously frantic as he shouted, "He's going down the road."

"Who? What in hell . . .?" I was confused. Turnbull was interrupting me during a crucial sales meeting.

"Dr. Rash is leaving." His voice crackled through the phone. "John . . . Goddamnedest luck. Some of the drug pushers that moved up here from Aspen bombed an undercover narc's camper in our parking lot early this morning. The Doc was walking one of his dogs. The explosion knocked 'em both on their ass."

I threw my pen onto the desk. "Sonofabitch!" was all I could say. I'd already decided to ask for Jack Rash's help, and under normal circumstances I knew I could count on him. But I knew even better his hatred of hippies, leftists, and addicts. His only criticism of me came when he thought I was under "liberal" influences. "Sonofabitch." This was a catastrophe, and it was magnified by Quarton's earlier report that the club needed an immediate infusion of $25,000 to keep operating.

Sweat marks on my desk top were a sure clue to troubled times, I thought. And today, no matter how hard I rubbed my hands on my trousers, they still left damp stains.

"Problems?"

I kept my hands in my lap as Rosenheimer came into the office. He wore the special grin that said "something big is up," and seemed in an unusual hurry. "You need an airliner," he said, thrusting himself forward until his bulging body was halfway across my desk.

The scene and the dialogue were so bizarre that I laughed and said, "Sure, why not?" Buying an airliner was the last thing on my mind; I was desperately broke; but I kept smiling and played the game. I'd quickly learned, long before, to hide all pessimism, pretend that every loan could be paid today, unless, as a "favor," Rosenheimer asked me to keep open balances for him to earn interest on. And when Rosenheimer said, "Buy," I would buy. That was the secret of handling the "Fat Boy."

He described "The Bird:" "A Martin 404 airliner. A fifty-two-seat commercial convert customized to carry twenty-one passengers in absolute luxury. Wet bars, television, stereo tape deck, even a telephone. It's a solid plane with a 2,500-mile cruising range, a service ceiling of 27,000 feet, and a cruising speed of 280 mph. No race horse, but known for untemperamental and dependable performance under all conditions."

"You're higher than that plane can fly," I told him when he stopped for breath. I recognized the 404: a prop job refugee from the 1950's, descendant of the 202, that had already been retired from general service because of its tendency to lose wings.

"The Bird is an exception," said Rosenheimer, chuckling. "And you can buy it with no money down."

"Helluva deal." I nodded, trying to think of a way to broach the subject of more plebeian loans. I looked for Higbie, who was supposed to be gathering financial statements, and saw that Rosenheimer hadn't come alone. A big, leathery man was sitting in the bull pen, upturned palms resting on his knees—a begging posture. "Who's he?"

"Dick Metcalf, president of Golden Sunset Mining Company— now it's Metcalf Farms–Hawaii." He motioned to the older man and pulled him into my office.

I wondered if there'd ever be a chance to ask about money for my companies, and then I tensed, feeling totally frustrated, when Metcalf began to talk.

"Mr. Rosenheimer tells me that Janeff Credit may lend me $100,000."

"Is that right?" I wanted to laugh or cry or break something; anything but sit there and listen to another new proposition while Diamond J companies were collapsing. But Rosenheimer, with a grin and a two-eyed wink, encouraged me to pay attention. I figured he was trying to tell me that my problems were "No Problem"—that money was on the way. I took a deep breath.

Metcalf gave me a confused smile, produced an agricultural magazine, and began telling me his problems. "Well, several years ago I came up with the first seeds that would successfully grow corn in Hawaii. So I leased 16,000 acres on Oahu and Kauai, and produced a crop, well . . . it was spectacular enough to make the front cover of this magazine." He shoved his agricultural journal at me.

"Fine." I fidgeted. It took the farmer forever to tell his story. He began every sentence with an endless "Well . . ."

"Well, the second crop was growing good. Well, then, you know we can get three, maybe four crops a year in Hawaii. That's good, well . . . if all goes well."

Rosenheimer listened, watching me. His hands were folded behind his head, elbows pushing backward, big gut poking in my direction. "Unbelievable profit potential," he injected.

I glanced from Metcalf to Rosenheimer and wondered: with "unbelievable profit potential," why hadn't the loan been made at his bank?

Metcalf continued, "Well, the islands have a lot of rain. And humidity, well, it breeds bugs." The gist of the story was: Bugs eat corn. Rice birds feast on bugs and corn—corn castrated before it can pollinate. No crop.

"So how do you make money to repay a loan?" I hoped the question would end the discussion.

"He's got a new spray to eliminate bugs," Rosenheimer said. "And the Audubon Society has declared the rice birds a varmint, so Dick can poison them. *No problem.*"

That seemed to be everybody's favorite expression today.

I called in the corporate secretary, "The Digest," and told him to take Metcalf away, study his supporting documents, and process a loan application. Because now, damnit, I was going to work on Rosenheimer for the money I needed.

"Jim," I told him, "you know there's no way to make this Hawaiian loan. It sounds good. So does the airliner. But before I add any frivolous debts I've got to have $100,000 myself."

"No problem," he chuckled. "I knew that before I came over. The Bird will fly you to money. Financing is prearranged." I could borrow twice the purchase price . . . unsecured. In addition, the seller would take an unfinished Thunderhead condo in trade. "If you give us one on the top floor you can free up another $58,000 for the Inn."

"What do you mean, 'us'?" I'd just discovered the reason for Rosenheimer's strange lending latitude at a time when the FDIC was ready to swoop down and take his bank away. "You've got money in the 404." I stood up and poked my finger into his chest. "Don't you?"

"Just a small loan at the Jackson Bank." He closed his eyes: not a wink this time, a study in nonchalance. "I'm doing the owner a favor. He's given me free rides and now he's short because McGovern's campaign committee hasn't paid their charter bill. The Bird's too big for him; it's just the right size for you." Rosenheimer explained that the asking price was in the middle six figures, but might come down a long way if I made a fast offer.

I was necessarily, and egotistically, interested. But I still didn't understand how it would be so easy to borrow twice the purchase price. The legal lending limit at Rosenheimer's banks didn't approach the kind of money he was talking about. I looked around and saw that he was watching me, smiling, as I thought. "You're a wild man," I said. Rosenheimer turned me on. Even in the face of big trouble, the FDIC's current investigation, he was enthusiastically working on big new projects—far-out and risky, to say the least. I couldn't trust him, but I was learning to understand and anticipate his deviousness.

"Don't worry, we'll get some quick money to tide you over the current crisis." Rosenheimer kept smiling.

The corporate secretary returned with Metcalf and a folder thick with data. "Looks good," he said.

Metcalf's weathered face flushed with hope. Rosenheimer folded his lower lip over the upper and nodded briskly. He looked at his watch and said that Metcalf had to catch a plane. I promised to give them both answers within forty-eight hours. As soon as they left, I realized I must see the 404 before agreeing to buy it; The Digest ran after Rosenheimer to make an inspection appointment. "As soon as possible."

Kritchner, who was spending most of his afternoons at the Diamond J offices, showed up the same day. When I described the airliner he sat down and shook his head.

"What's your hangup?" I'd expected him to be excited, but that took time and lots of talk. Finally he stood up and walked thoughtfully to the window. Dead leaves were blowing by outside. "Can the plane be ready by ski season?"

"I don't see why not." That was over two months off. "What are you driving at?"

"If the airliner's half as good as you say it is, and safe, I can fill it with skiers every weekend." Kritchner started making notes on his pocket pad.

"Hey, I hadn't thought of that." Then I realized that I didn't know the exact price either.

We figured that an airliner that was supposed to be the little brother of the Playboy jet had to cost half a million.

"If Rosenheimer gets us the money and you can make the 404 pay for itself . . ." I spread my hands, palms up, and let the thought dangle.

We inspected the airliner the next day. The Martin 404 straddled the runway. For me, whose ultimate plane had previously meant a fast single-engine four-seater, the Bird seemed almost too big for the skies. The self-contained loading ramp was down. A skinny kid wearing pressed jeans and a red cowboy hat with a Steamboat hatband stood at the base.

"Welcome aboard, sir." He almost saluted.

Rosenheimer and the owner were waiting in the cabin, already holding drinks. The tour began forward. The cockpit instrumentation wildly surpassed that of any aircraft I'd flown; and Kritchner, of course, was sure that half the gauges, switches, knobs, and blinking lights were fake, totally useless.

"But, Jesus, are they impressive."

"There's even radar!"

The galley had more lights, blinking to tell what was cooking where.

"The onboard luggage compartment has been modified," the owner told Kritchner. "Enough room to hold skiis for a mountain battalion."

"How about the toilets? They're old-fashioned." I pointed fore and aft, and told the owner that "twenty-year-old chemical toilets do not a luxury liner make."

Just as I began to think I'd made a point to use again during price dickering, the skinny kid, the owner's son, handed me a Cuba Libre. He had obviously been well briefed. I nodded and moved into the passenger section—now here was *something*. This area, in which originally everyone had sat facing forward, was now a super big boy's playpen—deep plush swivel chairs that reclined, sofas, booths with air maps laminated to the tabletops, duplicate instruments for passengers to study speed and altitude, a main bar with a wine rack and minibars scattered throughout the long room, and a host of audiovisual electronic gadgets.

"The couches at the rear make into queen-size beds," said the owner, twitching his eyebrows.

I took a second look at everything and doubted that the most fashionable whorehouse anywhere could boast accommodations to match it. I laughed aloud and leaned forward to tell Kritchner I had a name for the Bird—"The Flying Fuck."

Now I really believed I needed the 404. Eight mammoth projects requiring constant supervision were underway a thousand miles apart, I told myself. The club members were screaming to visit them. So when Rosenheimer announced that the purchase price was only $130,000, because the owner (he slapped his shoulder) had agreed to bail out below cost, it was easy to see that I'd soon be flying around my empire not much below and behind Hugh Hefner.

The airplane loan, plus $85,000 extra, was participated through Rosenheimer's bank to the Harris Trust in Chicago. Stock purchase notes from my associates were used as collateral instead of the 404 itself.

"The Bird is free and clear," Rosenheimer said proudly. He declared that he'd solved my money problems and given me an appropriate status symbol at the same time.

It had cost me the secret assignment of almost 20 percent of my stockholdings in the club, Dash, and Shadco, but actually I didn't mind. As Rosenheimer said, he was becoming a very important part of Diamond J. He leaned back onto the 404's cabin lounge and lifted his feet to the cushions.

"Late enough to have Higbie bring us a drink," he suggested, motioning me to relax also. "I want to tell you about Titan, my new enterprise, a loan brokering company operating part time under my secret guidance."

"Why tell me?" I asked, remembering Rosenheimer's habit of sharing information only as it benefited him.

"Because we can make a killing sharing our contacts. My friends have money and your friends need it."

Titan Enterprises sounded like nothing more than a loose conglomeration of talents like Topp and Henry. It didn't make sense. As far as I knew, their resources were drained beyond the point where more money could be effectively raised. "You got any new friends, new sources, in mind?"

"Certainly," he answered. "Pension funds." He didn't say any more, just lowered his eyelids and stared at me through the slits as if he expected me to understand.

My formula for controlling my responses had become more

refined, rendered with constant analysis and forced application until it was a smooth habit, a mental reflex. "No problem."

My reputation crossed state lines. A Kentucky oil operator, first introduced to me by Rash in the late fifties, called and suggested that we reactivate our "friendship." He sold me some oil wells and joined Lake, Sport, and Travel so that I could "squeeze him in" on our airborne elk hunt to Colorado. He bought two memberships, one for his "angel."

"Richest man you've ever met," he said.

Now that we had a "luxury liner," Lake, Sport, and Travel had begun to impress everyone. It was a "Nationwide Airborne Sports Club," according to Quarton's latest printed promotions. The annual elk hunt was filled the day it was announced.

I preceded the main hunting group to check accommodations and do my best to make sure that the oil man's "angel" would "get his elk."

The angel was Art Anders.

"A self-made multimillionaire," the oil man said, "who's built the third largest trucking company on the East Coast from scratch."

Anders was an avid outdoorsman who already owned land in Montana. He was a perfect prospect to head the new investors I needed to buy a 3,990-acre ranch with the North Platte River running through it.

"The river," I told him, "if measured around the curves, stretches nine miles through the property." It was a perfect opportunity to implement my subdivision plan and prove to the bankers that I could create instant cash flows, and it had the bonus leverage of probable oil reserves. The price was $390,000, with the usual 29 percent down.

I'd already arranged to borrow part of that from a new bank purchased by Lindsey; I had investment commitments from my regulars and some of Butters's friends; all I needed was one more substantial stockholder to close the deal. So I was going to make damn sure Anders got a shot at an elk. "And I'm your licensed guide," I said, hoping to impress him before I flew on ahead to make sure everything was ready.

The hunt's schedule was upset when the Martin 404 developed engine trouble. Quarton called me in Laramie to say, "It's minor, but Captain Feisty says our ETA is moved back four hours."

Quarton had nicknamed my pilot-in-command "Captain Feisty," and as I imagined him fussing over the repairs, I could see why. The pilot, Gene Harris, could not be described without a long string of clichés, and he mirrored every one of them. His graying, close-cropped hair stopped at ears flat to a large head, with square jaw and jutting chin. He was barrel-chested, heavy-armed, tall; one of those long-waisted, short-legged people who swagger when they walk.

Harris was a World War II pilot who had worked for the FAA and had run a cargo line out of Puerto Rico. He had flown over 12,000 hours in planes like the 404. He spoke with authority, and he was a "damn good pilot"—he never let anyone forget that. When he boarded the 404, Harris was In Command—total control. It was a "serious business flying the boss's ship." He may have been a pompous blowhard, drinking too much and bragging interminably on the ground (that's how he got the name), but in the air I trusted him completely.

"Harris has one flowing fault," Quarton observed. "He sweats constantly."

I laughed and nodded to myself. No reason. He sweat equally hard in serene and nervous times. But people got anxious when they saw liquid pouring out of him, so I hoped he stayed in the cockpit while the 404's engine problem was solved.

My ship finally arrived and I met the new angel. Anders wasn't what I had expected. I remembered Koziel, the first millionaire Rosenheimer had introduced me to, and wondered if all rich men were beginning to look like truck drivers. Anders, of course, was the real thing, and he gave the impression that he could still "wheel the big jobs." He also reminded me of Captain Feisty—a smaller, slimmer version—except that when he shook hands, his were very dry.

During the drive to Lone Tree I discovered that Anders loved to needle people. "You still guarantee me an elk. Good. No fish—no pay." He waited before smiling.

Anders called himself a trucker, or a truck driver, and did a superb job of concealing his wealth. I decided not to fence with him. When he mentioned the "beautiful country," I said flatly, "I'm going to sell you a piece of it," and dropped the subject.

Anders did not kill an elk. He got one shot at one from the side of the Jeep while the animal was running a quarter mile away. It might have been closer, but Kritchner (who rode along that day) and I mistook the elk for a large deer until its rump was turned to us. The next day I followed tracks in deep snow until they led to the oil man, who was also on a scouting expedition. And the day after that I skidded the Jeep off a cliff—If we hadn't hit an isolated tree twenty feet down, this story would be over.

The more Anders laughed, the better I liked him. He laughed at frustration and danger, and at my sorry joke about being Colorado's "most fucked-up guide." But he nonetheless agreed to buy a piece of the new Diamond J Ranch.

"He's perfect. Just what we need in Diamond J," I told Quarton as I took a second long look at Art Anders boarding the 404 to fly home to Pennsylvania. His skin was weathered like Metcalf's. His eyes were hard, but not cruel like O'Connor's. Anders had the best of many scattered qualities. He was strong and tough, with a sense of humor, and I bet he was tender with his children. Even though he ran a huge business, he seemed to know when it was time to relax. I wanted him for a partner and for a friend. He could help me in a very special way—by adding calm control to Diamond J.

I went straight back to Lone Tree and climbed the high hill to the solitary pine it was named after. I was tired and felt reflective. "I'm thirty-nine years old," I said, walking down toward the cabin where I had been conceived and wondering if my parents had ever dreamed of the demands their son would make from life. "Perspectives change." My head fell forward; I felt exhausted, mentally and physically.

One cure for drowsiness, I knew, was to test your vision to the furthest arc, strain to the peripheries. I stood up straight and turned in a full circle. I forced myself around, thinking that in my business I couldn't afford to be weary. Then I remembered that yesterday Anders had agreed to buy into the new ranch before Christmas. "Next year I'll probably own all of you," I shouted across the valleys, and listened to the echo as I ran down the hill.

Sue was waiting in the lodge, just finished cleaning up after the hunters. Wisps of quick-chilled body heat seemed to rise around her as I threw the door open and rushed in with a sudden high wind at my back. I squeezed her in my arms, in my strongest hug, while the snow blew in around our feet and beyond, making long white ridges across the pine planking. Neither of us bothered to close the door. We were holding hands now, still standing tightly together. And I hoped, as Sue looked up at me, that she could see how grateful I was.

"You make it all worthwhile," I said, as her eyes closed and a peaceful smile began.

Rosenheimer and O'Connor kept in constant touch. The former always had some new "big deal" to talk about; the latter rode my ass to be sure there was no delinquency at his bank that could be traced to credit originating with Janeff or Diamond J. "Buy back every account over sixty days behind payment schedule," O'Connor insisted.

Suddenly there were a lot of them. Many of the original club members were unhappy with our changing image ("Too affluent," said Padgett), and the Buyer's Club contracts we underwrote turned sour when stories about Consumer Sales Law violations began to hit the newspapers.

Janeff and Lake, Sport, and Travel ran out of money again, so O'Connor arranged personal unsecured loans to me and insisted I pay off the delinquency.

"Remember, I'll always take care of Johnny if Johnny helps keep a clean house," he said.

When O'Connor implied that Rosenheimer bothered him I began working to keep them apart. The million-dollar line of credit O'Connor promised was essential. "But so is Rosenheimer's regular assistance, which enables me, on any day, to walk into a given situation and come out with a handful of cash," I reminded myself. Enough, as it happened, to buy Padgett out of the club.

"Best thing you've done so far," said Kritchner.

Everyone else agreed. "A happy move."

Padgett even smiled when he said good-bye. "Lake, Sport,

and Travel's a fantastic operation. Just not my style."

I believed he meant it when he assured me he wanted to continue doing business whenever our interests meshed.

Kritchner wasn't so sure. "Watch him. And keep everything at arm's length. Anybody will be your buddy when you hand him a big enough check."

There wasn't time to argue. Early snow was falling, and I had less than an hour to drive seventy-five miles.

O'Connor, bright red from another trip to Florida, met me in Milwaukee, saying that it would soon be time to start the leasing company. "I've found a genius on the East Coast who wants to participate. But let's take an inventory first, people and things." Again O'Connor was implying that he had no use for Rosenheimer, and that bothered me. He didn't know yet that Jim Rosenheimer planned to be president of Janeff. I made a mental note that Rauterberg must find a way to soothe the rawness between them.

"Quit daydreaming," O'Connor hissed, jerking his head at me. "Got a current financial statement with you?"

I shook my head at him.

"Thought so. You've been moving so fast there's no way you can guess your net worth. Make a new one today." He smiled, advising me to show real estate values at their highest market price.

I went him one better. I listed everything at its maximum inflated value; it was credible because these were the top prices I hoped to get for my companies and properties if I sold them under ideal and optimum market conditions next year. When I finished, the bottom line showed that my net worth was $1,170,850.

"I'm a millionaire!" I called Sue and shouted the news.

The next morning I telephoned Judy and told her. Higbie overheard.

"Are you sure? And if you are, that's the best way I know to land back in court at a hearing to increase your support payments." He sounded worried.

"No way." I smiled and went on spreading the word. I was a millionaire. And any minute I would be able to prove it, with the impressively bound financial statement my personal CPA was adding his special touches to, making it official. I deserved to be proud—ecstatic—and I wanted Judy to know.

But less than an hour later, resting my voice with a cup of coffee, an undefined doubt began to nag. Higbie was still hanging around, puttering with a stack of snowmobile race photos scattered across the sofa at the far end of my office.

"What are you so Goddamn worried about?" I shouted. Then, before he could answer, I pinned down the doubt. Was my display of wealth exactly the same as Ingels's paper fortune? Were my million-dollar financial statements subtle evidence that I was losing sight of the practical limits of my energy and ability? Was I strong enough to turn the figures into true value?

"Goddamn right you are," I said to myself, slapping the desk top hard enough to spill the coffee and startling Higbie, who rushed toward me. I stood and held out my hands. "See. They're clean and dry. My head's clear and . . ."

Higbie cocked his head and blinked. "What do you mean?"

"I mean quit looking for problems. We've arrived on the first plateau of my latest Master Plan. Now everything's ready for the second stage." I walked around the desk and put my arm across his shoulders. "Now get to work on our race—make it the biggest fucking race in the world."

Higbie nodded, and when he began to grin I could see he now had enough new faith to accomplish whatever goals I set for him.

Rosenheimer and Rauterberg—I was calling them "R. and R." by now—usually popped into my office unannounced. Today they momentarily alarmed me by calling for an appointment. But with Higbie's happy reaction still on my mind, I was prepared for anything.

"So hurry up," I said. "It's getting late and I'm taking Sue out to celebrate tonight."

Rosenheimer opened the conversation with questions about his pending presidency of Janeff. "I've gotta figure out how to fit the loan company and Titan Enterprises together."

"Together?"

"They both lend money." He looked toward Rauterberg, who nodded. "Just a thought." He changed the subject to the Metcalf

Farms–Hawaii loan. "I've lent them over the limits at my banks, you know."

R. and R. kept glancing at each other. Now Rauterberg moved the topic to my money needs.

"You running out of funds again?"

I shrugged, thinking that the usual animation was missing from their conversation; Rosenheimer wasn't even chuckling. They were trying to prepare me for an important announcement. The mysterious pension funds? I wondered. I told them not to waste time.

"OK." Rosenheimer stood up and locked eyes with me. "Bob and I have been talking. You've got a good thing going, but we're worried. You're stretched awfully thin and you've used up the borrowing power of your present stockholders."

Rauterberg interrupted. "You can't absolutely count on a million from O'Connor without fresh blood in the companies."

"What about Anders?" I said. They knew he was about to join Diamond J—first the ranch, then probably everything else.

"He helps, but we've got someone better," Rosenheimer said.

"Who?"

"A really big man. With more connections and clout than you're accustomed to—a really big man." He saw that I was about to ask who again and continued quickly. "We'll tell you more later, after you've decided how much of Diamond J—every part of it—you're willing to contribute to a merger."

I stood and faced Rosenheimer. "Merger?" The word had an anxious rattle.

"Merging your interests is the best way to protect your position." Rauterberg leaned forward. "Better a small piece of a giant pie than a little uncooked cake that might not rise."

Now Rosenheimer chuckled. "Look at Walt Koziel and his merger into Beatrice Foods." He chuckled again. "Made millions."

I lit a cigarette and looked at them through the heavy smoke exhaled from my first deep drag. R. and R. were trying to double-team me.

They started to edge toward me, seeking a response.

"Let me think about it." I nodded, pretending interest in their idea; actually, I was hoping to buy enough time to create a counterstrategy. R. and R., two-thirds of my banking power, had to be kept in a compatible mood. If they had some special plan, I knew I'd have to use part of it. That was inevitable.

My last thought had been transmitted somehow, I figured, because they left with happy wrinkles at the corners of their eyes.

When Radisson Hotels Corporation submitted their contract to manage Thunderhead I turned it down.

"They're obviously trying to grab all the guaranteed profits of the Inn," I said to the stockholders. They endorsed my proposal that all surplus cash should be directed to payment of our burgeoning interest payments.

"I don't really think we need them under any circumstances," Hollis said. "Aren't we almost as big as Radisson by now?"

I told the Radisson executives that the only way Thunderhead's stockholders would sign was with a clause promising the replacement of all existing debt at low interest—"inexpensive long-term financing."

"Your power play is foolish," Ingels observed. "It may scuttle Radisson's plans for the Golden Triangle."

"Nonsense," I told him. "The competition—Ramada, Sheraton, even Hilton—will force Carlson and his Radisson Hotel Chain to play out the hand Bright Star dealt him. He's going to help us develop the Golden Triangle."

That didn't satisfy Ingels. "When? The richest land in Steamboat has lain idle too long."

"It takes money," I told him, pleased that for once I could pass the pressure of funding a development, and knowing that Ingels had to produce because he'd been bragging that Bright Star was his baby for too long. His image was at stake. And for the first time, I saw a bitter flicker in his eyes.

Rauterberg, who'd been quietly observing from a comfortable chair in the corner, salvaged Ingels's good spirits. "No problem financing the Golden Triangle. Bright Star's not recognized yet as part of Diamond J."

His remark reminded me that the Banking Commission's objection to my loans and even to my participation in Lindsey's bank had never been explained. It was my turn to play put-upon. "How did I get on the shit list?"

Rauterberg chewed the inside of his cheek before answering slowly, "The examiners follow your loans from bank to bank and know you understand the system for extending repayment indefinitely. Now only O'Connor's bank, with its nearly perfect portfolio, is immune to their criticism. O'Connor says he shakes his blank delinquency reports in their faces and laughs."

"How do I handle the other banks?" I asked, upset. "This can be a serious problem."

"National banks. They're supervised by different agencies," Rauterberg said, explaining that I could still borrow through state-chartered banks so long as they participated the new loan balances to nationals. "Or move your loans anywhere out of state —as Rosenheimer did with your loan to buy the Bird."

In a continued discussion the following week, Rosenheimer said that I shouldn't overlook leasing as a source of ready cash. "Anything you now own can be converted to bank balances simply by selling it on a lease-back contract. There's no loss of control."

I knew that from my discussions with O'Connor. Now I wondered if Rosenheimer was talking about the same thing, our own leasing company. He wasn't.

"My idea is to arrange lease-backs with established sources— about the same as an installment purchase since equity growth is still so important. At the end of the lease your property can be repurchased at a predetermined 'token' price." Rosenheimer strode back and forth, hands folded across his belly, punctuating his remarks with a halt and a profound cough. "The system also gives both the lessor and the lessee a tax advantage. The lessor, as owner, can depreciate the property, and Diamond J, the lessee, can deduct the payments as a business expense."

"Are you sure?" asked Kritchner. He'd come into my office to talk with R. and R. about moving the loan collateralized by his wife's inheritance to a new bank at lower interest rates.

"No problem, so long as the repurchase contract is kept separate and secret. That way the IRS watchdogs can't criticize the small 'token' buy-back until after the fact, if indeed they ever discover it."

Sounded good. And if it was workable, the Martin 404 was worth $150,000 any time I needed it—like now. The annual payment on Walton Creek Park was coming due, and unless I missed my guess, Thunderhead's and Shadco's bank accounts were overdrawn.

When Rosenheimer said, "No problem—no problem," he was right. Two weeks later I picked up a six-figure check at the Northridge Leasing Company, a subsidiary of the bank of the same name. While processing the lease, I changed the airplane's Federal Aviation designation to 404 LS and ordered Captain Harris to have the Diamond J logo painted on the fuselage along with the new number. Rosenheimer, as expected, came to "inspect the Bird's new feathers" and to tell me it was now time for him to assume the presidency of Janeff.

"Next year," I reminded. "As soon as I finish paying Sommers." And as soon as Rauterberg gets O'Connor in line, I thought.

Simultaneously, Ingels and I got the final word that the Colorado Referendum had rejected the '76 Winter Olympics. Ingels's year-round suntan faded completely until I pointed out that we had already known there was little chance to save them, and convinced him that the loss of the games could work to our advantage. "LTV, which has certainly counted on the Olympics more than we have and has spent a helluva lot of money already, will have to try harder now. We'll benefit from their increased advertising and promotion."

"How will the loss affect your plans to make snowmobiling an Olympic sport?"

"That was only a gimmick to get people's attention." I showed him the already published magazine stories and newspaper articles calling my race "The first of the super races." "Higbie's doing a good job spreading the word." Other headers said, "Gold in Milwaukee," "World's richest race," "Stone crazy or a genius?" I didn't show him the reports that the International Pro/Am Championships were an "impossible dream" because weather forecast-

ers saw no snow on the ground at State Fair Park in February.
The snow would come later, and afterwards I could prove that
certain speed sport reporters were full of shit.

Higbie was already lining up enough snowmaking equipment
to cover the mile-long, 140-foot-wide racetrack two feet deep with
snow.

"And if necessary," I laughed privately to my Brain Trust,
"Anders's trucks can haul more from Canada."

Ingels had heard enough. He left my office smiling, with a
pocket full of VIP passes to "the first of the Super Races."

I told my executive secretary to fix me an early Cuba; it was
becoming my habit to drink rum and Coke instead of coffee in
the late afternoon. I sipped the drink and studied Butters's
progress reports on the North Platte River acreage now referred
to, even on legal documents, as Diamond J Ranch. Stockholder
subscriptions—actually partnership percentages, since we'd decided on a limited partnership for tax purposes—were filled. The
general partners (Kritchner, Lindsey, and myself), with 20 percent each, controlled the venture. The others were my regulars,
plus The Digest; Butters and his friends, including a Las Vegas
county commissioner ("very useful fellow to be in bed with," Butters said); the Kentucky oil man, and Art Anders. The closing was
set for New Year's Eve or Day, whichever worked out better taxwise. We were receiving the recorded oil rights and a verbal
option ("Good as paper among mountain men") on a similar ranch
in the nearby foothills.

I pushed the papers back into their folder, there being nothing
I could add to them, and yelled for another drink.

"Goddamnit," I told my newest secretary, wishing Shari were
working in Madison instead of Denver, "we need an intercom."
I looked out to the desk-crowded Bullpen. "As a matter of fact,
we need a whole new office complex. Forget the drink. I'm going
on a scouting expedition." And, squeezing her arm on the way by,
I trotted out of our obsolete environment.

By 6:00 P.M. I'd found what I wanted, and by 9:00 A.M. the
following day I was closing a deal to move in.

The new complex was owned by the president of an advertising agency occupying space in the same building.

"I'm looking for exciting new tenants," he said, explaining that half the first floor was vacant and promising to redecorate to my specifications when he saw that I was ready to sign a lease.

"This is perfect," I said, wandering through the vacant space. There were four executive offices, two clerical sections, a large reception room, an employees' lounge, and conference room. I stopped in a huge private office. "I'll settle in here. Now all you have to do is sweeten the pot."

"Anything you want." His eyes twinkled as he lit my cigarette. "Built-in stereo, intercom, centralized IBM dictating equipment with jacks in each office, as many sign-designated parking spaces as you need, and every one of your eleven businesses and companies listed on the building directory."

He had almost started to rub his palms together when I interrupted. "I'll need more room later—offices for Toussaint, my CPA, and Butters, my attorney. So be sure I get first option on any future vacancies."

"For sure. Now, I'll send my decorator over with paneling and carpet samples next week."

"No good. I need everything finished in three weeks."

He choked, but nodded gamely.

"My people will need three or four days to move in and settle after that," I continued. "I'm giving a party, combination Christmas and the reintroduction of my companies to the public in the right environment."

Engraved invitations were mailed twelve days in advance. Ten days later the decorating was nearly done. And the afternoon of party day, my staff and most of the local stockholders finished the moving and arranging. I stayed in my own suite, personally hanging the plaques and photo blowups of my activities and accomplishments. There was almost too much wall space. Besides my mammoth private room with the carpeting running up the walls to the wainscoting, there was another smaller area for a private bar and my yet unnamed executive assistant, and another private reception room with ample desk space for my personal secretary. My offices were custom everything, especially my nine-foot-wide, half-circle desk with its inlaid parquet top.

"Damned impressive," I told myself, and decided to inspect the rest of the complex. Everything was nearly new, and perfect. "Good taste," I said as I passed through. "Your hearts are into it this time." I noticed that Quarton's office was the only one without photos showing him doing something. Instead, he had an antique rice paper drawing, a bronze sculpture, a western print laminated to barn board, and two Indian sand paintings that I had given him. "Got to have something of me in every room," I joked as I helped Quarton hang them.

I retraced my steps for a second look. Higbie's office was silver-toned, with dozens of snowmobile trophies lined up on specially built shelves. Some were mine, others had been won by Judy and Shari, and the rest were last year's unclaimed trophies and samples of next year's bigger models. My Storm Trooper's room was all fish, totally masculine, spartan fish. I knew it wasn't that he didn't like girls. He just never seemed to show any signs of sexual arousement. But muskies—gleaming, toothy muskies—that was something else. The room was full of them, and my Storm Trooper was sitting behind his desk looking at them with a rapt, almost sensual expression.

When he noticed that I was leaving he followed me to the conference room, which had originally been intended for all tenants in the building. Only its proximity made it seem like our exclusive domain, so the landlord had not consulted Diamond J on its decoration. The wallpaper was blue fuzz embossed on silver with fleurs-de-lis. The carpet was tripping-length violet shag. The supermodern, white, elongated oval conference table wasn't too bad, but the purple-and-white arm chairs mixed among fuzzy white mushroom stools created the immediate impression that we were in the display room of a cosmetic firm or the headquarters of the Gay Revolution.

"Fix it," I told my Storm Trooper. I knew he'd be the perfect person to give our conference room the macho image it needed.

Everybody on my staff, and every shareholder except Turnbull, came to the party. I noticed how my cast of characters had changed and enlarged as Diamond J's plotted Master Plans expanded. Turnbull, Kritchner, and I were still the Triumvirate, even though it seemed that Turnbull had become even more introspective out West. Uncle Willie and Rodney Vitner were on the fringe now, aware, I'm sure, that they were included only when money was needed. "That bothers me," I told Sue, "especially since Rodney's going through a divorce he doesn't want and has already used up most of the cash in his trust funds helping Diamond J. I don't think he's got enough left for a property settlement."

Sue smiled. "You'll help him."

And as soon as Vitner arrived, I did, pulling him aside to say, "Don't worry. Diamond J takes care of its own."

He shrugged out of his sleet-spattered overcoat. "You've just made a long, scary drive worthwhile." He tossed the coat over a chair, gripped my shoulders with both hands, and looked at me with bulging, brimming eyes. "Thanks, brother."

"He means it," said Sue, giving me the same moist look.

"Let's have fun." I turned into the crowded conference room and saw Hollis and most of the other investors, and, for sure, every employee, with pride glowing from their happy faces, each trying to show the others around the "fabulous new offices."

Perfect, I told myself. They feel a part of it. The times for doubt were over. The Brain Trust concept and every other concept were working. I bumped into Rauterberg, who said O'Connor was the only banker missing.

"No problem," he winked, and quickly told me that O'Connor had sent word from Florida again that my million-dollar line of credit was all set. "He's definitely impressed with the sizable share of business you've secured in Steamboat, and with the constant progress of Lake, Sport, and Travel. And he says it's OK for Jim Rosenheimer to assume the presidency of Janeff."

"Great." Now even Janeff was ready to break the restraints of tight money, rotten reputation, and low income. He had also observed (Rauterberg tried to repeat O'Connor's remarks verbatim) that because of the obvious success of our initial programs and the excellent publicity we were receiving, and just plain word-of-mouth enthusiasm, we could expect expressions of enthusiasm from a multitude of new investors.

"So sufficient cash flow to repay loans is assured, if not from profit, then from the sale and resale of our stock," I insisted, without smiling at first. Then, as I gave Rauterberg a smile I didn't quite feel, he pretended everything was still great.

Rauterberg moved on to greet other guests, and my mind locked back onto O'Connor's analysis of Diamond J. As relayed by Rauterberg, it raised some very disturbing questions. Sure, my credit was good. The bankers were excited and impressed. And, because I could assure them that new investors would bring me enough money to repay old loans, the bankers would let me borrow more and more. But I was also remembering R. and R.'s advice to be ready to merge with a "really big man," O'Connor's talk of importing a leasing genius from D.C., the constant shifting of the $3.8 million I owed to fourteen different banks, and the millions I'd guaranteed on top of that. And Kritchner's warning about the "point of no return." I shuddered. If there was a conspiracy among my bankers, I was dead; worse, they'd eat me alive, pulling off hunks of my stock until Diamond J was only a skeleton.

I drained my drink and lit a cigarette. There were defenses. I could slow down, admit how thin I had stretched myself, and seek Jack Rash's help to consolidate my position and realistically refinance along conservative lines. Or I could match power and wits with them. I had Anders and a horde of other investors and Brain Trusters behind me, and my ideas were, I believed, superb. My dream was nearly reality now. Certainly I was living on expansion.

"That's the name of my game." I chuckled to myself, ignoring the crowd. And my bankers' game also. They were money manipulators and barracudas, but I was their best chance to legitimately earn their fortunes fast. Right now they needed me. They could not replace me. And I didn't see any way they were smart enough to cope with the counterstrategies I'd devised to handle them in the future.

Sue jerked my earlobe and handed me a fresh Cuba Libre. "This is a party. Don't be so serious."

We circulated. I didn't have to pretend to enjoy myself now. I'd made up my mind, and every happy, enthusiastic man or woman I talked to helped firm the faith that I was right. No one was going to knock John Stone off his mountain.

Quarton appeared by my side, his eyes pulsing with the urge to do mischief. He knew I hated nicknames, but laughed anyway, and called me "God, little g."

"Not too bad," I said, laughing back. It was a strong, loud laugh sounding as if I was full of pride, anticipation, and just the tiniest touch of tension. All in all, I thought as I closed my mouth into a grin, the right laugh for the times.

9
January 1973

My breath frosted the inside of the window looking out on the frozen parking lot and distorted the figures hurrying from a long, dark automobile toward the warmth of my office.

"Damn." I sat down hard, making the air hiss from the heavy padding of my desk chair. I was nervous. I didn't know what to expect. I'd wanted a secret look at "The Big Man" before we met face to face, but now I had to settle for the sound of his voice echoing greetings from beyond the receptionist's desk. At the same time I could hear footsteps pumping along the deep carpeting and the high points of secretaries' whispered questions.

Who was this enterprising monarch of a business empire that seemed to dwarf Diamond J?

R. and R. had briefed me in advance. "The Big Man," Leo W. Roethe, was loaded with titles, accolades, and awards. He was president or chairman of the board of eight companies, enterprises that spanned the globe. He was chairman of Wisconsin's ORAP, the conservation committee that had spearheaded the state's impressive new antipollution and recreation program. He was founder and past president of the National Agricultural Hall of Fame and a founder of the International Conservation Hall of

172

Fame, had been named Wisconsin's Conservationist of the Year, and even held the coveted Silver Beaver Award from the Boy Scouts of America.

"No joke," Rosenheimer told me. "The Silver Beaver costs lots of time, effort, dedication, and money."

Weatherby–Nasco, Roethe's power base, was the world's leading manufacturer of big-game rifles and had also diversified into the mail order fields of farming, scientific, and educational supplies and equipment. The corporation was headquartered in Fort Atkinson, Wisconsin, and had branches in Modesto, California, and Guelph, Ontario. The company was, according to Rosenheimer, "merger-minded." Its latest acquisition was Amron, Inc., a munitions manufacturer, formerly owned by Gulf & Western. Roethe had traded the giant conglomerate a 26 percent interest in Weatherby–Nasco for control of Amron. R. and R. said it had been a "shrewd maneuver."

Roethe watched Apollo launches at Cape Kennedy by special invitation, corresponded in longhand with the likes of Haile Selassie, Spiro Agnew, John Connally, and Jomo Kenyatta, and headed a United States Trade Commission to East Africa.

Now, as Rosenheimer ushered him into my office, Roethe's presence seemed to force everything else from the room. His supercharisma exploded through the walls and rattled the entire complex.

"Great to see you," Roethe said, taking my extended hand in both of his and pumping it twice. Though his palms were cool and dry, I felt sudden heat rush the length of my arm, dampening my shirt. I stepped back to compose myself and saw that Roethe's smile wasn't really quite a full one. Still, the sparkling intensity of his gray eyes encouraged me to think that it would widen any minute.

I motioned for him to take the closest chair and sat down myself as Rosenheimer explained, "This meeting is probably the most important event of our lives."

"It well may be." Roethe's voice matched his stature, and it was magnified by his enthusiasm.

Ruddy, clearly an outdoorsman; thick hair many shades of steel gray; strong hands; straight back—Roethe was a tower even when seated. His ears, nose, and jaw were suitably oversized to match his frame. Though his clothes were years behind the style, his jacket pocket, I noticed, bore a superbly embroidered crest of the Shikar–Safari Club, the world's most prestigious hunting association.

"The boys tell me you're the most exciting young financier in Wisconsin, and I can see they weren't exaggerating." Roethe gestured to the pictures on the wall behind me. His cuff links were heavy gold elephant heads, ears flared at the moment of charge. His watchband, also obviously solid gold, was sculptured to depict other animals of the African Big Five. "Maybe my projects will seem dull, but I hope not." He patted the briefcase beside his chair. It was good leather, worn and bulging.

'I'm *sure* not," I told him, and I meant it. The fact that his shoes needed polish or that his tie was too narrow was easily lost in the subtle flow of gold.

When my secretary brought coffee, Roethe acknowledged the interruption with an appreciative nod.

"Now tell me about the Diamond J enterprises."

My secretary lingered in the doorway, eager, I was sure, to see the meeting of Titans. I suggested that Quarton and the other Brain Trusters join us.

"Together," I told Roethe, "we are expanding my plans to make a golden age of the decade of recreation."

Twenty minutes later I reminded myself that it was dangerous to oversell. "That's the gist of it," I finished, looking as far as I could into Roethe's eyes.

He answered without hesitation: "Greatest thing I've ever heard. A real winner. I want to join you."

That fast!

So Leo Roethe came to me, John Stone, and bought my dream. "Its greatness must be obvious," I thought, "because he's endorsing *my* Master Plan before explaining his. Hot damn."

"The next visit I'll show you my winners. Now I have to rush to another important meeting." He stood up, reached inside his jacket, and pulled out a checkbook.

"I knew this would be a perfect marriage of interests," said

Rosenheimer, his face flushed, eyes twinkling, lips twitching. A wedding kiss.

Roethe leaned over my desk and wrote a check. I watched to see how much it was for. He noticed me trying to read upside down.

"Not a big one, but enough to get me started, enough to qualify for the Lake, Sport, and Travel board of directors." Roethe finished writing and handed me the check. He was smiling his widest smile. "We'll talk about a much bigger investment very soon. Right?"

I nodded, trying to think of the right words, but he was out the door before I could reply.

Rosenheimer popped back into the room. "Send Leo written resumés of everything you've got. Like now."

For several minutes my office was quiet. Then everyone crowded around my desk in a crescendo of enthusiasm. I fingered Roethe's four-figure check, then held it high over my head. "Symbol of success," I shouted.

"Are we merging?" someone asked.

"Not companies, interests. And now we've got to show him that this overpaid, overstaffed operation means something," I said, trying to sound austere but unable to suppress a grin.

"Are we moving the offices again?" It was the same voice, dubious this time.

"Oh, for Christ's sake." I shook my head and told them to get out and get to work. I motioned for Higbie and Quarton to stay behind. "Looks like we're on our way. This is what I've been waiting for. Now, Goddamnit, don't screw it up. I'll need up-to-date reports, especially a list of all Lake, Sport, and Travel facilities—with details. And membership kits. Throw in everything we've got. Get me copies of all appraisals."

They rushed out. I buzzed my secretary.

"Start calling the stockholders. I want to talk to each one today." In the background I heard the Xerox machine beginning to click out promotional papers.

Turnbull was first on the line.

"We're about to be international," I began.

Telephone calls to Kritchner and the others followed. I carefully explained to each how R. and R. had delivered the greatest golden goose of all: "the most prominent businessman and biggest recreation buff in the state."

The Master Plan needed revising. First, Lake, Sport's facilities had to be expanded, then all Diamond J's holdings suitably enlarged so they'd be big enough to hold Roethe's interest, encourage him to want seats on all our directing boards.

"Afterward, we'll use his connections and assets to shore up our finances," I told my milling Brain Trust. "Now settle down so we can figure out the best way to redistribute the stock."

"What do you mean?" Higbie sounded anxious.

"We've got to dilute our holdings. . . ." My voice was hoarse.

"But what the hell. Remember when you said, 'Better a smaller piece of a bigger pie'?" The Digest said. He was really excited.

The excitement was thoroughly infectious; only Turnbull had lingering doubts. He called back, "Don't get so damn high on Roethe that you forget we're two months behind on the condominium construction loan at Columbia. They're making noises."

"This is a major breakthrough, Ed. Can you handle things for thirty days?" I knew he was living with the hour-to-hour pressures of a negative cash flow, even at the height of the season. His staff was rebellious because their raises had been postponed. They were blaming the high-living absentee owners for squandering cash reserves on self-gratifying glamour properties like the Diamond J Ranch and its potential oil interests.

Turnbull was working alone in Steamboat, trying to satisfy both sides. "Get me some help—first things first," he said. "I need $125,000, *now!*"

"Right." I got moving, maybe faster than usual. I called Rauterberg, who promised to telephone O'Connor in Florida and arrange an emergency loan, the first drawn on my million-dollar line of credit. Next I set up an evening meeting with Elliot Ingels to finalize borrowing plans for enough money to start developing the Alpine Village on the Golden Triangle and pay off Bright Star's debt to Lindsey, Kritchner, and myself. "We, in turn, will finish paying back Shadco for the original option," I explained to Turnbull in a return call.

Ingels beamed when I showed him my million-dollar financial statement. He handed me his statement to include with the Bright Star loan application. He was worth more money than I, but I couldn't help wondering if Ingels was also using inflated property appraisals.

I told Ingels about Leo Roethe.

He said, "I'm impressed. You've got to be the luckiest sonofabitch I know."

"So let's not waste time talking about it. Let's turn my good fortune into cash," I said, pushing him to finish the latest Bright Star development proposals. "Leo may like that too."

Roethe didn't waste time either. When he wasn't calling, "to apprise you of my new ideas to expand your horizons," he was dictating "informative memorandums." I averaged three bulging envelopes a day from him, and in less than a week I had a file drawer full of information on Roethe properties, companies, and pending investments. The list was astonishing, at least twice as long as I had expected.

In the continental United States, Roethe owned or claimed to control a lumber mill in Amasa, Michigan; sixty-nine acres of subdivision land in Fort Atkinson, Wisconsin (the site of Weatherby–Nasco's main plant); a creamery package building, also in Fort Atkinson and rented to a division of Quaker Oats; Big Mountain Country, a proposed year-round resort in the Wyoming mountains, which included among its assets a perpetual lease from the U.S. Forest Service on four million acres (most of the Shoshone National Forest); Wyoming Estates, which owned 640 acres of condominium land in the Tetons; and Sorini Foods, formerly a chain of pizza restaurants in Minnesota, now the parent company of Roethe's personal museum, The World Wide Animal Kingdom. Sorini Foods was planning an immediate merger with McNally Industries, "a maker of fine machine parts," and then a public issue of its stock. "Guaranteed to quadruple in value as soon as the merger is completed," Roethe said, referring me to the printed material, "which you should have in today's mail."

I couldn't find anything new about Sorini in the most recent envelope, but I did find plenty to reinforce some of my growing suspicions.

In Hawaii, Roethe owned a large block of stock in Metcalf Farms, which he had received from the merger of that company with his Wisconsin agricultural ventures, Greentree Forests, Inc., and Farm Corporation of America.

I'd been right when I'd guessed that Roethe and Rosenheimer had worked together longer than they admitted. The memorandum on Metcalf Farms was almost identical to the material Rosenheimer and Metcalf had presented to me five months earlier. The only new facts, and they were astounding revelations, were Roethe's position as an officer and director authorized to offer 40 percent of the Metcalf company for sale, and the price: half a million dollars. "Find out how Roethe got involved with Metcalf and check that price," I told Higbie, shoving the memo toward him.

"I'm too busy with the Pro/Am Race to check it out," he said, "but I'll put someone on it immediately."

My staff told me that Rosenheimer could deliver the same deal for a quarter-million. It looked like a hustle, but hustle or not, there was a definite communication gap between Rosenheimer and Roethe, who were, I was now sure, in cahoots. So what? If they were both going to solicit my participation, double-team me, that meant they needed me and my resources.

I told Angel Anders long-distance: "It's an even bet that Leo Roethe needs money, and that he's already borrowed all he can from my banker buddies."

Anders grunted his agreement.

Roethe delivered the next series of projects in person. "You're going to like these," he said, piling maps and color enlargements on my desk.

"Just a minute." I pushed the exhibits aside. "I want to know more about Metcalf Farms first."

"You mean Jim's earlier proposition." Roethe waved a hand in front of his chest. The elephant ears on his cuff links seemed to wave with him. "Just a misunderstanding. My fault. The memo you received from me was copied off the proposal we offer outsiders. Your original information is correct. You can have 40 percent for a quarter-million. Now look here . . ." He unfolded a map of Central America. "A complete sawmill and village built on the shores of the Caribbean. My company, Agricola Itzapan, has leases from the Honduran Government to harvest 500,000 acres of exotic hardwoods. And in the same area there's a beautiful white sand beach, a lovely resort for hunters and sunbathers and fishermen, and excellent jaguar, ocelot, deer, tapir, wild boar, and wild turkey shooting for Lake, Sport, and Travel Club members."

"Is it operative, the mill?" I had started to stammer, so I leaned back to light a cigarette while Roethe pawed through the rest of his material.

"As soon as I find a new partner," he said nonchalantly, lining up photographs of Africa. "Now, in Kenya . . ."

I felt flushed, like late in the day after too many early Cuba Libres.

Roethe continued: "I own 27,500 acres situated between the Tsavo and Amboselli Game Parks, where, on December 25, we finished two hotels of 125 beds each. One is called the Salt Lick Lodge and the other the Taita Hills Lodge, and they are now under a twenty-year lease and in full operation by Hilton International."

It was hard to believe—almost beyond my imagination. I couldn't even concentrate on the rest of the material, stories about a private island off the Washington coast stocked with exotic game animals. Munitions manufacturing, a 600-room hotel in Turkey, and something (I started to laugh) called Yoo-Hoo Chocolate Beverage. I couldn't sit still. It was hard to focus my eyes. Now I felt as if I were into the second stages of a rousing drunk. I knew that if I could effect an honest-to-goodness total business affiliation with Leo Roethe I'd be as big as I ever wanted to be— bigger. Maybe he didn't have as much ready cash as I'd hoped, but he had a big reputation, important contacts, and exciting business propositions to offer. That was all I needed. Hell, I'd sail right by Hugh Hefner!

Usually, when it came time, I slept. I was proud of my ability to sleep on command. That night I lay awake shuffling my Master Plan, refusing to let myself rest until I had found the right pattern to include everything Roethe had his hands on—and, at the same time, maintain my coveted control. But the size of Roethe's empire left me in its shadows, and I gathered from his conversation that he was not about to allow me to usurp its leadership without overwhelming cause and reason. Even in the partnership, he clearly suggested that I would be the junior. His primary weakness seemed to be a possible shortage of money, and my advantage, in that case, was entirely controlled by bankers who were probably already in league with Roethe.

I decided that my best counterstrategy was to use the bankers' loan pledges quickly and grow really big before they realized what I was up to. Then, when the assets under my control were more nearly the size of Roethe's, I stood a better chance to split the dream fifty-fifty with him.

I could match his energy. Hell, I was younger; my reservoir had to be greater. I lacked only his depth in braggable assets. The acquisition of the Diamond J Ranch seemed small tonight, when just a week ago I had boasted about closing the biggest deal yet. I remembered Butters nodding. "Limitless profit potential," he'd said. If my scheme to subdivide proved viable, sure —but now I had to acquire more property fast.

The first thing that came to mind was the Cowdrey Crossroads. The idea was to buy the Cowdrey Store, which at first glance was nothing but a sagging sixty-five-year-old building in a town in the middle of nowhere with the unbelievably tiny population of twenty-eight. Across the highway on one side was a creaking frame building probably older yet, occasionally referred to as the Guest House. On the other side was a vacant lot and the owner's residence, much newer, but still in the style of the town. I called it "run-down Rocky Mountain Dogpatch."

It all seemed worthless, but I knew about plans to construct a new highway leading from the point where the present one—the only artery from Laramie to Steamboat and Salt Lake City beyond—ran past the Cowdrey Store. When it was finished, the new road would be the back door to Steamboat Springs, winding its way past Lone Tree Ranch and the Big Creek Lakes Recreation Parks and up through the north end of the Mount Zirkle Federal Wild Area—a doorway to limitless outdoor vacation lands that in years to come would draw thousands of people.

Very soon the Cowdrey Crossroads would be a hot spot for investment in service stations, sporting goods stores, groceries, restaurants, and motels. And it was only the first step on my way to owning the county. The purchase of a second ranch like Diamond J was already in the works. The Big Creek Outpost was for sale, and it would be a simple matter to add Twisty Park, a privately controlled side valley with two man-made lakes and hundreds of cabin sites with a direct view of the jagged magnificence of the mountains. Contiguous to Lone Tree were another 240 acres now owned by the Climax Molybdenum Mining Company. The property included several obsolete gold mines, nonproductive since the twenties, when a prospector-promoter used them to float bogus stock issues.

There'd be no problem finding investors to join me in buying these undiscovered treasures. If necessary, I could always repeat my winning explanation to my associates: how any lands utilized by Lake, Sport, and Travel Club members would inevitably not only produce a good cash flow but, because of the public exposure, be easily marketable at far higher prices than their acquisition costs. *Capital gains.* And then there were the oil rights. My younger brother, a geology professor, had for years alluded to the possibility of oil reserves deep beneath the valley floor. Already major oil companies had productive wells in the eastern sector. The glamour of black gold was important; the possibility of gushers excited everyone.

I tingled with as much excitement as when I had read Roethe's letters and listened to him talk. I took a deep breath. Gulping air was therapy, just like when I drank too much and needed to make the bed stop spinning.

First thing the next morning I told Quarton and The Digest to start work on a total acquisition analysis of the North Park Valley.

"All of it?" Quarton asked.

"As much as we can get our hands on." I handed him my list.

The Digest screwed his face into a dubious expression. "How soon do you need it?" he asked.

"*Now*," I said. "And dig out that loan application from Metcalf Farms." I turned away to look for my file folder labeled "Pending

Possibilities." In it was a slip of paper with the notation "Lake Steamboat." I buzzed my secretary and told her to call Turnbull.

"When's the money coming?" he asked in a sharp voice.

I hesitated. I'd already forgotten Turnbull's problems. Fortunately, however, I knew that we'd closed a loan at O'Connor's bank several days before. I made a quick decision to use Lake, Sport's funds. "It's on the way," I told him.

"Good. I'm working, as you suggested, on Lake Steamboat, but don't count on anything soon. I have to concentrate my extra efforts on constructing homes on the lots in Steamboat II."

"How many we got?" I asked.

"Five under way."

"Good deal," I said. I shook my head. There were so many things going on that I was beginning to forget some of them. "What are they worth?" He didn't answer. "On the average?"

"Thirty-eight thousand on completion, maybe more."

I wrote $200,000 opposite "Steamboat II—five houses" on my inventory pad. "Any chance to pick up dude ranches in your area?"

"If I find one priced right I'm gonna keep it for myself. You guys are going ape back in Wisconsin. Getting too damn big. I've got to have something to fall back on." This was the first time Turnbull had vocalized his disapproval of my operation.

I wondered if he felt neglected, or if it was simply the fact that his original idea had been to move to the mountains and stay there.

"Don't get yourself so tangled up in scatterbrained ventures with highbinders that you fuck up Steamboat. I mean that, John."

I tried to explain once again that expansion was now my only method of raising money to make everything fly at once, and that included Thunderhead and Shadco. They drained more than their share of the money I borrowed. Janeff Credit, Dash, and the Club didn't begin to excite Turnbull until I made him understand they were the basis for most of our credit lines.

"OK. Great. They're our meal ticket. . . . you sure?"

"Damn right. O'Connor's million-dollar line is based on my ability to get new and old investors to sign notes for the purchase of stock. Right now that means Lake, Sport, and Travel, Dash, and the new Wisconsin companies, unless you want to dilute Thunderhead and Shadco."

"No way. I don't want the Colorado companies disturbed," Turnbull growled.

His attitude changed and his voice had a happy tone after I assured him, "Western operations are your baby."

"When are you getting married to Sue? As if you've got the time." He laughed.

"The day after my divorce from Judy is final. March third."

"Good luck." Turnbull hung up, still laughing.

Roethe was back in my office the next day. He said he'd reviewed the Diamond J information I'd sent him, including the lists of officers and directors. "The slate looks a little weak. Why not put the millionaire trucker Jim Rosenheimer told me about on your boards?"

"Anders? Fine."

"And I think you need a 'name.' Someone exciting. I can get Jim Lovell, the astronaut. He took the course at Harvard Business School, so he's a fine financial advisor, as well as the man with the most time in outer space." Roethe smiled and made a quick bobbing nod. "Yes, he'll serve. He's already on several of my boards."

My door was, by chance, open, and someone must have overheard our conversation, because once again I could feel excited vibrations as the news sped through the offices. Roethe smiled. He sensed the thrill, too, and probably read my mind. He nodded again. Our combined charisma was uncontrollably contagious.

Three days later I received a telephone call from Lovell at the Manned Spacecraft Center in Houston. It was hard to hear: half the office staff was on extensions. Captain Lovell's voice was an interesting combination of reserve and ebullience. He called me by my first name, but I hesitated to reply without using his full title. The commander of Apollo 13 said that he was looking forward to a fruitful association with Lake, Sport, and Travel and thanked me for the stock Roethe had promised I would give him.

"My pleasure, Jim." Once I realized that I was buying his

participation, my awe of Lovell's reputation quickly disappeared. I invited him to be a special guest at our upcoming International Pro/Am Snowmobile Championships. "We'll hold a board meeting concurrently." I said.

"May I bring my wife and son?"

"Certainly. My secretary will make arrangements." No one said so, but I knew expenses were also expected. "I'll confirm by letter, Jim."

"Very good, John. I'll do the same."

"Now we're buddied up to an astronaut," I told Sue, "and it's not hard to tell—the Diamond J family's walking on rarefied air." I was proud of myself.

The word spread.

Walter O'Connor arrived, beaming. Usually he didn't smile much, but today he almost looked as if he wanted to hug me. "Let's take a look at what Roethe's proposing." He moved toward the file drawer reserved for Roethe projects.

Has he got a homing device? I wondered, stopping him. "Can we talk first?"

Turnbull's problems were not completely solved. He'd called the same morning to tell me that Shadco needed more money to start a townhouse development at Walton Creek Park.

"Use as much of the million-dollar line as you need. We may even have to increase it now." O'Connor, still smiling, told me to make sure I had enough stockholder notes to grease the wheels of the money machine. Then he jumped up. "Let me use the phone." He went into Higbie's empty office and closed the door.

"Typical O'Connor," I said to the sudden void. I pulled out the Thunderhead and Shadco stockholder notes to be sure I'd held some back just in case Turnbull had more surprises. The worst thing that could happen was a financial disaster caused by shorts in Steamboat just as I was about to lock up millions of dollars in new worldwide assets.

O'Connor popped back into my office, saw the notes I'd laid out, and asked what interest rate they bore.

"Eight percent."

"No good. And the papers don't qualify for my bank. Get 'em

resigned on these at 10 percent." He handed me a stack of four-part Wisconsin Banking Association forms.

"Walt, we need funds *today.*"

"No way, but get 'em ready. I'm going to Algoma tomorrow; I'll take 'em with me. We can wire transfer if necessary. Hey, Bob."

Rauterberg stood in the doorway grinning impishly.

"High finance? I told you we could count on Walt." He didn't remove his coat. He paced nervously, not over the funding but obviously because he and O'Connor had something going that evening.

Both were night people. I hoped they wouldn't stay out until dawn—if they did, O'Connor would postpone his trip to the bank.

"We're going to a meeting," O'Connor corrected my thinking. "Get these signed, Johnny boy." He punched his fist on the blank notes.

They left as quickly and quietly as they'd arrived, and I got on the phone. There was a lot to do before O'Connor, I hoped, showed up in the morning.

Higbie ran notes to Kritchner and Hollis for their signatures. I telephoned Vitner. After some bantering and minor bitching he promised to drive down from Green Bay. His firm voice told me he was really in good spirits.

"Great. I can always count on brother Rodney."

Then Turnbull called again. "Better get it here by Friday morning; the coyotes are at the door."

"No problem."

Higbie was back by six P.M.

"Good work."

"Maybe . . ." Higbie looked worried, and I wondered if there was some problem with the snowmobile race that I didn't know about.

Kritchner followed him into my office, waving his note and shouting, "Why are we rushing to stick our necks out again?"

Higbie blinked his eyes nervously. "Dr. Hollis signed," he said, looking toward Kritchner, who scowled and said, "And mine's signed." Suddenly he was shouting again. "But Goddamnit,

Stone, let's make sure there's some control over how the money is spent." He waved a folio at me. "I'm going to call Turnbull tomorrow and verify a completion date for these condos. If they're not marketable soon, the interest will eat up all our profits."

I knew that two floors were nearing completion and that thirty-four units out of the seventy-five available had already been spoken for. "With a little luck we'll close out the project this year," I said. "That's another million in the kitty."

We left a note for Vitner and went for drinks and dinner at the Loft, the bar where I'd first met Sue. It had become our regular hangout.

Higbie started fretting about the race, complaining that we were spending too much time on Roethe and Steamboat.

"If we don't get moving, Dash is going to collapse. Some of the media people claim it's doomed anyway."

"Why?" Kritchner frowned.

I stared hard at Higbie, who should have known better than to inject another problem, and said, "Hell, you know what George said about the long-range weather forecasts. They were right last year." My brother was a handy, but totally unwitting, weather prophet. His job as a science professor made him the easiest of tools with which to allay the annual fears about lack of snow. "Besides, you've got snowmaking equipment."

"I hope it works."

"What?" Vitner had arrived, and was looking at me, eyes wide open at what must have sounded like a serious problem.

"Hi, Rodney. Want a drink?"

"Of course." He sat down hard.

Higbie, as if he were on the other end of a teeter-totter, popped up to go to the bar.

"Now what's up?" Vitner was flushed. Obviously he'd stopped for drinks on the way down.

I gave him two neatly organized portfolios; his notes were in the top one. "It's all here. Study these tomorrow; tonight you've got to sign this new note."

"Where's my old one?"

"Clipped to it."

He scrawled his name and pushed the notes back across the table. I slid them into the briefcase.

"How much is it for—my note?"

"Fifty thousand."

"Where's it going?"

"Algoma."

"No, the money?"

"Mostly Shadco, and part to Thunderhead, Lake, Sport, and Dash."

"Am I in all those?"

"Of course." Higbie handed him a drink.

"What were you saying about the race?" Vitner took a long swallow, watching us over the edge of his glass.

"That it's all set. But pray for snow." Higbie signaled the bartender for another fast round.

Vitner seemed to sober up as he finished his first drink. He shoved the second aside. "Something bothers me. This Roethe, the patron of Boy Scouts and astronauts, why does he need to associate with our little Midwestern conglomerate when he's got access to international consortium and the biggest banks in the world?"

I decided not to mention my conclusion that Roethe needed money as badly as we had in the two years just past. Instead I said, "Roethe's excited, and drawn—like so many others—to the magnetic reputation of Diamond J." I chuckled.

"Don't overestimate your charisma, John." Kritchner rattled the ice in his glass. "Roethe's accustomed to men with bigger, better reputations than yours. Be very careful."

Vitner nodded.

Too many people were beginning to say that. I worried most of the night again, flip-flopping from one side of my bed to the other, fretful also because Sue was still living in her own apartment. The next morning I shifted my thoughts to positive subjects and telephoned Roethe to request a strategy meeting. "Tomorrow too soon?"

He surprised me when he said, "I'll be right over."

Roethe was soon sitting in my office, answering my questions before I could ask them.

"If we're going to do business together you should know my entire financial position," he said, handing me a list of personal assets and liabilities showing that he owed nearly $2 million to eight banks. "Not so bad when you notice that my assets total over $6 million. And they're worth more, much more, if and when you and I get together and make the ideas really work."

"I think you're right."

"I believe I am. You're a bright young man. And you'll be able to turn a profit on everything I've shown you, especially if my businesses become part of your Master Plans."

"My Master Plans?" For a moment it was hard to believe that Roethe was subordinating his dreams to mine. Then, in his simple gesture of squeezing the tip of his nose, I saw that he was still unsure of my commitment. I could demand an equal share of our forthcoming partnership. "How do you propose to consolidate our interests?" I was too deliberately nonchalant.

Roethe noticed. "Come on, John, let's don't banter. I'm willing to put up everything I have to make this work. You don't have to match my contributions, just my energy and enthusiasm."

"No problem." I smiled and stood up, and walked around my desk, right hand extended.

While we were shaking, Roethe said he wanted to buy stock in all my companies but didn't have any immediate investment capital. He suggested signing notes in lieu of cash, "like the other stockholders."

I wondered who had tipped him off on that. One of my bankers, I presumed, had explained my system of selling investors, at a discount, notes to Janeff Credit. Janeff, of course, then resold the notes to banks at a further discount. Expensive, yes, but ultimately producing most of the money required in the first place.

"Why not run my note for $40,000 through today? I can use part of the proceeds to make interest payments to my banks and the balance to buy your stock." Roethe said.

"Why not?" I grinned. Why worry about the rest of Roethe's motives? He was my biggest catch yet, sitting in my office ready to sign notes. If there was a gimmick, if he was planning to use me, then I'd devise further counterstrategies to make good use of him also. The big, and bigger, bites I'd taken before made me think I was about ready to devour the elephant—not a bad metaphor after all, since Roethe was also a renowned big-game hunter.

His next request was for an introduction to Anders.

"For sure," I said. Anders planned to meet Dash officers at the race to be held by our largest competitor, the World Championships, in Eagle River, Wisconsin, the next weekend. I invited Roethe to join us. "You can meet Anders, and, much more important, help with the advance promotion of our Milwaukee races. I'll send my private plane to fly you up."

"Great." Roethe slapped both palms on my desk. "That's the way I expected you to operate. What kind of plane do you have?"

The day before Roethe arrived in Eagle River, the owner of the Chanticleer Inn, now an enthusiastic promotor of all the Diamond J ventures, burst into my room, panting, while I was talking long-distance.

"Keep alert and be good. I miss you," I told Shari, and turned to face him.

"Sorry to interrupt," he said, "but I thought you should hear this right away. Allen Dorfman wants you to join him for cocktails at the Jack-O-Lantern this evening!"

"You're kidding." I lit a cigarette, fumbling with my lighter, while I recovered from the surprise. Dorfman was supposed to be the financial brains of the Teamsters Union, and the Jack-O-Lantern Lodge was the mysterious hideaway of the Brotherhood's hierarchy. Few outsiders received invitations to the well-guarded retreat.

"The call was genuine. I took it myself. Five P.M., and you may bring your staff," the Chanticleer's owner said solemnly. Then he smiled. "Even Anders. Don't worry about his ownership of a trucking company. The event's strictly social, they said."

I felt as if I were walking onto a movie set when I entered the Jack-O-Lantern Lodge. We came in through a private doorway to the game room, which was big enough to hold a hundred people. The bar was a study of preserved mid-twenties opulence: warm, glowing woods mixed with the chilly patina of hard oak chairs where, as Sue whispered to me, "Al Capone might once have sat."

There were four men in the room. I met their eyes; each set was harder than the last. I grinned at them, then fanned my gaze across the room for a second look at the silver trophy collections, stuffed animal heads, and long rows of expensive liquor bottles. "Another adult playpen," I thought, "even if the occupants don't look playful."

Out of the corner of my eye, I noticed Anders staring apprehensively over the top of his glasses. He shifted his weight from one foot to the other and tensed as Allen Dorfman came through the kitchen door. Dorfman was wearing a big white apron and hat, and his lips smiled while his eyes matched the brooding mood of the four men, who had closed ranks behind him.

"John Stone. Good to see you." His hand shot out and caught mine unprepared for the knuckle-crushing grip. He pulled me with him as he turned toward Anders. "This guy work for you?"

"Don't I wish," I chuckled, pushing the sound into a laugh when I realized that both men had recognized each other instantly.

"He's a rugged negotiator. We've been on opposite sides of the table once or twice." Dorfman winked. "Now be good, Mr. Anders, or I'll strike you."

They started laughing, Anders's pitch higher than usual, and I could see that neither man thought the moment was funny. Then Dorfman moved forward and introduced himself to my crowd of Brain Trusters, finally settling beside Sue.

"I've only met your husband once before, last year at the press party, but now it looks like we may see a lot of each other."

Sue cocked her head, curious.

"Maybe we'll be partners." Dorfman reached for a drink from his closest man, and turned back toward Sue to explain what he meant just as a new flunky rushed in from a side door and waved a signal. "Excuse me a minute. Phone call."

I felt Anders move close to me.

"I'm *out* if you entertain any idea of a business association with him." Anders's eyes flicked toward the closing door. He whispered, more quietly with each word. "Dorfman's unscrupulous. He's already been indicted for some kind of pension fund loan fraud . . . or kickback."

"What if he wants to buy Thunderhead?" I tested Anders, knowing that he believed the Inn was the biggest lemon in my portfolio.

"Sell it. Cash at arm's length, a clean deal. But not mutual business. Period."

Dorfman returned and finished explaining his proposition: "a snowmobile racing team."

Later Anders cautioned that the race team was just a carrot dangling in front of the donkey. "Stay away from Dorfman, damnit!" It was one of the rare times I heard him swear.

Late the next morning, Roethe, wearing a red Hudson Bay blanket coat, red boots, and a beaver cap, swept into our VIP trailer and shouted, "What a great group of people!" He turned in a full circle, waving to racing celebrities, Dash employees, and stockholders. "And such a fine way to warm up! Where did we get this trailer?"

"From the Bosch Corporation, Dash's newest sponsor," Higbie told him, looking toward me for approval.

"We can thank Jim Higbie for bringing us the First of the Super Races," I shouted over the excited voices, hoping to impress Roethe and encourage Higbie at the same time. "The World Championship this afternoon is just a heat race before our main event in Milwaukee."

Moments later, as if by magic, Roethe disappeared. I pushed through the crowd looking for him and noticed that Anders was also missing.

"Outside," said Higbie.

"I didn't know they'd been introduced."

"They weren't. Just seemed to be pointed in the same direction. Probably had to drain their radiators." Higbie handed me a hot buttered rum.

I took a mouthful, burned my tongue, and spat it back into the mug. I ignored the sting as I tried to shake my suspicion that Roethe had come only to meet Anders. R. and R. had probably pushed him onto the plane. "Damn." It seemed that the bankers were helping to plot Roethe's movements. I couldn't be sure why, but I wondered how much more I needed to know about him.

Outside, I discovered Roethe and Anders standing in the snow, apparently comparing the financial structures of North Penn Transfer and Weatherby–Nasco.

"Goddamn, Leo, you move fast."

Anders looked my way, frowning. "Did you say that?"

"I've never been known to waste time," Roethe told us. "And this is as good a time and place as any to tell our big plans to our trucker." He laid his arm across Anders's shoulder and started with a description of his African game lodges.

The two men seemed oblivious of the crowds that swarmed past as the snapping roar of snowmobile engines signalled that the races were about to begin. I climbed to the observation platform on top of the Bosch trailer, alternately watching the track and Roethe pitching Anders.

"Men are more exciting than machines," I finally told Sue, standing beside me. I began to focus all my attention on the discussion below.

Anders was standing perfectly still; only his eyes moved, flashing in the sunlight reflected off the snow. Roethe was gesturing furiously, like an artist painting a picture on a deadline.

Later, I guessed that he must have done a good job on the illustration; Anders assured me that he was interested in everything: "Diamond J, the works . . . except Shadco and Thunderhead. Steamboat scares me." He pulled me away from the others and continued in a whisper. "And stay away from Dorfman."

"I promise."

"Then I think we're going to do a lot of business together." Anders peered over the top of his glasses and showed me the happy crinkles at the corners of his eyes.

Now all I had to do was improve the image of the Steamboat ventures. "Then I'll have a perfect setup," I told Sue on our way back to Madison.

"And maybe slow down?"

I stared into the oncoming headlights and pushed harder on the accelerator; I wished she hadn't said that. I settled my mind on next week's schedule. I could avoid a trip west by conferring long-distance with Turnbull. The only real problem in Steamboat was Sid Henry's defection to a private construction company that was planning to use our research and development data to put prefab houses on competing property in the vicinity of Steamboat II.

"So what?" I told Turnbull early the next morning. "He's not going to hurt us. No way. He's served his purpose and we're better rid of him now."

"He's a stockholder too, you know." Turnbull's tone was deriding, meant to jab me for selling Henry stock at cut-rate prices in lieu of paying his brokerage fees.

"So we'll pay him off, and I'll grab the money to apply on his past-due loan with Janeff. Now, damnit, doesn't that show you how all the companies can fit together?"

I started to give him other examples, but broke off the conversation when the morning mail arrived—another stack of Roethe memos repeating his enthusiastic descriptions of African Ponderosa and Agricola Itzapan (the Honduran timber business), and pushing for my approval to buy into Metcalf Farms.

"He must have dictated these before he came to the races," I observed, and ordered my secretary to put Toussaint to work with recaps of our cash and credit positions. "Leo's not going to rest until I start writing checks."

At the bottom of the pile was a letter from Lovell confirming his "delight to become a member of the board of Lake, Sport, and Travel, Inc. It sounds like a dynamic organization." He added, "Leo Roethe had dinner at my house and mentioned the snowmobile race that I am to participate in—stand by, Milwaukee!"

Higbie's eyes bulged when I showed him the letter, and I could hear his heart move into overtime tempo when I told him to use it for press releases: "The world's most travelled astronaut to host the first of the super races."

We needed that, Higbie said, because the Wisconsin press was hammering on the lack of snow and beginning to say, "Give Stone an 'A' for effort for trying something that could *either* be as big as all life, *or* a good idea that didn't make it." One reporter claimed I'd never pull it off.

"That reporter's an asshole. Did you tell him about our snowmaking equipment?"

I expected Higbie to smile. He bit his lip instead. "The snow-making equipment is useless until the temperature drops below 20°. We need five days of cold."

"You've got over a week left," I told him. "It gets cold in Wisconsin in February. Bluff it through. Tell the press that's what the NASA forecasts say. And that Lovell's bringing extra long johns."

A telephone call from Roethe interrupted our discussion. I told Higbie to "keep the heat on everything except the snow machines" and waved him out of the room.

Roethe said, "I've got to see you tonight. It's important."

I worried while I waited for him. Like me, Roethe was a dreamer. And also like me (only more so), he often believed that his fantasies were real, living, working, functional facts. I was sure that whenever anyone told Roethe an idea was viable, he reacted as if the deed were done. Roethe was no superswindler like Charles Ponzi. He was Barnum and Bailey and the Wizard of Oz. But, damnit, he sounded like he needed a lot of money in a hurry.

I guessed right. Roethe said he was still short of cash, even after using his share of the $40,000 I'd just got for him from O'Connor. He needed another $100,000, but said I could keep part of it for research and development costs on the properties he was offering. "They're my sure winners," he said. "You'll find out how good they are. We'll both make millions. Guaranteed. You're a bright young man. . . ." He began the next sentence.

And suddenly I realized that whenever Roethe cocked his head to one side and used that phrase he was about to bullshit me. But I was mollified when I heard him say, ". . . devote a small portion of your incredible intellect to solving my problems."

Roethe oiled my imagination. I began to think I could walk in the footsteps of Horatio Alger.

"I'll get the $100,000," I told him, "and use part of it, as you said." I winked to let him know I would always agree to a mutually beneficial system.

The moment Roethe left, Higbie rushed back into my office. "Were you kidding about getting Anders to truck snow from Canada?"

For months everyone had been consumed by the idea that our races were going to be the biggest, best, and richest in history. Now, if they lost the momentum those superlatives had given them, I'd have a faith as well as a financial problem.

"No," I told Higbie, "you better believe I'm not kidding. I can get snow."

Now he started smiling, nodding briskly and moving his arms in and out against his sides. First I thought he looked like a little boy. Then I realized Higbie was pumping himself up again. He showed me a new press release—"As a true sports club, Lake, Sport, and Travel is promoting and encouraging snowmobile racing. After all, that's what racing is all about: improving the recreation machine. Big-time racing demands big-time backers, so Lake, Sport, and Travel joins the Bosch Corporation (Germany), Bombardier, Ltd. (Canada), and a host of outstanding domestic corporations in building the biggest winter prize in history."

" '$18,000 in mechandise, ski trips, and elk hunts for the winners.' OK?" he said.

"Go, go, go." I slapped his eager shoulders and shoved him out of the room before he saw the worry lines I felt forming in thick, hard ridges on my face.

The problem of snow was not solved; only I knew that. I began visualizing sports page headlines: "Stone Fails." I couldn't stand that kind of publicity. Anything that made people think I was vulnerable, even to the elements, could destroy my charisma. I began calling the weather number hourly, my mind begging for a report that temperatures were dropping so the machines could make snow.

Sue said I was an edgy, intolerant sonofabitch, a fearful ogre when I saw my sons, an impossible leader. But surprisingly, as they realized the truth, my associates seemed to understand that I was carrying the mental burden for everyone. Maybe their faith was stronger than mine during those last three days. Then the temperature dropped to zero and the Milwaukee newspapers ran a front-page photograph of our snow machines running full-blast.

I hugged Sue, Higbie, everyone I met, and then I got drunk. I forgot about everything until my secretary told me the next nauseous morning that I had better get to Milwaukee to meet Captain Lovell.

I drove over alone, thinking all the way that this was the first time in my life I had felt hung over. My natural ability to avoid hangovers, no matter how much I drank, was another high point of my pride. "Not today," I moaned. And, on top of everything else, I was horribly depressed. I remembered Kritchner's admonition that alcohol was a depressant; it was a condition intolerable to my lifestyle.

I fought back, swallowing the bitter saliva, the gagging dejection, for another fifty miles, until, in a sticky bath of sweat, it washed itself away.

Captain Lovell looked like his pictures; he was everything I expected. His high, thinly lined forehead had to mean he possessed a quick, sure mind. Muscled forearms, a flat belly, and broad shoulders left no doubt that he was an active athlete. And he was usually smiling, emphasizing every happy contour of his face. There was something in the calm color of his eyes, the dry yet penetrating resonance of his voice, and his totally coordinated movements, even when shaking hands, that raised him above the other men I'd met. He looked and acted as if he'd been to the moon and beyond. Yet everything else about him was down-to-earth. Instinctively I knew that he'd repel any display of deference.

Lovell and his son took their first snowmobile rides at the racetrack while most of my staff and a huge contingent of professional racers watched, eyes popping as if they were seeing the first satellite launched.

The race itself ran perfectly, until, as I watched Lovell entering the crowds, I heard a gut-piercing moan rise from the stands. I swung around in time to see a driver's body hurtle out of a cloud of snow and bounce over the retaining wall. I choked, knowing somehow that the racer was already dead.

Two hours later Higbie told me that another driver had died in the hospital after a seemingly minor earlier accident—"The first female death in the history of snowmobile racing." He began to cry.

I was stunned. I had to force myself into action. The deaths were accidental, to be sure, but would the press say so? I was remorseful one minute, anxious and resentful the next. How could this be happening? The first of the super races could be the last, and at the expense of two lives. Judy, who had come to see my triumph, now came to build up my morale; I brushed her aside. I worked most of the night, planning memorial funds, issuing statements, and wrestling with a decision—should the final day of races be cancelled?

The early newspaper editions gave me the answer: the press exonerated Dash. Lovell became a working part of Diamond J when he suggested substituting a memorial lap, with snowmobiles arranged in the pilots' traditional "Missing Man" formation, for the celebrity race.

Later we held an impromptu directors' meeting. "Not an appropriate time, but the only opportunity," I explained, "to introduce Captain Lovell, and my latest addendum to the club concept." Acquisition and ownership of enough properties to satisfy our anticipated membership was impossible, no matter how much money we managed to borrow. The only way to fill a complete catalogue with recreational opportunities was to promote an affiliation of world-wide resorts, travel agencies, and tour organizers. This would become possible with Lovell's and other prominent names on our letterhead.

In addition to the telephone and the mails, I suggested that we use a field force to contact likely affiliation prospects. "Everyone can travel, charge off the expenses to research and development; build the club concept into a network of opportunity filling a book thicker than AAA's," I told them. "A million dollars' worth of benefits that will only cost us peanuts."

As usual, there were no objections. And, somebody said, it was time for a celebration. "Dash did the impossible."

Even the critical newspaper reporter, the one I had called an asshole, said, "It was the greatest snowmobile race ever."

I looked around the room. Lovell was gone. I wondered if I was the only one left thinking about the racers who died. I knew Lovell had; I had seen it in his eyes—the same look, I supposed, that was there while Apollo 13 burned its way back from the

moon. Maybe he knew what it felt like to die. "Someday I'm going to ask him," I promised myself. And then my mood changed
and the thought got lost.

A week later Quarton reported that I could buy three-quarters
of the Cowdrey Crossroads whenever I was ready. And everything else on my list of North Park properties was easily obtain-
able for 29 percent down. "Except the Big Creek Outpost. The
owner, the idiot caretaker of Lone Tree, wants cash on the barrel-
head. He thinks we're highbinders." Quarton took a long drag
from his cigarette and blew the smoke toward his feet. "He and
his wife are natural-born pessimists. Hell, I've heard her say, without even looking in the oven, 'the biscuits won't rise.'"

"Screw him," I said. "When we're ready, we'll pay cash. In the
meantime we're probably better off using him as an affiliate and
letting him babysit Lone Tree."

Rosenheimer, who was in the office picking up current financial
statements from my associates, stuck his head in the door and
said, "Cheer up. You're making lots of millionaires." Then he
gave Quarton a quick sideways glance and said he wanted to talk
to me alone.

"I've got no secrets from Bill."

Quarton left anyway.

"Good. I don't want anyone to know where this came from."
Rosenheimer reached into his briefcase and pulled out two slide
carousels. "There are photographs of the entire LTV Master Plan.
Top Secret."

I smiled. Top secret? They were available in printed form, anytime, to the right people. Turnbull already had a set. Rosenheimer
implied that he'd sent a pro to sneak into LTV's executive headquarters. I went along with his game, knowing that he loved the
glamour of nonviolent illegality. Now that it was over, I suspected
that he'd even gotten kicks from his hassle with the FDIC.

"You are at peace with the feds, aren't you?" Suddenly I wasn't
quite sure.

"Except for state requirements to put more capital into my
banks," he said, explaining that Rautenberg was going to arrange
a loan in Chicago so that he could personally buy up a new stock
issue. Then he assumed his familiar posture, leaning over my

desk, and said, "There's something much more important to talk about. Seriously."

"Problems at Janeff?"

"No way. This is much bigger." "Big," with all its variations, was another one of Rosenheimer's favorite words.

"It's time we considered forming a conglomerate."

"What do you think Diamond J is?"

"A bunch of companies with your brand on them, but with no formal legal connections, only interlocking directorships and the questionable practice of sharing money from a community pot." That bothered Rosenheimer, who pointed out how loans he arranged for one company might very well be used for another without his knowledge. He insisted that my companies had to be tied together, sorted out, and arranged in a legitimate package if I wanted to keep borrowing. "You've got a choice—either merge your assets or arrange for each company to guarantee the debts of the others. That includes Janeff. And cross-guarantees are dangerous. So conglomerate."

When I thought about it later, Rosenheimer's suggestion seemed sensible. It didn't require a counterstrategy because it was mutually beneficial. But I had trouble deciding which company should absorb the others. Some had to be excluded from a conglomerate. Janeff Credit, for instance, would lose the advantage of a middleman's position if it became part of the borrowing entity.

Lake, Sport, and Travel was the obvious choice for the conglomerate. It could absorb the real estate companies, which were used as affiliates anyway. It was headquartered and chartered in Wisconsin, where it was easier for me to maintain control—and, of course, I was still the biggest single stockholder. And a conglomerate paved the way for solid acquisition of the Roethe businesses.

I began to explore the legal ramifications and requirements of a conglomerate. Butters and Kanakis saw no problem. They told me to be careful, though, that my stockholders numbered fifteen or less. "Don't even imply the offer of stock to more than fifteen people," Kanakis warned, "or you're liable to end up in the slammer."

Turnbull didn't like the idea. "I want the Inn and Shadco kept separate from the Wisconsin whirlwind. The Steamboat ventures have to remain autonomous. That's it—or buy me out."

The conglomerate idea didn't impress O'Connor either; he thought it was too soon. "There's nothing wrong with doing what you're doing now, using a multitude of companies to cosign and guarantee each others' loans. It looks good when the bank examiners come around," he said. "The more financial statements, the better."

My mind was changed for me, and soon we were reviewing the Master Plan for the million-dollar loan scheme at the Algoma Bank. "The bank's legal lending limit is $75,000 to any one company or individual. Therefore, you have a choice. You can acquire the money through fourteen different companies or fourteen different people or a combination of the two," O'Connor said. Then, to be sure I didn't argue, he gave me another reason to postpone the conglomerate. He relisted his requirements for extending the line of credit. "The borrowers must have acceptable, preferably strong, financial statements. If some companies or people are stronger than others, then the strongest must guarantee the loans of their weaker associates. And you, Johnny, must prove and guarantee *everybody's* ability to repay."

"Out of profits, of course," I said, expecting that to satisfy the last requirement.

"Not good enough," O'Connor said. "Some of your ventures may not be in the black for years."

He thought he had the best brains, so I asked him, "What do you suggest?"

"Your personal stock's for sale, isn't it?" I thought O'Connor must have seen my jaw clench, because he started telling me not to worry about losing control. "So you only own 20 or 30 percent in the end—doesn't make any difference. You'll be guaranteeing all the loans and they'll be collateralized with the stock. So if and when a borrower doesn't pay, you'll be the one who redeems the note, and the stock along with it. I'll arrange for you to borrow the money, if you still need it by then." He smiled, squinting slyly. "Better yet, if some stockholder becomes a pain in the ass, fix it so he *can't* pay and force him out without an argument.

That's power." O'Connor's voice sounded as brutal as his scheme.

But it would work. I wasn't worried about the method; I was curious about the man. Of all the bankers involved I knew the least about O'Connor. And so, though I didn't enjoy his sloppy social style, I invited him for a drink, hoping he'd loosen up and tell me about himself.

In the beginning I thought my party ploy would work. O'Connor seemed to be an egomaniac as well as a greedy opportunist, just enough of a "Joe Lunch Bucket" to respond to Padgett's basic motivators.

"I'm a former military policeman with a law degree," he said, sipping a martini through his teeth. "Married to a banker's daughter. After I saved the family bank, I branched out in Florida real estate and politics. That's my legal residence, because Florida's got tax and other legal advantages over Wisconsin."

He didn't tell me where he came from, or anything more about his friends and family. And when I probed, he changed the subject.

"Did you know I fixed it for Padgett to buy Camp Dells?" he asked. His speech was slightly slurred from the alcohol, but his eyes followed every move I made.

"No." I leaned forward on the cocktail table to let him know that I was interested in hearing about it.

"Padgett's not so dumb. He's got a good thing in the Dells. Enough acreage on the Wisconsin River to build two, three hundred permanent campsites, along with a recreation building, bar, and restaurant."

I nodded. I knew the property.

"But, as usual, he's broke," O'Connor continued. "Too much screwing around with his Buyer's Club. But at the campground in the Dells, hell, he can sell memberships easier than you can. I think he's going to make a lot of money. So we're setting up a corporation...." He closed his eyes. "Padgett gets 10 percent free for engineering the deal. The resort operator gets 30 percent. The rest is for me and my friends." O'Connor's friends were his brother in Florida, a Milwaukee banker, a Miami lawyer, a former Miami policeman who was now O'Connor's right-hand man, and a mysterious character called "the Marlboro man."

I leaned farther forward—not to psyche him now, just to hear. The more O'Connor drank, the quieter he got, and so far, he hadn't mentioned any names.

Finally, barely whispering, he told me, "You've got to meet these people . . . and impress them good because . . . they've got connections, Johnny boy."

And then he pushed himself away from the table and rose to leave, nodding slowly and giving me a knowing smile.

10
Mid-February 1973

ASSETS—$1,352,600.00
LIABILITIES—$161,916.00
PERSONAL GUARANTEES—$5,250,000.00

Another cold front moved in overnight, frustrating my plans for a predawn meeting with the Brain Trust.

"My damn car won't start," I told Higbie, who had answered his phone on the first ring.

"The Digest has the same problem. He just called looking for a ride, afraid you'd blow your stack if he was late."

"Not today. His projects are at the bottom of my priority list," I said, explaining that I had new leads to follow in our investigation of O'Connor's mysterious activities. "And we've got Rosenheimer, Rauterberg, and Roethe to deal with before we spend any more money."

"I'll be right over," Higbie said. "You can use my car while I find a way to start yours." He was the only Brain Truster who seemed to understand that there was more to borrowing money from our friendly bankers than just signing blank notes.

As I skidded Higbie's yellow Corvette into the office parking lot, my mind was already recalling telephone numbers. First I called Padgett, who verified that he and seven other "big shots" were buying a resort complex called Camp Dells.

"Couldn't swing it without O'Connor," he said. Then, realizing

I was still ignorant of the details, he added, "Your pal Rauter-berg's helping too. The mortgage, a big one, is at his bank."

But still no names. He seemed to be evading them too.

"Thanks." I hung up before Padgett could question me about Diamond J's finances.

"Loves to trade information," I said to myself, and looked up to see R. and R.—their earliest visit ever.

"What information?" Rosenheimer was stamping the snow off his shoes.

"Just checking up on O'Connor's side deals." I scowled at the circle of slush staining my carpet.

R. and R. sat, side by side, on the sofa, Rauterberg staring at me with wide, angry eyes.

"What's Walter up to now?" he asked.

"You tell me."

Rauterberg confirmed the mortgage loan on Camp Dells. "A courtesy, but still a good loan, co-signed by the stockholders. One's that banker I got you a loan from last fall. Remember?"

I shook my head.

Rosenheimer blinked and leaned forward; Rauterberg loosened his tie and stretched his neck, apparently wondering how much to say in front of his associate.

"We're all part of the big picture," I said, and then, directly to Rauterberg, "Now jog my memory about that banker."

He stood, apparently having made the decision to talk freely. "O'Connor's new partner is the guy chartering a new bank on the west side of Milwaukee. I think it'll be my correspondent, and—" he grinned—"another good loan source."

While Rauterberg described the rest of the Camp Dells stock-holders, I leaned back in my chair and played with my pen, but as soon as I realized that he was telling me nothing new, and not mentioning names, I sat up straight again.

"Who are they?"

"All important people," said Rauterberg. "That's why my bank is lending money to them."

Still no names. Now the comment O'Connor made the night before, "They've got connections," was beginning to sound sinister.

"Just how far can we trust Walter O'Connor?" I asked.

Rauterberg looked surprised. He opened his mouth, but made no reply.

Rosenheimer stood up and walked to the opposite side of the room. "What difference does it make?" he said. "Right now you need Walter, we all need him, bad. So why make waves? Later, sure, but not now. We have to wait until Titan's operable and I'm able to place loans with the pension fund."

"He's right, John," Rauterberg put in. "And I'm sure O'Connor's straight anyway."

I started to ask if Allen Dorfman was involved with Titan, but Rauterberg, insistent now, said, "We're forgetting why we're here."

"Because I need . . ."

I slapped the desk, silencing Rosenheimer. "Because *I* want some reassurance." I looked back and forth to be sure I had their attention. "Diamond J is about to move farther and faster than ever anticipated."

"I know, I know." Rosenheimer came back to my side of the room.

I raised my voice anyway. "Well, maybe you don't know that there's a point of no return in this business. When it's passed you're either a multimillionaire and a hero or . . ." I cleared my throat, and slapped the desk again. "Or a failure, damned as a crook, a hustler; condemned to a death that lingers forever."

"So?"

"*So?* Is that all you can say, Jim? So, I think I'm passing that point, and I want to be goddamn sure I can depend on my bankers."

R. and R. exchanged worried glances.

"And can we depend on you?" Rosenheimer asked softly. "Can you stand the pressure?"

"Damn right." Neatly, intentionally or not, the burden of building morale rested with me again. I smiled. "OK, what's your problem?"

"The Banking Commission's back on my ass. They're checking all my loans. And they're about to discover my account with Roethe and Metcalf Farms." Rosenheimer's eyes twitched toward Rauterberg.

Rauterberg exhaled a deep breath and swung around to face me. "And they're watching your loans, too." He frowned.

"If I have to move my loans I will. You know how—O'Connor. He'll probably take Roethe and Metcalf in the same package, if everything you say about him is true."

R. and R. smiled. That's what they wanted to hear.

"Now can we talk about my situation, the real reason you're here?"

"Not yet." Rosenheimer reached for his briefcase. "I haven't been able to sell my Steamboat property, North Meadows and the Glover 40."

"And you need a favor." I knew Koziel was getting pissed because he saw no sign of the quick profit Rosenheimer had promised. "Want me to make you an offer, like ten grand an acre?"

"That's half-price, you fucker." Then, seeing my grin, Rosenheimer lowered his voice. "Seriously, I need help."

"Remember, if we work together we can't lose." Rauterberg began tightening his tie, expecting my cooperation, preparing to leave the meeting.

"You came here to discuss Roethe with me," I reminded him.

Rosenheimer moved between us and handed me a typewritten form. "First I need your signed offer to buy the Steamboat land."

I tensed when I saw the figures. "This is for double the market value."

"I won't demand performance. I only want to show it to Koziel, keep him happy. Then maybe I can get some of his money for Titan."

I pointed to Rauterberg. "You heard that. He won't make me honor my offer."

Rauterberg laughed. "You couldn't pay anyway."

"Don't make jokes," said Rosenheimer when he noticed my frown, my quick look at my watch.

"Time's running out. Roethe's due here in fifteen minutes." I signed the form. "Now what don't I know about him?"

"Leo's a good man. Put another good man next to him—*you*." Rosenheimer jabbed a finger at me, then picked up his papers. 'And we'll all get rich."

"Right." Rauterberg nodded, stood up. "Pure gold."

I shouted to let them know the meeting was not over. "You guys think I'm an alchemist?" I crossed the room and stood between R. and R. and the door. "Less than a year ago you told me to clean up my own act—find a cash flow. Now, before I finish saving myself, I'm supposed to salvage Roethe? Unassisted?"

They began to sit down, scared again.

And I began to laugh, uncontrollably. "Why not? I'm ready to take on anything." I knew I had no other choice.

R. and R. stayed for my meeting with Roethe, who didn't seem one bit embarrassed by his debts. He passed me loan lists as quickly as he'd previously provided information about his assets. His excuses didn't sound like excuses, more like a rational justification of his position, even bragging.

"I've had some bad luck, bad timing, and I've gotten screwed," he said, "but I wouldn't be as big as I am without some trouble. Now, you're a bright young man. I'm going to place myself in your hands." He nodded to me, then to the others.

And all of a sudden, Roethe was on his feet, moving toward the door with R. and R. following. He stopped to check the time. The gold animals on his watchband seemed to be staring at me. Then Roethe waved good-bye. "Take good care of our affairs."

"You can bet on it," Rosenheimer told him, chuckling happily on the way out.

I poured a fresh cup of coffee and began to study Leo Roethe's debt structure. The stack of papers he'd dumped on my desk was at least five inches high. I thought about calling Toussaint in to run adding machine tapes and work up an accountant's recap, but discarded the idea when I realized that Roethe's debt was big enough to boggle most minds. Toussaint's nervous temperament, uncontrollably contorting his normally worried face, might start a chain reaction among my staff and undermine their faith.

I shook my head and slipped the Roethe data into my drawer. "Goddamn," I thought, "if I'm going to be custodian of nearly $5 million of Roethe's money, plus $2 million of his bank debt and almost $3 million in personal guarantees, on top of my own growing millions, it's time to travel appropriately—in a car that starts." I canceled my afternoon appointments and rushed out, to buy a new Eldorado with white leather seats and a mobile telephone.

The day the Cadillac was delivered, I drove straight to the travel agency that handled my mushrooming transportation schedule.

"Listen," I told the owners, "I know how we can all make some extra money."

Their heads moved forward. "Like hungry dogs biting at a bone," I thought, happy that they were so ready to believe me.

"My staff, my stockholders, and the club members are traveling more and more, farther and farther," I said, throwing them extra goodies—"Africa, Honduras, and Hawaii. They're buying tickets indiscriminately, all over hell and back. I can run it all through you."

The senior partner lit my cigarette. His hand trembled. "It would certainly simplify your bookkeeping," he said.

"I suppose, but the main point is money. I can double your volume. What's your average commission?"

"Seven percent."

"I want a cut."

"We can't do that," said one, looking grim.

"Because it's illegal," added the other. "Federal regulations prohibit commissions to anyone but licensed travel agents."

I shook my head, watching their dull eyes and thinking how they reflected stagnant minds. "Not commissions. Advertising and promotion fees paid to one of my companies—the equivalent of one-third of everything you make off Diamond J."

Their smiles returned.

"Easy, huh?" I shook their hands.

"It's better than American Express," I told my staff. "Now why doesn't someone else think of something new and exciting?"

"I already have," said The Digest. He spread out descriptive data for a potential resort affiliate called Holiday Lodge. "It's got everything—a PGA-approved golf course, two lakes stocked with fish, and a landing strip . . . and . . ." he started to stutter.

"This has got to be good. I've never seen you so excited before."

"And it's got a great restaurant-bar complex that, during prohibition, was a gangster hangout."

"You've seen it?"

"No, but look at the brochures. I think we should buy Holiday Lodge to complement Camp Dells and the Kritchner farm. That way we can establish a chain of facilities along the interstate."

Quarton, listening from the doorway, yelled, "How much?"

"We can get control for pennies. The owner's pinched, nearly broke because he's a poor manager," said The Digest.

"So, as usual, we assume his debts or substitute our own loans." Higbie pushed past Quarton. "Sounds good. Even if we don't buy the place, we can use it for a party. It's time for a party."

"Why not?" I winked at The Digest. "If it's a bust, *you* pick up the tab."

He gathered up his materials and strode purposefully out of my office.

"It works," I thought. "Let every man contribute to the dream and they're loyal for life."

But Holiday Lodge, ten miles from the interstate in north central Wisconsin, was not the "Gateway to the Northland" the brochures promised, not the quaint and colorful haven shown in the photos, certainly not the winter wonderland The Digest imagined. It was winterkill, a complete disaster. Invited to the outdoor festivities—skating on ponds reminiscent of Currier and Ives, snowmobiling on endless white trails, cross-country skiing where the only sound was the squeak of clean snow—or the gala banquet, with good wine and slow dancing, club members were too shocked to be disappointed. As the guests arrived (even a carload of extra ladies imported from Chicago) the weather was damp, foggy, snowless, and gray.

"Chin up," I told The Digest. "Weather can change in a minute."

But the sun did not shine, and the snow did not filter down in dewy flakes. It stayed a total and absolute gray. Even the Lemonweir River was gray—and so was the Holiday Lodge. It was like a tumbledown, weather-battered barn with none of the charm of a really old barn, or even the sinister mystique of the Jack-O-Lantern Lodge—just a gray bar, gray formica-topped tables, gray curtains, gray windows looking out on the muddy landscape. At-

tached to the bar was a huge, drafty dining room, also gray.
Nothing promised much in the way of Diamond J's typical adventures in recreation.

Quarton wondered what to do with impressionable members
and investors in this grim situation.

"A stiff drink, a hearty drink, and another drink," I told him.
"Announce an open bar. The drinks are on The Digest."

"One thing," said Quarton later, "Holiday Lodge does serve
a good drink."

"And Holiday Lodge will never again have such a bountiful
till," I needled The Digest. "Thanks to you."

All of us ignored his scowl.

As the hours waned, the cocktails moved to the dining room.
Now nothing was gray anymore. The mayor, our honored guest,
arrived just in time to be seated beside me at the head table.

"Nice turnout." He swiveled his head and frowned into the
brimming glass I offered him.

The Digest noticed and beckoned me to meet him in the corner. "We're making a damn poor impression, and you're not helping. Hizzoner doesn't drink."

"So what the hell did you invite him for?" I laughed, amused,
but stopped quickly when I saw that The Digest was fighting to
hold back what would have been either tears or a tirade.

"I can't hack this," he said, waving toward the center of the
churning room. "You expect me to pay for a drunken brawl?"

"Who said you were paying?"

"I did." Higbie pushed between us. "It was his idea. That's the
way we do it in Diamond J. Right?"

I shook my head, but before I could speak, The Digest shouted
at us both.

"If that's the way Diamond J does it, I want out."

Higbie laughed; even to me, the sound was slashing sharp. "So
quit, and find another job to pay the notes you've signed. Or wise
up baby, enjoy, because you're with us for life."

I could see The Digest tense every muscle, and I half expected
him to smash Higbie's grinning face. Instead, before I could get
ready to separate them, he turned another shade grayer and
walked limply away to the bar.

Much later, and much drunker than the rest of us, The Digest came up to me and said, "You know, this could all be a nightmare." Then he shuffled back to the bar, seemingly prepared to forget the evening forever.

As I expected, no one came to work the next day. So I picked an easy project to work on, the new Diamond J letterhead, and began adding to the list of enterprises crowding the left margin below my logo. Lake, Sport, and Travel, Dash, and all the Colorado companies were already in place. I included Diamond J Oil, because I owned oil wells now; Diamond J Publications, because I was publishing a snowmobile racing yearbook; The Thundercats (our company-sponsored racing team); and Diamond J Imports, to emphasize foreign commerce, even though I hadn't yet decided what products to import from where. My forehead rested in the palm of my hand.

There had to be more, but I didn't feel like thinking. I knew I was tired, and I had been neglecting Sue. Our wedding was less than two weeks off. I decided to take the day off too, but it took a long minute to get used to the idea. Just before leaving I jotted down "Diamond J Aviation," meaning the 404, the planes Bindl had provided, and the Executive Twin I had told Captain Feisty to buy for me.

I tried to forget about business, but my association with Roethe was erasing the last traces of privacy, even in my moments with Sue.

"You talk in your sleep all night, every night," she said.

"What do I say?" I was more anxious than curious. As far as I was concerned, sleep talking was always dangerous—especially since I frequently called Sue "Judy" by mistake, even when I was just drowsy.

"You're running either a sales or a directors' meeting." Sue laughed, seeming to understand my circumspection. She rubbed the back of my neck, knowing that sometimes I could hear my temples pound from the pressure. Though she was busy with final wedding preparations, I knew she was trying to spare me additional burdens. I nearly crushed her in a bear hug, trying to thank her. "You're fantastic," I said, relaxing my hold. "Too good to lose, so I promise to take off two weeks for our honeymoon."

"Just us? Never happen."

Sue was right, but she never mentioned it again. And I never forgot.

"I love her most of all for that," I was telling Quarton early one morning as Roethe bustled into my office with a new armload of investment information.

"Glad to hear you're human," said Roethe. Then, after a short, smiling pause, "African Ponderosa needs your immediate attention."

"Problems?"

Roethe referred to the documents. Unless $300,000 was raised to pay the Asian contractors, the work on the game lodges would stop. Hilton International might cancel its management contract, and Chase International **Investment** Corporation and the Chase Manhattan Bank would call their loans.

"You can't afford to miss this opportunity to acquire the finest resorts in East Africa. And I can't afford to lose the image I've built during two decades and fourteen trips to Kenya." He handed me a large red-bound book titled, in gold embossing, "Leo the Lion."

I opened it to a prologue headed "We." "We" referred to Roethe and his son, who had died when his private airplane crashed on June 29, 1971.

"We shared many safari adventures," Roethe said. He reached across to turn the page to a photograph of Leo, Jr. standing in the curve of a mammoth elephant tusk. "His trophies are displayed at the World Wide Animal Kingdom. After college he was going to help me with African Ponderosa."

I looked at Roethe's eyes. He was hurting. He wasn't acting now.

"We'll go to Africa," I told him. "That's all I can promise."

"The grand opening of my lodges is next month," he said, sounding encouraged. "I want you and Anders and Kritchner to attend. And your wife. A honeymoon."

I nodded to keep him talking while I considered the merits of acquiring untested businesses half the world away—chancy at best. The African Ponderosa Lodges were already plagued with the same problems I'd met with at Thunderhead.

In the background I heard Roethe telling me again, "You're a bright young man; you should understand that the lodges mean more than a foothold in Africa. They're an opportunity to form a working partnership with Hilton and the international bankers." He stopped talking and watched me. He didn't smile until he saw me make a decision.

"I guess if I want to do business with Leo Roethe I have to start in Africa," I told him. The opportunity to gain international stature didn't come along every day. If I bailed Roethe out of his problems in Kenya, in Honduras, and at home, I'd be a hero on three continents. I told myself that that was what I'd been looking for since 1970. Maybe now the balls I'd bragged about were facing their first test. But I knew I was taking a big chance. Before I spoke, I licked my dry lips. "I'm going to bring Rauterberg along too. A majority of the decision-makers must see the lodges for themselves. I'm going to need backup votes on this one."

Roethe nodded, then said, "One more thing. On my last trip to Kenya I donated $20,000 to build a hospital in the Taita hills. That's the district where the lodges are located. Jack Shako, the minister of tourism, and I made the announcement to 50,000 cheering tribesmen. The check came through the other day, and it's NSF. If I can't cover it by the end of the week, my bank will send the check back to Africa."

"And then you'll have to stay out of Kenya forever," I told him. I laughed as I imagined the tribesmen—waving spears this time—chasing Roethe through the jungles. "Don't worry. I'll get the money from O'Connor."

"Good." He leaned toward my desk and began inscribing his book to me.

I could tell there was something else Roethe wanted to talk about. Still very serious, he was lingering too long. "What else, Leo?"

He looked up and smiled. "You guessed I needed another favor?"

"Sure, why not?" I was in a hurry now, anxious to tell Sue about our unexpected extra honeymoon.

"Look here." Roethe pulled a document from his briefcase.

It was an agreement to purchase 80 percent of the outstanding stock in Big Mountain Country for $1.15 million.

"You'd better not be serious," I said. "That's more money than Diamond J can get its hands on."

Roethe promised he would never execute the document. "It's only a ploy to keep the other stockholders happy."

I walked to the window and watched the snow falling on Roethe's limousine. I closed my eyes. Sometimes I had to close my eyes to sort out the ideas that whirled through the tornado in my mind. This was the same setup as Rosenheimer's Steamboat property gimmick. There had to be a conspiracy among Roethe and my bankers.

I told Roethe that I'd sign, but that I also needed a letter of intent from him, confirmation that he was going to buy 1,000 shares of Thunderhead at $100 per share (twice the original price).

"I have stockholders too," I smiled.

Somewhere, someone had gotten the idea for a bachelor party, and they managed to keep it secret until the last minute, when Quarton called me into the crowded conference room. Everyone was there except the bankers. I hoped that didn't mean problems. I nursed a drink, concerned about a visit I would have to make later to my mother, who was in the hospital. I watched the door until I saw Rauterberg come in. He waved, winked, and joined a group where Kritchner was describing plans for the next airborne ski trip.

"Lovell's flying copilot on the 404."

Suddenly all conversation stopped, and I saw that everyone else's eyes were on something behind me. I hesitated, expecting a practical joke. Then I turned to face Rosenheimer, who stood inches away—with a totally nude woman on his arm.

She stuck out her hand and introduced herself as if she were entering a directors' meeting. "I'm Judy Day, Miss Nude America."

Rosenheimer must have enjoyed my expression, because laughter rumbled up from his belly and he could scarcely get his words out: "My bank's bonus for a good customer."

Kritchner rushed across the room and introduced himself. "I'm a plastic surgeon and can't help admiring your breasts. Maybe I can use them as models for implants to your less fortunate sisters."

Miss Nude America seemed fascinated by his medical jargon. By the time Kritchner finished his examination every man in the room was calling himself "Doctor."

The wedding was also a company affair. When Sue brought home proofs of the wedding pictures, I couldn't help thinking how much they looked like a record of the nuptials of a "Godfather." Kritchner (my best man) and the rest of the Brain Trusters (groomsmen and ushers) wore chocolate-brown tuxedos, which gave the photographs a somber hue, especially since my men outnumbered the bride's brightly dressed attendants three to one.

My sons stood in the forefront of most scenes. I studied their faces and thought I detected a trace of sadness in their smiles. Then I wondered if it had been a mistake to make them altar boys. Maybe they would have preferred to fade into the background. My mouth turned dry and bitter; I knew I'd put John and George in a rough spot.

I carried a fresh drink into the bathroom and asked myself, "Why do you always see your mistakes with the people you love after it's too late?" I raised my glass in a secret toast to Judy. "You're better off without me, honey." Then, on the verge of tears, I drained the drink and ran back to Sue, holding her as long and as hard as I dared.

We left in the morning for a short, late, but very private honeymoon in Florida.

I had forgotten that Lovell was leading the club ski trip to Steamboat at the same time.

"So what? Nobody missed you either," said Quarton the day we all returned to Madison. He looked away, pretending to ignore me, but turned back again and, unable to suppress his grin, told me "the latest tale of Lake, Sport, and Travel."

Lovell, who, as a ski buff was fascinated by the Diamond J concepts, was just as excited about the trip as the other passengers, especially since he was going to get a first look at the Thunderhead condominium we were selling him at a special price. The condo was to be decorated in a red, white and blue NASA motif and called the "Launch Pad."

Marilyn Lovell accompanied her husband. They arrived at the airport at 3:00 A.M. on the bitter cold departure day. Everyone else agreed that Lovell was the perfect image of an astronaut. Besides having a commanding physique and steel-blue blinkless eyes, surrounded by the tiny wrinkles most pilots have (which in his case, someone suggested, may have been caused by pressure changes in outer space), Lovell was astonishingly alert for the early hour, and seemed impervious to the subzero temperatures. He introduced his wife, left her in the company of Mrs. Quarton (who was acting as stewardess), waved to everyone, and disappeared into the cockpit.

Quarton followed, curious to observe Captain Feisty's reaction to his famous copilot. Lovell looked at the maze of instruments, buttons, and levers and asked the pilot for a briefing. This was a smart move, Quarton said, because Captain Feisty was already in an abnormally wet sweat about sharing the command of "his ship" with an astronaut.

"Doubt you've ever seen the flight deck of a 404 before," Captain Feisty said, handing over a checklist and beginning to smile as he realized Lovell was only the honorary copilot.

Lovell read the checklist and instinctively followed the pretakeoff instructions. In minutes the props bit hard into the freezing air, and with snow billowing behind, the Bird lifted from the ground. Scant seconds later, and barely 100 feet up, everyone heard a strange thunk come from the vicinity of the left wing. Quarton saw Feisty furiously adjust the controls.

"Sonofabitch. Blew something on the engine. Help me bring her around for a landing," he growled to Lovell.

Quarton knew that my standing orders were not to alarm passengers with talk about mechanical failures on the Club's "Super-Safe Luxury Liner." He asked the pilot what to say.

"Tell them we hit a seagull," was the angry reply.

Quarton explained to every anxious face in the cabin that Captain Lovell could orbit the moon without incident, but had found the traffic a bit heavy in the skies over Madison. "We hit a seagull, and are landing to make a precautionary inspection," Quarton told them, happy to see that there was no sign of panic.

"I'll bet it was Jonathan Livingston," someone wailed merrily.

As the plane rolled to a stop, Lovell appeared in the cabin

doorway. His smile showed true cool confidence. He winked toward his wife. He said nothing.

The mechanical problem was quickly corrected and the flight resumed. No one ever asked what a seagull was doing in Wisconsin.

"The rest of the outing was great," Quarton said, "especially for the newcomers. Their faces reflected the sheer joy of being part of the Diamond J adventure, the excitement of watching kingmakers at work."

The last observation hit home, hard and happy. It was the kind of talk I liked hearing.

"Hey, wake up. I need a favor—fast!" Rosenheimer shouted from the doorway. I could tell by his heavy, nervous breathing that it was urgent and probably peculiar—impossible to grant immediately. I listened anyway.

"One of my banks, now run by a trustee as part of my peace treaty with the authorities, is pushing for the repayment of a loan I made to a country music nightclub. I want you to buy the place before the trouble starts."

"What trouble?"

Rosenheimer closed the door, then pulled a chair up to my desk and told me, almost in a whisper, that he'd had a bad loan with a nightclub called "Little Nashville."

"Little Nashville?" I started to smile about the name, caught myself, and fixed my eyes in a hard stare. "Are there any more setups like this?"

He shrugged. "Look, all you have to do is sign a mortgage. I'll get it funded."

"No way. My stockholders are getting nervous, warning me to slow down."

"Then talk to O'Connor for me. He could buy it out of my bank." Rosenheimer's voice was desperate.

"Leave O'Connor alone. He's got his hands full funding Diamond J." I clasped my hands behind my head and wondered why Rauterberg wasn't helping his friend.

When I asked, Rosenheimer told me, "I want to keep this private." He took a deep breath and bit his lip. "Forget it. I'll find another solution. Just don't tell Bob anything." He waved the peace sign and left, forgetting his portfolio.

I examined its contents: more data on Little Nashville, a packet of used airline tickets (to and from Hawaii), and a bank deposit slip with "Su Lee" and a phone number scribbled on it. I copied down the name and number and told Higbie to check it out. Then I telephoned and asked Anders, who'd been talking regularly to Rosenheimer about Titan and the Diamond J companies, if he knew anything about Little Nashville or the Hawaiian business.

"Nothing," he said, and allowed that he might have missed mention of those companies amid a staggering list of other businesses Roethe and Rosenheimer had described to him.

"When was that?" I asked.

Anders explained. "Both men made a secret trip to Pennsylvania earlier this month. They came to discuss Weatherby–Nasco and Roethe's battle for control with Gulf & Western. I've agreed to become a director and join the Roethe forces."

I took a deep breath and signaled my secretary to hold all calls and visitors; I saw a crisis coming. Roethe and Rosenheimer seemed to be working behind my back, trying to tap Anders's resources before I had secured his investments in the Diamond J companies. Sure, Anders already owned a share of the ranch, and stock in Janeff, Lake, Sport, and Travel, and Dash, Inc. But I wanted him to buy more, and to help me fund the purchase of the Cowdrey Crossroads, Twisty Park, and selected Roethe properties.

They knew that Anders was worth well over $5 million. When Rosenheimer had seen my copy of Anders's financial statement, he had remarked that it seemed purposely deflated, probably for tax reasons. I remembered how Rosenheimer's eyes had stretched at the time, but I'd missed that obvious clue to his intentions. Now, goddamnit, he and Roethe were deliberately burning the candle at both ends, and running the serious risk of scaring Anders away from all of us.

I decided to tell Anders everything I knew about them both, hoping he'd help me determine the best method of using their good points without being stabbed in the ass by the bad.

"Look," he interrupted, "I already know about Leo's debts and

Jim's problems with the Banking Commission. Like you, I'm sometimes suspicious, but I don't think they mean to cheat us. They're both just scrambling to save their life's work." Anders talked as if he appreciated men who faced up to adversity. "I want to help if I can."

"You mean that?"

He cleared his throat, and I imagined him smiling.

"Of course. They're a couple of good promoters. You should recognize that."

Now I was sure he was wearing a happy expression, and it didn't seem as if any damage had been done. Excited about our upcoming trip to Kenya, Anders said:

"Great chance to learn more about each other and discuss the details of expanding and merging all the businesses, except . . ." His voice trailed off to a reluctant tone. "I'm not too sure about the game lodges." Then, strong and cheerful again, he reminded me of the time I had driven the Jeep over a cliff. "And I'm absolutely sure you're not guiding me on a lion hunt."

In the midst of last-minute preparations for the trip, Rosenheimer burst into my office again. This time he wanted to know when Diamond J was going to move on Metcalf Farms.

"When I get back," I said, angry because there was already too much on my mind. I turned my back and continued to stuff my briefcase, paying special attention to copies of the office work schedules. While I was out of touch, totally unavailable for two weeks, my empire would have to function alone for the first time. That made me very nervous. I wasn't sure Quarton, the Storm Trooper, or The Digest could administer the loosely knit organization that had until now depended almost entirely on my off-the-cuff decisions.

Rosenheimer, still waiting, looked over my shoulder at the African Ponderosa papers I'd begun to sort. "Going to buy it?"

"I don't know." I started shaking my head slowly. African Ponderosa was an enigma. Apparently it had begun as a sisal plantation, owned jointly by Roethe and a professional hunter from Pakistan. Later, when nylon rope replaced hemp, it had been converted to a shooting preserve. And today, African Ponderosa was suddenly supposed to be a pair of totally cosmopolitan

resort hotels sitting in the middle of Kenya's largest outdoor un-
fenced zoos.

Roethe said that it was much bigger and better than Bill Holden's Mount Kenya Safari Club. It would outclass the famous
Treetops Game Lodge and would become an outstanding addition to the international conservation movement. "African Ponderosa is the logical hub for travelers making the Nairobi–
Amboseli–Tsavo Park Run, as well as for the German and French
tours that regularly use Mombasa as their base and then roam inland to see the game. A Mecca," he said.

That was why the president of Searle Laboratories, the chairman of White Trucks, and a host of other business and professional leaders were stockholders. That was also why the Chase
International Investment Corporation (CIIC), the Standard
Bank Finance and Development Corporation, Limited (London
and Nairobi), and the Chase Manhattan Bank had agreed to lend
the company up to $1,425,000 for the construction costs. The idea
was so good, Roethe said, that CIIC had also taken an investor's
position in the project.

"Everybody involved has more money than Diamond J, so why
does Leo need us on this project?" I looked to see if Rosenheimer
had heard me and, when he shrugged, turned back to my billowing briefcase. "The answer's probably somewhere in there, but I
think I can find it more easily in Africa."

I said the same thing to Anders as we boarded the Pan Am 747
to begin our trip.

"Maybe so." Anders seemed uninterested. He settled into a seat
beside Roethe and discussed Weatherby–Nasco in hushed tones.
The rest of us started a party at the bar; I finished two fast drinks.

"I need some time to myself," I told my group. "Not just business, business. Right, Sue?"

"This time I think you mean it." She knew that all my life I'd
dreamed about visiting Africa, especially Lake Rudolf on Kenya's
northern frontier. "Who but John would travel 6,000 miles to go
fishing?" she said, laughing about my promise to catch a two-
hundred-pound Nile perch.

"Perch?" Rauterberg giggled as he signaled the steward to refill
my glass.

I was more than halfway into a euphoric drunk when Anders patted the arm of his seat and beckoned me over. "I've been telling Leo how I don't mind a junket, but I wouldn't want to be along under false pretenses."

Roethe gave me a weak smile.

"No one's going to pressure me into a foreign investment that will sap our management strength," Anders said. "By the way, who bought the tickets?"

"I'm underwriting the trip, regardless of the outcome," Roethe said. He added that he would transfer the business expense only if, and when, Diamond J acquired African Ponderosa.

Anders picked his gums with a match and gave him a look that clearly meant "don't hold your breath," then turned toward the bar, where Sue, Kritchner, Rauterberg, and an *Argosy* magazine photographer were drinking faster and faster, their voices rising. He pointed at Rauterberg. "Never seen a banker like him before." He shook his head and began making biting jabs about booze and wasting money on a photojournalist who probably padded his expense account.

"If we're going to take advantage of this trip to promote Lake, Sport, and Travel Club, we need pictures and press," I said. "Bringing the *Argosy* man along was my idea. His specialty is perch portraits."

Sue laughed in the background.

Anders frowned and turned away to talk with Roethe about the struggle with Gulf & Western. "I'm going to enjoy that fight," I heard him say as I went back to the bar.

Our first stop, fifteen hours later, was Monrovia, Liberia. Because of the six-hour time change, it was early morning, but I felt no jet lag, no hangover as we all rushed into the transient section of the airport for our first look at Africa.

Roethe bought a round of local beer and raised his glass in a welcoming toast. He was wearing a rust-color safari suit festooned with club emblems. He was, in fact, the most exotic thing about the place: the airport was scrubbed colorless, and the locals spoke English and wore clothes we all saw every day at home.

Disappointed, I felt depressed as our plane took off, but as we flew east the sun stayed a steady twenty degrees above the horizon. Now it was bigger and hotter than I'd ever seen it before. Then, in Lagos, Nigeria, when Rauterberg and I tried to deplane during refueling, black soldiers carrying submachine guns shoved us back into the cabin and began to move up and down the aisles, taking a hard look at every passenger.

"They're searching for South Africans," Roethe explained, smiling when he saw the rest of us feel our first sense of adventure.

We met John Strohm, the editor of *National Wildlife* and *International Wildlife* magazines, and also one of the African Ponderosa stockholders, at the Nairobi airport. His wife and his attorney were with him.

A strange coincidence, I thought, carefully watching Roethe.

Roethe's reactions were normal: total command of the situation, wide smile, and happy voice. And the attorney said that he was representing Strohm and the other stockholders merely as a disinterested third party to give them a progress report.

That didn't make sense. I had a briefcase full of Roethe's data and correspondence, and they indicated that all of the stockholders had been informed of everything. The attorney was very cordial, but I could tell that he was observing and recording everything. I knew I was right when he was conspicuously absent during our introductory tour of Nairobi, even though Strohm had said it was his first trip to Africa.

But I was so excited by the opportunities for exotic shopping sprees, tours to the nearby game preserves, and our forthcoming departure to fish for marlin in the Indian Ocean that I almost overlooked the bizarre evidence indicating that Roethe had not told me everything about his businesses in Kenya.

First there was the matter of changing American money into Kenyan shillings. Prominent signs in the lobby of the new Stanley Hotel advised foreigners that all cash conversion must be made at government-controlled currency exchanges. The purchase of shillings on the black market was punishable by incarceration. The desk clerk implied worse. As soon as we got to our rooms, however, Roethe said, "I'll call one of my partners. He'll bring over Kenyan money, which you can buy for sixteen shillings to the dollar."

The posted rate of exchange was twelve to one.

The "partner," an Asian, told us, "I'll be most pleased to cash your checks, any amount."

Sue and I had already seen lots of goodies to buy, so I told her to hang on to our Traveler's Checks. "Personal check OK?" I asked Roethe.

"Certainly. That's what he wants. Just leave the payee space blank. He'll fill it in." Roethe advised everyone else to do the same thing. "Make the checks as big as you like."

After large packages of new bills were distributed, the Asian nodded to Roethe, who said, "Now it's time to look at tanzanite."

"What's that?" Sue asked.

"Blue gem stones from Tanzania. The scientific name is blue zoisite, very similar to diamonds. They sell for $1,000 a carat in New York. Look here." Roethe held up a stone that had to be three carats. "This is only $400."

"Isn't there a helluva duty on jewels?" Kritchner remarked, fingering the tanzanite.

Roethe and the Indian chuckled, and everyone in the room knew that they were about to explain the smuggling of tiny stones.

When Rauterberg asked what else was for sale, the Indian smiled, again deferring to his partner.

"Ivory," Roethe's voice rumbled. "Their company, our company, Elite Studios, sells photographic supplies, curios, and beautiful ivory. Tusks or carvings. Ivory's hard to get now, you know. Good investment. You'll see tomorrow—it's on the itinerary."

Sue smiled at me, and I realized that shopping was going to be almost as much fun as fishing. The fat wad of shillings in my pocket felt like a million dollars.

We met the Strohms for cocktails, and John told us, before Roethe arrived, that the reason the Asians, notorious sharpies, made such good offerings was because the government was squeezing them. The Asians, who controlled much of the country's commerce, were being persecuted by the native Africans. They were not allowed to take their money out of Kenya legally, so Roethe helped them find other means, such as personal checks (which were much easier to remove than currency) and exports to be paid for at their destination.

Strohm seemed talkative, so I changed the subject. "What's the real problem at African Ponderosa?"

He looked down at his drink, then straight into my eyes. "The original stockholders intended to invest in a game reserve, with a hunting lodge to be constructed." He sipped his drink, still watching me. "Not two hotels. Didn't you know?"

I shook my head.

"Roethe proceeded with the tremendously expanded project without telling the others about his ultimate plans. As a result, some stockholders unwittingly signed documents guaranteeing the payment of any construction costs exceeding the original estimates. And now the Asian contractor, who is hundreds of thousands over budget, is attempting to collect from them. African Ponderosa is broke. Whether that's due to dishonesty, mismanagement, or sloppy estimates no one knows. That's what our attorney is here to find out."

He watched as I made notes on my cocktail napkin, then continued, more slowly now. "There are other suspicious signs. Leo's managing partner, an interior decorator from Chicago, was very low on capital when he moved to Kenya, but now he supposedly owns a chain of Kentucky Fried Chicken restaurants in Nairobi. He's the one who broke our original construction contract with reliable builders and made the new one with Laxmanbhai, the Asian who's pushing for extra payments."

"And if Laxmanbhai doesn't get paid, I suppose he'll close down the job?" I asked.

Strohm nodded.

"And there will be no grand opening, and Hilton will refute the management contract, and CIIC will sue the shit out of everybody. Even you." I said.

Strohm, still nodding, said, "That's about right, unless, as Roethe told me, you can help."

I shook my head, half in jest and half in astonishment. Less than twelve hours after my arrival in Africa, I'd discovered that

Roethe had introduced us to black market money, gem stones and ivory, fried chicken, and heaven only knew what else. That didn't really bother me, but when I discovered that he was facing a shareholders' revolt, I decided I needed a local attorney.

But first I had to have another drink. Strohm, his wife, and Sue agreed. And so, by the time Anders arrived, I was sitting in the White Hunters Bar well into my fourth Cuba Libre, about to start pretending I was Robert Ruark. Anders smiled, switched to a straight face, and then gave in to the grin. He said, "I've quit worrying about having African Ponderosa shoved down my throat, because it doesn't look like anybody's going to do any business."

Strohm smiled.

The next morning I took early tea with the hotel manager, who said he'd also heard rumors about African Ponderosa and directed me to an "advocate." Just minutes after I had introduced myself to the advocate and was beginning to explain, he said, "I understand your problem."

"You do?"

"A crazy American dream!" he called it, and said he'd be delighted to represent me and investigate. His eyes twinkled with curiosity.

When I told Roethe about my serious doubts that African Ponderosa would survive as a business, least of all prove a profitable acquisition, he laughed. He kept laughing, not in a loud derisive way, but softly, intimately, like a close friend telling me how life played silly little jokes on everybody except us.

"Strohm and the other shareholders don't understand that CIIC arranged for the Chase Manhatten Bank to lend me an extra $300,000 to cover the current overruns," he said. "Don't worry about the grand opening. Some of the biggest people on three continents will be there: Kenyatta's personal representatives, the minister of tourism, the bank officers, Hilton's executives, foreign envoys, and," he laughed and slapped my shoulder, "the men from Lake, Sport, and Travel." Roethe cocked his head and pulled at his ear. "You know, I think we should begin calling our company 'Recreation International.'"

Next day everyone except Roethe hopped an East African Airways flight to Mombasa, where chauffeurs with tribal tattoos waited to drive us up the coast. Our final destination, the M'Narani Club, was a British colonial remnant sitting atop 500-foot cliffs facing the Indian Ocean. The buildings and grounds were old, blotched light and dark by alternating sun and rain. But like everything else along the Kenya Coast—the surf that crashed against the shimmering rock cliffs and seemed to leap higher than I'd ever seen surf before; the silver line marking the horizon and making a border with the Near East, where I could see the faint outlines of sailing dhows; even the dry green leaves forming a backdrop to the club compound—the place radiated an eerie excitement.

Our rooms had conical thatched ceilings. The beds were mosquito-netted. Servants were everywhere, standing behind each chair in the dining pavilion and at every elbow in the bar. It was impossible to hold an empty glass for more than the quick moment it took a waiter to replace it: "If you please, bwana."

"This is the real Africa," said Rauterberg, loosening a third button on the front of his sweat-darkened shirt, baring more skin to the faint breeze climbing over the cliffs from the ocean.

The M'Narani Club's managing director had been waiting quietly nearby for some time. He finally coughed discreetly and entered the edge of our circle, handing me a radiogram. "It says that the charter flight carrying your party to the dedication of African Ponderosa Lodges will be here three days hence."

I saw him step back, hesitant, waiting for a response.

"Please join us and let my husband tell you about our stateside club," said Sue.

"A pleasure." He signaled for a drink and sat opposite me, chin thrust forward in formal attention.

"Kenya seems to offer something for almost everybody," I began, explaining my plans to add the best examples to Lake, Sport's list of affiliates.

"Interesting." He began to be a buyer, relaxing, leaning back into his chair.

The conversation continued through dinner and resumed at

breakfast. Except when I was fishing, I spent most of my time outlining my concepts for the managing director, whose regular response became, "Astounding," and later, "I like it. I like it very much."

On the last morning he sent his assistant to wake me with an invitation to sunrise tea.

"Just the two of us," said the director, pulling back my chair.

I watched the Indian Ocean open like a huge sleepy eye, red, then slate-gray, then twinkling blue. And my teacup was cold before he spoke again.

"You'll see many more mornings here." He smiled and handed me an envelope.

Inside was a letter approving reciprocal memberships. "Great."

"There's something more, now that we have some light." He led me onto the veranda, where a freshly carved plaque had added my name to the club's record board. "Your striped marlin is the heaviest so far. You're the champion. That should impress your visiting members."

The *Argosy* man took pictures while the director shook my hand.

"Utterly astounding," he said.

"Total bullshit," said Anders during our flight to the grand opening.

He was referring once again to my new and bigger plans to expand into Kenya—"African Ponderosa or any reasonable substitute," I said, emphasizing that it was the country, not the specific projects, that excited me.

"It's his honeymoon," said Rauterberg. "Don't expect him to talk sense."

Anders ignored him and leaned forward to talk into my ear. "Five days ago in Nairobi you told me Leo's African businesses were a kettle of worms. What really made you change your mind?" His voice was very low, probing and suspicious.

I turned to reply and saw him chewing at the back of his hand. Then I felt Sue's eyes on us and knew they'd be worrying too.

Was Anders losing faith?

Maybe I'd made a big mistake. Perhaps the trip had scared

Anders about all of Diamond J. "But, damnit," I told myself, struggling for confidence, "the risk was inevitable anyway, and the odds had to favor me."

What was I worrying about? No way could I lose, even if Roethe turned out to be a cheat and a thief. Then every new problem would be blamed on him while I retreated comfortably inside the old, safe framework of Diamond J.

The important question—nearly overlooked—was, what advantages did African Ponderosa offer me? I didn't need any more headaches from businesses already in trouble unless they contributed substantially to my power or my personal image.

"Well, hell," I said aloud, then thought, the ultimate decision was obvious long ago. The lodges are great bait for raising money. They're exciting, and they'll help enthuse bankers, hotel chains, and the investing public.

I looked out at the bushy, rock-strewn wilderness zipping under the plane just as the pilot shouted above the engine noise: "Your lodge." He banked the plane, circling four stories of stone and steel that might have been imported from any American gold coast.

"That's Taita Hills?" Kritchner sounded amazed.

The plane leveled. "And just ahead is Salt Lick Lodge, an exact replica of a native village on stilts to protect it from the animals," the pilot said, banking into another circle.

"Hard to believe." Anders's voice had lost its edge.

"I wonder how many cheering tribesmen Roethe's trotting out to welcome us." Rauterberg's question sounded very serious.

"About $20,000 worth, all bed patients," Kritchner yelled back, then said quietly to Anders, "Remind me to look for that hospital we're allegedly building."

We settled onto a new airfield with assorted light planes clustered at one end. Coveys of shouting children rushed toward us and Sue gasped, fearful that the propellers would hit them. But as soon as they saw our faces behind the windows, they stood to respectful attention.

"About sixty of them," Sue giggled, watching Rauterberg's disappointed frown.

Leo Roethe met our van at the mammoth raw stone entry to the

Taita Hills Lodge. He was wearing a blue business suit with the ever present Shikar–Safari Club emblem on its jacket pocket, but he looked more like a rampaging tribesman as he charged through the milling crowd of workmen and red-coated retainers to throw open the door personally.

"My trucker has arrived," he bellowed, shaking Anders's hand and pulling him out of the van.

A wide canopy was being erected in front of the hotel, while television camera crews were moving their equipment into position before a banner-draped rostrum beneath it. Long rows of chairs, twenty deep, had been set up on either side.

A procession of waiters brought us coconut shells filled with fruit and what tasted like a combination of Scotch and rum and Coke.

"Sweet and musty," said Sue.

"That's Stone's style. He hates the taste of good whiskey so he's always bastardizing booze," Kritchner spat in my direction.

Roethe laughed. "Wait until you try the Masai drink, blood and milk." He shepherded us into the lobby, a madhouse. Dignitaries were shouting for room assignments while clerks scurried back and forth between a clattering telex and a radio transmitter squawking the arrival of another plane load of VIPs. Native music played somewhere in the background, the beat sometimes keeping cadence to clanging hammers as workmen hurried to finish their jobs. Roethe paused every few steps to examine papers thrust at him by men who must have been the resident junior executives. They all wore suits like the boss. Looking over Roethe's shoulder, I saw him initial forms that I guessed were payroll vouchers and purchase orders. And I marveled at his ability to project boundless enthusiasm while silently struggling to shove endless problems out of sight.

Soon we were swept outside again and seated in the first row of chairs beneath the canopy. I looked across the line. Anders was near the end, beside a man with nervous eyes and sweat beginning to stain his collar.

"He's a Chase International vice-president," Rauterberg whispered.

Our *Argosy* man knelt among the other photographers in front of the podium as the formal dedication ceremony began. The first speaker called it "The country's first step into the world of modern tourism."

The Cabinet Minister of Tourism and Wildlife talked next, finally introducing Roethe. The applause was long but polite, tapering to Rauterberg's last clap, as the big American began.

"Jambo." He said the Swahili word for hello and goodbye, friendly fire in his eyes.

"Jambo," shouted the crowd.

During the rest of his speech, which was a slightly exaggerated version of the usual pep talk, I studied the faces around me. The expressions were no different from those found in church on Sunday.

I ganced toward Anders. He was almost smiling. Anders never actually smiled; he just sort of screwed up the crow's-feet around his eyes to show when his humor was good. Today the little lines deepened and spread as we heard Roethe leading into his finale.

I looked back to the podium as Roethe waved his hands, palms up, gold brighter than ever before, and said, "This is only the beginning."

The applause was overwhelming now; it seemed to echo far into the Taita hills—almost as if the 50,000 tribesmen were really cheering.

11
March 1973

ASSETS—$1,480,000.00
LIABILITIES—$185,250.00
PERSONAL GUARANTEES—$6,000,000.00

Anders shook his head slowly and moved his lips silently, as if he knew there was no stopping us. He tried anyway.

"Absentee ownership scares the hell out of me," he said, looking first at Roethe and then back to me. His eyes were bloodshot.

The Nairobi Hilton's air conditioning didn't seem to work, or at least not sufficiently to handle the smoke from my lone cigarette. There'd been no time to talk serious business during our three days in the Taita hills. There had been too many receptions and tours, petty public relations and politics, and probably my own reluctance to face a showdown with Anders.

"But now," I said, "we're going to stay here until we make a decision."

"No way. We're just raking garbage." Kritchner walked to the window to check to see if it was open all the way.

Anders continued. "We're half the world away from home, in a country where the business methods, the morality, are totally foreign. The Asians"—he pointed at Roethe—"are stealing you blind."

"They tried, but we're going to beat them in the courts. And you're emphasizing just one case." Roethe stood up. "You heard

231

Jack Shako, the minister of tourism, telling everybody his good offices are always at our disposal."

"He's an African."

"Then consider my partners in the Elite Studios—completely honest. And besides," Roethe turned toward me, "John says he enjoys matching wits with them."

Rauterberg laughed. "Not with his own money."

I stared him down, ready to ask whose side he was on.

"I was just kidding."

"All we have to do is infuse another half-million to clear up odds and ends, show good faith to Hilton International. Then they'll run everything for us," said Roethe.

Anders rubbed his eyes. "Granted. But I'm still afraid of the politics here. The Mau Maus can reclaim anyone's land."

"Jomo Kenyatta is a personal friend of mine," Roethe shouted. "He sent his personal representative to the dedication, and," he lowered his voice and paused, obviously for effect, "next month I'm making Kenyatta the first inductee into the International Conservation Hall of Fame."

Anders cocked his head, still rubbing his eyes, which had begun to water.

"It's a sure winner," Roethe told him.

"He's right, Art." My voice was loud, enthusiastic, stronger than I remembered it. Africa still excited me more than any place I'd encountered previously. "And because it excites me," I rationalized to the rest, "it's got to excite many others. Any part of Kenya has got to be a valuable addition to Diamond J . . . Recreation International."

"Why don't you just agree to try . . . further consideration?" said John Strohm, who had been standing inconspicuously near the door. Now he stepped forward, head bobbing, eyes the brightest in the room. "I'm a stockholder, and I know there is a problem, so I'm going to stay out of the decision. Give everybody time to think. Keep working." He smiled. "You'll find the right answer."

"Right." Anders started for the door, slapping Strohm's shoulder as he passed. Then he spun around and told me, "Better call your office. Spend twenty bucks to find out if we're still in business in the States."

The telephone connection with Madison was fine, even with Higbie and Quarton on separate extensions, both talking at once.

They laughed when I turned Rosenheimer's favorite phrase into a question.

"No problems?"

"Absolutely none," said Quarton.

Higbie said that the only messages of note were from **O'Connor**. "He wants to see you about Janeff, but don't worry. He sounded happy when he told me."

"Is Anders having a *good* time?" Quarton asked, using our word code.

"Good enough." I laughed, thinking of funny stories I could tell them.

Then Higbie shocked me back to business. "Your trip to Germany the day after tomorrow looks really important. Our PR man says the Bosch Corporation is turning out en masse to welcome you to Stuttgart. Even the mayor's supposed to meet your plane."

I started a quick mental review of my schedule.

"You didn't forget?"

"I'll handle it," I told Higbie. And, to myself, "Somehow."

I *had* forgotten. On the same day I had scheduled a meeting with the African Ponderosa Limited creditors and bankers. Roethe was right. International finance was heady and hairy at the same time, and I loved matching wits with the African advocates and Asian businessmen.

My adversaries were absolutely amoral by American standards. Contracts by handshake were a joke, and formal documents were written with built-in loopholes. Negotiations with Laxmanbhai concerned the degree of unauthorized and illegal (by my standards) overcharges to be allowed for the work at African Ponderosa. I told my advocate and the representatives from CIIC that my style was different. "A man's word, his bond, is paramount." But what I really wanted them to know was that, because of me, Diamond J had the ability to bail out African Ponderosa.

During meetings with Roethe and CIIC, and particularly at a second meeting with Jack Shako, I had begun to see that my charisma was really envisioned by other financiers and promoters as an ability to sell myself as a promotional tool and thereby to produce dollars for investments. It was clear for the first time: I was the "money machine" Rosenheimer talked about.

Well, if it really works, use it, I thought. The Diamond J concepts—Roethe now habitually referred to them as Recreation International—would never fail to benefit from my reputed ability to raise money.

I sent Rauterberg to Stuttgart as my emissary, with the *Argosy* man to back him up, and I went fishing.

Our chartered twin Beechcraft, flightplanned for the southern Sahara, was taxiing for takeoff before Anders let me know that he didn't really approve of the junket.

"Who's paying for this?" he shouted from the back seat.

"Leo," I said.

The pilot announced: "Lake Rudolf lies in the Old Nile riverbed, one of the most isolated places in East Africa, and the best spot to catch 200-pound Nile perch."

I grinned.

Anders grunted. "This is a business trip?" Then he broke into laughter.

I winked at my reflection in the windshield and tuned him out. I was fascinated by the jungle fading beneath us—a subtle yet stark change from gentle greens to coarse browns—the approaches to the Sahara, endless variations of sand and stone. The pilot dove, buzzing the fringes of a village. No vegetation, just fragments of huts and the thin shadows of tribesmen popping from a shimmering haze.

I twisted for a second look.

"Turkana. The wildest nomads in Kenya," said the pilot.

"Desolate country. How come the nomads don't move on?"

"Wait until our destination, Ellye Springs. Did you chaps know that Lake Rudolf has over 500 miles of shoreline and only two settlements? There was a third until a fisherman was speared by the natives. Mind you, now, don't photograph the Turkanas. They don't like it. They think the lens eats their spirits."

I saw a shoreline ahead, and we dipped even lower over Lake Rudolf. The water was a chalky blue.

"Not fit to drink—high soda content," said the pilot, continuing his warnings.

Black treetrunks dotted the shoreline, but there was nothing but sand inland.

"No green trees at the oasis?" I said, as the fishing camp blurred below the plane.

A minute later we were taxiing across the desert, raising a miniature sandstorm until we stopped in front of a sun-scarred hut with a crude sign that made everyone laugh: ELLYE SPRINGS INTERNATIONAL AIRPORT, CUSTOMS AND IMMIGRATION. The place was deserted.

"Careful, everybody. The metal skin of the airplane will burn you," said the pilot, anxiously watching the dunes ahead.

The first breath outside scorched my nostrils. The sky was too bright to look at, and it was also painful to look down at the reflecting sand, so I squinted and finally saw a Land-Rover bouncing toward us.

Two natives speaking a flat dialect, not musical like Swahili, loaded our gear. Their skin was opaque black and their powerful movements gave only a hint of motion, as if energy were almost as precious as water.

The overseer, wearing a sidearm, waited motionless at the edge of our oasis camp.

"The only white man living near the lake," whispered the pilot.

I wondered if that explained the man's cold eyes, which never stopped moving, and his curt nod in place of a greeting. He led us to a cinder-block cabin, grunting as he worked the heavy brass bolt on the door. Inside, it was dark, but no cooler, yet I shivered when I saw that thick iron bars made black stripes on the sky. A sensation of danger seemed to stroke my body, almost sensually. I told Sue, and myself, "This is the farthest we've ever come from a world we know we can control." Strange vibes—an orgasm of emotion, in which my mind sailed into some strange atmosphere stronger than a drug, until I almost began to enjoy my sensation of fear.

The next morning, against the overseer's advice, Sue and I ordered a Turkana guide to sail us the forty miles across the lake to the Somaliland shore. There was no sign of human life. I stared at the glowing rocks and felt their heat penetrating my eyeballs. "We couldn't live half a day out there," I said. "It's crazy, crossing a lake where desert winds could raise six-foot waves in an instant, in a sixteen-foot boat with a native who speaks a language we've never heard before."

"It's the first time we've really been alone." Sue hugged me, and as our perspiring bodies clung together, she whispered again, "Alone."

We fished for the huge perch that seemed to steam the surface of the lake as they fought; watched the crocodiles that stared back from the shoreline; and saw a hippo pop up, wiggle his stubby ears, and snort before he disappeared again.

"I wonder if he's walking toward us under water?"

I took Sue's hand. "I think we've found our private place."

And then, with no warning, I was angry. Much as I wanted the moment to continue, I was beginning to worry. "I can't afford to forget Diamond J." Suddenly I was anxious to return to Nairobi, to get back to Madison.

Sue began to share my mood on the flight home. She was worried about my investors ("Do you really know who you can trust?"), and about money, and about buying Roethe's companies ("When are you going to stop expanding?"). Her questions were pleas.

And so were my answers. "Just give me time."

O'Connor was waiting for me in Madison. Quarton said he'd been roaming the offices much of the time I was gone. He hadn't fooled anyone with his casual drop-bys; O'Connor had been conducting a methodical inspection. The office tempo could have told him something, and most of his information came from his unique ability to read upside down, but one thing he couldn't do was read through opaque folders. Quarton chuckled when he told me how irritated O'Connor had become when he'd seen important papers being slid into folders every time he approached a desk.

I moved slowly through the outer offices, trailing anecdotes about my trip; I left zebra-skin cigarette cases on all the desks. As I approached my office, O'Connor appeared and motioned me inside.

"Finish the bullshit later," he said, closing the door. Then, instead of his usual hard-boiled expression, he forced a wide grin, and, without preliminaries, asked, "Are you ready, willing, and able to borrow the rest of my first million dollars?"

I was stunned. I began unpacking my briefcase; I didn't have an answer ready. There was a time when bankers looked for reasons *not* to make a loan. Now O'Connor was rushing me to give him any reason to lend Diamond J nearly one-fourth of the assets of his bank.

"I've found some big deposits to buy," he continued. "County money. And I need income from high-rate loans to make the deal viable."

"Sure, I can use it," I finally said. I explained my plans to acquire African Ponderosa.

O'Connor shared Anders's opinion of Kenya. "Why not examine Agricola Itzapan first? I've got a close friend who was an assistant ambassador to Honduras. He'll help you. I want him on your payroll anyway—to watch my investments."

"We'll try both. A million dollars goes a long way. OK?"

"OK." O'Connor smiled. "Rosenheimer hit me up to buy his nightclub loan while you were gone," he said. "I sent him someplace else. He's got some stupid deals." O'Connor shook his head, then looked away. "But I like his proposition to use Janeff to bail out Roethe."

My angry thoughts about Rosenheimer poaching on my money sources turned to astonishment. "He must have pitched Roethe to you at the right time," I said. "Just a month ago you wanted me to move Roethe's loans because they were red flags as far as the bearish banking authorities were concerned."

O'Connor watched me for a long time, and then, apparently convinced that I hadn't been totally overwhelmed by his change of heart, explained. "You can raise money for Roethe without involving Roethe's name and reputation. Use your own shareholders, the old standbys and the new faces clamoring to be part of Diamond J, to borrow the money for him. Pick up Roethe's collateral and magnify the security by making him sign a wraparound guarantee."

I took a deep breath, wondering what was next.

"Janeff and my bank will make a bundle on the discounts," he reminded me. "Ten percent each on top of the interest."

I nodded, still thinking. If I used up my line of credit on Roethe, the other Diamond J companies would suffer.

"I know it'll take two, maybe more, million." O'Connor was reading my mind again. "That's why I want to bring in another man to help you put Janeff's profits to work. I told you about him. The best lease man in the country."

Now I understood. O'Connor's friend, George Weast, had made a nondescript East Coast lease and loan company public in less than two years, and had made a fortune by selling off his stock over-the-counter. O'Connor figured to do the same with Janeff. I wondered how long it would be before they would make me a proposition to buy control of everything.

Higbie came in as O'Connor left. He too closed the door. "You were a damn fool to send Rauterberg on the grand tour of Bosch. They wanted to see you. Now we've got a serious problem, the Bosch management's loss of face."

"Send them honorary memberships, mementos of the Super Race, and invite them to Milwaukee next year at our expense," I said in a voice that told him I didn't want to be bothered.

All of a sudden Higbie's face was a blur. Jet lag, I thought, or my fast, forced readjustment to the world of Wisconsin banking. I shook my head and poured a cup of coffee, sipping slowly as I assessed the situation.

Rosenheimer had been elected president and director of Janeff Credit Corporation in absentia. Some of the older stockholders had hesitated to vote for a man they'd never even met, but they had seemed satisfied after I had made my pitch for him. Now there was no way I could dump him without embarrassing myself.

"Dig in some more," I directed Higbie. "Verify what you've got. And listen, I'm damn sorry about the Bosch fuck-up."

Rosenheimer showed up a week later, bragging that he'd found a new way to make a killing. "I've got a friend who will sell us or get us half a million dollars' worth of siding paper each month. We'll get an extra discount, and can write insurance on it too, and . . . and, keep all the commissions. Fantastic deal." He paused to catch his breath.

"No way," I said. One of the first things I'd learned as a loan company trainee was that the siding business is the highest-risk, poorest-quality financing on the market. I kept shaking my head. "Your friend hasn't any place else to sell his paper. That's no deal."

"Yes it is," Rosenheimer insisted. "Let's meet my friend for a drink and discuss the business firsthand."

Higbie came along, and I saw his brows furrow when Rosenheimer introduced us to Colonel Beauregard Nechy, also known as Henry. Nechy laughed a lot, mostly at his own jokes, and his voice was condescending. It was a case of instant mutual dislike.

After that night, which ended a few minutes later when Higbie and I left without saying good-bye, Rosenheimer stopped going to the Janeff office.

"You've got to have management," said Sommers. He had suddenly reappeared to remind me that he still owned some stock in the company. "I'm moving back to protect my investment."

"Not necessary," I told him. "I already have new management." I couldn't wait for Rosenheimer to resign, as Rauterberg had promised he would "once Titan can support him."

"If he doesn't leave of his own accord, I'll fire him," I told O'Connor. "I'm ready for your man now. Fast, before Sommers retrenches."

The break with Rosenheimer didn't seem to bother anyone else.

"As a matter of fact, it's only a short separation." I said to Quarton as we watched R. and R. coming across the Diamond J parking lot, O'Connor right behind them. Inside, the three bankers surrounded my desk, and one at a time said, "What are you waiting for?"

I knew they were referring to my delay in using the multi-million-dollar line of credit. And I was worried. I hadn't used it because I knew that during loan processing someone was bound to discover that the old problem of negative cash flow had never been solved. My companies were really in no better shape than Roethe's.

Thunderhead had failed to meet its profit projections for the ski season just past. High interest rates were slowing Shadco's land sales. The condominium construction was still falling farther behind schedule as building loan interest ate into our estimated profits from the sale of finished units. The Cowdrey store, Diamond J Ranch, and Lone Tree were all suffering from a recent drought of Lake, Sport members traveling west in the winter.

As a matter of fact, the club just wasn't recruiting the hordes of new members I'd predicted. Sure, after several screaming harangues followed by sweet talk and backpatting, I'd been able to satisfy myself that everything was moving ahead again. But still, it would be another year before all my companies got out of the red. O'Connor's multimillion-dollar loans would keep them solvent, but I knew he'd bug me about the negative cash flow. He'd insist that I improve my balance sheets by selling more stock. And soon I wouldn't be able to offer any more stock without the expense and delay of registering a public stock issue with the state securities commission or the federal SEC. Otherwise I'd be breaking the law, exceeding the "Blue Sky" limits of fifteen stockholders per company in Wisconsin.

There had to be another way, but right now my head was beginning to ache, and I could feel the bankers' hard eyes watching for my answer.

"I'll be ready to use the million-dollar line any day," I promised. I was relieved when they nodded and began to file out.

Then I packed two briefcases with financial projections, appraisals, and every scrap of data on Roethe's companies, and left for Denver. I hoped that if I isolated myself in the penthouse I'd be able to discover the right way to proceed.

The first night I couldn't get started. I sorted my papers on top of the grand piano. But soon I realized that I was just shuffling folders from one side to the other. I gave up and climbed the back stairs to the Playboy Club.

I drank a lot that night, but the Cuba Libres had no effect. It was impossible to hide from the problem. I was glad I was alone— no need for anyone to see me running my finger endlessly around the rim of my glass, head down and jaw hanging loose, stumped for an answer.

Sale of assets? I believed that the immediate sale of Thunderhead would net a million, and Rauterberg said we could probably clear a quarter-million on Janeff. But if I moved in that direction, I'd severely erode my power base in Colorado and throw away the key to my borrowing power in Wisconsin. I could merge with a larger, stronger entity that had money in the bank and earned regular profits. Maybe?

As I finished my drink, the idea hit me—Metcalf Farms. The Hawaiian venture had debts instead of bank balances, but it also had pro forma statements promising a profit in 1973, it was a public corporation, and it was available. And both O'Connor and Anders had said it looked good.

"Lucky I'm alone during my moments of insecurity," I thought. Everyone else would keep the faith as long as they believed I could, and would, find a way. "And maybe I have." I nodded to myself. Metcalf Farms was, as I knew Roethe would say, "a sure winner."

As first light reflected off the mountains, I called United Airlines and bullied a seat on the first flight back to Wisconsin.

Metcalf flew in from Hawaii two days later, and the deal was closed in my office within four hours.

"Just in time for a celebration," said The Digest, pointing to my perpetual clock.

"Ten minutes until cocktail hour," I told him, thinking the man was beginning to depend too much on booze. "The rest of us want to make sure Mr. Metcalf hasn't slipped one by on us." I winked at the farmer, whose leathery face was beginning to lose some of its frantic creases.

Lake, Sport, and Travel was agreeing to pay a quarter of a million dollars for 40 percent of Metcalf Farms–Hawaii common stock. This would give me complete control as long as I was teamed up with Metcalf and Roethe, who owned an equivalent amount between them. I would also have the right to select two members of the five-man board of directors. Roethe and Metcalf would nominate two more. And a fifth director, ostensibly independent, would be chosen from my list of candidates. We later agreed that I would name the chairman of the board and the corporate secretary, and approve all major disbursements through the Madison office. Since it was a public corporation, all such changes had to be disseminated via proxies to the stockholders, and ratified at the annual meeting in June.

"Too slow," I told my associates as they toasted the transaction, "but an unavoidable requirement, now that we're under the auspices of the SEC."

Metcalf motioned me aside. "Well, this is great, but . . . well, even though it's not official yet, I've got to have operating funds immediately if you expect me to plant a current crop."

"That's the whole idea," I said. "Sow it, harvest it, sell it, and send me money."

"Right," shouted The Digest, who'd been standing behind me.

Toussaint, the CPA, was right behind him.

I whipped my head back, signaling them to move closer. "Give Metcalf whatever temporary financial relief he needs, but make damn sure every penny goes into the ground."

Then, with an exciting background of enthusiastic Brain Trusters' voices, I began telephoning my stockholders for approval of the acquisition.

The doctors said, "Fine."

The rest fell into line, including Anders, who said, "You having a party already? Might as well. Metcalf is a much happier investment than APL."

As soon as Roethe heard the news he told me it was time to change the corporate image. "Beginning with the Diamond J name. Too personal."

So we followed his example and started saying "Recreation International." I telephoned Jack Rash to tell him about my progress.

"Be careful," he said. "Be very careful."

I knew he was thinking of my best interests, but I wanted him to stop sounding so pessimistic. I started to tell Rash about "eating an elephant," but stopped myself when I realized that he was not pessimistic, just conservative. That started me thinking about my entire organization. I knew the corporate structure was infantile, a bunch of loosely connected companies with uncharted management. At this point the Brain Trust concept was really formless, nothing I could put on paper.

Maybe, I thought, I've kept it that way to be sure that everything depended on me.

If so, I was being childish. Size alone dictated formal organization and the addition of heavyweights to my staff.

I tried to tell Roethe the next time he came to see me about the need to reorganize Recreational International's management.

"I've got more important matters to discuss," he said. "The First Annual Conservation Hall of Fame Awards, sponsored by the African First Shotters, are being presented next week at a gala dinner in New York."

"Who are the First Shotters?"

"I told you in Africa. A hunting group, conservation-oriented." Roethe grinned as he handed me a brochure with titles embossed in gold. "The recipients will be Jomo Kenyatta, the Grand Old Man of Kenya, Prince Bernhard of the Netherlands, Governor John Connally, General Jimmy Doolittle of World War II Tokyo raid fame, and William Holden." Roethe puffed his cheeks and pointed to the impressive array of names. "I'm presenting the Kenyatta award, and our man Lovell will do the honors for William Holden."

"And you want me there?"

"It's important. I reserved a table in your name. Now I need a check for $1,000. Anders and anyone else you select can join us. It will be an outstanding opportunity to promote Lake, Sport, and Travel," he said, and then winced. "We should do something about that name too. It sounds plebeian."

"How about 'Compass'?" I said. I'd been thinking about changing to the "Compass Club" for some time.

"Great," said Roethe. Then he moved quickly on to the next subject, his war with Gulf & Western. "Charles Bludhorn, president of the conglomerate, is notorious for his raids on independents. And now he's after Weatherby–Nasco."

It sounded as if Roethe, believe it or not, was in over his head. "How did you get involved in the first place?"

"As I told you and Anders, Gulf & Western owned Amron. I wanted it. Munitions is a good business, worldwide today. So I traded them stock. A broker friend of mine, the brother of a man who had arranged some of the Metcalf Farms financing, arranged everything—even a loan from Gulf & Western to Weatherby–Nasco."

I asked him who the brothers were and what Metcalf financing he was talking about. Roethe ignored my questions.

"The only thing that's saving me is the acquisition agreement that forbids Gulf & Western from buying up more stock. But they have two men on my board of directors who are screaming about the $340,000 I owe Weatherby–Nasco as a result of my generosity when I underwrote the Stone Bridge Press losses." Roethe paused. "I underwrote the advances made to the now defunct affiliate because they exceeded the amount anticipated by my board of directors."

I knew that "anticipated" meant "authorized," and that the losses must have resulted from Roethe's exceeding his authority. So Gulf & Western did have a club over his head.

"I have to pay off the debt," he admitted. "And I have to clean up my loans with the banks, especially the million-dollar judgment the Midland National Bank didn't have to take. Gulf & Western's using that against me too."

I stood up to pace and think.

Roethe moved toward me as if he was going to shove me back into my chair. "Understand, the judgment is a big mistake. I provided two good cosigners in lieu of making a principal reduction when the loan came due."

When he told me that one of the cosigners was Walter Koziel, Rosenheimer's partner in the highly leveraged Steamboat Springs land deals, I wondered just how many times the man had been used by Roethe and Rosenheimer.

"How did the million-dollar loan originate?" I asked, hoping to receive an explanation of the entire transaction.

All Roethe told me was that he'd arranged to merge Weatherby–Nasco with a Milwaukee department store chain, and had had to bite the bullet himself when the other directors turned down the deal just before the company went under. It took all my self-control to keep from calling Roethe an idiot. "No one should stick his neck out that far."

Just like O'Connor, and sometimes R. and R., Roethe seemed to read my mind. "I've learned my lesson. Now I want you and Anders and Kritchner to take my power of attorney and straighten out my affairs."

I sat down again, astonished by Roethe's offer of a power of attorney. Why total control so suddenly? I wondered, and I took

my turn reading his mind. A lot of money was needed—millions.
Roethe was in a tough spot.

"I can repay your advances and all my other debts within five
months."

"How?" His answer had better be good, I thought.

Roethe cocked his head, differently from the way he did when
he was about to bullshit me. His eyes narrowed and he laid his
hands on my desk. "This has to remain top secret," he said softly.
"I'm getting a consolidation loan from a pension fund."

"What fund?"

"I can't tell you now. But it's all set." Roethe trapped my next
question when he said, "The only thing that will queer my deal
is disclosure of the money source."

I guessed that the source was the Teamsters Union. I wondered
if the unexpected invitation to Dorfman's Jack-O-Lantern Lodge
last winter was tied into Roethe's strategy.

"How much can you handle now?" he asked, meaning, I was
sure, "How much money will you borrow from O'Connor and
relend to Leo Roethe?"

"Not over a million," I told him. Something had to be reserved
for my companies. I knew Turnbull was going to ask for at least
$200,000 soon, because the Thunderhead condominiums were still
behind schedule, and the Cave Inn was out of business; LTV was
reclaiming the leased land it sat upon.

"I have to have more," Roethe demanded. Then he suggested,
"Why don't you consult with Anders?"

The three of us talked about another million in New York, during the International Conservation Hall of Fame festivities.

Anders said he had an idea for raising money to help Roethe.
"I'll check it out in Philadelphia."—nothing more, but that seemed
to satisfy Roethe, who then introduced us to General Jimmy
Doolittle, William Holden, and General Joe Foss. "They should
all join our club," he said.

None of them seemed to know which club he meant, so I
explained, and I was elated when they all agreed that Compass
sounded great.

"They should all be on the Compass Advisory Board," Roethe
said next.

"Sounds interesting." Foss nodded to me.

I nodded back, starting to smile. Compass didn't have any such board yet, but I'd damn sure create one—*now*. I raised my Cuba Libre in a silent toast to Roethe's quick thinking. Holden, winking, parroted my motion with his bottle of Heineken beer.

After the formal dinner, Sue and I attended a private party in Roethe's suite. While I continued to describe the Compass and Recreation International concepts to Foss and a new listener, John Connally, Sue talked Africa with Holden. I suppressed a grin. She was telling him how the African Ponderosa Lodges were going to take all the business away from his Mount Kenya Safari Club. Governor Connally, like the other men in my group, seemed surprised that my innovative ideas for outdoor recreation had originated in the Midwest.

"Why not?" I said. "That's Roethe country."

"Hear, hear," someone shouted from across the room.

I met General Foss for breakfast the next morning. He listened carefully, definitely interested in our association, but said he wanted more details, in writing, before he'd lend his name and reputation.

Foss's remarks confirmed my decision to organize and record my concepts, and I began charting the chain of command on the flight back to Wisconsin. There was an obvious hole in my executive format. I needed another strong leader. My Storm Trooper was a benevolent dictator who tended to hire stray dogs, and would rather feed than fire them.

"They're part of his retinue, along with the several camp followers he shares among his subordinates." I was thinking out loud, hoping Sue would come up with something.

She put her magazine away and lit a cigarette before she said, "I think he's afraid of the unaccustomed power and prestige."

"That makes sense. And he lacks the sophistication required to move in my newly developing, internationally oriented circles. The rest of my men are good troops, but no more. Even Quarton —he'll never deviate from his decision to keep out of top management."

"You need a qualified second-in-command." Sue was emphatic, eyes flashing.

I asked Roethe to help me find the right man. He already had someone in mind.

"Rick Murray's about your age. He was a vice-president of Weatherby–Nasco, resigned to run for public office, lost, and was appointed director of the SBA (Small Business Administration) in Wisconsin. Now," Roethe smiled, "he's looking for a new challenge."

Murray turned me down at lunch the next day. "Your proposition's the second-best idea I ever heard—almost as good as my plan to buy the bank at Fort Atkinson, near Madison, and the land surrounding it." He laid down his fork and leaned toward me. "I'm going to build an honest-to-goodness fort in Fort Atkinson, a shopping wheel with an American frontier motif, my bank at the hub."

"I guess I'm a little late," I said, impressed with Murray's imagination and intensity, and more than a little annoyed that he wasn't available. My mood changed when he told me how he could help anyway.

"My bank will lend you money. And don't worry. Leo's the greatest promoter I know. He'll find the right man for you— lucky man; I don't see how your companies can miss."

Coming from the chief of the Wisconsin SBA, that was quite a compliment, I thought. Murray reminded me to "get in touch as soon as I move into my bank."

I was surprised to find Roethe waiting for me back in the office. He scowled when I told him, "Murray's out," but quickly brightened when I explained the bank venture.

"I knew he was working on that, but never thought he'd put it together," Roethe said. "Great. He'll be a bigger help in a bank than he was at the SBA." He walked to the window and looked at the string of laughing employees returning from lunch. For a minute his mind seemed to wander far away. Then he snapped around and told me, "I'll have another good candidate in a day or two. Now let's talk about Honduras and Agricola Itzapan."

I shrugged and slouched into a comfortable chair, and I might have passed up the tropical hardwoods business if Kritchner hadn't arrived and overwhelmed me with his enthusiasm.

"This thing can make millions the first year," he said, tapping the thick folio of research and development data he was carrying. He handed me a folder from it. The guts were a report by the Forest Products Laboratory, with addenda from the U.S. Department of Agriculture and the University of Wisconsin. "Now look at the feasibility study." Kritchner slapped another folder into my hand.

"Better read it," said Roethe.

The introduction claimed that there were a quarter of a million acres available for cutting, mostly virgin timberland with ten marketable species. "All in great demand." Roethe was reading over my shoulder. "See where it says that Evans Products—they're a big outfit—wants everything we can harvest."

"All the major U.S. lumber companies are vying for Mahogany and Santa Maria." Kritchner sat down in the closest chair and added that Agricola Itzapan was unquestionably the best of Roethe's offerings. He held up a pro forma financial statement showing that the operation could be in the black six weeks after it began, and would then start to turn a $60,000 a month profit. "Cash flow—that's what we need." I studied the rest of the material and discovered that Roethe was tied into the Honduran president's brother-in-law, who was a sort of silent partner.

"How can we lose?"

The Digest rushed in. He reported to Kritchner: "We can hire the best production engineer in this hemisphere, one of just a handful of men who know the secret of profitably harvesting hardwoods in the jungle. As you told me earlier, doctor, everything is ready. Honduran attorneys are standing by, Price Waterhouse will handle the accounting, and General Oswaldo Lopez's government is anxious to issue long-term cutting permits with very reasonable stumpage fees."

I lit a cigarette and blew the smoke at The Digest. "Sounds like someone finally got you off your ass."

He raised his eyebrows and looked toward Kritchner, who rose defensively.

"He's doing a good job. Aren't you ever going to forget about Holiday Lodge?" Kritchner stood up and slapped The Digest's back. "That place isn't as bad as you remember. Oughta see it with a coat of snow."

"I think we've got enough to work on already." And then I saw that The Digest was still smarting. "The gray party wasn't your fault, and Kritchner's right. This is a damn good job."

I saw Roethe smile and winked back. We both knew that most of the research had been completed long ago, but we were also of one mind when it came to manipulating our employees.

Several days later the production engineer, R. E. Rubeaux, arrived for a contract and operations conference. His face, pocked and scarred, made him look as if he'd always lived on the edges of civilization, but his ponderous, flabby body made me wonder if he could boss lumberjacks in Caribbean rain forests, where the temperatures pushed 100° and the humidity was heavy enough to crush every drop of moisture from an athletic gringo. Rubeaux was flaccid, and I noticed he was short of breath when he lumbered across my office to find an ashtray.

"Am I supposed to believe you can run lumber camps spread over 200 square miles of mountainous jungles?" I said. I closed one eye, letting him know that I was going to doubt any answer he gave. But my words bounced right off the man.

"Come to the Mosquitia Coast with me. We'll see who keeps up with whom," he said, grinning. Rubeaux had obviously fenced with international entrepreneurs before. "Half the last bunch was crawling in the mud before we reached the first timber stand."

His English, I now noticed, was quite proper, with only a trace of Spanish and New Orleans creole. He probably cheated by riding a mule through the jungle, but I was going to like this guy. I turned away from him, thinking how I'd already made plans to visit Honduras—not for the timber, necessarily, but because my private research revealed that it was just emerging from the Central American Dark Ages, and might be the perfect place to develop low-cost Compass Club tropical hunting and fishing facilities.

"Am I hired or fired?"

"You'll get your chance to try dragging me through the mud." I smiled over my shoulder. "But your contract's going to have enough loopholes so I can bail out if it's *you* that ends up crawling."

Rubeaux laughed. "I think I'm going to like this job."

He stuck out his heavy hand, and I was about to shake it, hard, when my private phone rang.

"Glad to see you're working." Roethe shouted through a poor connection.

"Where are you?"

"New York, fighting with Gulf & Western."

"Call me back on a better line." I hung up quickly, anxious to finish with Rubeaux and be alone.

I turned the Honduras deal back to The Digest just in time. The phone rang again.

"Bludhorn's closing in." Roethe, for the first time, sounded really desperate. "I've got to get my personal finances handled. There's no time to waste. My reputation's on the line. And you know, John, how much this can affect you, too. One thing depends on another, right?"

Roethe was right. Everything depended on saving him. I'd described my original Master Plan many times, and in every conceivable fashion, so that he'd have opportunities to add ingredients as the mood and the opportunity moved him. In spite of the financial skeletons marching endlessly from every closet in Leo Roethe's mansion, I was convinced that he came closer than anyone else to bringing three-dimensional life to my paper projections.

"We work well together," I told him hopefully. "We'll work it out." I was past the point of using Roethe. I *had* to believe in him, as so many others did, because I was well past the point of no return. And Roethe's reputation *was* important. It was the pass to closed caucuses with powerful politicals, giants of industry, and magnetic celebrities. "I'll get on it now."

I telephoned Anders and asked how he suggested salvaging Roethe, "his assets, contacts, and charisma."

"I can arrange a million-dollar loan at the Philadelphia National Bank, but only because I'm a member of their advisory board, a position honoring long-term and large, very large depositors," he said. "Leo will have to provide the same collateral held by the Midland Bank. And the doctors, plus the rest of your key partners, should guarantee the loan to make it look good."

No one argued when we asked them to sign. Vitner and Hollis

laughed. "Anders's signature is the only true strength behind the loan; then comes Leo. We're just little guys."

While I worked on the details of the million-dollar loan, Anders transferred an extra quarter-million of his own cash to a savings account in Roethe's name at the Waukesha, Wisconsin, Savings and Loan.

"I'm going to assign the account as collateral on my Weatherby–Nasco debt," Roethe said.

"That will keep Gulf & Western quiet," added Anders.

Both sounded as if they were ready to fight Charles Bludhorn, and as if they were happy about the prospect.

In quick succession Roethe called a secret Weatherby–Nasco directors' meeting (minus the Gulf & Western representatives)—where I gave a pep talk about Leo's problems ending and everyone's future holding new opportunities in the wild world of Compass and Recreation International—notified his creditors to "call John Stone and you'll get paid;" and, "for one dollar and other good consideration," issued two-year options on Weatherby–Nasco stock to Anders (30,000 shares), Kritchner (10,000), O'Connor (10,000), and me (10,000). The options were at $5 per share (the present market value, Roethe claimed), and represented approximately 30 percent of Roethe's holdings in the company.

"Now we have a solid reason to make Leo's businesses run," I told my associates: "hard currency."

The day after the Philadelphia National Bank loan was closed, Roethe began passing out Weatherby rifles and shotguns. The doctors, all smiles, called them "our first dividends."

12
May 1973

ASSETS—$2,168,446.00
LIABILITIES—$191,420.00
PERSONAL GUARANTEES—$9,800,000.00

Every outside line was lit on the other phone as I hurried to finish a call from Turnbull to my private number. I waved my secretary in from the outer office and scribbled "Who?" in four-inch letters on my pad. She looked, leaned across my desk, and, exaggerating the movements of her lips, whispered, "Mr. Roethe's creditors."

I muffled the phone to Turnbull against my thigh and told her, "Take messages, damnit, and find O'Connor. Tell him I want to meet today." Then I told Turnbull, "You think you've got problems? Steamboat's frantic? Hah! Try Madison for a week!"

O'Connor sauntered in during the lunch hour. He brought an assistant. "From Florida," he explained, "to help part-time administering the first multimillion-dollar loans."

"How did . . ."

They both winked, and the new man said, "We always know when you need money."

"Today that's good, because I'm passing the word—Compass and Recreation International are selling stock on notes, no money down."

Frowning, testing to see how far he could push me, the

Southerner stepped forward and said, "What the hell is Recreation blah-blah?"

O'Connor cocked his head, watching over the top of his glasses.

I poured fresh coffee for myself. O'Connor's assistant had said he was an ex-Miami vice squad detective, but as far as I was concerned, Huffman looked and acted more like a high-class thug. His muscular body had the beginnings of a beer belly. He greeted everyone with a practiced, too strong handshake and a smile that meant, "I'm a helluva nice guy so long as you don't cross me."

"A catchall for the Diamond J companies. Come to the staff meeting tomorrow and listen when I explain everything to the rest of the troops."

"And now give us five minutes alone," O'Connor told him.

The assistant nodded and marched out. O'Connor sat on the edge of my desk, eyes darting, reading upside down again.

"Sure you've got enough stock, and is it registered to sell?"

"No problem."

"Save some for me . . . and my other friend from Washington."

When O'Connor left I poured more coffee, sipping and chain-smoking as I pondered the hidden problems I'd have to solve before banking his first million. Everyone worth a damn already owned shares in Lake, Sport, and Travel, Dash, and the Colorado companies. Now I was encouraging the same group, mostly employees and board members, to buy part of the new Compass Club. But the incorporation in Illinois, where securities laws allowed twenty-five initial stockholders and ten additions each succeeding year, was incomplete.

I buzzed my Storm Trooper and asked when the final forms were being filed.

"Should be official this week."

"Good. How much did you decide to buy?"

"I'm still thinking." He paused. His voice, always agreeable face-to-face, cooled over the intercom. "I've never heard of signatures on five-figure notes being a job requirement."

I sucked my gums. That was the big problem, the reason I'd called a general meeting—to be sure there'd be no other reluctant investors.

And so as I opened the meeting the next morning I told my

associates, "Compass Club and Recreation International, the Diamond J concepts, are not just jobs, not just investments. They are a way of life." I paused for effect, and saw that I wouldn't need the long-prepared pep talk lying untouched on the desk in front of me. I'd said just enough to fire imaginations and assure myself of everyone's signature, as well as everyone's best efforts eighteen hours a day, seven days a week. I rubbed my chin and sat unnaturally quiet as I watched my audience straining to hear more. I marveled at my powers of mental manipulation. I could dispel doubt and encourage devotion with less than twenty words.

" 'Joe Lunch Bucket' and 'The Family Man's Country Club' are forgotten forever," I said softly. "Now let's refurbish every visible detail of the greatest business endeavor this country's ever seen." I stood up to close the meeting while my associates clamored for their fair share of the sophisticated stepchild of Lake, Sport, and Travel.

And they were there for hours, everyone taking his turn to ask, "How much can I get? When?"

Quarton and I were the last to leave the office. It was long past the time I'd promised to meet Sue for dinner.

"Hurry," I told him. "We both need a drink, and maybe you can help pacify my wife afterwards."

He didn't answer. He fell behind, fumbling to lock the front door. When I turned back to hurry him again I saw his head bobbing while he talked to himself:

"And the loan orgy begins."

O'Connor, who was spending most of his time in my office now, insisted that the job of overseeing the note processing was too delicate for Toussaint and The Digest. "I suggest," he stated in a clipped tone that left no room for dispute, "that *you* hire my man from Florida full-time. He'll act as liaison between the borrowers and me, the lender."

Quarton called my newest employee "a runner," and when the "runner" overheard the remark I got a fast idea of his potentially violent nature. He snapped a pen between his fingers and sent the pieces clattering onto the nearest desk top.

"I'm working for you and O'Connor, period. I'm not another animal in this zoo."

I saw trouble coming, and decided that Huffman should be utilized elsewhere as soon as the first million dollars was disbursed. "How'd you like to ride herd on Honduras for me?"

"No, at least not alone," he said. "Walter's sending another man for that job."

The next day he brought the aristocratic Edmund Carter in for a job "interview." Carter was the "assistant ambassador" who, O'Connor had previously told me, would grease the wheels of the slow-moving Honduran Government. He was lean and white-haired; he puffed on his pipe while considering his responses, which were always delivered in a thoughtful drawl; and despite his age (I took him to be over sixty-five), he stood ramrod straight.

"I prefer not to be seated during important meetings."

Carter, who spoke for O'Connor as well, agreed that an inspection trip was mandatory before any big money was invested in Agricola Itzapan. I suggested that he and O'Connor's other man leave for Honduras at once, and breathed a deep sigh of relief when they acted as if they were already packed to go.

O'Connor joined us later, happy, saying, "I'm glad things are finally moving. Now the next project is to buy Padgett out of Camp Dells."

"What?" I'd almost forgotten the rumors that there was trouble at Camp Dells.

"Padgett's a pain in the ass. I want you to replace him as an officer and a director." O'Connor cleared his throat, staring straight at me. Then, much louder, he said, "And as a stockholder. Don't worry about the money. I'll make you a private loan." He made the word "private" sound like it meant "free."

"You got a deal," I said. I didn't ask the terms. Why bother? It wasn't costing me anything.

We shook hands, a quick, meaningless movement forgotten when O'Connor turned toward Huffman.

"Do you think Johnny can use more help now?"

I knew it was only a matter of time before O'Connor put his eastern friend, "the leasing genius," on my payroll too. But before that I wanted to fill the administrative gap in my Brain Trust. So as soon as they left, I called Roethe.

"Did you forget about . . ."

Roethe interrupted. "Come to my house Sunday afternoon. I've found your new exec."

According to Roethe, Luther Dickson Griffith was a better choice than even Rick Murray—"nearly as good as yourself." He patted my shoulder as we walked onto his sun porch.

Griffith stood in the center of the room, reaching for my hand, already addressing me. "Jim Lovell says you're quite a guy. And I know Joe Foss and Governor Connally were impressed at the Hall of Fame Dinner."

"I came to hear you praise yourself." I winked at him.

"I wasn't sure where to begin." Griffith responded.

His credentials came close to equalling Roethe's. As a matter of fact, I noticed, many were identical. They were members of the same big-game hunting clubs. They seemed to be on a first-name basis with the same celebrities.

Griffith was currently the president of Griffith Broadcasting, Inc., and LDC, Inc., operating radio stations KHOB and KLDG in Hobbs, New Mexico.

"Funny," I thought as he interrupted the résumé to pour himself a glass of white wine, "Griffith doesn't look or sound like a Southwestener." His almost white hair was too properly in place. He wore an outdated, thin-lapelled, navy blue suit similar to Roethe's, but just slightly—perhaps intentionally—rumpled. His voice was soft, almost musical when he injected Hawaiian phrases into his conversation, and it also bore traces of coarser East Coast accents. He laughed a lot, but his laughter was artificial. I had a hunch that I was not meeting him at the peak of his business life.

Griffith continued to tell me about himself, as Roethe nodded and grunted to affirm each new success story. "I was a commissioned navy pilot, a founder of Chicago Helicopter Airways, a senior vice-president of Kenyon and Eckhardt. . . ." He paused, shifting to a lower octave. "One of the country's leading advertising agencies, you know. And I was president of the Columbia School of Broadcasting, running offices in Cincinnati and Honolulu. I still own part of that company."

I stood up to pour myself a drink, and noticed how suitably he waited until I sat down again and gave him my full attention. He handed me a fat folio of stories he'd written for outdoor magazines, then said, "You can read them later if you like. Now then, where next? Oh, I gave the principal address at the 1966 World Travel Congress in Hong Kong."

"See, Dick's quite a guy, too." Roethe passed me another folder opened to a letter of commendation from the congress. The next sheet mentioned his "good work producing 'Congo Adventure,'" starring Robert Stack and Joe Foss, for TV.

"And I've appeared on the 'Today Show,' the 'Roy Campanella Show,' and 'To Tell the Truth,'" Griffith said, suddenly increasing his tempo, "and campaigned with Ted Agnew, and . . ."

"Whoa. You're hired," I said, looking toward Roethe to let him know that Griffith had said enough.

"As I told you, Dick, John makes quick decisions."

I smiled at them. I'd been a little hesitant moments before, because, I knew, I didn't want to hire a really strong competitor. But now I was convinced that Griffith would be easy to handle—a pushover, really. Griffith obviously needed a new job desperately, and he was depending on Roethe and me to find a way for him to reestablish his has-been glory. There was, however, enough ego in the man to assure me that he'd do anything to get back on top and stay there. And there was no denying he had the qualifications I'd been looking for.

Quarton, however, wasn't so sure.

"Looks like a candyass. He's out to use you."

I laughed. "Let him try. Before I'm finished with . . . candyass," I laughed harder, "he'll melt himself down to a skeleton."

I told Griffith to give the club a totally new image. "Your job is to break into the national membership markets. *Now.*"

Griffith impressed everyone when he presented his plan to sell Compass Club memberships by direct mail. He had a knack for preparing visual aids, usually giant poster displays, that made his material seem like accomplished fact. According to Griffith, Compass Club would have 100,000 members, and turn a million-dollar profit, within the year.

"The direct-mail approach, utilizing the skills of the country's top direct-mail company, is foolproof." He put his arm around my shoulder and gave me a "you understand—you're my kind of person" squeeze.

Under other circumstances I would have figured him for a fag, but in the intensity of the Compass–Recreation International offices I knew he was simply trying to tell me that I was the only other person capable of visualizing our companies in the rarefied atmosphere of Big Board business.

"Wall Street is our next destination."

I hoped he was right, because I'd just run into another pack of money worries. O'Connor had held me up for a bigger discount fee before starting to disburse the proceeds of the second million-dollar loan line. Roethe's bankers, sensing the opportunity for a complete bail-out from his debts, hounded me for more and bigger disbursements. And a host of Metcalf Farms's hidden credit troubles crashed down on my desk and almost cracked my touted investment portfolio wide open.

"We need your money *now*," I told O'Connor, arguing that he'd promised to grant loans for another million under the same conditions as before. "Twenty percent, split equally between Janeff Credit and your bank, is all we can afford to pay."

O'Connor shook his head. "I need another 5 percent to cover my expenses," he insisted. "It costs a lot of money to process and supervise loans to businesses that are as complicated as yours."

"My costs are rising, too."

O'Connor smiled, and when I demanded looser loan requirements in return for paying the higher fee, he finally relented. "Suppose I return a third of the extra discount fee to you . . . to help cover your expenses?"

Now it began to sound like a kickback scheme, especially when O'Connor admitted that he planned to deposit the extra fees in a personal "expense fund" account. "You'll get paid from that."

I lit a cigarette and pondered the proposition. It seemed to violate several banking regulations. I asked O'Connor, "How do you have the authority to pay yourself and me a commission?"

His eyes narrowed. "Because Janeff and my bank will authorize payment of *expenses*." He raised both eyebrows. "Not *commissions*. Then everything will be legal."

I wasn't sure, but since it seemed that I had no other choice, and the other creditors were screaming louder than ever, I nodded. "OK." I rationalized that my side of the deal was within the law, because I planned to return my share of the "expense fund" to the company treasuries anyway.

As soon as O'Connor began to provide more funds, I was able to quiet Roethe's creditors, and I discovered that there was a loud ring of truth to the philosophy that "Where there are problems, there are opportunities." The bankers I paid off seemed only too happy to consider my requests for new personal loans, so long as I kept helping them bury their garbage. Some months before I'd decided that it was impractical to borrow from a long list of small-town banks. Now I discovered that most of them were interrelated by loan swaps and other financial favors.

"As a matter of fact," I told Toussaint, "it isn't always necessary to use cash when we pay off Roethe's loans. A fresh substitute, paper from an unfamiliar name with an acceptable financial statement, serves the same purpose. The bankers are happy so long as their examiners don't find the same borrowers that caused them to file damning reports in the past."

"You're right. And you may have found the solution to our problem with Metcalf Farms." He produced an analysis that clearly showed the relationship between the Metcalf Farms loans at the American City Bank in Milwaukee, the State Bank of Mount Horeb, and another smaller bank, owned by a group from Janesville, Wisconsin.

"The group from Janesville bought the Mount Horeb Bank from Roethe."

My coffee splashed on Toussaint's papers when I shoved the cup aside and leaned across the desk to be sure I hadn't misunderstood him. "Roethe owned the bank?"

"Sure. Didn't Lindsey ever tell you about the time he worked for them?"

I shook my head, the spilled coffee dampening my elbows.

"Roethe had to sell out when the Banking Commission caught him lending most of the money to his own companies and business associates. So he made a deal with the Janesville group, headed by a guy who just happened to be a director of Weatherby–Nasco —and an investor in Metcalf Farms. And his group owns a holding company that controls several other banks."

I mopped up the coffee and refilled my cup. "What you're

saying is that we should have no trouble borrowing from one of these banks to pay the others."

Toussaint nodded solemnly, a little nervously, I thought.

Roethe thought my ideas were great. He brought Stuart Shadel, the man who had engineered the Mount Horeb Bank deal, to an immediate meeting at my office.

"I haven't much time today," said Shadel, smiling as if our yet-to-be-discussed association were a foregone conclusion, "but I'm sure we can arrange to do business."

After he left Roethe asked how Recreation International was developing.

"It still lacks something," I said, as he settled comfortably onto my black leather sofa. "Form." I let the word dangle.

Roethe nodded. He understood my worries about lack of total control and violation of securities laws, and began explaining. "A shell is a company with stock registered for public trading, and with some assets but no active business operations; a legal corporate skeleton that can be the easiest and fastest means to a functioning conglomerate. And, most important, a shell eliminates the tedious problems of starting from scratch."

I put my feet up on an open desk drawer and listened happily while Roethe listed the rest of the pluses.

"The expense of securities registrations is eliminated, assuming the shell is public. Most shells have no active business purpose, but they do have *liquid assets*. That's the clincher."

"Where do we find one?" I asked, my feet back on the floor.

"I have one," said Roethe. "Sorini Foods. It's already documented in your file of my assets."

"How much money does Sorini Foods have?"

Roethe smiled. "Very little today, but my man, who'll be in Madison any day, will tell you he can raise over $1 million tomorrow."

His "man" was Allen Quello, a Minnesota attorney. Roethe said that Quello was prominent in the complicated business of mergers, acquisitions, and shells. "I can assure you he'll have the solution to all our problems."

I hung a lot of hopes on that remark, and I was grateful for the temporary peace of mind—until I met Quello, several days later. He looked sloppy.

Roethe's deferential demeanor in Quello's presence was almost ludicrous. Quello's suit was threadbare and in need of cleaning. His wing-tip shoes were a study in scuffing. His fingernails were irregular. His glasses were dirty, and his tie was the wrong shade for the suit. I stared at him, but I couldn't get him to look me in the eye, and he clutched his bulging briefcase as if he were afraid someone would discover what was concealed inside. "He should be working for Padgett and the Buyer's Club," I thought, about to make up some excuse to avoid having to listen to him. Then he began to speak.

Quello's mind, unlike his body, seemed to be precisely organized. Apparently he knew everything about the Diamond J companies and how to make them fit into a conglomerate under the umbrella of Sorini Foods. He used the expression "not difficult" instead of "no problem," but he meant the same thing. "I can raise a million and a quarter in the Twin Cities as soon as your conglomerate outline is on paper."

"How?"

"Private funding. Notes and debentures at the start. Later we can sell stock for as much money as you'll ever need. Right, Leo?"

Roethe nodded.

"Is Sorini Foods public?" I wanted to hear it from somebody besides Roethe, because I wasn't sure he knew what "public" meant.

Quello said it was, "in Minnesota."

"That's as good as national registration with the SEC, because Minnesota has the fastest-moving penny stock market in the world," said Roethe, adding with a smile, "We can register the stock nationally if you like. That's why the next man I'm going to introduce you to is my broker from Delafield Childs. They're a brokerage in New York, members of the New York Stock Exchange."

My mind was racing. Roethe was throwing new people at me faster than he'd tossed off corporations. I knew they all had their place and purpose, but I also knew Roethe's trick of using sheer quantity to win overwhelming decisions.

"One man at a time," I told him.

We spent the rest of the afternoon listing the companies to be included in the Recreation International conglomerate: all my Wisconsin and Colorado companies; African Ponderosa, Metcalf Farms, Agricola Itzapan, Big Mountain Country, and Wyoming Estates from Roethe's portfolio; Anders's farm in Kentucky and Resort Lane in Montana; Kritchner's farm—even my Storm Trooper's wilderness ranch in British Columbia.

"Enough to keep everybody happy," Roethe said.

Quello, in spite of his appearance, made the future look brighter than ever. Each project, he was sure, "is in its proper place, ready to turn a profit tomorrow."

More important, after the Recreation International conglomerate became reality, the whole would be much greater than the sum of its parts—an automatic capital gain which would at least double my net worth. Or, as I told the doctors in deliberately heavy jargon, "The results of the Recreation International mergers will be multiplicative rather than additive."

"Like a snowball," Hollis grinned.

"A fucking pyramid," said Kritchner.

I knew that my life was a travelogue about to become a fantastic odyssey. "Happy days are here again," I told Sue.

When Roethe called for more money, and told me in the lower tone he used to mean "urgent—personal and confidential" that he'd forgotten several creditors, I said, "Hurry over. That's what I'm here for."

He rushed into my office, after driving the thirty miles from Fort Atkinson in a scant half-hour, and listed numerous unexpected problems, starting with loans made by "Jim's banks," which were now in the custody of a trustee and being scrutinized by the Banking Commission for the umpteenth time. "I want you to pay off all my loans from the Jackson and Fredonia Banks, and another one Jim arranged at the National Boulevard Bank in Chicago."

"Goddamnit, that's one you never mentioned before," I said, and threw my pen onto my desk. I was acting, playing a game.

But Roethe missed the twinkle in my eyes, and I could feel him reviewing his previous disclosures. He didn't want to risk any more "white lies," so, in a voice that was uncommonly soft and deeply accented with sincerity (the way I suppose he spoke in church), Roethe told me about Smith and Vernath and Amasa Lumber.

Smith and Vernath were investors in Agricola Itzapan who'd never received their stock certificates. They had to be paid off before they filed charges. Amasa Lumber was supposed to be merged into Weatherby–Nasco, but, like the department stores, the transaction was rejected by the board of directors. As a result, Roethe was being sued by the Amasa Lumber Company stockholders for his failure to perform.

"That's more dirty linen than I expected. What else?" I asked, staring hard into the back of his eyes. I tried to project all my energy in a single short look that might wring the total truth from him.

"Nothing." Roethe was obviously nervous. He pulled at his ear before he made a final attempt to extricate himself. Then, in his normal, firm voice, he said, "This is all temporary. My pension fund loan will be completed soon. Then all our money can go for expansion."

I smiled; I'd learned more than I had expected, without really trying. "Send your bankers to me and have my people issue what checks you need," I told him. I kept smiling, wickedly now; it was fun to play the benevolent despot.

Two bank presidents and a bank executive vice-president arrived early the next morning. My secretary, amused by their anxious expressions, deliberately kept them waiting in the Board Room.

"Can't they trust the mails, or is one day more going to break them?" she asked me with a wide grin.

She had given me an idea, and I told her to ask if they were members of the Compass Club. The answer, of course, was no. Then I sent her back to the Board Room to tell them that only members were admitted to the Inner Sanctum, my office, where the checks were kept. Then, within minutes, my secretary had sold her first three memberships in the Compass Club—one for cash, one charged on BankAmericard, and the other (after credit approval) on an open account.

"The beauty of the drill," I told Quarton later, "was that all three seemed to appreciate their memberships."

"And Leo seems to appreciate your quick attention to the money details. He's waiting to see you again."

"Jesus Christ." I opened my door to wave him in. "What now?"

Roethe started to chuckle. "Nothing. Can't you stand good times? I only wanted to thank you and tell you that if ever you need funds for private investment . . ." He looked toward Quarton, wondering, I supposed, if he could be trusted.

I nodded.

"If you need any money, let me know." Then, in a very soft voice, Roethe explained that the Weatherby–Nasco corporate deposits were a wonderfully effective carrot that generated considerable clout with hungry bankers. "Can't use them for myself anymore, but you . . ."

My private line rang. It was O'Connor, wanting to know if I needed more money.

"Not today, Walter. I'm beginning to feel pretty flush." I turned to Roethe. "And I think I'll start spending some on the old Diamond J gang."

"You deserve it."

"Damn right."

So Lake, Sport, and Travel bought an executive aircraft—a six-passenger, twin-engine Aero Commander painted red, white, and blue, with 1776X for a registration number.

"If times ever get tough, I'll fly it to Philadelphia for sale during the Bicentennial," I told Anders, talking long-distance, with a superwide grin.

When Vitner told me he was $50,000 short on his divorce settlement, I slapped his back and said, "So what?" I handed him a blank note to sign and promised him the money. "More, if you need it, will be in your attorney's hands within forty-eight hours."

Metcalf flew into Madison, shaking from jet lag fatigue and panicked because his farms were being water-tortured. "Hawaiian weather can be a cruel tease," he said. He explained that when rain did come it was too heavy; the fertilizer flooded away. The rest of the time, the stationary clouds emptied a tantalizing mile beyond the edge of his dusty fields. "We'll never harvest four crops a year now." He looked ready to cry.

"Four was only a wild hope," I consoled him. "Three will be exceptional." And then, to show that I wasn't the least bit perturbed, I told Metcalf I would send The Digest to Hawaii, to handle public relations at the annual stockholders' meeting and to investigate the purchase of irrigation equipment.

When he finally smiled, I told him about my special surprise (it had even been a surprise to me when I had first thought of it). "I've selected the biggest nit-picking sonofabitch I know to help you handle obstinate creditors and solve the farms' bookkeeping problems. Feldher Sommers, the former president of Janeff, is going to be chairman of your board," I announced as my secretary, by prearrangement, ushered Sommers into the room.

Sommers was smiling, anxious to be working again. The two men hit it off perfectly, and when they left together chatting happily about profit projections, I was sure something divine had intervened to keep Sommers around until I had found a place for him to retire gracefully and profitably. Now everybody felt good.

My relaxed enthusiasm was contagious. Nobody mentioned money anymore. Roethe's next visit concerned only Anders's official election to the Weatherby–Nasco Board before Gulf & Western could mount a campaign against him.

"Everything's arranged," he said, "faster and easier than expected. One of Shadel's partners, a man who's been splitting his allegiance between Gulf & Western and my management, resigned from the board without argument. He's the perfect person for Anders to replace. That done, you and Dr. Kritchner should replace two other dissident directors."

"What about Bludhorn's boys?" I said.

"The first battle with Gulf & Western was won as soon as we covered my debts to the company. Now, as long as we move fast, we should have our own way with everything. Maybe even consider the eventual merger of Weatherby–Nasco and Recreation International."

"Go, Leo, go." I toasted him with my coffee cup.

For months I had contemplated opening a West Coast office next, and I now literally stumbled over the opportunity when Marv Rand, the public relations man who had recommended Bosch's sponsorship of the Dash race, told me he wanted to quit his job and move to San Diego. I couldn't help liking Rand. He had a flair for making me feel important.

"And he's so pure," I told Sue, anxious for her to meet him. I believed he was one of those rare urban birds who never screwed outside the nest. Most men like that annoyed me; on Rand it wore well.

He started as editor of the Compass Club newsletter, and had my carte blanche to open a full-scale office in San Diego as soon as possible.

"Why don't you tour the West and line up new affiliates?" I suggested. "Maybe even hit Baja." I thought for a minute. "My wife and I will even go with you," I added.

Before we left for Mexico, Roethe insisted that I personally inspect his World Wide Animal Kingdom and arrange for my office to manage it. As far as I was concerned the museum was a joke, a waste of time and an unnecessary money-loser. The huge steel building, filled with hundreds of rare trophies, priceless oddities, and artifacts collected on Roethe's journeys, was located in the midst of the Coney Island atmosphere of the Wisconsin Dells. It might have been a success in different surroundings, but never there, across the road from a go-cart concession and within sight of an artificial dinosaur park.

I wanted to reject the World Wide Animal Kingdom, but I knew that it was dedicated to Roethe's dead son; was shared with his best friend, who owned equal interests in several of the other businesses I was acquiring; and was now, since Roethe had already merged it with the shell, the primary listed asset of Sorini Foods. To reject it would be to reject my continuing alliance with Roethe and the expansion he offered.

I shrugged. My holiday mood made it easier to say, "Yes, I'll put a crew to work developing an international gift shop and promoting group tours."

Actually, it might just turn profitable, I rationalized. "If nothing else," I told my staff "it finally justifies the name 'Diamond J Imports' on our letterhead."

On our trip to Baja I saw an opportunity to make a contribution to the conservation movement, and perhaps to promote my nomination to the International Conservation Hall of Fame. Mexico enforced a law limiting the taking of salt-water sport fishes. I wrote to Luis Echeverria Alvarez, the head of state, asking his assistance in encouraging the same regulations in the United States. Later, when I showed the carbon copy to Roethe and Griffith, they suggested that our companies sponsor the movement.

"Maybe then you'll be wearing a watch like mine," Roethe smiled; copies of his watch were presented to everyone inducted into the Hall of Fame.

"Goddamn," I thought, "sometimes he sees right through me."

Quello flew into Madison for an investors' meeting the following evening. He'd prepared an agreement of owners' interest for Roethe and me, as well as for all of our major investors, to sign.

Sorini Foods, the agreement stated, had already resolved to authorize a six-million-share increase in its issued common stock. The new stock was to be issued at $1 per share and was to be traded for the complete assets of all the Stone and Roethe companies. Even Thunderhead, with assets valued at $1 million, was listed. I wondered if Turnbull would agree to the proposition, then forgot about it: Kritchner was president of the Thunderhead corporation. He could sign instead as long as the other doctors approved, and that, as usual, would be no problem. Everyone seemed frantic to be included. Even before I finished reading my copy of the document, all the other key individuals were committed.

The agreement also required a $1 million cash investment for working capital and expansion of operations.

"Where's that coming from?" someone asked.

Roethe and Quello explained that it would be borrowed from private sources, per a prior agreement with me. That seemed to answer all questions. Once again I began to feel like a money machine.

After the others left the meeting, Roethe pulled another agreement from his briefcase, saying that he needed to have it signed as verification of his net worth. The contract called for Recreation International (the new name for Sorini Foods) to purchase, on demand, three-quarters of a million shares of Recreation International from Roethe at $4 per share. There was a separate guarantee of the obligation at the bottom of the page. My name was typed below the signature block.

"What the hell is this?" I demanded, raising my voice to tell them that I wasn't about to endorse an automatic $2,250,000.00 profit for anyone.

Roethe repeated his statement, which he now made sound like a promise, that the agreement was only to be used to prove his net worth, just as I'd done for him and Rosenheimer the winter before.

"Good trick," I thought, "an easy way to increase the bottom line on a financial statement. Simple."

As soon as Roethe left with his signed document, Quello pulled out another set of papers and explained, "We need to select officers for the new conglomerate, open a bank account, and execute borrowing resolutions and notes to raise the first quarter-million of operating cash. But John, since you're already chief operating officer of most of the merging companies, I think it would be better if someone else was president, temporarily, while we arrange the mergers. Of course you won't lose any income. There won't be any until everything's completed. Then you can have, or *be*, just about anything you want."

Quello talked as if the presidency were more important than the power and the money. And I played along, because I still didn't trust him and I figured it was an advantage to let him believe he could buy me with a title. We made my Storm Trooper the temporary president. Kritchner became treasurer, and The Digest was secretary, as usual. Quello said he'd meet any two of our new officers at the bank tomorrow and close the loan.

"What bank?" I asked him, wondering which one of my sources he intended to tap.

"First Bank of Grantsburg," Quello said. When I didn't show any recognition, he said, "It's the primary depository for two of Leo's other companies."

"What companies?"

Quello didn't answer.

Late that night, after Quello had gone, I researched the files for the information I remembered Roethe had included with his initial salvo of business data. He owned interests in many companies that, as yet, were not part of our conglomerate plans. Some had question marks penciled in beside their names, and I knew it was only a matter of time before they'd be presented as candidates for acquisition by Recreation International.

Two businesses, a machine factory and an exporter of grain to Russia, looked as if they might carry accounts at the bank in Grantsburg . . . big accounts, especially the grain exporter, which I remembered John Strohm telling me about when we were together in Kenya. He was on its board of directors, and knew that the company was about to realize a large profit from sales to Russia.

Quello, the corporate memorandums showed, handled the legal work for that company and for most of the others. Apparently Quello was using them all to help each other.

"I'll be damned," I said softly. "My company may get a quarter-million-dollar loan because somebody might have sold grain to Russia and stashed the profits in a little bank in the northwest corner of Wisconsin."

Then, as Quarton came in, I shook my head. I didn't trust Quello, but I wasn't sure why.

"Let's get a drink."

"Right on. I want to wash out the sour taste of Quello."

Quarton could tell when I was pissed, so even though my remark drew a curious glance, he changed the subject and reported on Griffith's progress. "A mammoth kickoff is scheduled to introduce the newest Chicago and Milwaukee offices. Lovell's appearing again, along with several other astronauts, and I saw a letter from Bill Holden's office enclosing clippings from the African press and indicating, so Griffith said, that Holden might also be present."

"What about your other projects?"

"Everything's in good shape. Membership sales haven't picked up yet, but we can't put the cart before the horse. Have to build and polish the product first." Quarton looked happy. He was doing his thing.

I finished my drink, ordered another, and had a brainstorm. "Your club facilities division is shorthanded, isn't it?"

Quarton nodded.

"Then I'm going to hire Judy to run that department."

He cocked his head and started to tell me I was crazy. Then he grinned. "Maybe that's the best way to beef up my staff and bring your ex-wife halfway home." He bought the next round.

I knew I was going to get drunk. I owed it to myself.

O'Connor's assistant, the ex-vice cop, returned from Honduras the next morning. "Carter's staying behind," he said, "to cement our relationship with the government." He handed me a short written report verifying that the lumber venture was underway and should be "highly successful," and tapped my shoulder "Better get down there and let them all see the boss. Meanwhile I've got to go run Camp Dells."

He started to leave, then swung back to my desk. "Walter says you're giving me a company car."

"That's the first I've heard about it." All I knew was that O'Connor divided his share of the extra discounts with the man; he, like the rest of us, was supposed to use the money for expenses But I shrugged. "Why not?" I threw him the keys to my year-old yellow Oldsmobile, which sat in the parking lot, unused, behind my Eldorado.

"Thanks." He sauntered out of my office.

I sighed, and glanced from the zebra-skin appointment folio to the perpetual clock to the Masai spears guarding the trophy-covered wall. I figured that I was prepared for anything, and since the rest of the day was open I decided to relax, study, and think At about 11:00 A.M. I fixed my first Cuba Libre, noting with satis-faction that Higbie kept my office bar stocked with every key in-vestor's favorite liquor.

Everybody had to be happy now, not just content. Our lives were too intense for mere contentment. Yes, even Turnbull had sounded happy yesterday when he'd called to tell me that the

Thunderhead condos would definitely be finished in time for the 1973–74 season.

Now I sensed that his elation went beyond that news; he must be intoxicated by the thought that he could get all the money he needed, anytime. Like me, he knew that Roethe's banker friends, especially Shadel, promised extra lines of credit totaling more than $1 million. "Extra, extra, extra," over and above the first and second millions from O'Connor and the third million I knew he would provide as soon as I hired his leasing genius and expanded Janeff Credit into the commercial lease field. On top of all that was the million and a quarter Quello had promised to deliver via the Sorini Foods–Recreation International mergers. And I was beginning to believe that he could and would do it. The first $200,000 was already in our new account at the First Bank of Grantsburg.

My Storm Trooper, who had represented the Diamond J interests at the loan closing, reported that Quello had deposited nearly half a million dollars in mysterious checks to open a separate compensating balance account, a sort of bribe to assure the bank's continued cooperation. I laughed. I was sure the checks represented the proceeds of grain sales to Russia and had to be used with the blessing of John Strohm. "Now, by God, I've got a direct fiscal connection with the editor of the world's most prestigious nature magazines, and I'm indirectly involved with East-West détente." It sounded great.

I flipped through the latest copy of *Playboy*, saw Lovell's name, and read his candid quote: "We fully envision that in the near future we will fly women into space and use them the same way we use them on Earth—for the same purpose."

Now that was the kind of eye-catcher we should be printing. I scribbled "Buy a magazine *now*" on my list of urgent projects.

Then I remembered my idea to hire Judy. Judy and I had had a good working relationship as parents, and now we were friends. She was at last learning to understand me. Today, because I was so obviously successful in so many endeavors, she could certainly cope with my lifestyle.

Sue knew that I would always love the happy memories of

Judy, and that I would never break the new bond between us. And she seemed to accept Judy's important place in my past. So there was no reason she'd object to Judy's safe new niche in my future business world.

Judy would be an extra set of eyes, too. And extra binocular vision was very important with new vistas appearing in startling, superfast succession.

I added Judy's name to the list, and, without thinking, wrote my brother's beneath it. With success seemingly assured, I wanted, finally, to include him. I needed more of my own people to counterbalance the waves of self-serving associates Roethe and O'Connor had rolled through the gates to my empire.

I poured another drink and buzzed for Quarton to join me, then told my secretary to gather the rest of the Brain Trust. "It's time to show them all how there'll be moments now when everybody can relax and share some good, old-fashioned, purposeless bullshit."

I shouldn't have been, but I was bright-eyed and bushy-tailed the next morning when my visitors, O'Connor and George Weast, the "genius," arrived. I sized up Weast: he was a perfect banty rooster. I bit the inside of my cheek to keep from laughing at my unavoidably funny first impression: every feather on his head was in place. The blue-black mohair suit was perfect plumage for the little man. Manicured nails, styled blonde hair, and smooth skin that looked freshly massaged completed the image of a creature who demanded first class, regardless, with more elbow room than he could ever use.

Weast squinted at me. He was sizing me up too. But I had to bite harder on my cheek, fighting a real belly laugh, when I thought that he must be deciding how tough it was going to be to rule my barnyard. The urge disappeared when I remembered that O'Connor had begun calling my offices "the zoo." I finally introduced myself and shook Weast's small, hard hand.

He looked me straight in the eye, still squinting, and said, "So you're John Stone." Then he sat down and waited for me to do the talking.

He knew how to handle himself. When he did speak, his questions showed that he'd analyzed everything I said. He succeeded in controlling the conversation with a minimum of words. And I changed my mind—Weast turned me on. I could tell that he was a tough human being who usually got everything he wanted, a fighter with real smarts. Maybe even a genius.

Long before lunch, Weast, O'Connor, and I had agreed to change Janeff's name, relocate the home office, and give Weast, the new president, free rein to develop an international leasing company with public stock selling on a major exchange.

When Weast asked about stockholder approval, O'Connor chuckled. I said, "It might take half an hour on the telephone. But before you start moving American Leasing and Financial Corporation to Washington, D.C., I have a special mission for you." I handed him my carefully prepared outline of the Metcalf Farms operations.

I didn't have to tell him that this was his first and only test when I explained that he was already scheduled to join Sommers and The Digest at the important annual shareholders' meeting in Honolulu. "Another banker, Stuart Shadel, has personally invested $350,000 in Metcalf's equipment. See if you can set up our first lease on that equipment. Name your own lease rate; Shadel and Metcalf will cooperate."

Weast cocked his head, "Are you sure?"

"Damn right." I walked across the big room and used the heavy silver lighter on the end table to light my cigarette. I wanted Weast and O'Connor way behind me while I chuckled softly over the deal I'd made with Shadel.

He'd agreed to lend me "whatever is needed" if I guaranteed to help him recover his risky personal investment in Metcalf Farms. Actually, all I'd be doing would be helping Shadel move his money from one pocket to the other. The $350,000 he wanted Metcalf to repay would come through American Leasing and Financial, but it would originate with loans at his own bank.

I turned back to the others. "You can be sure Shadel will cooperate."

Weast gathered up the paperwork and started out after O'Connor on a tour of the office complex. I stayed behind, wrestling with the sudden premonition that these men were very hungry and that I was about to be their elephant.

During my duty calls to the controlling Janeff stockholders, Anders said, approvingly, "It's about time you added some financial brains to your staff." He liked the sound of "American Leasing and Financial," and he was particularly pleased that the home office was moving to his part of the country. "Now I can personally supervise the money."

I could see him smiling.

Kritchner and the others liked everything I told them, especially the fact that I was now free to go to Honduras.

"That's our best bet yet," Kritchner reminded me.

Honduras was like a replay of Kenya, almost. Rubeaux was patiently waiting on the observation balcony of the weather-beaten airport when Sue and I arrived, two hours late. The sun was setting behind rugged mountains. It was chilly, and there wasn't any more jungle atmosphere than you'd expect to find in Colorado. As a matter of fact, Sue and I both seemed short of breath.

"Why not?" said Rubeaux, when I told him that the air seemed thin. "Tegulcigalpa is over a mile high." He wasn't breathless at all.

Before I had a chance to test Rubeaux in the fields and forests, he proved to be a superb host in the city. We were quickly passed through customs and delivered in a chauffeured car to the only truly modern hotel I could see.

"The interior of the Honduras Maya looks like Las Vegas," I told Rubeaux.

He nodded and said, "You're right." Then he whispered: "The hotel was built in anticipation of legalized gambling. You're not the only *Norte Americano* setting up shop in the country."

Our accommodations were the VIP Suite. "Seldom used," the bellboy told me, "except by government officials, gangsters, and movie stars."

While Rubeaux showed Sue the rest of the rooms, I inventoried our central lounge. A row of rum and Coke bottles long enough to quench my thirst for a year was lined up on the back bar. There were gigantic bowls of fresh fruit, and more flowers for Sue than at our wedding.

Rubeaux returned, and I forced the grin off my face and asked for an immediate appointment with our attorneys and the Price Waterhouse accountants. I didn't want anyone thinking that I could be lulled into a vacation mood by squandering expense account money. The trip was a welcome change of pace, but during my moments of reflection on the flight down I'd realized that I was indeed a money machine, and therefore could allow myself only a very few days away from the crucial financial maneuvering in Madison.

Rubeaux grinned. "You'll have to change your ways. Haven't you heard that business is transacted slowly and decorously in Tegulcigalpa?" He must have practiced that sentence for some time.

I slammed down the rum bottle I was opening and shouted, "Bullshit."

Rubeaux's head jerked around.

I had his attention, so I smiled, but I made sure my voice was biting when I told him, "If my money backs the timber business, then the business is going to run my way. My favorite words are 'fast' and 'now.' My least favorite word is 'mañana.'"

I allowed thirty-six hours for small talk, cocktail parties, and diplomatic dinners before I told the attorneys to brief me on their progress with incorporation and government contracts and asked to see the financial analysis from the accountants. Nothing was ready.

"Nothing?" I exploded. I didn't even try to be polite. That was Carter's job. "And where the hell is he?" I demanded.

And when the attorney said Carter had returned to Florida to wait while the Honduran government and business community digested our proposals, I explained the American expression "shit or get off the pot."

"I'm trying to help improve your country," I said.

He nodded.

"That's why the unexpected delays are so frustrating."

He kept nodding. I knew I was going to have a rough time teaching him my favorite words.

Rubeaux chartered an ancient-looking airplane to fly us the 500 miles north to inspect the lumber mill and the timber tracts on the Mosquitia coast. He told me not to bother packing tackle, because the promised "good year-round fishing" petered out during the early summer. But we did transport all of our food; the wild bananas, pineapples, avocados, and grapefruits Roethe talked about were forty miles down the trackless coast, and the motor of the company's boat had been stolen.

"I had anticipated a few exaggerations," I quietly told Rubeaux, whose expression reminded me of a little boy with wet pants. "Any more?" I was smiling now because he was beginning to choke up; I simply hadn't wanted any surprises when we landed in the jungle.

Rubeaux said the purported population of "2,000 happy, friendly people" in the company village of Iriona actually might be a bit rebellious, because Roethe still owed a substantial payroll debt for construction of the sawmill and lodge. The lodge, once very beautiful, was badly run down, nearly engulfed by the creeping jungle, which the villagers refused to prune back.

"What about the landing strip?"

"We'll make it," Rubeaux said, beginning to relax.

Sue laughed as we approached the coast. The land below was a tangled mass of steaming treetops. You could see the surface beneath only when the cover broke onto the dull shine of stagnant swamps. "I'd love to be along when the doctors inspect their investment," she said.

After our pilot set the plane down on a 900-foot field of yard-high saw grass, I jumped out and ran into the nearest bushes to empty my bursting bladder, strained by too much coffee and some anxious airborne moments. But once I saw the size of the mosquitoes, I was afraid to open my fly for fear that they'd castrate me.

"There's no way Agricola Itzapan will ever become a haven for Compass Club members," I shouted.

But the timber was there. Rubeaux told me how he planned to get the logs out. "We'll float them downstream to a harbor I'm going to build, and load them directly onto the ships. Never been done here before." He made the project sound totally feasible, and led me two miles through the jungle to view the harbor site.

Now I was excited, sensing the same soaring emotions I'd encountered at Lake Rudolf. Agricola Itzapan and Rubeaux offered a chance to challenge raw nature. "Here nothing is impossible," I thought. "How many others would ever meet such opportunity?"

Sue must have felt the same way, because her question "Do you think it will work?" was asked in a way that demanded an affirmative answer.

During the return flight Rubeaux showed me a tattered telegram, three months old, in which the Evans Products Company offered to buy every foot of lumber produced at Iriona and promised to issue irrevocable letters of credit to back up their word. So it was easy to say, "Problems provide opportunities," when Rubeaux told me that Roethe owed his silent partner, the president's brother-in-law, $20,000.

"So pay him," I said. I was still excited—but, the next moment, very tired when I realized that I was facing the outcome of decisions based mostly on dreams.

I slept hard. Sue told me the next morning that I'd been tangled in sweat-wet sheets all night. But the next day I felt completely rested.

When Rubeaux and I met our attorney for breakfast, I told him that I still wanted to proceed, "*Now* and *fast*. Form a new corporation. Use any name you like. You (because his father was a Cabinet Minister), Rubeaux and I will be the directors for now. Later, when they visit Honduras in person, we'll add Captain James Lovell and my other prominent partners."

The attorney's eyes glowed. Rubeaux's reflected hope. They both appreciate authority, I thought, patting their backs. "Get it done. I'll be back in two weeks."

In Madison, everything was running on schedule. Butters reported that the Cowdrey Crossroads purchase was legally closed. Quello flew in from the Twin Cities with Sorini Foods' final stockholder proxies. They were ready for ratification at the annual meeting, where the name would officially become Recreation International; new stock would be registered for public sale; and

O'Connor, Weast, Griffith, Anders, the doctors, Lovell, three Brain Trusters, and I would become the new board of directors, along with Roethe, his friend and partner Earl Jordan (I made a mental note to meet this mysterious man), and a Minnesota county commissioner representing the minority stockholders.

"No need to attend the general meeting," Quello said. "We'll hold the directors' meeting down here later. That's the important one where you'll be elected president." Then, quickly, he suggested that the company should make "investments of opportunity" in the Trans Polar Snowmobile Expedition—good publicity value—and in a venture importing Eskimo stone carvings, prestige items to sell at the World Wide Animal Kingdom.

Before Quello had finished, Higbie interrupted, "to deliver important news." A national magazine, available for immediate purchase, had been discovered. *Four Seasons Trails* was a trade publication for camping vehicle dealers. It could easily be converted to the national voice of Compass Club.

"Better yet," said Higbie, "an *international* publication. That will be easy, because John Strohm is part of the magazine's present publishing group."

It was late afternoon, several days later, before I had time to read my accumulation of mail. I marked most of the correspondence for dispersal to the Brain Trust, but held two envelopes to enjoy with my Cuba Libre. The first contained the finally approved plat for Walton Creek Park, and a note from Turnbull: "The last property to be zoned for multiple housing before Steamboat Springs slapped a moratorium on new construction." I felt like shouting when I saw that Turnbull had named streets after Vitner, Hollis, Kritchner, and me. "The last remnants of Diamond J are still hanging together."

The second letter was from Roethe. It confirmed my forthcoming meetings with the executive vice-president of CIIC at One Chase Manhattan Plaza, and with the president of Hilton International Hotels at the Waldorf Astoria.

"*Now* and *fast*." I finished my drink and rushed out to tell the rest of the world. "My dream is coming true."

13
Mid-June 1973

ASSETS—$2,416,212.00
LIABILITIES—$274,300.00
PERSONAL GUARANTEES—$11,300,000.00

The speaker on my mobile telephone squeaked "Good-bye" as Sue, twenty-five miles away, hung up, sounding annoyed because I was going to miss dinner. I switched off the receiver and turned into the Weatherby–Nasco parking lot, empty now except for Roethe's Cadillac in its usual spot near the main entrance of the sprawling building. The only light came from a window in the south wing. I pulled up beneath it and stepped out into the yellow glow as, inside, Roethe's shadow crossed in front of me.

He opened the front door. "Thanks for coming. I've got something great to show you. A surprise."

"Another dream about to come true?"

"This is no dream." He pushed me into the center of his office and pointed to the letters and brochures laid along the front edge of his desk. "This summer I'm leading the world's largest safari. Here it is." He thumped the nearest papers. "You and I, our families, astronauts, nobility, and selected business leaders are going to Kenya, under the auspices of Jomo Kenyatta and the African First Shotters."

I gulped a deep breath. "We are?"

Three days later Roethe delivered a huge gold-lettered membership certificate to my office.

"Welcome to the African First Shotters, the finest hunters ever assembled. Maybe soon they will affiliate with the Compass Club." He smiled so widely that his eyes squinted, and then he excused himself to check the safari roster with Griffith.

I knew Roethe meant that soon my club membership roster would include many of the names I'd read about in *Outdoor Life* and *Sports Afield* and *Time* and *Newsweek*. Roethe's powerful cronies and contacts seemed limitless; most of them were listed on the boards and committees of the organizations he promised would become part of Compass or Recreation International.

The African First Shotters Club was actively served by governors, U.S. senators, a count, airline presidents, and numerous other tycoons whose names were household words.

On top of that, according to Griffith, there were smatterings of media VIPs, like Roone Arledge, the ABC sports program producer, who might be invaluable promotion tools.

Griffith's associates were equally impressive, and had apparently evolved from the same recreational activities as Roethe's. I gave myself a big mental pat on the back. My original concept to create a massive, all-encompassing sportsman's lifetyle was tailor-made for these men.

Recently I'd sent the Martin 404 to fly eighteen Western bigshots, the entire operating committee of the One Shot Antelope Hunt, to a foofaraw (Roethe's name for an elite picnic-festival for his favorites) at Shagbark, a private hunting preserve near the Wisconsin Playboy Club. My plane had landed on the "Bunny Strip" in front of a crowd; word had spread that it was the biggest airliner ever to use the Playboy airfield. I remembered the surge of pride I had felt when the Bird taxied up to the waiting limousines and everyone from Playmates to press could see the four-foot-high Diamond J emblazoned on its nose.

I had soon discovered that a foofaraw was not just a fun time. Roethe's mysterious partner was there, Earl Jordan; he owned Shagbark and was also a Weatherby–Nasco board member and a principal in Wyoming Estates and Big Mountain Country. Two of the One Shot executives, an attorney and a bank president, were also partners in the Wyoming ventures. After the food and games, and speeches lauding everyone for something, we had had a private meeting in Jordan's nearby condominium complex.

Roethe, seeking another loan extension, had tried to convince the banker that Recreation International and/or Compass planned to buy Big Mountain Country for three times its appraised value, and then to spend $5 million developing a major ski resort. Jordan had lent the only air of fiscal respectability to the incredibly reckless proceedings.

A prominent general agent with Massachusetts Mutual Life Insurance Company, he had addressed our business with the same analytical persistence that, I supposed, he used for selling corporate retirement plans. He was the elder statesman, to be sure, who pictured himself a man of integrity, dependability, accomplishment—the wise, faithful friend, the experienced traveler—a man of quality. The image he projected was incongruous with what I knew to be his highly leveraged and hopelessly entangled position in the deficit financing of the Wyoming ventures as well as of his own Shagbark and resort condominium projects. He was also Roethe's quiet partner in the World Wide Animal Kingdom, now part of Recreation International.

I had enjoyed myself, thinking over and over again that "problems lead to opportunities." As the meeting ended, I had assured everyone that my companies offered their best solutions, and I could tell by the big smiles and happy handshakes that everyone had agreed.

"As a matter of fact," Roethe later said, "you're the best thing that ever happened to them."

Now, as Roethe and Griffith returned to my office, I felt my hands tingle with a sense of intense power—as if I could lift anything and everything from the dull shadow world of probable failure into the bold and brilliant atmosphere of the dreams I made come true. I wasn't walking in the footsteps of Horatio Alger; I was running past them.

The three of us reviewed the safari schedule and the guest list. Kritchner, representing the investors because Anders didn't want to go; the ever-present *Argosy* magazine photographer; the editor of *Gun Digest*, my latest addition to the Compass Club advisory board; and Sue and I joined astronauts Ron Evans and Joe Engle as VIP participants ("Lovell," said Roethe, "went on his freebie last year.").

When I turned the discussion toward the upcoming meeting of Recreation International's new directors, Roethe and Griffith acted as if every merger candidate should be acquired instantly.

"We have to show the bankers and stockholders some positive action," Roethe said. "The time for talk is past. We have to start merging or we'll lose our momentum."

"And now I'm ready to expand Compass Club, implement the direct-mail program, and open offices in New York."

"We'll need more money than we have now," I said. Here was the perfect opportunity to pin down the date for Roethe to repay his advances. "When will the consolidation loan proceeds be disbursed?"

"Soon, soon. Before we leave for Kenya." Roethe reached into his briefcase. "Now here you can see pictures of last year's less elaborate safari."

"Hold it," I shouted. "I want the rest of the answer to my question. An exact date—and the name of the lender. You'd better understand," I slapped my palm onto the album in Roethe's hands, "unless my companies and my investors get paid off, no one goes on the supersafari."

Griffith, unaccustomed to anyone bullying Leo Roethe, cleared his throat and tried to intercede. His lips made nervous, smacking sounds.

I stared him down and pointed out to Roethe that the millions promised by O'Connor, Shadel, and Quello all depended on proof of our ability to repay. "And your consolidation loan closing has got to be the first major evidence."

Roethe looked to see that the door was closed and leaned forward onto my desk. He looked back over his shoulder at Griffith, seemed to decide that he could keep the secret, and said, "The money is coming from the Central States, Southeast and Southwest Pension Fund. I'll have it all by the end of July."

I wanted to ask more, but, seeing how painful it was for Roethe to talk in front of Griffith, decided I had enough to begin my own private investigation. I knew Roethe realized I wasn't kidding about "no money—no safari."

And Roethe had already changed the subject. "Jordan thinks it would be a good idea to insure our key men," he said.

That made sense, especially since many of us were guaranteeing each other's notes. We decided, for starters, that the companies should cover me for $2 million, Roethe for half a million, and everybody else for at least $100,000.

"And Jordan gets his first dividend from Recreation International," I smiled. "Membership in the insurance million-dollar Round Table."

Griffith, now relaxing, suggested that Recreation International issue stock options to the members of its board.

"A good idea," I said. O'Connor, Weast, and Topp, Rosenheimer's old buddy, the mortgage banker, who had all demanded directorships, were now complaining that they needed a bigger piece of the action.

"I'll see that Quello takes care of the paperwork," Roethe said. Then he changed the subject again, passing me a list of new bills to pay. One was for legal fees incurred during the struggle with Gulf & Western.

"Everything okay now?" I inquired.

Roethe said that he, Anders, Lovell, and Jordan controlled the Weatherby–Nasco Board of Directors, and that Charlie Bludhorn had learned his lesson. "We're merging a new company into ours," he bragged. "Plastics manufacturer in New Jersey. Anders's country. They make pool balls."

"Pool balls?" I looked at my watch; it was 5:15 P.M. I went to the bar and began fixing drinks.

"None for me," Griffith said abruptly. "There's a lot of work left to finish today." He smiled in Roethe's direction, and both men began gathering their papers from my desk.

The next morning Griffith's secretary delivered a freshly typed memo advising all executives to clean house for a forthcoming visit by the head of KLM–Royal Dutch Airlines.

"Tell Griffith to be damn sure he coordinates this with my schedule," I said, passing the memo to Quarton. "Looks very important."

If the head of an airline was coming to *me*, either Griffith was a better salesman than he had said, or I was bigger than I'd thought, or the man from KLM had a problem.

"Opportunity knocks," I told Quarton. I packed my briefcase while I talked. "Tomorrow in New York I'm meeting with Curt Strand, president of Hilton International Hotels, to discuss the worldwide promotion of African Ponderosa, and with the senior officers of CIIC to plan our purchase of the game lodges. Then I'm making a quick flight back to Madison for an urgent meeting with Weast, Huffman, and O'Connor about American Leasing and Financial before I hop into the Aero Commander and continue west to fish with Anders on the Diamond J Ranch and inspect Big Mountain Country. Then I sneak away for a few days with Sue and my sons at Lone Tree."

Quarton frowned. "You've got to slow down, have some fun, get off alone somewhere."

"Don't need to. My business and pleasure are an easy mix."

Thirty-six hours later, as the Aero Commander hummed west high over the darkened plains, with only the red instrument lights and the flashing strobe beacon to distract me, I took a long mellow drag on my cigarette and let my eyelids slide nearly closed. I felt great. "Quarton should see me now."

The results of the meetings had been almost perfect. I could have African Ponderosa whenever I wanted. CIIC was treating me like a partner already, and was sending their senior vice-president, John Perfumo, to help with final details in Nairobi during the supersafari. Hilton had promised to give the operation its best shot. Strand had introduced me to his department heads and told them to work with my staff.

My biggest encouragement had come during the stopover in Madison, when O'Connor had stopped referring to my offices as a zoo and said, "I'll send Carter to Africa as your leg man. Quite possibly there'll be future opportunities for leases in Kenya."

In the meantime, Weast was moving fast, to establish our new headquarters in Washington, D.C., to finalize the Metcalf Farms lease of Shadel's equipment, and to sort out dozens of other "good lease applications" he'd already received from private referrals all over the country. And American Leasing and Financial's credit was assured. I was carrying loan guarantees for the lease lines. All of the important investors, including my brother, George, who was gratefully taking an active interest, had signed, except Anders. He would be added during our fishing trip, and, at the same time, would probably agree to help Weast secure another multimillion-dollar line at the Philadelphia National Bank.

Only one small, and probably insignificant, incident bothered me. In our scheduled "quick" meeting that afternoon, O'Connor had been called out to take a call from his bank. Even though he knew I was anxious to head west, he'd talked for nearly an hour behind closed doors, and when he came out I had noticed that he was toying with his glasses more than usual. And for the first time ever, I had seen sweat glistening on the palms of his hands. Otherwise O'Connor had still worn his expressionless mask. But it worried me.

Mild turbulence near the edge of a thundershower scattered sparks from my cigarette onto my suit. As I smelled the cloth burn, I remembered the time the kids and I had flown under a lenticular cloud hanging over the Rocky Mountains. Terrible turbulence had sent the altimeter spinning upward a thousand feet per second, finally flipping the light plane on its back at 25,-000 feet. It had been a terrifying experience, even for me, and after we were safely on the ground in Denver I had taken my sons aside to reassure them. There were no tears as we talked about fear and death, and I would never forget the wry little smiles and the words one of them had finally whispered: "When you die, you die."

I was anxious to see them again, and I needed to hold Sue; when the mountains made that first dim bulge on the dark horizon I let out my patented whoop and holler, loud enough to rattle the pilot into gyrations on the controls that almost duplicated the effects of a lenticular cloud. When we were straight and level again he looked at me, knitted his eyebrows, and asked what was going on.

"All us entrepreneurs are half nuts," I told him. "Better get used to it."

"I already am," he said.

And I detected a higher pitch to the engine as he eased the throttle forward. I didn't have to tell him that I was in a hurry.

Anders and I finished our business quickly. Neither of us was impressed by Big Mountain Country, even though Roethe's banker partner spared nothing on our celebrity tour of Lander, Wyoming, and the Shoshone National Forest. We were both invited on the One Shot antelope hunt and treated to a very private view of the inner sanctum of frontier banking. The banker's office was a combination club room with private bar, art gallery, and miniaturized World Wide Animal Kingdom; the bank's public areas were almost as opulent.

Anders shook his head. "I'll never borrow money in Wyoming. The interest rates have got to be too high."

The banker smiled. "Not for you. Now, what are you going to do about buying Big Mountain Country?" He leaned forward anxiously, seemingly ready to tell us that we could borrow the entire purchase price of the resort from him at no interest whatsoever.

"Let us think about it," I said tonelessly. "Right now we've got to get to the airport. I don't like to fly in the mountains after dark."

We left immediately.

"I've got a surprise for you," said Sue when we landed in Jackson County.

She was restoring the old homestead on Diamond J Ranch. Some of the same sons and brothers of my investors who'd rebuilt Lone Tree were already at work. I held her hand and watched John and George running around the dilapidated buildings. Smelling the pine pitch oozing from fresh-cut logs, I could easily envision the place regaining its rustic grandeur. I heard the North Platte River's subtle currents moving through my valley; I felt the prairie winds carry snow-crisped air from the nearby "Never Summer" range.

And now I've got another home, I thought. Five in all: the townhouse in Madison, the condominium in Steamboat, the penthouse in Denver, Lone Tree Ranch, the homestead. Too many, too close together along the backbone of the continental divide? Hell, no. This was my country—literally.

I went back to the Jeep, took Higbie's and Butters's latest reports out of my briefcase, and double-checked to be sure that they weren't neglecting to buy up the rest of Jackson County.

John and George said they had a surprise too. "A maverick bear is raiding the spring house at Lone Tree."

They'd tracked and marked his nightly path down from the hills, past the Outpost, stopping to raid the garbage dump, and through the willows to our compound. The caretaker had been alerted, they said, and was waiting up nights to shoot the "sonofabitch."

I started to deliver a lecture about bad language, but, hell, it was man talk in mountain country. So I smiled and told my sons, "I'll get you a bear rug."

"OK, Dad, but first let's go fishing."

By bedtime I'd forgotten every detail of my businesses except the nagging question of O'Connor's nervous hands. The more I worked to find an acceptable explanation the more I began to worry. As I peeled off my tight leather shirt, I swore and finished the sentence in my mind: "it isn't fair to ruin such a beautiful day."

John and George were chattering in their cabin and I was crawling into Sue's double sleeping bag when shots cracked from the direction of the Outpost. I dressed again, jumped into my Jeep, and tore along the dark road until I found the caretaker shining a dim flashlight beam into the willows along the stream.

"Missed, I think. Light's too weak," he said, leaning unconcerned against a fence post.

I switched on my own sealed-beam torch and saw tufts of fur on the barbed wire and fresh tracks in the mud. The caretaker and I had never talked much, anyway, so I didn't waste time with him. I turned off the light and crawled under the fence and into a tunnel made by cattle foraging in the bushes. Everything was suddenly very quiet. Even the stream, not more than thirty yards ahead, made only the faintest misty hiss, like soda effervescing in the bottom of a tall glass.

Gradually, easing forward on my elbows, I picked up a sound that was the funniest noise I'd heard all year. The bear was up ahead somewhere, chomping on the twins' stolen watermelon, smacking and sputtering; it sounded as if he were spitting out the seeds. I must have chuckled, because the willows suddenly cracked as the bear charged through them on his way toward the denser cover ahead. I crawled after him until I could feel moss along the streambank.

I smelled the bear. His odor was almost the same as that of a greasy frying pan lying in a sinkful of dirty water. I flashed my light until I saw red eyes on the opposite bank. I aimed my revolver below them and shot until there was only one cartridge left. The bear disappeared.

I tracked the bear for hours, crisscrossing the willow swamp, groping through the thickets until my light began to dim and Sue's shouts, mingled with the staccato honking of the Jeep horn, convinced me I'd better give up. I switched off my light and stood in total darkness for a moment, wondering how I'd explain my foolishness. Why was I chasing a wounded bear, at night, with just one bullet and a sheath knife? Because, Goddamnit, I had promised John and George a bear rug. And because it was fun to face a simple danger, where "when you died, you died."

Sue reminded me later, "You can't afford to get hurt."

On the way back to Madison, I stopped in Denver to check on Ingels's progress with Bright Star. The attorneys told me that he was considering an immediate cash sale rather than risk the cost of development.

That didn't sound like Elliot Ingels, and I started wondering if he was having trouble with his other investments. Rauterberg had mentioned that Florida was going to restrict condominium sales, which would definitely jeopardize Ingels's projected profits from the Commodore Club on Key Biscayne and the Tennis Club in Fort Lauderdale. If Ingels got panicky he might, in turn, frighten our mutual shareholders.

I telephoned Lindsey, who was still an investor in Bright Star and who was usually imperturbable, and asked him to nose around the banking community. He suddenly changed the subject. "What do you know about Leo's involvement with John King, the oil entrepreneur who's trying to usurp Bernie Cornfeld's mutual fund empire?"

"Nothing. Where'd you pick that up?"

"Rumors."

I figured that the source was someone in the Janesville group; if so, the rumors might be based on facts. So I went nosing around Denver, King's home base, and discovered that Griffith and several astronauts had lost money investing with King, who had sold them oil stock on hunting trips. Roethe wasn't involved, but had, on another occasion, solicited King's help in raising money for many of the ventures I was now backing. King had promised to provide collateral for Roethe's loans. He had failed to deliver when he became embroiled with Cornfeld. Soon after that, R. and R. had introduced Roethe to me.

I intended to get complete answers from Roethe when I returned to my offices the next day, but I wasn't able to see him alone. He was waiting with Richard Sleavin, the senior vice-president of Delafield Childs, to discuss a $6 million private placement of our securities.

"Very possible now, because Delafield Childs is a member of the New York Stock Exchange," Roethe said. He nodded and adjusted his French cuffs; the animal heads on his watchband seemed to wink at me again.

Sleavin interrupted. "No fund raising now. My company is only prepared to begin work as your consultants, corporate planners."

"Fine."

"Just as long as you understand, Mr. Stone, that we need more details, sufficient memorandums to assure an investment placement, before we undertake to help you secure financing." Sleavin's expression was a practiced mixture of bland, straight lips and serious, watery eyes.

"Yes, and . . ." I could tell there was more.

"Recreation International must contract to pay our standard

fees and expenses, and tender commissions and stock options when money is located."

"Expensive." I suppressed a grin and nodded toward Roethe, referring to his recent letter on my desk. "Leo tells me that Governor Knowles called and said there was a company in Minneapolis that has $15 million and wishes to invest in a business here in Wisconsin. He thinks maybe they might be interested in Recreation International." I cocked my head. "So you see, Mr. Sleavin, you're not the only one working for us."

I agreed to his terms. "But not exclusive."

As Roethe and Sleavin left together, O'Connor drove up, and my secretary paged me to take a call from Anders.

"It's going to be a busy week, Art," I said, grabbing the nearest phone.

Anders was worried about the lease guarantee signed in Colorado. "It was not completely filled in."

"Of course not. We're not sure when, where, and for how much," I said.

"Well, make damn sure it's not over a million, and only for leases." He still sounded perturbed. "Remember I've already had almost $2 million tied up in Roethe, Stone, and companies."

I tried to make him laugh. "You're our golden goose."

Anders grunted.

O'Connor wanted the guarantees at once, and I was suddenly reluctant to give them to him.

O'Connor insisted. "Weast shouldn't lose his momentum." He positioned his half-moon glasses low on the bridge of his nose and stared over the top of them.

"What's the problem?" I asked slowly, because O'Connor knew that when I spaced my words I was hanging tough too.

"No problem."

I should have known that it had been too easy to overpower him, but the next new order of business was too much a pleasant surprise.

"I used $50,000 from my extra discount-expenses fund to buy stock in a new bank for Janeff." He smiled and corrected himself. "American Leasing and Financial now owns part of a bank."

That was hard to believe; O'Connor did not usually share his profits. When I made him explain the transaction, he said that a mutual friend of his and Rauterberg's had chartered a bank on the west side of Milwaukee, misjudged the investor interest, and sought help meeting capital requirements.

"So I reinvested some of the expense money in American Leasing's name. It's all in the family," he said. "My banker buddy's already made loans to you through his other bank."

Now I understood. O'Connor had come to the aid of a banker who was always available to participate in the chain of loan shufflers. By opening another bank, he'd provided just one more place to move and hide unpaid, unsecured loans when the regulatory authorities complained.

"As a matter of fact," O'Connor told me, "this is the same banker who helped with the original Camp Dells purchase. You guys are fellow directors."

I nodded, waiting for him to say more. He seemed to be leading up to something.

"The bank stock will beef up American Leasing's financial statement. That will make it easier for all the bankers to process the loans all of your companies always guarantee."

"So?"

"You need more banks you can depend on," he said, "because I'm running out of money."

"Really?" I smiled now, thinking he was teasing.

O'Connor pulled his glasses down to the very tip of his nose and glared at me. "Be serious. The most important project is American Leasing and Financial. They must have a million to buy leases with, right now. That's why I need the signed guarantees today. . . . You're sure you have them?"

I nodded, but didn't speak right away. I was angry; O'Connor was placing the fortunes of Weast and American Leasing ahead of Compass and Recreation International. "But what about the other ventures, Walter? They're going to need a lot of money too, and I had counted on another million from you."

"You weren't listening." He raised his voice. "If emergencies arise you can borrow from the new bank, and hell, there's always

Roethe's friend Shadel. I can help you make more deals with him."

I kept staring at him, still upset.

"Don't worry," O'Connor said as I bit my lower lip, "Johnny won't suffer."

All I had to do was deliver the guarantees, and execute an inch-thick stack of documents, to tie up the loose ends I'd overlooked while I was running around the world, leaving, as O'Connor put it, "poor Walter to cover my six-figure bum checks."

"Where did all your other money go?" I wanted to know, now. And I wouldn't let O'Connor beg off with a cliché about not putting all his eggs in one basket.

Quietly, with many pauses, he told me that there were other large loan commitments to a developer friend of Rauterberg who was buying the King's Gateway, a resort hotel in northern Wisconsin, and building a resort subdivision called Wild River, patterned after Sun Valley. Both were good prospects for Compass Club affiliation. Then he reminded me that my own CPA, Toussaint, was referring his clients for financing.

"You get a fee from that," O'Connor noted.

That didn't pacify me. O'Connor seemed to be playing games. I kept staring at him, feeling my face redden.

"Tell your boy to get his ass moving before I have to say no. Look, John," and now O'Connor seemed more sympathetic and sincere than before, "I have to spread my money around. Otherwise the Banking Commission will shut us down. I'm trying to take care of you. Better a few extra dollars on Toussaint's deals than nothing."

"OK, but I want assurance that the American Leasing commitment is firm and that you *will* arrange another million from the rest of the banks." I started to tell him we could be bankrupt if just one segment of the multimillion-dollar money package was lost, but he had read my mind; he said it for me.

"Make sure Roethe pays you off, and Quello comes through with the Minnesota money. You're barely making your interest payments, and one of these days soon you'll have to knock down some principal."

O'Connor gathered up the signed papers and left, and I rubbed the moisture off my own palms as I wondered how long it would be before I had the actual ability to crack a $10 million debt.

The nicest fringe benefit of my business was the built-in mechanism to defer depression. Too much was always happening too fast to leave time for sustained worry. Today, for instance, Griffith had put everyone to work readying our offices for the visit by KLM's chieftain—"That's the word he used, chieftain," said Quarton facetiously.

F. O. Kielman, who immediately insisted that I call him Fritz, was the most magnetic man I'd met so far. Unlike Roethe's charisma, which bombarded me with frenzied dreams of power, Kielman's charm enveloped me with a sense that, standing close to him, success was safely assured.

Fritz was about fifty years old, and his face combined the wind-burned lines and craggy, sun-bleached highlights of the frontiersman with the quick, wide-set eyes of the connoisseur and the large, sculptured lips of the continental stud. He was very tall, with wide shoulders, big hands, and head solid with sandy hair. He spoke slowly to cover a stammer that really only added to his magnificent image—it became a human weakness perfectly controlled. The man was beautiful and he knew it, but I was comfortable and felt no awe as I casually studied him.

Griffith winced when I ignored preliminaries and said, "A man of your stature, Fritz, does not fly to Madison, Wisconsin, without a good reason. What is it?"

And I saw that that had been the best opening possible when Kielman smiled and, talking as if I were the only other man in the room, said "I do have a problem, which, very possibly, you can help me solve."

I clasped my hands behind my head, leaned back in my chair, and listened as Kielman, after waving down Griffith's attempted prologue, told the story of Continental Royal Services, CRS.

In addition to his public position as director of KLM's operations in the western hemisphere, he was the power sub rosa and the primary silent investor in CRS, a wholesale travel agency that also packaged private tours and controlled a retail tourist business, in Florida. He was similarly involved with the Hotel Bonaire in the Neatherland's Antilles. The hotel, of course, obtained most of its bookings from KLM and CRS.

"All of these companies involve Dutch-oriented travel and tourism, but"—Kielman spread his hands—"there are many ripe opportunities to expand. German and Japanese tourists are clamoring to visit the United States because of the monetary advantages of spending the deflated dollar. And American travelers, apparently unconcerned with their inflation, are anxious to broaden their horizons within the U.S. and to every other continent."

By using KLM, Martinaire (one of the world's largest charter airlines), which was closely associated with CRS, and other scheduled airlines with which he had private agreements, Kielman intended to reap a worldwide travel harvest. He.knew exactly how the system should operate, and he apparently had the right contacts to make it work.

"Fantastic." I couldn't restrain myself. "What's the problem?"

Kielman explained that he had a partner, with whom he had had a disagreement, and that he was delaying negotiations with Gulf and hiding the key ingredients to a "guaranteed success."

" 'Tropics,' " whispered Griffith, looking at Kielman for acknowledgment. A weak, stupid power play, I thought. He'd been briefed beforehand when he had arranged the meeting, and now he was clumsily trying to assure himself of a share of the spotlight. I ignored him and focused on Kielman.

" 'Tropics,' " he repeated, stammering on the second syllable. "The software to a computer system that offers instant, on-location, total trip planning, scheduling, reservations and ticketing."

"He means everything—air, ground transportation, hotels, meals, supplementary tours if you like," said Griffith, enthusiasm pushing his voice well above its normal pitch.

The "Tropics" system, simplified for universal usage, made it possible for ordinary ticket and travel agents to compute an entire itinerary on a remote unit, confirm, and issue complete tour packages on the spot.

I took a deep breath, stretched my eyelids, and stared at Kielman. He was talking about a process that could eliminate travel agencies, as I knew them, and make billions for the men that introduced it. "How do you know 'Tropics' will work?" I heard myself stammer and hoped Kielman wouldn't think I was mocking him.

"It *is* working, in Europe. KLM owns the software," he said, smiling. Waiting for my next question, he seemed to be enjoying my excitement.

I had many questions, but I didn't ask them. First I had to unscramble the tumbling ideas from the dollar signs whirling through my mind. I forced my attention to focus on one and took a very deep breath before I said, in a carefully level voice, "Let me rephrase my initial question. Why do you need me? You can't need my money. You can pick from the biggest money machines in the world, and find new front men at the same time."

"Certainly the concept can be sold," Kielman said very slowly. "But I want to keep it myself and share with just a small group. Dick Griffith's convinced me that you are small enough to share, yet big enough to make everything work." He paused and tapped the new Compass Club folio on my desk. "And I happen to like your ideas." His smile broadened.

I ran my hand across the plastic-coated folio and looked down at the three-color logo imprinted in the center of the simple off-white cover. Very tasteful, but portending the powerful contents. Griffith and Quarton had really produced a winner. Monthly tabloid newsletters, four-color brochures, a list of properties and affiliates that rivaled the Triple A roster, decals, embroidered shoulder patches, gold-embossed membership cards, a mock-up of our national magazine, *Four Seasons Trails*. Very impressive, very expensive. A rich package with an advisory board almost beyond cost, authenticated by memos from governors, letters from tycoons and bank presidents, telegrams from Lovell and three new astronauts (Ron Evans, Joe Engle, and Stu Roosa) recruited to promote my "celestial" concepts (I dug that bit of Quartonesque), and even a hand-written note from Ernest Borgnine telling me he'd serve. And another long list of participating international sportsmen, most of whom were already Kielman's friends.

"I'm sure we all agree there can be some tremendous mutual

benefits in the merger of our interests," said Griffith, who now acted as if he were representing CRS and Kielman instead of me, his employer.

Kielman must have noticed this too, because, with an apologetic look, he asked, "Would you consider combining our concepts and efforts on a fifty-fifty basis?"

"Certainly," I said, hiding my amazement. "You'll get an honest front, an organization that functions smoothly and adapts easily, the use of my total facilities, and the support of Recreation International. And I'll have the opportunity to leapfrog half the hurdles I face making my companies the leaders of the Decade of Recreation."

"Good speech."

And I knew we had a deal.

Griffith took Kielman to lunch alone, explaining as they left that "John never eats until evening."

He was right, and I welcomed the time alone even though I realized that Griffith wanted this chance to politic a bigger role in the Compass-CRS reorganization. It didn't matter; I was sure Kielman abhorred ass-kissing.

I closed my office door and began wandering from one long wall to the other. I looked at the rows of identically framed photographs of my properties and projects, my maps and Master Plans. There were more stacked in the closet, but no place to hang them. "So what?" Anyone could see that I was in big business—and, from the look of it, that I owned a little bit of everything. More than a little bit. But what had happened that morning seemed unreal, even to me. In less than three hours I'd accepted an unexpected proposal to do business with some of the largest companies in the world. It happened so fast it might have been preordained.

Now my future was irresistible. I telephoned Judy.

"I need you on my staff."

She'd been reluctant when I had asked her to work for me several weeks earlier, but now something in my voice must have been overpowering.

She said, "Yes. How soon?"

"Need you ask?" I laughed. I hung up when I saw Kielman's

assistant returning from lunch with the rest of my Brain Trust.

I buzzed my secretary and told her to fetch him, realizing, when she asked, that I'd forgotten his name. He was plump and rosy-cheeked, shorter than I was, with close-cropped, dark-blond hair. He spoke precise English with just a trace of guttural accent, and he made a quick short bow as he introduced himself.

"Henk Guitjens, sir." His eyes drifted downward after a moment of direct contact.

Guitjens was my idea of a classy assistant, and I was both excited and possessively proud when he said he looked forward to working for me.

"There'll be a lot for us all to learn," I said, "so I'll arrange for you to spend as much time with me as necessary right after my return from Africa."

He laughed. "We'll see each other much sooner. Didn't you know, sir? CRS is handling all the arrangements for the safari."

I started laughing too.

Kielman came in. "May I join the fun?"

"I should have known you'd be overseeing a *Super* Safari," I told him.

"Yes, you should have known," said Griffith, interrupting in a prissy tone. "Fritz is a past president of the African First Shotters."

Guitjens blinked, and I knew that my real power struggle with Griffith had begun. I smiled at Guitjens and cocked an eyebrow toward Griffith. Stupid sonofabitch, didn't he know when to back away from a fight he could never win?

Kielman and I scheduled a formal meeting with Kraemer, our attorneys, and my man from Delafield Childs the following month —"the first week we'll both be in the United States at the same time."

We spent the rest of the afternoon until plane time talking hunting. Kielman told me not to miss the One Shot antelope hunt.

"An excellent opportunity to meet men who may be able to assist us," he said.

"I'll be there. Leo Roethe's arranged for me to hunt as a special guest of the Wyoming game and fish commissioner."

Kielman scowled when he heard Roethe's name. He and Roethe were involved in many of the same recreation and conservation projects, and moved in similar circles; they were supposed to be personal friends. Yet it was obvious that Kielman was angry. I'd been holding my close association with Roethe as a trump card. Now I was grateful that Kielman had telegraphed his feeling before I played it.

According to Kielman, Roethe had promised to arrange special financing for the Hotel Bonaire but had never produced. He had also, a year earlier, offered Kielman an unsolicited, custom-built Weatherby rifle, "a one-of-a-kind;" it had had not been delivered either.

"I didn't want the rifle, but I can't tolerate broken promises," Kielman said.

Then I saw Griffith jot a note and knew that Kielman would have his rifle shortly. I also knew that I should never use full shit on Kielman, no matter how positive it was, and though money had not been mentioned, I knew I dared not arrive empty-handed at our next meeting in New York. That made Roethe's repayment of advances even more important.

Later, when I called to ask about the exact closing date, Roethe said, "Any day."

At first I was relieved and satisfied. Then, after a moment's thought, nothing made sense. Every lender, especially the big boys, verified their collateral well in advance of a closing. But I had not been contacted yet, and I had accumulated most of Roethe's securities in the process of paying off his debts. Also, the lender had to determine the payoff balances before any loan proceeds could be disbursed. Considering Roethe's list of debts, that was a week-long job in itself. "Any day" began to sound like more bullshit.

I dialed Roethe back. "Talk is not enough. I've got to see proof: a letter of commitment."

"That's impossible. And if you don't stop asking questions you're liable to queer the deal."

That made me more suspicious. No one loaned $10 million secretly and unsecured. "If I have to fuck up the deal to get straight answers, I will. Because either way it's beginning to sound like a loser."

"Take it easy. I'll be right over to explain."

Ten minutes later Rosenheimer phoned. His voice was higher than usual. "Roethe's loan is a sure thing. Only you can't push the Teamsters around."

I hadn't had time to investigate the Central States Pension Fund. I hadn't been sure it was part of the Teamsters. Now I had my answer, and I was sure that something was wrong: The Teamsters couldn't afford to overlook loan documentation. I'd read somewhere that all their loans were being investigated by the feds, and that Dorfman had been sent to jail for loan kickbacks shortly after I had drunk with him at the Jack-O-Lantern Lodge. I wondered if he had anything to do with Roethe's loan. Had there been an ulterior motive behind my supposedly social invitation to the Teamsters' playpen? I called Higbie in, and was explaining how I wanted to use his neglected investigative talents when Roethe arrived, watching us suspiciously.

The minute Higbie left Roethe's expression changed quickly to anger, then again to a mixture of sympathy and anxiety. Deep furrows appeared on his forehead.

"I know you're trying to do big things," he said, "but don't work yourself up over matters you know nothing about. And no counterintelligence tricks. My loan's too vital for both of us." He patted my shoulder. "Now, I need my Metcalf stock today to show the pension fund men. Then you can make a complete list of all the collateral for me tomorrow."

"Everything?"

"That's right. The loan was approved on the basis of my pledging everything I own."

"You'll have your list tomorrow, but what about my written proof of the loan?"

"Didn't Rosenheimer call you?"

"Yes, but what's he got to do with this?"

Roethe looked around the room with the same suspicious expression he usually reserved for Higbie. "Jim helped me find the loan brokers. You've got to have faith, like I told everybody else."

He made me promise not to make waves with any more questions until the loan was finalized.

"I'll tell you all about it on the way to Kenya." Roethe took his Metcalf stock and walked out, looking as confident as I'd ever seen him.

"Either he's telling the truth or he's lost his mind," I told Higbie. He was already back in my office, with the report that some newspaper reporters thought James Hoffa owned part of the Jack-O-Lantern Lodge.

"Do you think Anders, because of his trucking business, is mixed up in this?" he asked, nervously fingering his tie.

I shook my head. Then I took a long look at Higbie and smiled. He'd made a big change recently; he had discarded his idea that color coordination meant using the four basic colors all at once, and his slicked-down hair was now fluffy, styled mod. He looked as if he could keep fitting with my fast flying plans, especially since he'd acquired the loaded yellow Corvette, which gave him the first semblance of prosperity.

"Stop checking on Roethe for the time being and concentrate instead on O'Connor and Rosenheimer's activities." I could afford to gamble on Roethe for a little while longer, but not if I got any unpleasant surprises from my bankers. I decided to give Higbie some help, by canvassing my own sources of information.

Lindsey told me that he'd confirmed Elliot Ingels's plans to dump Bright Star, "because rising construction costs have eliminated the quick profit potential of building Alpine Village." There was nothing adverse on the Tennis Club.

"But you may have a problem," he said. "The state banking examiners are checking everywhere and criticizing your loans. Right now, it would be good if you paid me off."

Lindsey sounded very concerned; I knew he'd never ask for a principal payment unless it was urgent.

Rauterberg echoed Lindsey. The state bank examiners were beginning to raise hell because the Diamond J–John Stone–Compass–Recreation International loans seemed to appear on the books of almost every bank they inspected. Rauterberg said it was time to start paying them off.

"Damn good thing Leo's getting his money soon," Rauterberg said. "After you spread some of it around there'll be no problem."

When I called a hasty meeting with O'Connor and Shadel, to be sure that they still agreed to provide the next million, Shadel seemed very nervous. He hadn't been bothered by examiners, but he expected them. Nonetheless, he promised to honor his commitment so long as I kept reducing the debts Metcalf Farms owed to him. And O'Connor guaranteed that if Shadel made the loans as scheduled he would move them out of Shadel's banks by winter. After they shook hands to seal the bargain I began to relax.

Then, as he was leaving, Shadel said, "I'm doing this because I know Leo's loan is going through."

And I was really content, enough to take the rest of the afternoon off and visit the twins, who were just back from Colorado.

"The bear's still prowling around instead of being a rug," they told me.

"I'll bring you a lion from Africa instead."

The Kenyan Ambassador to the United States appeared at my office several days later, a surprise visit arranged by Roethe. He seemed overwhelmed by the Compass and Recreation International concepts, and, without any solicitation, promised the complete cooperation and assistance of his office.

"Very impressive," he repeated as he toured the complex, leaving a trail of hyperenthusiastic Brain Trusters and speechless secretaries behind him.

Later the same day McCaskill, who said he had stopped in because he was curious, told me, "I've never seen so many companies, interlocking so many motives, beliefs, and purposes, move so far and so fast before. It's a gathering of eagles."

And I, having fired McCaskill because I thought he was the world's weakest sales motivator "who couldn't even sell his own pseudopsychological services," made a note to rehire him, retrain him, and make him a success, too.

Now I felt able to do anything.

It was difficult to withhold public announcement of the pending venture with CRS, but Kielman and I agreed to wait until more details had been decided and a memorandum of intent

signed. My key investors and Brain Trusters knew the funda-
mentals, and, in spite of my warning not to leak anything, could
not help displaying outrageous enthusiasm. They all looked ready
to explode, and soon the word was out that "Stone's about to do
it again."

My spirits soared higher, my ego so strong that when Roethe
told me that the Teamsters deal had been delayed slightly and
that his lawyers (using a power of attorney) were going to close
the $10 million loan while all of us were in Africa, I never said a
word.

14
August 1973

ASSETS—$2,612,400.00
LIABILITIES—$476,405.00
PERSONAL GUARANTEES—$14,650,000.00

Five minutes after the KLM DC-10 lifted off the runway at Kennedy Airport I'd forgotten everything but having fun.
Griffith, who, as usual seemed willing to be anybody's man but
mine, helped settle the rest of the African First Shotters and
tagged after Roethe while he welcomed the astronaut VIPs. I ignored everyone but Sue and Henk Guitjens, and, between gulps
of Heineken beer, which the stewardess delivered to us two bottles at a time, listened to him describe the grand tour of Amsterdam that "I'm taking you on during our first overnight stop."

I don't remember sleeping during the next forty-eight hours.
We drank and laughed and traded stories.

I told about the time I had pacified a screaming mob of irate
mothers who were demanding admission refunds from the World
Wide Animal Kingdom because, they said, "The collection of 200
Ethiopian songbirds shot by Leo Roethe is a disgrace, a terrible
example for our impressionable children."

When I had explained that the songbirds were not shot by Mr.
Roethe, but were rather collected in a butterfly net during months
of safari hardship by a man who devoted his life to the profitless
preservation of beauty. the women had immediately promised to

303

recommend the Museum to their friends—and had all bought memberships in Compass Club.

Someone else, pointing to the astronauts, said, "I know a fool-proof method for any man to screw his way across Europe and then Africa. All he needs is to travel with a man who's been to the moon, and a pocketful of pebbles picked up in any parking lot."

A piece of gravel bounced into Sue's lap, and another voice said, "Moon rocks, baby."

"Try that in any bar in any language, and you'll have to run or be raped," someone shouted.

At our "In touch with the Dutch" banquet in Amsterdam, Griffith and Roethe gave everyone a title. Sue was "the first lady of recreation," and O'Connor's man Carter, who had begun the trip as a business advisor, was elevated to "ambassador."

"You might have been Secretary of State, but 'no bullshit' is the rule," I told him.

The next morning, wandering along the canals, we found a Sex Supermarket, complete with grocery carts. I walked out with a shopping bag full of French Ticklers, psychedelic dildoes, and an electric vibrating penis with a Santa Claus head. I wondered what Kenyan customs would say when they opened my suitcase.

"They'll either lock your ass up or beg to join Compass Club," said Kritchner.

"No problem. Leo's leading the way," leered Carter.

I grinned. Carter was at least seventy years old, and usually stodgy. That had to be his first sexy line since joining my staff.

"See, Compass is a way of life."

We did some heavy shopping during our next layover, Munich, and must have been 200 pounds overweight when we boarded the final flight to Nairobi.

Henk Guitjens said, "No problem."

"Thataboy." He was a great luggage handler and an efficient assistant, and he was learning my language.

I stopped drinking and eased out of the games somewhere high over the Congo. When Sue reminded me that John Perfumo from CIIC was meeting me in Nairobi to finish negotiating the purchase of African Ponderosa, I sobered up in a hurry.

In view of the rumors that state banking officials might try to shut off my lines of credit, and with O'Connor's long-term financial commitments somewhat doubtful, I knew that I somehow had to delay obligating myself to bail out APL.

I poked at the ice cubes in my empty glass and finally popped one into my very dry mouth. Anders was still opposed to any investment in Kenya, so I couldn't count on him. And the day before I left, Sommers had told me that my companies had better be prepared to pump another $200,000 into Metcalf Farms or face a total loss; maybe the bastard still hated me for grabbing Janeff.

Sue looked worried. "Why don't you cancel your itinerary and stay in Kenya for the full two weeks? You're edgy and exhausted."

"Hell."

"Listen to me. You can't cram a vacation into two days of drinking. You'll have a breakdown."

I laughed, but I *was* envious of the time Roethe and company would spend playing white hunter, and I *was* tired. My schedule —working two days in Nairobi, hunting two days, working another day in Nairobi, and then catching a flight to London to meet CIIC's British associates, on the way back to ten solid days of appointments in America—was no vacation. I was afraid, however, to be away longer. These were critical times.

Sue wanted to return with me. Her eyes were sad as she pleaded, "We're so seldom together—and never just by ourselves."

"Someone's got to bird-dog Roethe," I told her, nodding toward him and Griffith. They were huddled over the safari camp assignments sheets, probably plotting who would sleep next to the astronauts.

"You have to stay for the whole safari," I told her again. "I need you to represent me."

Sue stared at me.

"Remember, there's that private audience with President Kenyatta toward the end of the trip. Only the astronauts, the Roethe family, and you are invited."

"OK, OK."

She didn't sound convinced. I felt my voice shift into its selling range. "I need you. For God's sake, can't you see that right now those three words mean more than 'I love you?'"

Sue closed her eyes and nodded slowly, but I knew she didn't buy my premise. She understood that she was being used, accepted her role, and enjoyed the prestige, but she was beginning to tell me in many different ways that she needed something more than power and glory. I closed my eyes too and lay back, nervously picking at the loose skin on my neck. Was it possible that the disastrous days with Judy might be repeating themselves with Sue?

The jet landed in Nairobi just after midnight. Carter, Sue, and I zipped through customs and immigration inspection ahead of the others, and because our travel arrangements were supplemented by orders for VIP treatment from Hilton International, we were quickly chauffeured to our suites at the Nairobi Hilton. A lucky break, I discovered an hour later, when I went down to the lobby to look for Roethe. Seventy-five overtired and very angry African First Shotters were crowded around the reservation desk as the night manager tried to explain to Guitjens, Roethe, and Griffith that Telex communications had never confirmed their reservations for the first night of the Supersafari.

"The hotel is booked solid."

Since I didn't want so many potential promoters and investors to connect me with their problem or to envy my comfortable accommodations, I eased into the nearest shadows and sneaked back to the elevators. Then, as the doors slid closed, I laughed aloud. What a perfect time for Griffith to assume command and learn his first lesson on how to lose a power struggle!

Perfumo called me early the next morning. "Take a cold shower to fight off jet lag so you'll be sharp at our 10:00 A.M. meeting with the local bankers, attorneys, and securities registrar."

It was urgent that the APL acquisition arrangements be completed before Roethe's disaffected shareholders notified the Kenyan creditors that they were assuming a hands off policy. If that happened, Laxmanbhai was certain to begin involuntary bankruptcy proceedings.

On my way to the meeting I ran into Carter, who was window shopping.

"Have fun," I said.

I didn't need him to back me up today. Everything was perfect.

The pressure was on CIIC. They stood to lose their investment—and, more important, much face.

"And that's something Chase and David Rockefeller can't afford," I told Carter.

He patted my shoulder. "In diplomatic circles, they'd say you were about to pull a coup d'etat."

At the meeting I made it clear to everyone: "Recreation International's directors are not about to be pressured into a hasty agreement." I made Anders the badass, explaining that he was privately supporting many other Roethe ventures and was ready to recommend dumping APL. "Unless all the existing creditors, Chase included, are willing to sweeten the pot."

"Aren't you the financial director?" Laxmanbhai's attorney asked.

Perfumo's icy stare seemed to question my authority to speak for Anders or Recreation International, and I knew I had to avoid a "yes, but" answer.

"I agree with Anders," I said. "You seem awfully desperate. What are you hiding?"

Perfumo's face tightened into an angry mask.

"I'm here to complete the investigation of African Ponderosa," I told them, "not to buy a pig in a poke."

Then I waited for the Asian businessman's advocate to explain the expression to his client, and stood up to emphasize my next statement.

"Edmund Carter, formerly with the U.S. State Department and now representing my banks, is here to supervise the preparation of a complete financial analysis when all your ducks are in a row."

Again I paused for breath, reviewing the impact of my statements as the advocate explained my slang. I hoped Perfumo realized what a great stalling technique I'd discovered. But I swallowed hard when it occurred to me that he might also figure out the real reason for my delaying tactics—doubts that I could find enough money to close the deal.

"We are anxious to have all the facts," I resumed. "Then we will move quickly to assume ownership of the lodges. As a matter of fact, I'm already working on the master management plan with the president of Hilton International."

I looked to Perfumo for verification, because now it seemed sensible to offer some concrete evidence of my intentions to eventually buy APL.

Perfumo nodded. "I'm satisfied." Afterwards he shook my hand and, with a comradely grin, showed his respect for my ability to deal effectively in the African business climate.

That gave me the chance to tell him privately, "Everything I said was preplanned to iron the kinks out of APL. Carter should have everything we need within two weeks, sooner if he gets some extra help."

I assumed Perfumo would take the hint and work with Carter while I went hunting.

The safari moved into the bush the next morning, and by mid-afternoon I was shooting my first African game. That day I killed record impala and eland. The second day I added record Grants and Thompson gazelles, and could have shot almost every other species of African game.

Roethe's safari, as far as I was concerned, was perfectly organized—instant exposure to every experience Hemingway ever wrote about. I didn't have to go into the bush looking for Masai warriors. They came to our camp to see Ron Evans, "the man from the sky," and I did my share of pointing to the fading daytime moon in the cloudless, pale-blue yonder.

While taking a shower in the topless canvas bathhouse, I saw a pair of giraffes walk by, so close it seemed they'd come to look in on me. Lions roared each night, so close that I joked that Roethe had sent half of our huge staff of native attendants to herd them in while the other half stood guard to keep them out of our tents.

Roethe apologized because I hadn't had the chance to shoot an elephant or a lion.

"No problem," I grinned. "Next year we'll do it right. I may even buy a hunting license."

I made Ron Evans promise to look after Sue and Roethe ("Remember, you're the Boy Scouts' idol").

And just before leaving camp I looked at my lineless face in our tent mirror and said to Sue, "Who ever said you can't cram a lifetime into a few days?"

As soon as I returned to Nairobi, I called the Madison office, where Higbie must have been waiting at the switchboard.

"Roethe's loan isn't closed yet."

The telephone suddenly felt slippery in my hand. "What does Rosenheimer say?"

"Any day now," said Higbie, mimicking Rosenheimer's daily report. Then he said, "I'm worried."

"So am I," I responded. "On the other hand, Roethe's on safari without a care in the world. It seems unlikely that he could be so Goddamn happy unless the loan's a sure thing. What else?"

"Everything else is perfect. No shit. No new rumbles from the Banking Commission. All our loans are current, and we've got all our checks covered."

I could see him smiling and pushing Quarton away from the phone.

"Tell him to stay over there an extra week and give us a rest," Quarton's voice yelled in the background.

If Quarton was joking, everything *had* to be all right. I decided to save a day and fly directly from New York to Houston, where Lovell and I were scheduled to visit the Y-O Ranch and sign up "the biggest and best hunting reserve in Texas" for Compass Club, as John Connally suggested.

"Send my Aero Commander to Houston. It'll give me mobility."

"What crew?"

"Captain Feisty," I paused; a wild idea had hit me. "And the new director of affiliates as copilot. She's qualified."

"Judy to Texas." I heard Higbie talking to himself as he made notes. Then he chuckled. "You want me to send Shari to carry your bags off the plane in New York?" Quarton was on the extension now, laughing. "Have fun," he said, "and don't hurry."

Perfumo's return trip tickets were first-class; mine were tourist.

"I work for a first-class company," he said, as I sent Carter to upgrade my reservations.

I anticipated a happy flight.

Perfumo and I reviewed the proposal to transfer control of APL.

"As soon as you're ready." He hoped that was soon, because CIIC had other problems for him to solve. Next week he was going to Korea to troubleshoot a factory investment, and then there were South American problems.

I listened carefully. Although Perfumo was using vague and guarded language, it sounded as if CIIC was an extremely loose lender. I figured that after we were better friends I'd find a way to talk him into increasing the APL loan so I could end up buying the lodges for nothing.

Perfumo shot down that daydream when he said he hoped the APL problem got solved fast. "There's another CIIC officer's job riding on the outcome." In fact, he began to talk as if the loan should never have been made in the first place. His opinion of Roethe paralled Kielman's. The CIIC man who'd handled Roethe's account had been conned, along with the other industrialists who'd guaranteed the construction overrun agreements, and, according to Perfumo, Curt Strand and Hilton International were also disenchanted with Roethe's dream merchandising; they were only hanging on for my infusion of new blood and fresh capital. Perfumo emphasized "*fresh capital*," and he made his point.

No new money from Chase. CIIC wanted to bail out of a bad deal, but if necessary, they were plenty big enough to let APL sink into the sands of the Taita Hills, fire the men responsible for buying Roethe's bullshit, and forget me and my companies.

As we carved our filets and sampled each others' vintage wines (his red, mine white) and chatted like old buddies, I realized the important lesson I had just learned. There were no opportunities to be found amidst the problems of bigger organizations with bigger money, unless . . . I sipped my wine and pondered . . . *unless* their obvious problems were only the tip of an iceberg of trouble.

I told Perfumo the story of Roethe's $20,000 donation for the hospital in the Taita Hills. "Jack Shako, the minister of tourism, handled the funds. But there's no sign of a hospital. We looked and looked, and finally my investigators discovered that Shako had begun construction of his own tourist lodges at the edge of the Tsavo game preserve just after Roethe's check cleared the bank. But no hospital."

Then I switched gears: "Here's an astonishing revelation. My contact at the Nairobi Branch of the Stanley Bank says that Tanzania, the country bordering Kenya to the south, is teaming with the Red Chinese, who financed a railroad—a line from the inland mines to the coast—after American money magnates refused to help."

Perfumo, chewing on his steak, nodded.

I spoke faster, louder. "So what's Chase's real reason for fooling with Roethe's game lodges when they could be playing with railroads next door?"

Perfumo, obviously shaken, quickly redirected our conversation to the details of transferring Recreation International's pending investment capital to Kenya.

I told him that I didn't understand international monetary controls, and would "leave that up to Chase," but, just as there'd been no response to my previous loaded question, Perfumo now ducked the assumption of any further financial responsibility and began talking about his art collection.

Patience, I told myself, sipping more wine. I wished I were through with London and New York, finished with the Houston trip and back in Wisconsin, where I could work with my own bankers and hopefully pick up the proceeds of Roethe's consolidation loan. And then reopen our discussion of APL, when I had plenty of cash in the bank.

Three days later, jet lag—or maybe the emotional strain of flying ten hours from Texas in a small plane with Judy—left me with a weary depression. I wasn't ready to tackle the latest unanticipated problems stacked up in my office.

"Rubeaux's been calling twice a day from Honduras," Higbie said, "demanding money for the unexpected expenses of hiring government foresters to make a 'feasibility study' of Agricola Itzapan. He even sent a cable: 'No money, no cutting permits.' "

Sommers had left numerous memorandums explaining why Metcalf Farms had to have immediate funds for seed, fertilizer, and payroll. Then he telephoned: "The business will be bankrupt if you don't disburse now."

Kielman waited on another line to confirm an earlier date for our next CRS meeting. He was canceling an overseas journey to make the time. "For important financial matters," he said.

Then Rosenheimer stopped by. "Now don't make any trouble

by screaming for answers," he implored. "There's no real problem, but the closing of Roethe's consolidation loan has been
delayed again until he comes back from Kenya and straightens
out some small details."

"Goddamn it. I should never have let him go on that fucking
safari," I shouted. Kicking my desk chair into a wobbling spin, I
ran out of the office to find Quarton.

"You dumb sonofabitch." I charged into his office. "Why did
you give me all those idiotic assurances during the long-distance
call from Nairobi? You said everything was perfect, when I'm almost bankrupt, for Christ's sake. Were you hiding the problems or
just too lazy to look for them?"

Quarton had a helluva temper, which he worked hard to control. He usually managed to disguise it with a practiced easiness
that was sometimes quite incongruous with his quick vitality. But
when he blew, nothing was withheld. Now the muscles in his
neck were fanned out like the head of a cobra ready to strike.

"What about the other terminal assholes on your payroll—
Weast, Huffman, Carter? Your fucking Digest and Storm
Trooper?" Quarton spat the names at me. "Bad enough they all
freeload on useless 'business trips,' but now . . ."

He shoved a handful of recent travel vouchers under my nose.
They showed that the Brain Trusters, married or not, were now
traveling with their wives.

"They've started dragging their cunts along, leaving me and
Higbie to babysit the business." Quarton glared at me, seething
silently, before he said, "And you set a rotten example taking
Carter to Kenya. He's nothing but fodder for your ego. And pulling Judy off company projects to play copilot for Captain Feisty
when he flies your toy airplane to Texas."

"Shut up."

"Hell, I'm just the grunt and go-fer. Don't blame me because
your big shot bankers' highbinder buddies don't tell me their
problems." He walked out of his office and slammed the door.

I caught Quarton in the front entryway. "You're fired," I
screamed, as he left the building.

The offices were very quiet then. It was only 5:15 P.M., but
everyone else had drifted away during my tirade. I took a deep

breath and whistled it out between my teeth as I poured a weak Cuba Libre. I drank it quickly, made another, and sat down to study my accumulated correspondence. The letters rattled in my hands.

Turnbull had written that the condominiums construction was delayed again. The earliest completion date would be after the first of the year. The interest on interim financing was due now. He needed more money. I tensed my hands as I refilled my glass. And after I went back to my desk and read Weast's memo telling me that American Leasing should find an immediate substitute for the credit lines at Algoma, my entire body began to sweat.

I left the office and drove toward the Loft, still trembling, now chilled by the early fall air rushing against my sticky shirt. If I knew Quarton, he'd still be at the Loft, mellow and ready to hear my apology and maybe help conquer my debilitating depression. He *was* there. We drank together, and for a while I forgot my depression.

But late that night, when I crawled limply into bed, the premonition of disaster returned. I slept scared, and bolted awake when my phone rang in the predawn darkness.

"John? Were you asleep?" Sue's voice was coming through clearly from Nairobi. "Can you hear me?" Her tone seemed terribly controlled.

"Yes."

"Leo Roethe was attacked by a wounded lion."

My reaction was the same as when I dove into a cold mountain stream: after the shock, complete control.

While Sue explained the nearly fatal events I switched on the lights; I began dressing with one hand while I carried the telephone from the chest to the closet.

Roethe's teenage daughter had shot at a lion, grazing its neck. Backing her up, Roethe had shot it in one paw. Several hours later the lion had charged unexpectedly out of deep brush; it was on top of the tracking hunters before they could protect themselves. Roethe, in front, had struggled beneath the 400-pound animal, saving himself by jamming his feet into the lion's mouth. But before the lion had been killed, Roethe's thumb had been torn off and both his legs badly mauled—bones crushed and flesh torn by many deep and dirty gashes that had already required three and a half hours of emergency surgery. Bone chips and infection from the carrion between the lion's teeth made his recovery questionable.

"Leo's really tough," Sue said. "He refused to let me use morphine. He stayed conscious and helped me dress the wounds while we waited for the bush plane." She said that there was some chance that he'd survive.

I told her to report twice a day—immediately, if there was any important change in Roethe's condition—and then hung up and dialed Quarton's home.

His wife answered, her voice thick with sleep.

"It's important. Wake Bill," I shouted. "Leo's been mauled by a lion."

I heard rustling noises, and her voice, now giggling, in the background. "Wake up. It's John and he's drunk; he says Leo's been balling a lion."

I allowed myself one good laugh before Quarton's voice, low and level, came on: "Explain the problem." When I'd finished, he said, "I'll have everyone at the office by 6:00 A.M. Maybe we can avoid a financial panic."

While I was starting my new Continental Mark IV, I suddenly felt a twinge of compassion for Leo Roethe. Most of us were obviously more disturbed about the destruction of a money machine than that of a man.

Later, when Sue called to say that Roethe would pull through with months of rest and reconstructive surgery, I realized that his accident provided a perfect—and crucial—opportunity to stall the creditors. I proceeded to postpone my meeting with Kielman, delay our answer to CIIC, and make arrangements to visit all of the Wisconsin banks involved.

The bankers were sympathetic, especially the big Roethe creditors, and many offered to increase my credit.

"I'll lend you whatever the law allows," said Rick Murray, now president of the Bank of Fort Atkinson, who was nearly ready to begin construction of his own "Shopping Fort" project. "Just be very careful. You're stretched about as thin as you dare."

He was absolutely right, and the money crunch continued in

spite of his help and an assist from Lindsey. Everything was teetering on a makeshift scaffolding.

"Make sure you pay me back by December, before the bank examiners come around again," Lindsey said.

Quello was no help. He couldn't raise money in Minnesota— "My hands are tied until Leo returns."

And Sleavin at Delafield Childs claimed that it would be at least three months before a private placement of Recreation International's securities was feasible.

Even that, it soon became apparent, was doubtful. I decided that the only way to handle my mounting financial problems was to use the proven method of raising money—by expansion. Unfortunately, I had no pending acquisitions except APL, Agricola Itzapan, and the Holiday Lodge (which The Digest was still touting, in spite of its drab prospects), and they all needed more money than their refinancing would generate. I considered accelerating the merger with CRS, but that was much too sensitive to disturb.

O'Connor suggested that I buy his bank.

"Why not? You're already using most of its money," he told me, pushing the glasses down on his nose and trying out his intimidating stare.

Elliot Ingels called a minute later, saying that he needed help finding financing for the Tennis Club. I suggested a meeting with O'Connor and Topp, the mortgage banker, hoping that their contacts (especially the rich Florida friends O'Connor talked about) would lead Ingels to money, some of which I might siphon into my projects.

"Why don't we all meet in Fort Lauderdale?" I said.

A minute later I remembered my promise to John and George: "Dad's going to have Captain Lovell arrange a special tour for you to see the Skylab III vehicles at Cape Kennedy."

"I'll meet you there next week," I told Ingels. "I'm making an important stop en route."

When I arrived in Fort Lauderdale, I saw Topp drinking alone in the Patio Bar as I entered the Tennis Club. Ingels was already on his way back north, and O'Connor had moved on to Miami.

"The meeting is a bust." Topp frowned. "Just as well. I won't do business with O'Connor, and Ingels is crazy if he gets involved."

Before I could get Topp to explain further, the club manager asked me to describe the benefits of Compass Club affiliation. When I had finished, we all had more drinks. That led to a party. So I was halfway back to Madison and Topp was off in another undisclosed direction when the frightening undertones of his remarks hit me.

I was still edgy when Sue arrived home from Nairobi.

"Now we're going away alone," she insisted before she unpacked. "Plenty of time. Leo will be hospitalized in Kenya for another three weeks."

At that point I was beginning not to give a damn about keeping promises to pay on time, and I knew I needed rest.

"Good idea."

Sue hugged me. "Let's go back to Baja."

I changed my mind an hour later. "I just can't afford a complete vacation now. How about mixing some fun time into a scouting expedition to Colorado?" I figured there might be some new land acquisitions available to use for a fund-raising base.

Sue pinched her lips together.

"It's important, honey."

"OK, John, but why bother pretending we'll have fun?"

The Aero Commander landed hard at North Park. We drove silently toward the Diamond J Ranch, somehow sharing a hunch that there was trouble ahead.

As we pulled up, I saw Butters's buddies—the men he had brought in as ranch partners—drinking beer in front of the ranch house. A sizable mound of dead prairie chickens lay in the sun beside their pickup truck.

Diamond J Ranch had the largest sage grouse population in northern Colorado, and I had been planning to protect it until licensed perpetual hunting of the relatively rare birds was assured. Now the outsiders, Wisconsin swingers I'd never liked and couldn't understand why Butters tolerated, were drinking beer while the illegal, uncleaned birds rotted in the hot sun. I was in a

fighting mood anyway. Suddenly I was so angry that I drove my
Jeep crashing into their truck.

Everyone but Sue and I thought that was very funny. They
ignored my lecture about breaking the law and my sarcastic references to the "prop-jet set." When the beer ran out, we all drove
to a bar in town.

"If you don't like us shooting your birds," said Butters's buddy,
"buy us out."

"How much?" I demanded. I wanted him out now.

The asking price was three times his investment.

"Write him a check," I told Sue, who carried our only checkbook.

She edged closer to me in the booth and whispered, a bit
loudly, "That will overdraw my account."

"She's kidding." I winked without a smile, then told Sue, "I'll
transfer plenty of money to cover it."

"How?"

"Leave that to me." I stared at her, exhaling a long, deep
breath.

Sue scribbled her signature and slammed her drink down on the
table beside the check.

"You're paying too much."

"Knock it off."

The sellers were beginning to smile at each other.

"I guess we can wait if you've got the shorts, John."

"No way." I glanced toward Sue. "She doesn't understand
what's going on."

I felt Sue's body tense beside me. "I'm not going to sit here and
watch you make dumb deals . . . and I'm tired of being treated
like a child." She jumped up and stormed out of the bar.

The man who was about to be my ex-partner picked up the
check and examined it. "Good?"

"Damn right."

The Jeep tires squealed as Sue drove away.

He started to laugh. "She's mad."

"Fuck you." I stood up, about to say more, then turned and
walked out to watch the taillights of Sue's car disappear down the
road.

I hitchhiked to the air strip and told my pilot we were leaving immediately for Denver. He was still tired from the trip out, so I flew while he dozed. I drifted upward on the thermals and was higher than the approaching mountains before I realized that it was late at night and I'd been drinking since early afternoon. The pilot hadn't noticed, probably because my breath often had the smell of a single social drink; and tonight my anger must have masked any sign of real intoxication.

But now the altitude was multiplying the beer's effect, and I felt a tight, tingling numbness in my hands. I was losing control. Still I was too proud to wake the pilot. I fought the feeling, and as I struggled, my tense hands exerted a slight back pressure on the controls, pushing the plane even higher. The front range passed far below, and then Denver radar picked up my transponder signal. The radio told me to identify myself and change frequencies, and when I worked the mike and dials I realized that my hands were nearly useless. I requested a straight-in approach to Stapleton Field.

"Say your altitude," squawked the controller.

"Twenty-three thousand feet," I answered, staring at the red-hazed instruments. Seven thousand too high, and without oxygen. No wonder I was lightheaded.

"Too close and too high," said the tower.

"That's what you say, fella." I extended the flaps to act as an air brake and pointed the airplane's nose at the black ground just beginning to be dotted by the lights of suburban Denver.

On the way down, just as the tales tell, much of my life over the preceding three years passed through my mind, clear and brilliant. And I was able to analyze it so easily. I'd set my goals too high maybe, an instant route to failure. Just like tonight, my head becoming lighter and lighter as every second I came closer to the moment I would crash. Unless, as my father had told me long before, I "conquered myself" and admitted that I'd passed the point of no return. Then I could recapture my faith in the future.

"A drunken dream?" I wondered aloud as I jerked the plane into level flight and then shouted, "No way," to wake my pilot.

And while he turned us into a sweeping, gradual descent, I suddenly sobered and felt my confidence return. Once again there was "no problem."

Shadel, urged on by my enthusiastic descriptions of the CRS merger and the "Tropics" system (and his own faith in Roethe's ability to consummate the Teamsters' loan), introduced me to the bigger bankers that bankrolled his bank. The American City Bank of Milwaukee was a national bank, and was thus unaffected by the Wisconsin Banking Commission's admonitions to "beware of Stone's loans."

It was an easy source of new money, especially when I learned that the bank already had problems collecting real estate mortgages on Farm Corporation of America and Greentree Forests (the properties Roethe claimed had merged into Metcalf Farms).

I could help them there. It was my idea to demerge the properties from Metcalf Farms and refinance them at the same bank under a new name. That way the bank could avoid immediate criticism from its examiners.

"No problem," I told Anders and the doctors. "Roethe and Metcalf will do whatever I say, and the American City Bank has already agreed to lend whatever money we need."

They smiled.

I laughed. "On your personal signatures, of course."

In the meantime I made a quick trip to New York, where Kielman and I agreed "to be in business together by year's end."

When I announced that at a special meeting of my bankers and investors, everyone was speechless. I could see, as I described "Tropics," that they were overwhelmed by greedy enthusiasm.

"Imagine you decide to take a trip. Let's make it hard for the system. You want to catch the first flight for Los Angeles tomorrow morning. You want a rental car on arrival, reservations for two nights in a first-class hotel. Then a continuing evening flight to Houston, another car, a room for one night, and a morning flight out to New Orleans, where you won't need a car but will require two more nights' lodging. Then the fastest air connection back to Wisconsin."

"So?" Kritchner grinned. "How do I get going?"

"The agent punches the information into the 'Tropics' computer unit, which immediately responds with the availability and cost of your requested itinerary. If specified flights or hotels are unavailable, the system makes comparable substitutions. When you approve, the operator punches another button and the machine prints out tickets that cover everything."

Kritchner, and now the others, seemed ready to go on grinning forever.

I broke the silence: "The 'Tropics' system is worth millions."

"No shit," said a banker.

"This is more like it," said Kritchner.

And so I began scheduling regular meetings, "to firm up the future of all our ventures."

Money was always on the agenda, but whenever it was mentioned, somebody inevitably said, "No problem." And others were sure that Roethe's loan would close any day.

I put up a confident front too, but I couldn't shake off the nagging apprehension that there were many hidden problems.

Sue noticed my changing attitude. Our flare-up in Colorado was long forgotten, but now she said that my preoccupation with misfortune worried her.

"You're so insecure lately." She reached across the dining room table for my hand.

"Insecurity is the catalyst of greatness," I said, and squeezed her hand while I thought of a way to drop the subject. "It's been a long day. Let's take a shower together . . . a sudsy shower."

Sue laughed and stood up, still holding my hand. "You haven't suggested anything like that for months. Go get the water adjusted. Warm." She pushed me toward the bedroom and bath.

As I passed her desk, I noticed that she'd been balancing her checkbook. I paused to thumb through the piles of canceled checks, stopping when I saw the ones we'd cashed with Roethe's partner on our first trip to Africa. The payees' names, which we'd left blank, and the endorsements were written in as twelve-digit figures. I sucked my lower lip, thinking. "What does this mean?"

"Ready?" Sue came up and hugged me from behind.

I turned around, waving the checks. I had my answer. "Look here. They've finally cleared, through a secret Swiss bank account."

"I guess most of the rich Asians have foreign accounts. That's how they hide their money from President Kenyatta's tax collectors. Now forget about looking for problems. It's shower time."

Early the next morning, before catching the 7:00 flight to New York, I looked at the checks again; I wondered if I was getting paranoid, seeing sure signs of devious maneuvering behind my back. I dropped them back onto Sue's desk and quickly left the house. I had more important things to think about: the biggest meeting yet with Fritz Kielman.

No one was admitted to the executive sanctuary of KLM without a confirmed appointment or preferred personage status; a phalanx of secretaries and administrative assistants saw to that. With Weast and Griffith in tow, I walked right in. The gallery atmosphere at Kielman's office, reflecting his personal blend of the best of the old and the new worlds, had been achieved with superbly lustered antique furniture, paintings by contemporary Dutch artists, contrasting Western Americana bronzes, and an assortment of porcelain and crystal—Delft ashtrays, Steuben bowls, and Lowestoft trays used as correspondence catchers—that made me jealous. A mounted rhinocerous head hung over the entry, and there were just enough photographs of Kielman hunting, fishing, and mountain climbing to make visitors immediately aware of his reputation as a sportsman and adventurer.

"Be comfortable, gentlemen."

Kielman's secretary served coffee while we waited for Warren Kraemer to arrive.

Griffith was impatient. He began describing Compass Club's plans to cope with the energy crisis.

"Not to worry," Kielman told us. He didn't anticipate serious problems. "We do have some special arrangements with the oil-producing powers."

That didn't make sense. "I thought the press said Holland was going to suffer because the Arabs didn't like the way the Dutch 'pampered the Jews.'"

"Don't believe everything you read. We are prepared." Kielman leaned forward, both hands planted on the center of his desk. "And, just like you, I have plans to turn the energy crisis into an advantage."

I nodded as he spoke. He made sense. When gasoline prices skyrocketed, overseas vacations would cost no more than a trip to Yellowstone Park or Miami Beach.

After we had finished our coffee and were making plans for lunch at the Netherlands Club, Warren Kraemer rushed in and the formal meeting began. Kraemer, perhaps because of Kielman's stammer, did most of the talking.

"It is urgent that we outline the terms of the CRS–Compass merger." Gulf Oil was ready to participate in the joint venture to bring "Tropics" to America, then spread it worldwide. The joint venture would include Gulf Oil, KLM, and CRS (after the Compass merger) as equal partners. CRS's cash contribution would be nothing, since the "Tropics" system more than balanced the larger corporations' financial resources.

"So all we really need now is a quarter-million dollars from you." Kraemer smiled in my direction.

"CRS," Kielman explained, this time without a hint of a stammer, "has numerous unpaid debts to the Holland River Lines, KLM, Martinaire, and other foreign service corporations. For the last year, because of our front's mismanagement, CRS has been forced to live on the 'float' between its customer receipts and remittances to the companies providing the transportation and lodging."

Simply, CRS was tapping its own till.

"Living on the float" was an accepted procedure, Kielman and Kraemer both explained, so long as the delinquency didn't exceed "normal limits"—ninety days.

I assumed from Kraemer's next remarks, "Our financial status is strictly confidential," that KLM and Gulf Oil were unaware of this activity.

"The balance sheet has to add up before I sit down with our potential partners again."

Unconsciously I began to shake my head; then, noticing the various faces flashing in front of me, I stopped and focused my eyes on Kielman. I knew that if I could pick the right words to tell how my companies offered the perfect solution to everyone's problems, I'd finally be in business with true titans.

"We can fund CRS," I said, without bothering to consider how I'd raise the money.

Kielman nodded.

I turned toward Kraemer, who was also nodding and smiling broadly. Henk Guitjens, sitting behind him, stood up.

"We may need more funding later," Guitjens said. "At least another half-million U.S. dollars to expand into the international retail market and revitalize the Gulf Travel Club."

Guitjens was certainly not, as I'd first assumed, present only as an observer. His jaw was jutting, and, like his eyes, demanded a credible answer.

And I could feel Kielman and Kraemer watching for my reaction to the sudden increase in the ante.

Weast came to my rescue. "We'll sell debentures," he said. "Cumulative, convertible debentures. They won't immediately dilute your stock, and on a deal like this it will be easy to find a market for them."

"That's a brilliant suggestion," said Kraemer, turning to smile in my direction. He was thinking, I hoped, that I'd picked good men for my staff.

"Can you do all this?" asked Kielman, standing up to indicate that the meeting would be over if I gave the right answer.

"Certainly," I said, grinning to hide my confusion. I felt confident, but I didn't know why. It was almost like booze talking and yet I was cold sober. I didn't even feel the need of a drink.

I was still exuding the same uncontrolled audacity when I met John Perfumo and his assistant for dinner.

"Chase International can look forward to closing the African Ponderosa deal with us as soon as Roethe is transferred from the Nairobi hospital to the Mayo Clinic," I told them.

"Are you sure this time?" Perfumo leaned back in his chair, squinting at me.

But when I laid out the mockup for our first edition of the new national magazine *Four Seasons Trails*, and pointed to a full-page ad for the game lodges, Perfumo rocked forward until he was leaning toward me with both elbows on the table. His eyes widened as he concentrated on the ad.

Finally he said, "Nice." He seemed satisfied.

There was no reason to linger in New York now, and plenty of work to do in Wisconsin.

"Like raising another half-million or more to bankroll CRS," I told Quarton when I called long-distance to brief him. "I missed the last direct flight, so have Captain Feisty meet the late plane into Chicago. He'll have to fly me on the final leg."

The Aero Commander homed in on Madison long after midnight, with Captain Feisty talking all the way—a rambling monologue to keep awake. Watching the headlights on the interstate below, I didn't pay much attention until he began describing how his assistant had recently flown Walter O'Connor to Florida.

"He thinks there's something mysterious about O'Connor. He's not telling you everything."

I loosened my seat belt and turned toward him. "What do you mean?"

He didn't answer.

I began to nod, and was about to ask again what he meant, but as the plane settled toward the deserted Madison airport, his movements of the controls were uncommonly abrupt, and I decided not to disturb him.

It was impossible to sleep. Finally, after fitful hours of struggling to find a comfortable position in bed beside Sue, I rushed to my office. The hands on the reception room clock were close to 6:00 A.M.

I thought about calling Rauterberg, but since I didn't know where he was spending the night, I dialed Jack Rash's Florida number instead.

He answered on the first ring; he was wide awake. "Just in from an early walk with my Irish setters."

Rash laughed when I told him about my hectic schedule, and after I finished briefing him on my progress he said, "You just might pull it off after all."

"Maybe. Still, I need your help." I asked him to recommend an investigative attorney in the Miami area.

"I know a good man." He paused, and I wondered if he sensed my anxiety. "Keep me posted . . . and John, be careful."

I swallowed hard as I hung up. I looked at my watch. It was only 6:15. I wandered around the offices, nervously clenching and unclenching my fists, angry because none of my Brain Trusters would arrive for an hour yet. There was no way to begin dissecting O'Connor's past.

I went back to my desk and started shuffling a stack of memos from Roethe and Quello. I talked to myself. I laughed.

"That Goddamn Leo. He's promoting even from his hospital bed."

The topmost paper was a list of new companies he'd submitted for my review—all possible acquisitions: a safari island, a synthetic oil company, a dog food processing plant.

"Shit." I threw the papers toward the wastepaper basket and began pacing again. My shoulders hunched. I felt the muscles knot beneath my collar, and I knew I was beginning to fight fear on top of the frustrations of trying to guess the true motives of my associates.

I was trapped. Even if I discovered that Bill Topp was right when he implied O'Connor was not telling me everything, what could I do? I was married to the sonofabitch, and a divorce would bankrupt me.

The same was true with R. and R. And most of the others were a dangerous enigma. Roethe and his banker buddies were either acting from desperation or weaving a fantastic web of lies, or else they actually did have an inside track to the Teamsters' money. But the Teamsters made me nearly as nervous as the Mafia. How in hell had I gotten mixed up with these people?

I punched the button that activated an automatic coffee machine, watched while the first pour slopped over the edge of the cup, and carried it, hot and dripping, to the nearest desk. After one sip I pushed the cup away and cradled my head in my hands. My index finger rolled a hunk of hair, unrolled it, rolled it again.

When I finally looked up it was nearly 8:00 A.M. I walked to the window and saw Higbie's Corvette, parked, heat still rising from the hood. Ingels's white Continental, identical to mine, was pulling up beside it.

Good, I thought. Maybe Ingels had sold Bright Star. Probably at a loss . . . certainly at a loss. I was sure that company could never show profits now. Bright Star was a failure, because its principals were divided, uncommunicative, unable to decide what risks to take. That was Ingels's fault.

Higbie came in quickly, shrugging off his topcoat. "Elliot Ingels is right behind me. Maybe he's got good news." He nodded as if trying to convince us both.

"Hell, I probably wouldn't believe it anyway. I don't know who to trust anymore."

Higbie stepped toward me. "John, what's the matter? You can depend on . . ."

I winked to stop him. "I was just kidding." I'd almost forgotten that the leader never lets his pessimism show.

Suddenly Ingels was in the room, his face lit up like a kid rushing to a Christmas tree.

"I'm your new boss," he announced in a voice that sounded somewhere between drunken amusement and hung-over sick humor.

I didn't respond. I was straining to hear the rest.

Ingels raised his chin and tilted his head back. His eyes twinkled over the bridge of his nose. Then he snapped his head forward and said, "I just bought the Algoma Bank from Walter O'Connor."

15
Mid-October 1973

ASSETS—$2,739,265.00
LIABILITIES—$489,600.00
PERSONAL GUARANTEES—$18,750,000.00

There was no public announcement, no story in the newspapers, yet within twenty-four hours everyone seemed to know the Algoma Bank had changed hands. And most of them seemed to think Ingels's latest big deal was going to be good for everybody.

"It's certainly to our advantage," said The Digest.

I agreed. If Walter O'Connor had sold his bank to anyone else I might have been badly shaken. As it was, the transaction seemed timely, a lucky break.

Shadel didn't think so. His lips were blue from overexertion, twitching with panic, as he hurried into my office less than an hour after he heard the news.

"Unless someone honors O'Connor's commitment to move your loans, John, my bank faces collapse." He was gasping; saliva ran from the corner of his mouth.

"Hold it." I held up my hand, then guided him to a chair. "Elliot Ingels is already associated with me in other businesses. He can't afford to make any new problems for Recreation International and Compass."

"You sure?"

"Yes."

Shadel began to relax, sinking deep into his chair, then rose quickly. "I've got to get out of here and see my directors, calm them down." He reached for his coat and was working an arm into it as he went through the door.

My private phone rang. Ingels's secretary said he was on the way over.

"Why?"

"I don't know, but it's probably important." She sounded more businesslike than usual.

I poured rum into my coffee and buzzed my secretary.

"Don't disturb me until Mr. Ingels arrives."

According to Rauterberg, the bank deal was fantastic. But that's all he'd really said when I'd called him for an insider's view. His voice was cheery but his answers were guarded.

I needed to know more before I was truly as satisfied as I'd led Shadel to believe. I sipped the rum off the top of my coffee and refilled the cup. A new premonition, the bad kind, began to throb high on the back of my neck. I could feel it. I rubbed the spot. I was perspiring.

Rauterberg was hiding something.

"Damn right he is," said Ingels as soon as I told him. "If word got out about the package he arranged for me, everybody'd be bugging him to buy a bank."

"I want to know all about it."

"That's why I'm here. Then maybe you'll stop digging for answers. Remember, you've got a bad habit of making waves." He started to frown but couldn't control himself. He chuckled instead. "Listen, but don't repeat what I say, hard as it may be."

Ingels explained that Rauterberg had arranged a purchase loan package that allowed him not only to buy the bank with no money down, but also—because he used a limited partnership in the Tennis Club for the down payment—to walk out of the closing with "a big wad of cash." His face was contorted by the intensity of his bragging.

"O'Connor's bank stock is so valuable, on account of the big profits from his loan portfolio, that I was able to borrow enough money from Rauterberg's Marine Bank to even help with other projects."

I wondered if he meant Bright Star.

He stuck out his hand as if he expected me to shake it. "And I unloaded part of my Tennis Club problems."

"And you got stuck—worked over by pros," I thought, as Ingels gulped for breath. Now I understood why the transaction had been kept so secret—hidden from me and my associates, who might have tipped Ingels to the fact that a third of Algoma's "profitable loan portfolio" involved my ventures, businesses that depended on continuing cash advances from the same bank.

Ingels knew nothing about O'Connor's promises to pay off Shadel and fund American Leasing. He thought my loan balances were insignificant—"no problem." And he was unaware of the Banking Commission's pressure to close down my credit and demand payment in full. His eagerness to trade stagnant Tennis Club equities for the prestige of a bank presidency had made it easy for O'Connor to bail out before Algoma's real problems became common knowledge.

Rauterberg had fucked his buddy when he engineered the deal; I wondered why. Rauterberg had always seemed much closer to Ingels than to O'Connor. He was involved with Bright Star and other Ingels enterprises, and was Ingels's regular party partner and confidant. While O'Connor, as far as I could see, was just another useful link in Rauterberg's chain of swinging bankers. There had to be some secret benefit in Rauterberg's unmistakable allegiance to O'Connor. Or hidden pressure.

I knew that my face reflected my concern, and there was no need to alarm Ingels. He might be a dumb sonofabitch, easily motivated by all of Padgett's old standbys (ego, greed, sex, and envy), but now he was also the controller of my currency. I laughed, and told my secretary to fix a round of drinks.

Ingels laughed too. "It feels great to be a bank president."

When I finally tracked O'Connor down, he also laughed, and told me, "You had your chance. Now, while I retire to Florida, you make damn sure your loans get paid." His voice was as cold as

I remembered his eyes had been when he had warned me, "Don't ever screw me, Johnny boy."

O'Connor was still watching every move I made, and of course I was still working with his associates: Weast on American Leasing and Financial, Huffman on Camp Dells, and "the ambassador" on the Honduran and African projects. So I placed a call to the attorney Rash recommended. I still needed to know about O'Connor's other activities.

"He's out of town for the week." The secretary asked me to leave a message.

"No message." I hung up hard, the phone slipping from my perspiring hand, as I noticed activity in the parking lot outside my window.

"Bigfoot" and "Yeti" had arrived, just in time to add a few hours of desperately needed levity. They were the products of my imagination, the taxidermy skills of Klineburger Jonas Brothers, and a faked research program—the first and only lifesize representations of the legendary gigantic apelike creatures purported to roam the Pacific Northwest and the Himalayas. I ordered their uncrating delayed until the office parking lot was filled with press photographers. Then Judy and I posed with the furry giants.

"The taxidermists didn't miss a trick," someone yelled pointing to the big male mounts. "They've even got balls."

"Who was the model?" Quarton asked, poking at the discreetly small genitals, which were meant to be hidden because "Bigfoot" and "Yeti" were to be displayed to mothers and children at the World Wide Animal Kingdom (I hadn't forgotten the Ethiopian song bird incident). I raised my hand and grinned at Judy when Quarton whispered, "There's a little bit of John Stone in everything we do."

Roethe was scheduled to be back in business as soon as he checked into the Mayo Clinic, and it wasn't long before he sent word that his Teamsters loan would close by the end of the month. There was a communal sigh of relief heard by everyone, and everyone smiled and said it was because Roethe sounded more believable now that he was nearly home.

"We can thank you for that," I told Sue, when she returned from a lonely trip from Honduras.

She tried to smile, a tiny twist in her lips.

I knew she was tired, strained from long days of arguing for answers about the progress of the timber venture, frustrated by endless double-talk. I wondered if she understood.

"If you hadn't saved Roethe's life—"

She interrupted me. Her voice was lower than usual, her eyes listless. "It's a strange quirk of fate. Leo's alive and the business goes on, and I hardly see you anymore. Everyone is getting what they want except me." She paused. "I'm becoming part of the business machine."

"No way. No way." I hugged her tightly and stroked her hair, and promised her she had the wrong idea. But I wondered if maybe she was hitting the truth, if I was becoming as phony as my boasts.

I flew back to Honduras with her to discover that the cabinet minister of tourism wanted to help promote the Compass Club but that the rest of the government needed greasing before our cutting permits would be issued. I left Sue behind again to secure the Club's position and to keep her eyes on Rubeaux, while I moved on to New York.

The attorneys and Delafield Childs were nearly finished with the CRS merger documents. Kielman and Kraemer said that they were about to succeed with the forced removal of the old fronts and that soon there would be nothing to keep us apart. I promised to send my entire staff to New York for a final briefing and to help with last-minute details.

"The merger *will* be completed by New Year's Eve," said Kielman.

With that assurance, I called Perfumo and told him to send someone to Wisconsin to attend a special directors' meeting, where the final decision on APL would be made.

"CIIC will wash its hands of APL unless your money is transferred within two weeks," he said. The precise, perfectly level tone to his voice told me he meant it. "No extensions."

I grunted a meaningless answer. By now I'd decided to dump APL unless Quello came through with the million-dollar capital contribution he had promised. And I'd also decided to bring my entire business to a boil.

Before leaving for Wisconsin, I telephoned Higbie and told him to schedule a series of board meetings.

Quello came to the first session two days later.

"I'm still looking," he said, "but money's tight now. Be patient."

"No time," I told him. Now that I knew he and Roethe were quiet partners in other private ventures (synthetic oil, dog food, mining), I was certain that the promise of $1 million was only a stall. Quello's motives were entirely selfish. He was trying to force me to override Roethe's failures.

"You're wrong," he said, as if he knew what I was thinking. "There's still a good chance to raise fresh capital any day."

Nonetheless, we voted APL down as soon as Perfumo's assistant arrived for the next meeting.

Even John Strohm, who, as a stockholder in APL, stood to lose a lot of money, said, "We can't afford it now. It's not practical."

"Sounds like your decision was made a long time ago. You've just been playing games," said the man from CIIC. He said more, implying that I was a con man, but no one bothered to listen. He left with his shoulders sagging, hands clutching his portfolio, and I guessed that he knew he'd be the scapegoat when his superiors heard the news. I felt sorry for him.

"But, damnit, he's expendable," I told Anders.

He shrugged and said, "We've wasted too much time on Africa already."

Weast attended the next meeting, and demanded permission to buy leases on the East Coast.

"What will you use for money?" I asked.

"We may have to go slow for a little while, but I've been looking for a substitute for the Algoma credit lines. I've made other connections."

It was then that I forced him to admit he'd anticipated the Algoma Bank sale. "You're O'Connor's partner. You owned part of that bank."

"So what?" Weast smiled as he stepped toward me. "You'll still get what you want. I'm still going to put meat on the Janeff bones, issue public stock, make a killing in the market."

Weast's smile broadened. His mouth widened. "But . . . I want 51 percent of the Janeff Stock."

Anders and I held a fast private caucus in the men's room.

"Tell him to shove it," Anders said. His lips turned down as he bit on the last word.

And he was unnaturally quiet until I drove him to the airport later that afternoon. He shook his head as we pulled into the parking lot.

"I don't like this."

"Weast? We handled him."

"No. Everything. I understand Sommers needs another $50,000 before Metcalf can harvest a crop."

I shut off the engine and twisted to face him. "Yes, but then we'll have a guaranteed profit."

His head kept shaking as he reached for his carry-on bag. "I'm tired of guarantees."

"You've seen the progress reports, the projections."

He opened the door. The first winter winds whistled into the car. Anders raised his voice.

"Don't count on me for another cent. Don't try to tell me how much I stand to lose if we belly up." Anders stepped out of the car, then shouted back to me. "I can afford to lose—what is it?— two million. It'll hurt, but I'm done being stupid."

He walked away toward the terminal. The car door swung, still open in the wind. My eyes watered. Even under a heavy fur-lined coat I was freezing, numb.

Much later, back at the office, my body began to thaw. My face stung at first and then began to feel feverish.

"The golden goose flew," I told Quarton.

"We'll make it without him." Somehow I knew that Quarton wasn't as sure as he tried to sound. "Look, John, we still have plenty of people blowing into the balloon."

Suddenly I began to laugh. "Hot air. Or should we call it hot breath filled with great ideas?"

Quarton said, "Why not?"

I tested him. "I *have* to believe, but why you and the others?"

"Because we want to. We have a prophet—John Stone."

I started laughing again. "You're sure?"

"Remember, God, little g."

Quarton seemed to be right. The Digest said he was. "The

American City Bank has faith. Their vice-president told me you
were a genius. They'll agree to lend us another quarter-million."

Griffith rushed into the room and listened while The Digest
described how the bankers believed that "Tropics" was the greatest money-making scheme ever discovered. Then, after everyone
else left for happy hour at the Loft, Griffith pulled a chair close to
my desk.

"Be sure to save enough to deliver what we promised Fritz
Kielman," he said. "I'm worried about the way you spend whenever there's money in the bank."

He pointed to "Bigfoot" and "Yeti" and waved a voucher for
the latest expense account transfer to Honduras.

"No problem." I stood up, hoping he'd leave.

"There is a problem—many problems." He hesitated.

I could see that his mind was searching for the right words.

"Frankly, John, I have a problem. I need $50,000 personally."
He rubbed an eyebrow, thinking again. "The sale of my radio
stations has been delayed by FCC red tape. I've got to pump
more in or lose them."

"Delayed? What about your friends in Washington?"

"They've got their own problems. Look here." He reached for
his briefcase and pulled out a Xerox copy of a letter to Spiro Agnew, which he handed to me.

Whenever Griffith needed to impress me, he produced letters to
or from prominent people: Curt Gowdy or Harry Tennyson at
Coca-Cola (describing how Roy Rogers, Prince Bernhard, and
Griffith should choose the future inductees for the Conservation
Hall of Fame), or the astronauts (usually suggesting new candi-
dates, including me, for the Confederate Air Force).

His latest letter to the vice-president read, "Rest assured that
Joe Foss and I, along with the greatest majority of my friends, are
appalled at the continuing efforts to discredit you. . . . We are sick
to death of Watergate and the sick reporting in some journalistic
circles. Keep in there fighting." It was written on the Recreation
International letterhead.

I looked across my desk at Griffith. He was sucking his lower
lip, waiting. Once again he was dangling his carrot before me,

offering access to his powerful friends. I waved the letter at him.

"So what does this mean? You just told me he can't help you."

"I wanted you to see that we all have problems. We *must* help each other."

"Goddamn it, Dick, Recreation International and Compass are not Watergate."

He winced.

And then I winked. "But I'll do what I can for you."

In spite of his fast talk and his obvious intention to steal command of CRS and Compass, I knew I needed Griffith. He was the only other administrator capable of the sophisticated maneuvers needed to beat the energy crisis. His programs included the subtle pressure we could exert on ticket profits as we used the Club's leverage to determine load factors on competitive flights, and the development of a complete Compass mail-order service to take advantage of the public's reluctance to drive to points of purchase. He was working with Warren Kraemer, whose best guess was that it would be seven to ten years before the nation was self-sufficient in terms of fuel. In the meantime, organized pleasure travel could be exploited to give Compass–CRS a constant flow of profitable options.

"Make us a drink."

"Cuba Libre." Griffith began to smile.

"Right." I took a long, slow drag on my cigarette.

The Fort Atkinson bankers approved more loans that week, even some extra money for Griffith. They reasoned that I'd be able to repay them before the end of the year.

"Especially since Leo Roethe's back. You've got too much going for you ever to fail."

I wondered if their logic was flawed by a preponderance of faith in Roethe's loan from the Teamsters. The closing was always being delayed. Roethe, who talked to me only by phone, made one excuse after another; paperwork was incomplete, key officials were called away unexpectedly, the participating banks were revising the loan documents.

"I need proof, Leo, something in writing to show that the loan has been approved."

"Be patient. I told you before that questions and demands for proof can cause problems, more delays. Now, believe me, I'm going to get my loan any day. Ask Art Anders. He knows."

Anders wasn't sure. He hadn't seen any proof either. So I finally sent The Digest out to investigate.

He met with Stanley Shafer, President of the First National Bank of Fort-Atkinson ,the primary participating bank, according to Roethe).

"Shafer doubts that the loan should be made," The Digest reported. "But he also said that other, more powerful, people insisted that Roethe should get the money. So one way or another, it looks like the loan may go through."

"Who are these other people?"

The Digest shrugged. "We're still checking, but we know they're big shots."

"Um hum." It sounded good. Then The Digest broke in.

"There's one more. Roethe's loan broker is a guy named Joseph Balistreri."

"So?"

"He's family." And, when I didn't react The Digest whispered, "Well, there's a possible connection with the Mafia that you should be aware of. Senator McClellan has stated on the floor of the U.S. Senate that Frank Balistreri, Joe's father, is the head of the Milwaukee family. This of course doesn't mean Joe is Mafia."

The Digest was too nervous to be dependable. so I gave the story to Higbie. "Get me the facts."

Then I called Roethe. "I want some straight answers."

He sounded as strong as ever when he guaranteed, "We'll all have our money on December 22—a Christmas present."

"How?"

Roethe refused to discuss details over the phone. "Come to my house next week." he said.

"That's too long to wait."

"Have some faith. Goddamnit." Roethe hung up.

"Nobody hangs up on me," I screamed at the telephone. I pounded my fist on the desk. I knew it was useless to call him back.

Quarton overheard. He came into my office.

"Hey now, you need a drink."

I stood up. "Damn right I do. Let's go to the Loft."

The vice-president of the American City Bank drove up as we walked out of the office.

"Thought I'd stop by to say hello w̶i̶s̶l̶ was in town on other business." He studied us carefully.

I doubted that there was any "other business." My companies had reached the point where they needed watching. He was a spy.

"I need to talk to you," I said, turning back into the building.

"Everybody's beginning to wonder," he said, when I exposed my doubts about Roethe's loan. "So let's find out once and for all."

He called the American National Bank in Chicago, where a friend, George Jacobsmeyer, was the officer in charge of administering disbursements for the Teamsters Pension Fund.

I fixed drinks while they talked, gulping my first one.

"Whoa. Doesn't look too bad, John. He says the collateral is insufficient, Roethe's a poor risk, but nonetheless the powers to be say the loan is going to be made. The board's decision is final. The bank only does what it's told."

"He said that? The loan's a sure thing?"

"Sounds like it." The banker sighed. "Now let's all have a drink."

His business trip turned into a party.

I came to work whistling the next morning. It was a bright, cloudless day. "And a happy day," I told myself. The CRS–Compass merger was almost ready. Enough assets had been transferred from the old Lake, Sport, and Travel structure and enough money had been borrowed to bring the Compass financial statement up to par. The first quarter-million was in the banks, ready for transfer. And all of my regular investors (except Anders) were willing to subscribe to the CRS debentures.

"I'm carrying a lot of financial clout." I patted my briefcase as Higbie drove me to catch a late flight to New York. "Kielman's got to be impressed."

"Damn right." Higbie loosened his tie. "Say, John, do you still want me to check out Balistreri and the Teamsters?"

"Yes, but be careful not to make waves."

I dozed on the plane and in the cab on the way in to my hotel, and then left a late call and stayed in bed until ten the next morning.

"I've never seen you so relaxed," said Kielman when we met for lunch at the Netherlands Club.

"I'm ready to finalize the merger," I told him. "Now."

"Can't wait to be president of the world's largest travel development company, eh?" He smiled and ran his tongue across his teeth. "I'm glad you're ready so soon. I just heard Cook's Tours is available. Maybe we can buy it."

That sounded like too much more money. "Impossible."

"Nothing is impossible. I thought that was your credo."

"I guess it is." But the words didn't sound right when I spoke them.

Kielman didn't seem to notice. "Shall we go back and review the merger documents?"

My premonition passed. The documents contained millions of dollars' of projected income. Their heft alone was enough to restore my confidence. Then I noticed that Kielman's name appeared only on the preliminary confidential papers. The master contract, the debenture agreements, and the other public papers listed D. J. Chandris instead.

"What does he do, besides being your personal representative?"

Kielman looked at me, squinting as if I'd made a dumb joke. "Greek friend of mine. Shipping and other enterprises."

"Of course." I remembered that Griffith had dropped his name, compared Chandris to Onassis. I pointed to the thick stack of papers. "I forgot. I've had a lot on my mind."

The documents were in order, and I offered to sign at once.

Kielman shook his head. "We should all sign together at the official time. I'm going to arrange a celebration, and, of course, there must be news releases."

It occurred to me that his legal preparations were still incomplete. I hadn't seen any confirmation that the fronts had relinquished control. There was no proof that CRS owned the rights to "Tropics."

"I suppose you're anxious to visit your new offices in Amsterdam and London," said Kielman, pressing a buzzer on his desk.

Guitjens appeared in the doorway. "Would you like to see the suite we're redecorating for you here?"

I looked out on Fifth Avenue from my windows one floor below and thought, "Why worry? And why did I ever bother worrying about what went on in Wisconsin?"

But when I visited Sleavin at the Delafield Childs offices later that afternoon I was shocked back to reality, and I realized again that I should remember to pay more attention to premonitions.

"It's going to take a long time and a lot of money and work to find venture capital for you," he said. "Next summer is the earliest you can hope to sell Recreation International stock. There's nothing available to you now."

"Have you talked to Quello?"

"He can't raise a cent."

I blinked. I hadn't expected a million, but I had counted on something.

Sleavin stared at me. His jaw was set, making hard, straight lines along his cheeks. "Look, John, you're dealing with the SEC. You can't play games. After the CRS merger, if it works, you'll have to keep your other proposed acquisitions in mothballs for a while." He cleared his throat.

"What about Thunderhead?" I lit a cigarette. Sleavin knew that Thunderhead was facing foreclosure unless our delayed payments were made.

"Use Roethe's money to keep everything afloat," he said.

Apparently Sleavin was in touch with Roethe, and knew as much about the Teamsters loan as I did. He began to sound encouraging.

"You'll make it," he told me on the way out.

I wasn't sure I believed him.

New York was the peak of my roller-coaster ride, I thought, as I boarded my flight to Chicago fingering the "urgent" messages handed to me by the reservation clerk. Now I was on the way down.

There wasn't time to call Ingels and Higbie back. I wasn't sure, but I had a sour feeling; my stomach twitched. They'd never bother to track me down at La Guardia unless there were serious problems. I moved back and forth in my first-class seat. I couldn't

get comfortable. I needed time desperately. If any one of my
biggies—American Leasing, Compass, Recreation International,
Roethe's loan—got born sound and healthy I could forget the re-
curring nightmare about the living death beyond the point of no
return. *If.*

I stopped at the first phone booth off the plane at O'Hare, but
moved on to the cab stand without placing the calls. I couldn't
concentrate. My vision was blurred; I was afraid to answer my
messages. I needed to talk to someone. I thought about Judy. No,
she was still too detached. Quarton? Not yet. He'd tell me about
all the new problems, and then maybe I'd have real trouble getting a hold on myself.

At my hotel I placed an overseas call to Sue in Tegulcigalpa.
The connection was terrible; I could barely hear her. But she
must have heard the desperation in my voice.

She interrupted to shout encouragement. "Everything's going
well here." Sue told me that Senator Robert Knowles (president
pro tempore of the Wisconsin Senate) was in Honduras helping
her promote Compass.

I shook my head. She was hard to believe sometimes, too much
like me, an alter ego instead of a wife.

"Hang on, John, we're going to make it."

If a twenty-four-year-old woman, privy to all my problems, had
faith, why couldn't I? For a minute I felt confident again, and so
I called Higbie.

He didn't have to say there were serious problems; his quick
breathing was sign enough.

"Turnbull called. He got served with papers. They're foreclosing on Thunderhead."

"You sure?" My question sounded stupid, but it was out before
I stopped to think that Higbie never told me about problems until he'd verified them.

"Turnbull said you shouldn't come West until you bring enough
money to redeem the mortgage. They might serve you personally."

Ingels's news was worse.

"The bank examiners want me to enforce collection of your
loans. I promised to make my initial report in the morning."

My throat felt as if it were filled with mucus. "Stall them until next week." I began to gag.

I hung up the phone and walked to the window, and looked across Michigan Avenue toward my dad's church. I thought about praying. And I conjured up a new commandment, the eleventh— thou shalt not pretend.

If my business was failing I had to do something about it. I stood to lose a profit recently estimated at $20 million.

The shower started cold, then turned to steam. I'd forgotten to adjust the temperature. My shoulders stung as I dressed, and I had to knot my tie three times before it hung straight.

My cab was creeping out into the avenue before I decided where to go for dinner. "Riccardo's."

Many years before it had been my favorite hangout. Now, when I walked into the bar, I wasn't sure I belonged anymore. One minute I felt too big for the place, the next too small—a counterfeit tycoon. My first drink was sour, the same gut-squeezed flavor I'd been tasting since I left New York. I lit a new cigarette, chain-smoker style, and listened to a conversation down the bar.

Somebody was talking about Sid Luckman and the days when quarterbacks were first experimenting with the split T. I recognized the story and realized, with an eye-watering start, that I wasn't a young man anymore.

After dinner I walked north along Michigan Avenue, pondered the goodies for sale in the shop windows, and took deep breaths of Chicago. The sour taste was still there.

I fell asleep as soon as I lay down, but soon I was awake again and analyzing the real reasons for my divorce from Judy.

Mismanagement of that relationship had started before we were married, more than twenty years before when I'd stood on my homemade pedestal and declared that I'd be a millionaire before I was thirty.

"Phony." My voice echoed on and on across the darkened room.

I fell asleep wondering if my life with Sue was only a replay.

When I awoke it was raining and the skies were nearly black, almost as if there were no day. But my travel alarm said 9:15 A.M. There was no time left to worry. Rain in Chicago could mean snow in Wisconsin, and I had to be in Fort Atkinson by early afternoon. Today was my big meeting with Leo Roethe.

Except for a hip-high cast and naked scars streaking his other leg below the bottom of the bathrobe, Roethe looked the way I remembered him. He was thinner, perhaps, but his fantastic energy still vibrated into my body as we shook hands.

"Thank you for coming. We need to talk."

"Yes, we do." I smiled, thinking that Roethe was making it easy for me to interrogate him. But that wasn't it at all. He used his usual strong offense to defend himself against my questions about the delayed consolidation loan.

"Why did you reject African Ponderosa?" he asked, clenching his teeth and staring at me.

"The board decided it was too expensive, too risky."

"No one consulted me." He kept staring, stroking his nose. "And what's behind the big slowdown in Honduras? Isn't the president's brother-in-law helping? Or aren't you paying attention to Honduras?"

"Now wait a minute."

"No." If he'd been able, Roethe would have risen from his chair. "I've had a lot of time to wonder how you're spending our money." He started to shout.

"Goddamnit, Leo." I raised my voice to match his. "You've been advised of every move I make. Stop fencing with me. You know why I'm here. I'm the one who needs answers."

"I've told you before, don't disturb the Teamsters loan with your questions and investigations." His face reddened. "I heard about the man you sent to see my banker. That sort of meddling is another cause for the loan being delayed."

Roethe struggled in his chair, forgetting that it was impossible for him to jump up.

I stood over him. "When *will* you get your money?"

"I told you—December 22."

"You'd better. Otherwise we're going to be out of business. And in the meantime I've got to have proof, something to show our creditors."

"All I can give you is my word. That should be enough."

"It's not." I took a deep breath. "We're in trouble, Leo. I'm afraid to go back to the office. The process servers . . ."

Roethe spread his arms wide. "I'm immune to fear and silly insecurity. I'm living my second life," he told me. "Ever since I beat the lion in hand-to-hand combat."

Others would undoubtedly have laughed when he said that, but I didn't. Roethe sounded like a Masai mystic; he looked like an adversary instead of a partner. He locked his eyes onto mine. They widened and refused to blink. The cords in his neck bulged.

His voice was many octaves lower when he said, "Get back to work now, and remember, you and you alone will queer my loan deal if you keep needling people."

And then we talked about the safari, and the one he planned for next year.

"Bigger and better than the last. And the lions be damned."

Roethe was chuckling when I left.

I shook my head. How could I cope with an adversary who thought he was immortal?

Quarton grinned when I told him about Leo's second life. "You should tell him to try a water walk next. Hell, Little g, you can join him." He threw a punch at my shoulder.

I started to laugh. "Why not?" But my private line began to ring.

It was Walt O'Connor."I'm coming to see you tomorrow. Stay put. It's important."

O'Connor arrived before dawn the next morning. He was angry because Ingels had complained about the whitewashed loan portfolio at the Algoma Bank.

"Get the damn things paid. Sell something."

"Like Janeff?" I saw a squeeze play coming.

"Whatever is marketable."

"Not yet. Roethe's loan is due to close this month."

"You can't depend on that."

"I have to." I reached for my briefcase and began filling it with folders from my desk, hoping O'Connor would take the hint.

"I'm telling you it's smart to start selling out now." He tapped the desk for attention.

"And I told you, I don't agree." I smiled. "Why are you so anxious?"

O'Connor snarled. "Don't make trouble for yourself." He always

snarled when his opinions were questioned. Like his partner,
Weast, he was the kind of man who considered questions as crit
icism, and he never accepted criticism gracefully.

I went to the closet and took out my coat.

"I've got another meeting, Walt." I walked out without waiting
for his reply.

Since I had no place to go, I drove south toward Fort Atkinson.
I decided en route to visit Rick Murray. He might even be willing
to increase my loans, I thought. Certainly he could tell me something about Roethe's prospects. I knew they kept in close touch.

Murray surprised me when he said, "I'm sure Leo's going to be
okay. As a matter of fact, I lent him some more money." He
showed me the collateral, the same Metcalf Farms stock certificate that Roethe had taken from me to show the Pension Fund.

"That belongs to me, and why did you lend him money now?"
I asked angrily.

"Leo needed $50,000 for the front money on his consolidation
loan." Murray didn't think anyone would object to that, and said
he needed to keep the stock certificate because "I'm a bank. I
need it more than you do."

I smiled and said I understood. "I know the bank examiners
watch newly acquired banks very closely. But look, are you sure
Leo's big loan will go through?" I was hoping to take advantage
of Murray's vulnerability to see some hard evidence.

Murray, cooperating from an obvious sense of urgency, showed
me an unsigned letter to the Central States, Southeast and Southwest Pension Fund's Chicago headquarters; it outlined the terms
of Roethe's loan for $10 million. Several paragraphs startled me.
The loan required no principal reduction for the first two years,
set the interest percentage at whatever prime rate the Continental
Bank of Chicago was currently charging, and listed among the
collateral "all notes, debentures, and securities purchased with
the proceeds of the loan."

"That's a damn cheap rate even with banks involved," I said,
and then, raising my voice to be sure he'd respond to my last
statement first, exclaimed, "I didn't know Leo was buying anything."

"Look at the second page where it says most of the funds will be used to obtain over 50 percent control of Weatherby–Nasco. Leo's no fool. He wants a hammerlock on the company."

"You mean the Teamsters do."

Murray shrugged.

I pushed my advantage and bombarded him with questions. "Who got the first fifty? Why isn't the letter signed?"

All Murray would tell me was that he thought the money had gone to a Milwaukee attorney named Balistreri, and that the letter was unsigned because his bank wasn't big enough to be involved. "Leo's using the First National Banks in Fort Atkinson and Waukesha."

That made sense. Both banks were Weatherby–Nasco depositories.

"Participation is a good deal for them because Leo is going to protect them with Certificates of Deposit he'll buy out of the loan proceeds."

"So what's holding it up?"

"I don't know," Murray said, "but I am sure he'll get his money."

He reaffirmed this belief when he gave me another $60,000, to be repaid after Roethe paid me.

Some of my confidence was coming back, and yet, as I drove to Madison, I was still worried enough to decide that the time had come for a mass meeting. I didn't trust Leo Roethe anymore, and now I was afraid to ignore O'Connor's advice. But if someone had to sell out, let it be Roethe.

I called my investors, Brain Trusters, and bankers together. "A gathering of eagles," I said. "We're all rather majestic, predatory —and *vulnerable*. And it's a long fall from our eyrie."

Then I explained the details of our problems and called for a vote.

"Do we sink Leo Roethe, sell his securities, and save ourselves, or do we gamble on keeping him afloat until Christmas when his loan is guaranteed to be closed?" I looked directly at Shadel, who'd been screaming louder than all my other creditors.

He voted to save Roethe, and all the rest followed suit.

Everything seemed to improve after the meeting.

Ingels stalled the bank examiners. The American City Bank said they'd "lend a little more." And Roethe, still confined to his home, sent more memorandums showing that the conservative estimates for investments in recreation during the next seven years were over $200 billion—$2.8 million had already been committed by the International Finance Corporation for hotels in Kenya.

"That's probably because the International bankers toured Kenya after their convention last fall," said Griffith. "Most of them visited the APL lodges at the invitation of Rockwell, CIIC's president. Maybe we should reconsider APL. It's not too late."

I saw Griffith's angle. He was trying to earn a pass into Roethe's camp.

"Forget APL. Concentrate on closing the magazine deal with *Four Seasons Trails*," I told him.

And then there were new problems. I dissolved the partnership to buy Greentree Forests and Farm Corporation of America when Sommers told me Metcalf Farms was bankrupt.

"Bankrupt?"

"Bankrupt." Sommers seemed to smile.

"Then we'll have to take our licks," I told him. He was bluffing with the bankruptcy. Metcalf himself had just told me that the farms were considered an essential industry and might get a remedial loan from the state of Hawaii. I hoped Sommers, shocked by my apparent indifference, would cut and run.

I shooed him out of my office when a call came through from Turnbull.

"I'm dodging process servers again. They're after Shadco now."

"Hold on two more weeks, Ed, and when Leo gets his loan we've got it made." I noticed that my voice sounded confident again.

The atmosphere at our annual Christmas party was heavy. My employees knew their bonuses would be paid only after there was money in the bank. My investors made weak jokes about tax write-offs and tried to kid the bankers about "high interest—high risk." Ingels and his attorney asked probing questions, and the

Milwaukee bankers wandered through our offices looking as if they were taking inventory. R. and R. left early. Shadel didn't even show.

Griffith seemed the happiest of the group as he passed out his new Continental Royal Services business cards.

"Why isn't Compass on them?" someone asked.

"Compass is only a division," Griffith smiled.

I heard a secretary tell my Storm Trooper that she had a feeling "some of us won't be around much longer." She looked at me. Her strained face told me that she thought I was letting her down.

I studied the rest of the room: everyone was beginning to look haggard. A premonition of the worst hit me. There wasn't much faith left.

I couldn't reach Roethe on the twenty-second. Late that night I found Rauterberg at another office party.

"Don't panic. It's hard to do business during the holidays," he said.

"I'm beyond panic, I hope. But I need to know what I'm facing."

I munched on an hors d'oeuvre and wondered how I could sound so calm.

16
Two Days After Christmas 1973

ASSETS—No Change
LIABILITIES—No Change
PERSONAL GUARANTEES—No Change

The Board Room was silent, so quiet I could almost hear the ashes falling from the cigarette in my shaky hand. I looked down the long table, my eyes darting from one frozen figure to the next. Each man seemed to be holding his breath; no motion, no sound. I counted six Brain Trusters, all of the original Thunderhead investors except Turnbull, and three bankers. Like Kritchner, whose year-round tan was suddenly fading to gray, the others wore a pallor of defeat.

Leo Roethe's consolidation loan had not materialized. Now, though he may have been "living his second life," whatever influence he had had was fading fast. Rumors that he was in terminal financial trouble had spread quickly, and my empire, trapped in the darkening shadows of doubt, was beginning to crumble from within. Time had about run out. I pushed damp hair off my forehead. Time was terror—unless Roethe's loan closed soon, or the Compass–CRS merger generated more investor interest and quick cash than I anticipated, or—

"Gentlemen, I have an idea," I shouted.

Vitner and Hollis's heads snapped toward me. The rest turned more slowly.

"What now?" said Kritchner, frowning as he rolled a pen between his fingers.

I talked fast, faster than usual, hoping everyone would accept my desperate solution. "I'm going to arrange our own super-consolidation loan. Our equities add up to over $10 million, and the personal net worths of the individuals available to guarantee a loan bring the grand total of our security to over $30 million. If that doesn't qualify us for an all-inclusive second mortgage . . ."

I didn't finish the sentence; I watched my associates' faces instead. They mirrored my counterfeit confidence.

"Great," said The Digest, smiling and looking around the table. "Just like the guys at American City Bank told me last week—you're either a genius or a wizard. They still want to go along with us, all the way." Once more The Digest was certain there was "No problem."

Higbie agreed. "Maybe Leo's loan was only delayed by the holidays, the Christmas spirit. So maybe we were worrying prematurely. And, if not, maybe your new idea will work."

The others nodded. They were obviously as desperate as I was.

My Storm Trooper stood up. "Maybe this is the wrong time for a meeting."

I could see he was anxious to adjourn, afraid something discouraging might be said to shake our tenuous enthusiasm.

Kritchner must have been thinking the same thing. He swallowed hard and said, "It would be nice to leave it at that, but we've been kidding ourselves long enough. What happens if your idea doesn't work and Roethe's money is delayed again?"

"Then we have to consider sacrificing Leo Roethe to save ourselves." I was ready to offer any alternative but bankruptcy, because I was really beginning to believe in myself again. It felt good not to be afraid for a change. My palms were drying as I spoke, and there was more momentum behind every new word. "We hold most of his assets as collateral. We can always sell him out."

No one nodded now. There was no sign of encouragement. In spite of public opinion, the rumors, and their own inside information, Leo Roethe was still the hulking shadow of success that moved, sometimes quietly, sometimes vigorously, through our offices. No one seemed to realize that Roethe was a false prophet, as much a false prophet as I might turn out to be—unless the next move was the right one.

I wanted to tell them what I thought: "Maybe Roethe was a liar and everything about him was deliberately exaggerated." But they should have known of that possibility by now, known that Roethe's charm had given him opportunities to transfer the burden of his debts to the eager advocates of the Diamond J lifestyle —all of us. Maybe he'd meant no harm, maybe he'd listened to his own sales pitch so long that he was beginning to believe it too.

But he wasn't truthful with himself when it came to the challenge of turning dreams into reality. John Strohm must have understood that the summer before when we had met at the *National Wildlife* publishing offices and he had told me he liked the idea of Recreation International but would never invest in it until I proved that we could meet the challenge with more than excited chatter. He must have seen that Roethe could never do the job of living up to his dreams.

I wanted to tell my associates, but I didn't, because another realization began to hammer my mind. I was just like Leo Roethe, maybe worse. I was one of the users that got used. I had made it easy for Roethe and the bankers to bury their bad loans, to pump my friends' fresh blood into dying debts.

My hands began to sweat again, but I forced a smile and hung onto my enthusiasm.

"Okay, we'll give him one more chance."

The others look relieved.

"And, if worse comes to worst, I'll put everything I have up for sale," I told them, standing and raising my voice. "I'm prepared to sell my share of the holdings to any of my partners at 50 percent of appraised value and use the proceeds to save our empire."

"What more can we ask?" said Vitner.

The meeting ended as Quarton whispered to me, "Good speech. You're beginning to glow again."

While everyone else began preparations to celebrate New Year's Eve and the Compass–CRS merger simultaneously in New

York and Wisconsin, I wrote a seven page confidential memorandum to Rick Murray.

"It will be hand-delivered today," I said when I called to alert him. "I know I'm imposing when I ask you to study the figures over a holiday, but you'll see how important they are. If we can get a loan for $1,976,500, everything will be saved, even Leo."

"Sounds viable," he said. "Real good."

So it didn't bother me when Lindsey called to warn me about rumors that the bank examiners were telling the banks I was in trouble.

"One day soon we're going to shove those opinions up their ass," I told him, reaching at the same time for the drink Quarton offered. "Right now I'm going to toast a fantastic New Year and head for New York."

The Telex in my new Fifth Avenue offices made a happy sound as it clicked out congratulations. I saved the messages, shoving all but one into my briefcase.

"To show my sons how Dad's doing business all over the world," I told Guitjens. Then I asked him to explain the last transmittal.

It read: "Looking forward to rewarding cooperation from both sides. Stop. Awaiting your telegraph transfer U.S. dollars 115,000.—Prompt Action." It was signed Arnold Duyf, President, Holland River Lines.

I knew CRS owed them the money, but I couldn't understand the urgency of the payment request.

Guitjens explained that the Holland River Lines was trying to merge with NSU. "The Netherlands Shipping Union is one of the biggest businesses in Europe, and Holland River Lines needs to have its accounts in order before submitting its current financial statement." He looked a little desperate when I laughed and said, "Doesn't anyone, even the giants, have a pot to piss in?"

Guitjens suggested that he and Griffith could just as well hand-carry the funds to Amsterdam when they flew over to present our expansion plans to KLM's home office.

"He means Prince Bernhard," Griffith added. I nodded, ignored him, and smiled. I was studying my new employment contract, which called for $40,000 per year from CRS. My smile broadened. That sum, added to the income I expected from the other companies, would put my spending money at more than $100,000 a year.

On the way back to Madison, Griffith and I talked about his role in CRS. He didn't want to be executive vice-president.

"If I'm going to represent CRS in high-level negotiations with KLM and NSU, I need an appropriate title," he said.

"How's 'king'?" I kidded, knowing that I was about to lose my title.

"You've already got too many burdens. The presidency of Recreation International will require your maximum efforts if the company's going to go public on schedule. If you make me president of CRS you won't give up anything," he explained. "You can draw the same salary as chairman of the executive committee. And, after all, that's the real power base."

I didn't feel like arguing, and, when I thought about it, that was a good way to get Griffith out of my hair and put him on one of my hot seats. "OK."

Griffith's face looked as if he'd just discovered the secret to eternal life. The radiant change in his skin tone, the clarity in his eyes, made me realize I'd just made his dream come true.

Mine slammed into another obstacle the moment I entered my office. My secretary handed me a stack of certified mail, all legal forms demanding payment in full of the assorted Algoma Bank loans.

I placed a quick call to Ingels.

"He's unavailable; in an important meeting," his secretary said.

I was shocked. Ingels was never "unavailable" to me. Never. I called Rauterberg; he was busy too. And so was Roethe, although he returned my call minutes later.

"You've made trouble," he said. "My Teamsters loan has been postponed indefinitely, and I think that's because you made a public issue of it. Now I want you to stop your crazy counter-intelligence operation and work on important matters while I try to salvage my loan."

I didn't respond, hoping he'd keep on talking and tell me something I could check out.

But all he said before hanging up was, "Art Anders and Earl Jordan agree with me."

Murray told me the real story. The Teamsters had caught Roethe secretly pledging part of their loan proceeds as private collateral (Certificates of Deposit) to the participating banks. Apparently this violated the federal law as well as the contract, and now Roethe had to find a new way to satisfy them.

"The banks won't participate without extra collateral," Murray said, "so now Leo's talking about using insurance policies."

"Insurance." That was another new lead.

I drove to Chicago to see Jordan. While I was waiting in his private conference room I noticed that one wall was covered with autographed photos of the Apollo crews, the same "astronaut wall" I'd seen in the Wyoming bank president's office and the offices of all Roethe's business associates. A sure sign of financial problems, I thought now.

Jordan was as worried as I. He didn't know anything new about Roethe's loan.

"Leo hasn't talked to me about any insurance. He's kept me in the dark too. But I think he's involved with some pretty questionable people."

After that my enthusiasm came only in spurts, and my depression deepened as I began to see Leo Roethe's face in my mirror.

There were some ups.

The director of Bougainvillea, Ltd., a vacation concept paralleling mine, suggested a joint venture with his clients' money.

The Playboy empire finally proposed an affiliation with my Compass Club. They were eager. "Time is of the essence, Mr. Stone . . . looking forward to a mutually successful program . . ." they wrote.

But there was no more time to squeeze into my frantic search for money.

And there were mostly downs.

Murray said he'd keep trying, but so far he couldn't find the place for my super second mortgage loan. We flew to New York together for a meeting with Anders, Kielman, and the attorneys and securities experts. Anders and I suggested substituting Murray for Roethe as President of Weatherby Nasco.

"Maybe that way the company can wash off the stigma of Leo's personal financial failure, and the resulting rise in the price of his stock will save us."

"There isn't enough time," said Murray.

I knew there was another reason. Federal authorities had begun investigating Murray's directorship of the SBA, and he wanted to avoid the taint of any further connections with Roethe or his companies. There were already enough questions to answer about an SBA loan involving Metcalf Farms–Hawaii. First it had been rejected because the operation was out-of-territory and not a qualified applicant. Later it had been granted to Metcalf's personal farming venture in Wisconsin.

"Which overnight became a feedlot. They qualified; farms didn't," Metcalf toid me confidentially.

When I explained this to Anders he said, "I'm Goddamn glad it happened before we got involved. I don't like to fuck with the feds."

I noticed that Anders was swearing a lot lately.

Murray left the same day, and I was certain he'd made the trip only to judge the possibilities of collecting my loans.

When Kielman said that it was imperative to sell the CRS debentures, I told him my investors were in no position to pay for their subscriptions.

Kielman and Kraemer, whose money was entirely tied up in "offshore" ventures, did agree to sign notes totalling $125,000 each, and I promised that discounting the notes with my bankers would be "No problem."

As it turned out, the only way I could use the notes was to substitute them for existing past-due loans. That was no good, so I told Griffith to return the paperwork.

Kielman called as soon as Griffith reached New York. The Dutchman couldn't understand why his signature was valueless.

"Why haven't you been able to arrange the loans you promised?" His question was nearly lost in an angry stammer.

"Wouldn't it be easier and cheaper to borrow the money through your friends at New York banks?" I countered. "We should have done that in the first place."

"We can't." Kielman dropped his irritated tone and changed the subject. "Dick Griffith seemed to do a good job for us in Amsterdam."

Maybe so, but Kielman's strange reluctance to involve New York banks made me wonder if he was hiding something.

I flew back to New York the next morning.

"What the hell happened to our money?" I asked Griffith.

"$115,000 was wired to Switzerland," he said, "and the rest went for bills. There wasn't enough because you"—he pointed a finger under my nose—"kept too much in Wisconsin." He reached into his pocket and handed me a confidential memo demanding salary cuts and terminations of half my staff, plus the closing of our San Diego office. My Storm Trooper was to do the dirty work.

"Just a minute, you silly sonofabitch, I want answers before orders. You sent money to Swiss bank accounts?" I was half out of my chair and ready to bust his finger.

Griffith put his hands in his pockets and backed away. "Most big European companies funnel their funds through Switzerland."

I didn't believe him, but decided to drop the interrogation and investigate privately. Griffith was still too important to antagonize.

"Sorry I blew off. Pressure." I smiled. I wanted his report on the trip to Holland.

Griffith said that the KLM executives were disappointed because David Eller, head of Gulf Oil's consumer service operation, had missed the meeting, but that they seemed satisfied with the proposal for a joint venture.

"Where was Gulf?" I was still smiling, but beginning to shout.

"Unavoidably detained." Griffith sat down, then stood again. He walked across the room and peered out the door. Then he motioned for me to lower my voice. "You're tired. I know the problems you're facing. Now's not the time to become embroiled in the details of the CRS operation."

It certainly was the time. CRS was beginning to smell. But Griffith was right about one thing; I did have other problems. And since I knew he was going to be evasive and I was getting too weary with frustration to argue effectively, I let him leave gracefully.

An hour later I caught the North Central flight to Milwaukee, then to Madison. Higbie met me at the airport. It was 7:20 P.M.

"Had dinner?"

"Just drinks." I took a deep breath, hoping Higbie wouldn't notice that I was beginning to feel them. "Dinner can wait. Right now I want to go back to the office and talk about the second of the Super Races."

"Good idea."

Higbie sounded enthusiastic and looked confident, so I didn't bother with questions. I just listened as we drove across town.

The race would be held in two weeks, bigger and better than before. Everything was ready. Sure, Higbie was short of cash, but Dash's credit was still good.

"Nothing can stop the Super Race, not even the weather. We have new, better snowmaking equipment this year. Don't worry, John, State Fair Park is one place we're going to make some money."

The Corvette's wheels spun as we turned into the parking lot. Quarton's car was still in its usual place.

"Why's Bill working late?"

Higbie shrugged.

I went straight to my office and got out the rum and Coke. Quarton came in as I was pouring my drink.

"You're going to need that." He poured a Scotch for himself.

Word had just come over the grapevine—bartenders who served us as listening posts—that Walter Koziel was in serious trouble. I took a long swallow of my drink.

"How come? Isn't he the guy with the big block of Beatrice Food stock, Rosenheimer's partner in the Steamboat land deal?" Higbie squinted at Quarton. "Hell, he's a millionaire."

My hand began to twitch as I tried to light a cigarette. Koziel had started with a lot more money than I had, or even Anders—some said $15 million.

Quarton tossed his glass into the wastebasket. "Sometimes, when I drink and worry, I get angry. So I'm going home," he said.

Higbie sat on the sofa and watched me with half-closed eyes.

I began to wonder if the snowmobile race was really going to make money. "What do you expect the gate to be, Jim?"

"Close to $200,000 if the weather's mild. Look how the World

Championships in Eagle River broke all attendance records. Remember two weeks ago, when Allen Dorfman predicted the International Pro/Ams would do even better."

I felt a surge of confidence, then a deeper depression when I remembered Dorfman's other remarks. I'd been trying to take advantage of his second annual invitation to the Jack-O-Lantern Lodge to sneak in subtle questions about Roethe's loan from the union. Dorfman had dodged away from the answers I wanted, allowing only that these were tough times for entrepreneurs. The authorities were clamping down on loan manipulators, borrowers and lenders alike.

Dorfman had spoken with authority. He'd just spent the better part of a year in federal prison as the result of being convicted on loan kickback charges.

"And it's no fun," he had told me in a heavy voice.

Now I shuddered. Dorfman had seemed to be a decent guy, and, in spite of rumors I'd heard, not the kind to be a convict. A shrewd businessman, sure, but I enjoyed his company, and I'd already thought how much alike we were. I shook my head, banishing the idea.

I stood up and walked to where Higbie sat. "I hope you're right about the $200,000 gate. We can use that money." I slapped his back.

"I'll do my best." He rose and gave me a small smile.

After Higbie left I found myself back behind the desk with my feet on the drawer and my hands pouring the last drops from the rum bottle. I looked at the unnatural emptiness of the desk top: my personal financial statement was the only document in sight. It was always at hand now. I realized that I'd been studying it constantly, looking for liquid assets and mentally inventorying everything that might be converted to cash to live on if my expense accounts and paychecks stopped.

Maybe my consideration of total failure was subconscious, but I was nonetheless preparing to weather the worst storm yet. It never crossed my mind that the Diamond J ventures would fail forever and the $20 million profit I counted on would fade with my dream. Sure, I damned Roethe's false hopes and excuses, his constant promises of "tomorrow, tomorrow." And I noticed that some of my friends were disappearing. The pragmatists were hunting a safer dream merchant. Most of the rest were already empty of illusions, floundering and beginning to blame me because they were losing the security they thought my lifestyle had promised them.

Sometimes, in the days just past, I had thought I'd seen hate in their eyes. Certainly some of their voices were beginning to sound bitter. But I was more frustrated than angry. I wanted to protect my people from the hurt that was destroying their faith. Our business and our lives had to improve—I still believed that. But the others seemed to be hurting more every day.

Usually I tried to strike a ruthless pose. Let them direct their hate toward me, I figured, instead of toward concepts that were good and still might work. But there were other times, like tonight, when I hated and was bitter, too, and when I felt like screaming or crying or running away.

Several days later Rauterberg took me to see Rosenheimer, who claimed that he could arrange the super second mortgage loan with a mysterious "fund."

"Not the union and nothing like Rick Murray could find for you, but it's money," Rosenheimer said, as he and Rauterberg studied my rumpled memo.

I figured they meant to try, hard, because they'd be in serious trouble if I folded. Their old loan schemes couldn't stand the bright lights in a bankruptcy court. And I knew that Rosenheimer needed the huge finder's fee to help pay the loans Rauterberg had arranged to refinance his banks. Those couldn't stand scrutiny either.

"But no dirty money," I told them, my voice much louder than usual.

Minutes later Turnbull arrived at Titan Enterprises. He said he was making a separate attempt to save Thunderhead.

Rosenheimer smiled weakly. "Maybe by working together we can save everything, even my Steamboat properties." He looked from Turnbull to me, his damp hair falling forward, nearly obscuring his eyebrows. "They're foreclosing on me, too, you know."

"Then let's get to work." Turnbull snapped open his briefcase.

It sounded as if his old vitality was still there, and I left the meeting later with a glimmer of hope that Turnbull would help me put a solution together.

That evening I flew East to another salvage meeting with Kielman, Anders, and Griffith, but I felt like a stranger when I walked into Anders's office the next day. The three men looked at me without speaking or blinking, and there were no smiles. Anders finally spoke.

"Fritz says CRS is bankrupt because you didn't deliver the money you promised." He was referring to the initial quarter-million.

"Some had to stay in Wisconsin," I said. I spat out the words and glared at them. "A merger includes assets and liabilities. We have bills too. Don't throw the onus on me. Fritz and Warren can't even pay for their debentures. And you," I pointed at Anders, "won't buy any, and . . ." I was sputtering now.

"Pay me back some of my money and I will," Anders said in an even voice.

"You know I can't, and that my people can't help. Roethe's breaking us." I tried to control myself. "If Leo had gotten his loan . . ."

"He's getting his loan," Anders insisted softly. "But CRS can't wait. I'm going to lend Fritz my own money, but it's for his use. John, you've got to cut your expenses in Wisconsin to the bare bone."

As if on cue, Griffith pulled out another confidential memo and handed it to me. I read that my reduced salary was to be paid "at the end of the year, out of profits, if any," while Griffith was to continue earning $35,000 plus expenses, paid monthly. I felt an explosion coming. I couldn't stop it.

"Conniving sonofabitch." I directed my bitter words to Griffith, but I meant everyone in the room. As far as I was concerned the CRS merger was definitely a ripoff. Griffith had delivered most of what he'd promised to Kielman, and now John Stone, the vehicle, could "be damned and departed." I shook the memo at them and shouted. "I suppose while my people are being laid off, Kielman's kids, Billy and Bjorn, will be hired and moved in to take their place."

"Be quiet or I'll throw you through the wall," Kielman snarled with no trace of a stammer.

I'd regretted my remarks the minute I made them, and, as I rode to the airport—sitting up front with the chauffeur—and overheard the hushed discussion between Griffith and Kielman behind me, I realized sadly that I'd lost another biggie forever.

"But it doesn't really matter," I told myself. I repeated it to Higbie, when I returned to the Madison office. "Let the East Coast big shots screw each other. We'll stick with *this*." I waved my original Master Plan. "We'll dump everything except Dash, the Colorado companies, and what's left of Lake, Sport. . . ."

"Diamond J rides again!"

My secretary and Quarton looked in with puzzled expressions. "Good news?" Quarton asked.

I explained, and concocted a new plan. We began a list of disposable assets: my Aero Commander, the 404, Kritchner's farm.

"And every Goddamn Roethe relic," said Quarton.

"But slowly and quietly, with our heads held high. Keep everyone thinking that all the ventures are still flying. No crash alarms. We'd lose our ass at a fire sale." I was thinking about the bankers. "Some people would rather grab the goods than the money."

"Cookie monster banks. They want every crumb," said Quarton.

That became obvious. One of Shadel's banking partners, tough because he was not directly involved, began summoning my investors to a new series of salvage meetings. There was nothing we could do now. The alarm had gone off.

My friends, my followers, everyone who had once had faith, now showed up with their attorneys and let their attorneys do the talking. "Your explanations explain nothing," they told me. "They're excuses."

Captain Feisty, one of the few representing himself, mumbled, "What am I doing in this chicken-shit outfit?"

Roethe didn't come to the meetings. He was hard to reach. When he finally answered his telephone and told me there'd be money "any day now," I shook my head.

"Too late," I told him. "We're being evicted, and they're cutting off the phones."

"Tell the men to work out of their homes," Roethe shouted, as if any stoppage, even after paychecks ceased, was a personal insult to him. "I can't be bothered now. I'm too busy talking to the biggest people in the world about a new way to save the same businesses you are so foolishly forsaking."

I didn't answer Roethe. He sounded immortal—beyond doubt, beyond belief.

"He'll always have a dream for sale," said Quarton, trying to smile.

Toussaint, my CPA, came in carrying the first reports from the Super Race. "We lost our ass again," he said, scowling at me.

"Get out of here!" I screamed.

Quarton winced; Toussaint, eyes twitching, slowly strung his words together.

"I think we've all had it."

I swiveled my chair around so I couldn't see him. The entire office complex was hushed. I knew that my staff was only pretending to finish the day's work. Earlier, when I'd made my usual noontime tour, I'd noticed the typewriters tapping to a funeral tempo. The sterile desk tops were polished, ready for the marketplace. The Brain Trusters spoke to me, but there was no eye contact. The news had leaked long ago. Diamond J was totally broke. Worse than that, broken.

I was sorry for my followers, but I envied some of them too. All things considered, it would be easy for the secretaries, the staffers, and the junior executives. Simple—go out and find another job. Their problem was temporary, merely a disruption. But for me, the truth was unacceptable, Kritchner's prediction coming true— living death.

Slowly, sullenly we began clearing the offices. And then, sadly, I saw Brain Trusters packing office supplies and equipment along with their personal effects. Some were carrying the furniture away. I stopped Toussaint's assistant, leaving with a parquet conference table.

"I'll store it in my home," he said, "until the company makes restitution for the notes I signed to buy the stock I never got."

His face was full of hate, his brows fiercely furrowed and his eyes set in slits.

I closed myself into my office and tried to pack my pictures. I heard my secretary leaving, but she didn't buzz me to say good night as she always had. I tried to make myself a drink. There wasn't any rum left, no Coke, so I poured myself a straight slug of Kritchner's special Scotch. It burned going down.

I poured another anyway, and stood at the window watching the cars pull away. The Brain Trusters look like lemmings now, I thought. I was thankful that my mother had moved to a nursing home near my brother in Oklahoma. There was nothing, no matter how hard she tried, that she could say about her eldest son now.

Driving home, my mind concerned itself with Sue, and my sons, and Judy. I had to talk to someone, but not to any of them just yet. I swung back to the Loft looking for Quarton. He was hunched in a corner booth thinking about the same thing.

"My wife and kids" (he called them his "troops") "are used to ups and downs and sideways," Quarton said. "They know things are bad and they seem to be coping, but I'm worried that they can't conceive how bad. I don't think they understand how many notes I've signed, what that means. But, Goddamnit, John, I'll explain automatically over and over until they do understand, and then we'll hang together. We'll make it. Now get out of here and look after yourself. You'll make it too."

"I suppose." I began to smile as I watched Quarton sipping his drink placidly. He could be violent, but he had a habit of handling big problems with what I figured was quiet strength.

The bankers' salvage meetings continued. They emphasized quiet, out-of-court settlements.

"No need to broadcast the trouble or write the Attorneys' Relief Act of 1974," one said, noting that there were probably more lawyers in the room than debtors and creditors. "I'm sure everyone is willing to make a mutually beneficial deal." His eyes checked every face in the room for signs of agreement.

I watched the other bankers. They were all straining to hear someone say that the problems could be solved before news of the crash reached the press and was spread to the public, the banking commission, and the FDIC.

The room was silent until the scraping of chairs signaled that the meeting was over. Later, when I phoned him about the meeting, Roethe enthusiastically suggested that the bankers would settle our debts, "maybe for fifty cents on the dollar."

"How? We haven't got *any* money." I spoke slowly, already weary of his delusions.

"I'll be closing my loan soon," Roethe promised.

"That's bullshit." I began to shout, anger driving my voice higher and higher.

"I'm sorry you believe that. I had expected better things from you, John," he sighed, "but now I guess there's nothing more to say."

Roethe's low voice seemed to echo from the phone even after he had hung up. He really believes he's immortal, I thought, and he's still sure that he will succeed. Goddamnit, why can't I be sure, too?

The middle of the next week we held a smaller meeting at my Storm Trooper's house. Only one banker, an associate of Shadel's, was present. The others there, waiting silently for words of encouragement, were Kritchner, his attorney, and myself. Kritchner's face had lost its year-round tan, and his bare scalp was showing where he usually combed his hair so carefully.

He shook his head. "I just don't understand what happened."

"That's because no one ever told you what was going on," said his attorney.

A preview of the stockholders' legal position, I thought.

We were still wondering how to begin the meeting when Griffith arrived. He ignored me and told the others, "Leo's still going to get his loan. So stop worrying and let me tell you about my progress with the new CRS."

My God, I thought, the silly dreamer is going to make another sales presentation.

Griffith had barely started when Kritchner's attorney asked, "Are you making any money?"

"Soon," said Griffith, smiling.

"Bullshit," I shouted.

The banker finally spoke, nearly as loudly as I. "Something had better be done, soon. Unless you straighten up this mess, I think someone's going to jail." He turned to me. His eyes were hard, his look noncommittal. "You've been stupid. The Weatherby–Nasco board of directors knew Leo Roethe was insolvent a year ago when you and Anders started handing him your money."

Kritchner asked how he had known that.

"I was a director until Leo asked me to resign," said the banker.

If that was so, I wondered, why hadn't he warned us long ago? Why hadn't Shadel warned us? He'd been on the board, too.

"Because they had more to gain than we had to lose," my Storm Trooper said, when we talked privately in the kitchen. "You were really stupid to trust them—then and now."

The meeting broke up with a tentative agreement to hire CPAs and an independent administrator to make a final attempt to salvage our assets. But that idea proved fruitless when the best troubleshooters we could find shook their heads and agreed that there was no hope.

Sleeping became a problem. I was always tired. I tried to rest in bed one morning, but the winter winds, reminding me that they weren't quite ready to go away for good, billowed the drapes and swept across the bedroom. The sweat-wet sheets, sticky when I had first awakened, now felt frozen to my skin. Tremors started in my shoulders, and before I could roll toward Sue's warmer body I was shaking all over.

The phone rang. One of O'Connor's associates asked me to meet him, *privately*.

"Why?" I barely knew the man.

"It's very important, so let's get together right away."

He wouldn't tell me any more, but I agreed to see him.

"What have I got to lose?" I told Sue as I left for the deserted Diamond J offices.

O'Connor's associate said that he was a real estate developer who also dabbled in money brokering. "And I've got a deal that may bail you out, or at least give you enough money to hide comfortably for the rest of your life."

"Hide?" It sounded like a bribe, a payoff. "Why should I hide?"

He shrugged, smiling painfully, and explained that the "deal" involved the purchase of a movie studio and acreage in Carefree, Arizona.

I laughed uncontrollably. "Is Carefree for real?"

"Certainly." His eyes admonished me for the giddy outburst. "It's near Phoenix. Now all you have to do is sign a contract to buy the place for $5.4 million and send along your financial statement . . ."

"Financial statement?" I started to laugh again.

"It's just window dressing," he said in a raspy voice, beginning to gesture with both hands. "Just do what I say and within a week we'll pay you a half-million-dollar commission . . . just for selling the property to yourself."

I lit a cigarette and walked to the window, taking deep drags. I looked out onto the empty parking lot and wondered what new problems I could make for myself if I accepted the deal. Obviously it was phony. I began to cough, my eyes watering as I imagined what sinister powers might be behind the offer. The premonition was ominous. No deal, I decided.

I wondered if I'd made a mistake the next day, when Rauterberg made a special trip to Madison to tell me sadly not to count on *any* help from Rosenheimer. No, I thought, feeling some pride in the fact that I could still act without desperation. But Rauterberg was pacing, avoiding eye contact as he talked, reminding me that the other bankers were beginning to turn on me.

"They're scared," he said. "Your failure may cause trouble for a lot of them. They can't understand how you managed to suck them in on so many sour loans."

Now I knew that I was marked to be their scapegoat—the conniving bastard who had robbed the banks.

In the weeks that followed, the crash of Diamond J and all its enterprises caused a chain reaction of evasive maneuvers. A telegram arrived from Guitjens, who had been sharing Griffith's administration of the new Continental Royal Services: "Since directors have not provided financing for operation . . . we are therefore out of business as of March 19."

"No way." I dialed the CRS number in New York.

"Royal Caribbean Services," came the answer.

I hung up. "Of course," I thought aloud, "that was another Kielman company, run by his sons. I'm out of business, *but they're not.*" I knew there was nothing I could do about it.

Roethe refused to talk with me. Griffith disappeared, and Anders insisted that I communicate with him through his attorneys. They tried to interrogate me instead of offering assistance. Quello double-talked and finally refused to take my calls. Sleavin said Delafield Childs was not involved anymore, and was not responsible for past participation because my companies had supplied confusing and incorrect information. Even the doctors, when I called to take their temperatures, avoided conversations, saying only, "See my attorneys."

Only Turnbull (telling me, "We may still have a slim chance to salvage something in Steamboat Springs.") and Jordan (insisting, "Leo Roethe may be able to renegotiate the union loan or find new sources of money in Europe.") kept my hopes alive.

It would have been easier if the crash had been complete, final; if there had been no hope at all. But for another month I was tortured by the painful shred of possibility that Turnbull might find an angel or that Roethe's littered trail would lead to a pot of gold.

One week I heard that Roethe was in Pennsylvania ready to close a deal with a syndicate, headed by Anders, that planned to buy Weatherby–Nasco and every other business Roethe had promoted. The next, word leaked that Texas tycoons were going to buy Thunderhead's unfinished condominiums for their appraised value and lend us money to save the Inn. Yet there was nothing on paper, and no money ever changed hands.

The litigation began. I got to know the process servers by their first names. A forced smile to greet them, the offer of a cup of coffee, and the passage of a summons became a daily ritual.

"You'd better find yourself an attorney," said Sue. She was constantly at my side.

She drove me to see Kanakis, who had handled my divorce from Judy; he was familiar with the Diamond J companies but had not been burned like Butters and other attorneys.

"Don't be ashamed to tell him you need help," Sue said. I left her waiting in the car.

Kanakis asked me if I expected criminal charges to be filed.

"I don't know. But there's more than one kind of thief," I said. I thought Kanakis was a religious man, so I used a theological metaphor. "I think I've been a party to stealing men's souls."

I saw that he didn't understand, and I knew it would take a long time to explain and longer to make my position clear in the courts. I also knew his time was expensive.

"I don't know how to pay you," I said.

"We'll work it out," said Kanakis. "How about Lone Tree?"

I winced. That was where my life had begun.

That night, during the dark private hours, I finally realized that the crash was complete. Diamond J was finished, and I felt small and incomplete. My body seemed to be shriveling. I felt my wedding band begin to slide off a sweaty finger, and when I clenched my fist there wasn't much strength in my hand.

I needed to talk. Sue was sleeping peacefully, so I dialed Judy on the living room phone. She sounded serene when I told her that I was going to lose everything.

"Not everything, John. Your lifestyle, yes, and your money, power, and prestige . . . but maybe now you'll have the time to find yourself again."

I sensed that she was somehow relieved, and, since she didn't offer advice, she must still believe I could salvage myself.

"I'm going away for a while," I said softly, tentatively. "Hug the boys for me."

"I'll be here whenever you need me, John."

And then, in spite of everything, I felt a moment of pride. I guessed I hadn't lost Judy after all.

Early in the morning I woke Sue and told her I was flying West. "I want to be by myself at Lone Tree."

Tears welled in her eyes as she nodded. Several times before I'd tried to protect her by talking her out of my life, but she had refused to move away.

"I can wait," she said now, and I knew she would.

Spring rain began to drizzle down as Quarton drove me to the airport. He didn't slow the car, even on corners, and I knew he understood how anxious I was to be gone from Madison.

"But you'll be back," he said, reaching for my hand as I got out of the car at the terminal.

I smiled my thanks and quickly turned away before the smile faded. I was already sifting my alternatives.

I could easily rent a small plane in Denver and fly alone into the mountains; everything would end quickly if I crashed against the peaks. No suicide stigma then; even the insurance companies, covering my life for millions, could never disprove an accident. The financial futures of my family would be secure, and even my investors might benefit. And I'd be following the captain's creed—going down with my ship.

"No way," I said softly to myself. "It's not my style."

Or I could run, far and fast. There would always be a home for me somewhere in the Compass world, a job in Nairobi or Tegulci-galpa. I shook my head as I approached the boarding ramp. That wasn't my style either.

"Well hi, John," said the stewardess, guiding me to my usual first-class seat.

I shook my head and walked past her into the rear of the airliner.

ASSETS—$800.00
LIABILITIES—$535,000.00
PERSONAL GUARANTEES—$19,575,000.00

Epilogue

By August 1975 the African hotels, the farms in Hawaii, the Inn at Thunderhead, Dash, Janeff Credit, and Lake Sport were bankrupt or in receivership. Compass and Recreation died without benefit of legal license. Headlines screamed "International ventures fail," and the news columns beneath chronicled a financial disaster that left a dozen banks shaken and scores of people insolvent, out of work, even homeless.

The Governor of Wisconsin ordered investigations by the Attorney General and the Banking and Securities Commissions. Probes by the U.S. Department of Justice, the FDIC and the FBI quickly followed. Grand juries were convened. And everyone started shouting the big question, "What happened to all the money?" As the legal process of discovery snowballed, more than a hundred new lawsuits were filed. Partner turned on partner. Debtors and creditors attacked each other. The banks and Leo Roethe were the prime targets, but I was the bull's-eye.

I knew then that my desperate acts would bring criminal charges and that I was faced with three choices: find new money to pay off the scandalous debts, stonewall it, or cooperate with the law. The first was impossible and the second unthinkable, so

I turned myself and my records over to the authorities. Later I pleaded no contest to charges of being a party to bankers receiving kickbacks, of securities fraud, of failure to register stock, and of filing false financial statements. My penalty for causing a crisis among Wisconsin banks, the hardest hit of the group, was a $50,000 fine and 90 days in jail. On March 8, 1976, I began serving my federal sentence of one year and a day at Sandstone (Minn.) Federal Prison.

Leo Roethe was impossible to pin down until new headlines suddenly appeared—"Roethe deals for billions"—and the story of how he was keeping creditors at bay while he tried to wrangle loans for Mexico and other foreign countries emerged. The money, $27 billion, was reported to be coming from the Arabs, with Roethe receiving brokerage fees that would pay for an end to everyone's problems. But the Mexican Government denied the transaction, and the financial drama ended as the international cast (sheiks, foreign ministers and a Swiss industrialist) faded away.

On August 16, 1975, the Chase International Investment Corporation led a creditor group that placed Roethe in bankruptcy.

"But I'm still going to find enough money to pay off," he insisted.

Nonetheless, the Algoma Bank and later the American City Bank failed, the latter the largest bank failure of 1975 and the fifth largest since the Depression. The investigations accelerated. Walter O'Connor was charged with receiving kickbacks, misapplication of bank funds and felony theft. A jury found him guilty on two counts of the kickback charge at his first trial: eight others are pending. O'Connor's assistant Huffman pleaded guilty to aiding and abetting, and the president of Camp Dells admitted to forgery. Jim Rosenheimer lost his banks and was charged with misapplication of bank funds. Robert Rauterberg was charged with perjury for lying before a John Doe investigation when he denied receiving kickbacks on bank loans. The license of a brokerage firm was revoked because Recreation International Stock had been sold illegally. Their salesman was found guilty of theft by fraud in connection with the sales. Toward the end of 1975 the

Wisconsin Justice Department created a new White Collar Crime Bureau that asked again and again, "What happened to all the money?"

I passed a lie detector test to prove I didn't have it, took a deep breath, and continued my search for the answer

Index